Advances in the Theory and Practice of Smart Specialization

Advances in the Theory and Practice of Smart Specialization

Edited by

Slavo Radosevic

Adrian Curaj

Radu Gheorghiu

Liviu Andreescu

Imogen Wade

ACADEMIC PRESS

An imprint of Elsevier

Academic Press is an imprint of Elsevier
125 London Wall, London EC2Y 5AS, United Kingdom
525 B Street, Suite 1800, San Diego, CA 92101-4495, United States
50 Hampshire Street, 5th Floor, Cambridge, MA 02139, United States
The Boulevard, Langford Lane, Kidlington, Oxford OX5 1GB, United Kingdom

Notices
Knowledge and best practice in this field are constantly changing. As new research and experience broaden our understanding, changes in research methods, professional practices, or medical treatment may become necessary.

Practitioners and researchers must always rely on their own experience and knowledge in evaluating and using any information, methods, compounds, or experiments described herein. In using such information or methods they should be mindful of their own safety and the safety of others, including parties for whom they have a professional responsibility.

To the fullest extent of the law, neither the Publisher nor the authors, contributors, or editors, assume any liability for any injury and/or damage to persons or property as a matter of products liability, negligence or otherwise, or from any use or operation of any methods, products, instructions, or ideas contained in the material herein.

Library of Congress Cataloging-in-Publication Data
A catalog record for this book is available from the Library of Congress

British Library Cataloguing-in-Publication Data
A catalogue record for this book is available from the British Library

ISBN: 978-0-12-804137-6

For information on all Academic Press publications visit our website at
https://www.elsevier.com/books-and-journals

  Working together
to grow libraries in
developing countries

www.elsevier.com • www.bookaid.org

Publisher: Candice Janco
Acquisition Editor: J. Scott Bentley
Editorial Project Manager: Susan Ikeda
Production Project Manager: Punithavathy Govindaradjane
Designer: Mark Rogers

Typeset by Thomson Digital

Contents

Contributors

Liviu Andreescu, Institutul de Prospectiva, University of Bucharest, Bucharest, Romania

Bjørn Asheim, University of Stavanger, Stavanger, Norway; Lund University, Lund, Sweden

Louis Brennan, Trinity College, Dublin, Ireland

Aleksandrs Cepilovs, Tallinn University of Technology, Tallinn, Estonia

Adrian Curaj, National University of Political Studies and Public Administration (SNSPA), Bucharest, Romania

Dominique Foray, Federal Institute of Technology in Lausanne, Lausanne, Switzerland

Radu Gheorghiu, Institutul de Prospectiva, University of Bucharest, Bucharest, Romania

Ksenia Gonchar, Institute for Industrial and Market Studies of the National Research University Higher School of Economics, Moscow, Russia

Markus Grillitsch, Lund University, Lund, Sweden

Thomas R. Howell, Dentons LLP, Washington, DC, United States

Erkki Karo, Tallinn University of Technology, Tallinn, Estonia

Rainer Kattel, Tallinn University of Technology, Tallinn, Estonia

Henning Kroll, Fraunhofer Institute for Systems and Innovation Research ISI, Karlsruhe, Germany

Yevgeny Kuznetsov, Migration Policy Institute and The World Bank, Washington, DC, United States

Keun Lee, Seoul National University, Seoul, South Korea

Justin Yifu Lin, Center for New Structural Economics, National School of Development, Peking University, Beijing, China

Nikos Maroulis, Technopolis Group, Brussels, Belgium

Slavo Radosevic, University College London, London, United Kingdom

Ruslan Rakhmatullin, European Commission, Joint Research Centre (DG JRC), Seville, Spain

Alasdair Reid, European Future Innovation System Centre, Louvain-la-Neuve, Belgium

Charles Sabel, Columbia Law School, Columbia University, New York City, NY, United States

Michaela Trippl, University of Vienna, Vienna, Austria

Lena J. Tsipouri, National and Kapodistrian University of Athens, Athens, Greece

Imogen Wade, University College London (UCL), London, United Kingdom; Institute for Statistical Studies and Economics of Knowledge of the National Research University Higher School of Economics, Moscow, Russia

Charles W. Wessner, Georgetown University, Washington, DC, United States

Marian Zulean, Institutul de Prospectiva, University of Bucharest, Bucharest, Romania

Preface by Editors

Smart specialization (SS) is a major industrial, innovation, and regional policy activity in the European Union and in the world and has huge transformation potential for both developed and less-developed EU countries and regions. It is also a prime example of a new industrial and innovation policy that requires in-depth scrutiny for two major reasons. First, its intellectual and conceptual novelty demands a detailed comparative exploration. Second, the policy significance of SS and the sheer scale of funding and expectations make it worthy of an in-depth and comparative assessment.

The current book project has gathered together an impressive group of experts on these issues with the aim of contributing to a better understanding of SS as a newly emerging industrial, innovation, and regional policy.

The aim of the book is to position the European Union's SS policy, as the biggest ongoing experiment in industrial and innovation policy globally, within the context of similar approaches that belong to new industrial and innovation policies. The volume synthesizes our knowledge of new industrial and innovation polices and, against this background, assesses SS policy as the European Union's version of a new industrial and innovation policy. We believe that these aims have been achieved by a carefully edited volume written by 23 experts in this area who explore the relevant issues from both academic and policy perspectives. The comparative analyses presented in this volume have broader ramifications for an understanding of viable industrial and innovation policies in other regions of the world.

What distinguishes this book from other recent contributions to its field is: first, its global outlook on the European Union's SS as a large-scale industrial and innovation policy experiment; and, second, its development economics and industrial/innovation policy angle. The 14 chapters of this volume were produced over a 1.5-year period as part of a project financially supported by Romania's Executive Agency for Higher Education, Research and Innovation Funding. The book's authors and editors are grateful to the Agency for its interest in the volume and the process that generated it.

We met at three workshops held in Bucharest on September 3–4, 2015; November 12–13, 2015; and March 3–4, 2016. The preliminary results of the book were presented at a high-level workshop entitled "SS in a Comparative Perspective: Challenges and Ways Forward" held on June 27, 2016 in Brussels under the auspices of the European Commission's Directorate General for Regional and Urban Policy. We benefited from the presence of three external discussants: Jan Larosse and Marek Przeor (both from the European Commission), and Ricardo Crescenzi, from the London School of Economics.

Our ambition was to not only produce an academically excellent, but also a policy-relevant volume that would advance the theory and practice of SS. We hope that we have met at least some of our initial high expectations, but readers and time will tell whether we have succeeded.

We are grateful to Alexandra Roman from the Romanian Executive Agency for her logistical and other support during the work on this project.

Preface by Peter Berkowitz

Head of Unit G1 (Smart and Sustainable Growth), Directorate General for Regional and Urban Policy, European Commission

This book comes at a timely moment. Since the emergence of the smart specialization concept within the European Commission's high-level expert group "Knowledge for Growth" in 2005–09, the policy space and environment-shaping innovation policies in the European Union and beyond have evolved substantially. Indeed, the expectations from policy makers, program, and project managers, as well as the networks of researchers and businesses that drive the generation and implementation of new ideas are greater than ever.

In their original paper, Foray, David, and Hall proposed an entrepreneurial process of discovery, a learning process to reveal the research and innovation domains in which a region can hope to excel. The role of government would be to supply incentives to encourage public, private, and knowledge actors in regions to become involved in the discovery of the regions' respective specializations; to create a process of evaluation and assessment to optimize the use of public resources; and to identify complementary investments both within and outside the region, in particular to link leading and lagging regions (Foray et al., 2009, p. 4).

In parallel, a process of policy reflection was taking place at the European level about how the effectiveness of Europe's policies for economic, social, and territorial cohesion could be increased. This debate expressed several distinct concerns, but focused on the need for the EU budget to deliver European public goods (the Europe 2020 strategy), the importance of institutions in economic development, the role of "place" and proximity in creating the conditions for successful regional and urban growth, and the need to increase the effectiveness of public spending through a greater use of policy conditionalities (Barca, 2009). In particular, smart specialization was seen as a way of increasing the effectiveness of spending on innovation and achieving the Europe 2020 objectives. At the same time, it linked closely to ongoing discussions in economic geography about the role of technological relatedness, embeddedness, connectivity (McCann, 2015, p. 174), and governance in regional economic performance that allowed the new concept to be easily translated into terms that regional policy makers understood.

For the Commission, too much funding had been allocated to overlapping projects or to priorities where regions lacked relative strengths. Regions should, therefore, redirect funding based on a smart specialization approach and focus on relative strengths where they can become excellent (EC, 2010a, p. 22).

This would require focusing the role of the Cohesion Policy on spreading and applying innovation across the European Union at the regional level and on supporting investment in basic infrastructure, institutions, and human resources in less-developed regions, so that they can participate fully in the knowledge economy (EC, 2010b). Smart specialization strategies would ensure a more effective use of public funds and stimulate private investment (EC, 2010c, p. 6). This refocusing of regional innovation spending took the form of an introduction into the regulatory framework governing the Cohesion Policy for the period 2014–20 of a conditionality that required the development of a smart specialization strategy before the agreement of a program. What then can we say after 7 years in what Slavo Radosevic calls in his overview a "massive experiment in innovation and technology upgrading policy"?

First, the new mechanism has had a profound effect on the terms of the discussion of regional innovation policy between the Commission and Member States and regions. This conditionality was applied in 169 out of the 205 programs making use of the European Regional Development Fund (ERDF), and resulted in the development of 93 action plans designed to better target spending, address institutional weaknesses in innovation systems, and improve governance. While there has been a great variation in this discussion, depending on the willingness of Member States to engage fully in the process, this new conceptual framework and the categories and norms it implies have been broadly accepted across Europe.

Second, all involved Member States have engaged, to a greater or lesser degree, in an entrepreneurial discovery process to prioritize support. In all, 121 RIS3 strategies have been agreed, establishing priorities for research and innovation investments in 2014–20. They will receive more than EUR40 billion from the ERDF. Support to research and innovation in the programs is expected to deliver 15,000 new products to market and lead to the creation of 140,000 start-ups, giving rise to 350,000 new jobs by the end of the program period.[1] In addition, EUR1.8 billion have been programmed under the European Social Fund (ESF) for strengthening human capital in research, technological development, and innovation.

Third, a process of policy support and benchmarking has been established by the European Commission, which set up a Smart Specialization (S3) Platform in 2011, providing methodological guidance and hands-on support and facilitating mutual learning, data gathering, analysis, and networking opportunities to around 170 EU regions and 18 EU national governments. Over 1300 national and regional priorities have been identified and mapped in the process of designing RIS3 strategies.[2]

Finally, smart specialization is also now attracting the attention of countries outside Europe. Smart specialization has, therefore, been recognized by international organizations, such as OECD (2013), World Bank (2014), and the United Nations Economic Committee. From the Western Balkans to Asia, and

Latin America, many countries have expressed their interest in learning from and exchanging knowledge with European counterparts that are implementing smart specialization strategies.

The first signs are positive, but we will need to wait for more detailed evaluations of the real impact of these changes, as projects start to be delivered on the ground. These evaluations will have to address the behavioral changes triggered by the new approach, whether new governance structures have led to better choices, and whether smart specialization strategies have led to better economic outcomes for the regions concerned. There are, nevertheless, lessons that can and, indeed, should be drawn from experience to date, which are summarized as follows.

- First, how effective have mechanisms to implement smart specialization in the European regions been?
- Second, has the design of the approach been sufficiently robust to deliver significant technological upgrading, and innovation production and diffusion?
- Third, what policy space does smart specialization occupy and how should it adapt to the challenges facing Europe in the coming years?

The chapters in this book make an important contribution to answering these questions and understanding the lessons that should be drawn for the design of innovation and technological upgrading policies in Europe and beyond. The conscious decision by the authors to assess smart specialization in Europe in the light of new industrial policy frameworks and experience outside Europe throws into sharp contrast achievements, but also weaknesses.

At the level of implementation, the advantages of using conditionality to encourage policy change needs to be weighed against the risks of shifting the focus of national and regional actors toward process and compliance. The institutional context of regulatory politics in the European Union in which policy design is a quality majority bargaining process between principles and agents means that there have been significant buy-in to mechanisms, such as conditionalities. Indeed, several Member States saw the smart specialization conditionality as a way of organizing and disciplining subnational governance of innovation policy. Nevertheless, there was a significant variation in the extent to which conditionality led to changes in prioritization, governance, or stakeholder involvement.

By its nature, a process built on the cooperation of different actors requires not just consent, but a willingness to engage actively in the sharing of knowledge and resources. Solving these collective action problems is a political process. Kroll highlights the challenge of politics and the need to be sensitive to the national or regional context building on processes of exchange between different actors. It is very difficult to reduce strategy building and prioritization to a purely technocratic process as shown by Gheorghiu, Andreescu, Zulean, and Curaj. In the absence of momentum for change, established policy and political routines tend to push choices back to existing the equilibria. Even where strategies and action plans are implemented correctly, there is, as Tsipouri shows for Mediterranean countries, a risk of falling back into the business as usual paradigm, once formal compliance is achieved.

In other cases, there is a risk of capture by one set of policy objectives, such as research in the case of the "scientific" push–based approaches highlighted by Karo, Kattel, and Cepilovs. This reflects a more general concern about ensuring that strategy building and implementation are driven by a genuine partnership including all actors. Weak involvement of the private sector will significantly undermine the entrepreneurial nature of the discovery process. Indeed, a strong and inclusive partnership operating transparently is the best guarantee of the long-term buy-in to the process, and of its strength beyond the formal compliance phase. As several authors highlight, it will be important to reflect on both sticks and carrots in incentive design to ensure effective implementation. While some mechanisms are currently available to provide positive incentives, such as peer learning, benchmarking, and policy support, a broader reflection on how to accompany conditionalities will be necessary for the next generation of smart specialization strategies in Europe.

As Foray highlights, perhaps the key policy design issue is finding a balance between the need to provide government with tools to make strategic decisions and the need to ensure that decentralized entrepreneurial dynamics are the main engine for innovation. Closely linked to this is the engagement of the private sector in creating an "industrial commons." Wessner in his examination of smart specialization in New York shows that to achieve meaningful economic benefits, R&D and research facilities necessarily involve close and multilayered cooperation with industry, and ideally include industry contributions in finance and equipment. In this respect, the design of policy measures to promote smart specialization needs to be seen in the context of a long-term process of reengineering of national and regional innovation ecosystems, rather than simply strategy building and prioritization of public spending. An exogenous agent, such as the European Commission, can play an important role in incentivizing change, but it is only a realignment of interests and incentives within existing national and regional laws, norms, and practices that will lead to durable change. Reid and Maroulis show quite clearly the difficulties in moving from a public agency– to a stakeholder-driven model in regions with weaker institutions. The question of policy design, therefore, becomes how instruments that encourage changes in institutions, behavior, and incentives among a broad range of actors can be developed.

Three clear messages for policy design come from the authors in this collection: a need for greater differentiation, stronger mechanisms of learning, and a simplification of the mechanisms to deliver public support for innovation. Many of the authors highlight the differences between more- and less-developed regions in implementing smart specialization policies. Gonchar, Kuznetsov, and Wade argue convincingly that the policy agenda for advanced and less-developed regions must be designed and implemented quite differently. At a European level initiatives, such as the RIS3 Support to Lagging Regions Pilot Project, seek to test ideas about support for selected low-growth and low-income regions through capacity-building measures, administrative reform, and peer learning.[3] A second key driver for change is policy learning. Kuznetsov and Sabel argue that experimental governance can drive the evolution of public sector agencies toward a more flexible provision of public goods. They highlight the importance of diagnostic monitoring of a project portfolio, rather than focusing on vision and strategies. This implies complementing the classic public policy monitoring and evaluation cycle with a process of learning embedded into the decision-making procedures of both the public and the private sector. Third, many authors highlight the tension between the timescale and deliverables of innovation projects and the eligibility rules and reporting requirements, which are part of the accountability mechanisms of the European funds. It is, therefore, necessary to reflect on how to better design the delivery mechanisms for innovation in the context of smart specialization.

What then is the policy space that smart specialization should occupy? It is clear from the earlier discussion that it goes far beyond research and innovation or regional policy. In the European Union, innovation is central to at least three core policy objectives: creating growth and jobs, future proofing Europe's economy and society, and addressing economic and social disparities and the legacy of the crisis.

In the developed and middle-income countries that characterize the European Union, a key driver of growth and economic convergence will be policies working together to encourage knowledge absorption (Aghion and Jaravel, 2015). According to some estimates, more than half of the total potential for productivity growth in developed countries comes from "catching-up" innovation. Growth in less-advanced countries, where most sectors lie farther behind the current technology frontier, will rely more on imitation (McKinsey, 2015). In both cases, it is necessary to fix the innovation diffusion machine to ensure that economies adopt new technologies and the best practices (OECD, 2016, p. 29). This will require a broad-based policy effort focusing not only on STI policies, but also accompanying them with the upgrading of institutional capacity, structural reforms, and investment in human capital.

However, beyond economic growth, innovation policies need to meet broader societal challenges. This will determine whether growth is sustainable and inclusive in the context of decarbonization, the transition to a circular economy, growing interpersonal and territorial inequalities, and the transformations brought by digitization, demographic change, and new work and consumption patterns. In Europe, this will mean building on research excellence to bring innovative solutions to market, at home, and abroad, and piloting solutions that reflect the diversity of Europe's societies and territories.

Finally, it will be necessary to address the needs of the less-developed economies in Southern, Central, and Eastern Europe. As Radosevic has argued elsewhere, existing policies in Eastern Europe do not sufficiently promote technological innovation, and need a stronger focus on encouraging improvements in production capacities (Radosevic, 2017). It is, therefore, not sufficient to simply improve capacities in relation to research-driven growth, but rather to draw the lessons from the more-developed regions that Asheim, Grillitsch, and Trippl identify, to look beyond traditional science, technology, and innovation policies.

In addition to a broad-based approach to innovation, new industrial policy can provide new tools to address the needs of middle-income countries. Lin argues for a more active role of the state in the design of modernization strategies based on national and regional endowments and comparative advantage. Lee shows how it is possible to propose specific strategies for middle-income countries facing increased competition and entry barriers in high-end segments of the international division of labor. In a European context, this would imply a stronger coordination between smart specialization strategies and the European Union's industrial and competition policies. Brennan and Rakmatullin draw our attention to the importance of positioning sectors in relation to global value chains, and the necessary linkages with initiatives to map their coverage. There is, therefore, clear scope to reinforce policy mechanisms that aim at strengthening complementarities between the European Research Area and the Single Market to create economies of scale and improve access to new ideas. Together, these different elements suggest that smart specialization represents, as Radosevic notes, an incomplete new industrial innovation policy.

The richness of the contributions to this book bear testament to the distance that the concept of smart specialization has traveled since its introduction into the Cohesion Policy in 2010. They add important conceptual and empirical depth to our understanding and help us to draw some preliminary lessons from this European policy experiment. Perhaps the most important lesson for the implementation of the approach is that the fulfillment of a conditionality is only the beginning of a process that involves delivering better innovation outcomes on the ground. This will require political commitment at all levels. For the next generation of smart specialization policy, there will need to be a greater focus on sustainable innovation ecosystem change, built on a greater differentiation of approaches to better target the different needs of regions, embedded learning, and simpler delivery mechanisms. Finally, there is a growing expectation in European policy circles that smart specialization should play a greater role in increasing productivity, meeting societal challenges, and reducing economic and social disparities. This will require a broad-based approach to innovation that is closely linked to policies for skills and education, institutional capacity building, reforms in product and labor markets, and industrial modernization. This book is an excellent starting point for policy makers and academics to reflect on these issues.

DISCLAIMER

The views expressed in this chapter are those of the author, and may not be regarded as stating an official position of the European Commission.

ENDNOTES

1. As planned in the national or regional operational programs for 2014–20 (https://cohesiondata. ec.europa.eu/themes).
2. EYE@RIS3 database: http://s3platform.jrc.ec.europa.eu/eye-ris3
3. http://s3platform.jrc.ec.europa.eu/ris3-in-lagging-regions

REFERENCES

Aghion, P., Jaravel, X., 2015. Knowledge Spillovers, Innovation and Growth. Econ. J. 125, 533–573.

Barca, F., 2009. An Agenda for a Reformed Cohesion Policy: A Place-Based Approach to Meeting European Union Challenges and Expectations. European Commission, Brussels. Available from: https://ec.europa.eu/migrant-integration/librarydoc/an-agenda-for-a-reformed-cohesion-policy-a-place-based-approach-to-meeting-european-union-challenges-and-expectations-barca-report.

European Commission, 2010. Europe 2020 Flagship Initiative Innovation Union, SEC(2010) 1161. Communication from the Commission to the European Parliament; the Council; the European Economic and Social Committee; and the Committee of the Regions, Brussels. Available from: https://ec.europa.eu/research/innovation-union/pdf/innovation-union-communication_en.pdf.

European Commission, 2010. Investing in Europe's future: Fifth Report on economic, Social and territorial Cohesion. Report from the Commission to the European Parliament; the Council; the European Economic and Social Committee; and the Committee of the Regions, Brussels. Available from: http://ec.europa.eu/regional_policy/sources/docoffic/official/reports/cohesion5/pdf/5cr_part1_en.pdf.

European Commission, 2010. COM(2010) 553 Final. Regional Policy Contributing to Smart Growth in Europe 2020. Communication from the Commission to the European Parliament; the Council; the European Economic and Social Committee; and the Committee of the Regions, Brussels. Available from: http://ec.europa.eu/regional_policy/sources/docoffic/official/communic/smart_growth/comm2010_553_en.pdf.

Foray, D., David, P.A., Hall, B., 2009. Smart specialisation—the concept, knowledge economists. Policy Brief No. 9. Available from: http://ec.europa.eu/invest-in-research/pdf/download_en/kfg_policy_brief_no9.pdf.

McCann, P., 2015. The Regional and Urban Policy of the European Union: Cohesion, Results-Orientation and Smart Specialisation. Edward Elgar, Cheltenham and Northampton, MA.

McKinsey Global Institute, 2015. Global growth: can productivity save the day in an aging world? Available from: https://ec.europa.eu/futurium/en/content/global-growth-can-productivity-save-day-aging-world.

Organisation for Economic Co-operation and Development, 2013. Innovation-Driven Growth in Regions: the Role of Smart Specialisation. OECD, Paris. Available from: https://www.oecd.org/innovation/inno/smart-specialisation.pdf.

Organisation for Economic Co-operation and Development, 2016. Regional Outlook 2016: Productive Regions for Inclusive Societies. OECD, Paris. Available from: http://www.oecd.org/publications/oecd-regional-outlook-2016-9789264260245-en.htm.

Piatkowski, M., Szuba, T., Wolszczak, G., 2014. Review of National and Regional Research and Innovation Strategies for Smart Specialisation (RIS3) in Poland. World Bank, Washington, DC.

Radosevic, S., 2017. Upgrading technology in Central and Eastern Europe economies. IZA World of Labour 338, 1–11. Available from: https://wol.iza.org/uploads/articles/338/pdfs/upgrading-technology-in-central-and-eastern-european-economies.pdf.

An Overview

Smart Specialization (SS) as a policy concept has been developed by the high-level expert group "Knowledge for Growth" (K4G[1]), as an independent advisory body for the European Commissioner for Science and Research. Subsequently, this approach was taken up by the Commission as a core element of the 2010 Communication document "Europe 2020 Flagship Initiative Innovation Union" and "Regional Policy Contributing to Smart Growth in Europe 2020," the major EU policy instrument for stimulating knowledge-based growth. It was also endorsed by the EU Council in its Conclusions on the Innovation Union for Europe (2010).

Based on this approach, a practical guide has been developed on how to organize the SS process of analysis and implementation (Foray et al., 2012). To support countries and regions in implementation, the European Commission (EC) established the supporting center and IT platform located at its Joint Research Centre Institute for Prospective Studies (IPTS).[2] This has led to a series of policy support activities and exchange of knowledge on the experiences related to SS activities. As part of these activities, a handbook on "Implementing Smart Specialisation Strategies" has recently been produced (Gianelle et al., 2016).

Developed SS Strategies with implementation plans are preconditions for the effective and efficient use of all EU Funds accessible to less-developed countries and regions in the areas of R&D, innovation, ICT, and low-carbon technologies. However, this by itself would not be a sufficient reason to embark on an in-depth academic scrutiny of SS. Two additional factors have motivated us to explore the European Union's SS experiment.

First, the sheer scale of activities and investments that are being mobilized under the banner of SS is huge. Overall, funding for this area in the 2014–20 period is estimated to total around EUR120 billion, which probably makes it the largest innovation policy experiment in the world.[3] The funding requires 121 national/regional strategies tailored to specific regional strengths and potentials aimed toward innovation-driven growth.

Second, SS is a further step in the evolution of the European Union's regional policy and its approach carries several important features, of which the most important is the idea of the so-called "entrepreneurial discovery process." As defined in Gianelle et al. (2016) "the term Entrepreneurial Discovery Process (EDP) is about prioritising investment based on an inclusive and evidence-based process driven by stakeholders' engagement and attention to market dynamics. The EDP is the motor of the S3 methodology" (p. 13). So, the methodological novelty of SS as a form of new industrial/innovation policy calls for its academic examination within the context of similar emerging approaches. We intentionally label it an "industrial innovation policy" to distinguish it not only from the old type of "sector"-focused industrial policy, but also from the horizontal (generic) type of innovation policy that has been in practice in the last 30 years. The term "industrial innovation" highlights that the area of innovation application (domain) is context dependent (such as industry, technology, and sector) rather than generic. For example, instead of ICT as a generic area, industrial innovation policy focuses on the fields of application of ICT (e.g., ICT in the fishery industry).

SS merges components of industrial and regional policies, but its novelty is in the specific blending of new conceptual features, which it shares with other "new industrial policy approaches" developed elsewhere (see Chapter 1). Its main challenge lies in coupling it with the administrative requirements of the EU Structural Funds.

This massive experiment in innovation and technology upgrading policy takes place within the increasingly divided EU "core" and "periphery" regions/countries. The case for industrial and innovation policy is stronger in the periphery than in the core due to less-developed financial, labor, and other markets and capabilities. However, while SS (explicit or implicit) works quite well in advanced EU regions where "thick networks" of implementing organizations exist, the real challenges are in its application in the periphery. In that respect, SS reinforces the issues recognized some time ago in the notion of "regional innovation paradox" (Oughton et al., 2002).

SS has emerged in the post-2008 context of a revival of industrial policy for which the 2008 global financial crisis, followed by the Eurozone crisis, served as an impetus. This has been further reinforced by the realization of the limits of market and framework conditions (structural reforms) to generate growth and recovery post-2008, as well as by increasing pressures to find alternative ways to stimulate the growth of the green economy and to address climate change challenges. Moreover, several parallel events led to the greater political receptivity of this new policy concept. First, there has been a recognition that much of "the free-market innovation machine" rests on public support to RDI (Mazzucato, 2013). Second, policy makers have realized the limits of horizontal policies (spray gun approach) to promote structural change in the European Union, which legitimized new approaches in industrial policy (EC, 2014). This shift in thinking has been further supported by new approaches in industrial policy (Aghion et al., 2011; Rodrik, 2007), but in a dominantly "Hayekian political economy" (Streeck, 2014) (markets rule) context. Finally, the growth of China and the New Structural Economics (Lin, 2012) as its ex post rationale and policy model have offered conceptually new avenues for thinking about industrial and innovation policy.

In summary, this book is about the emerging new approaches to innovation policy, which can be described as the "new industrial innovation policy." The contributions are focused on the European Union's SS as a large-scale policy experiment but in a comparative global context. In that respect, the book is of high relevance for those interested in new developments in innovation and industrial policy in the world, not only in the European Union. Although the European Union's SS is *de facto* a form of regional policy, this volume takes an innovation and industrial policy perspective, rather than a regional policy perspective. The reason for the relative neglect of spatial effects is not their lesser importance, but the conceptual novelty of SS, which lies not in its spatial focus, but in its design and in its focus on specialization choices.

The volume represents a highly coherent research effort, which has emerged as an outcome of a year and a half–long cooperation of a diverse group of academics and consultants, who are the leading experts in their respective areas and interested in the issues of innovation policy and development.

The book is aimed at researchers, enlightened policy makers, administrators in innovation, industrial and regional policies, consultants, and students. Its focus is both on the conceptual side and on the practice of SS. Moreover, its comparative focus on similar emerging approaches in the world will be relevant to those interested not only in the EU context, but also in emerging and other developed economies.

In what follows, we provide a brief overview of the book.

The book is structured in five blocks, each focused on a specific dimension of SS.

Chapter 1, by Slavo Radosevic, positions EU SS within the context of the six other newly emerged approaches to industrial and innovation policy. These approaches—binding constraints to growth, product space method, new structural economics, the neo-Schumpeterian and the Schumpeterian approach, and process (evolutionary) view—are briefly explained and comparatively analyzed. Within this context, EU SS is defined as the European Union's version of new industrial innovation policy. This chapter also outlines the policy implications of each of the seven emerging approaches of new industry and innovation policy and elaborates the key challenges of the EU SS.

Two chapters in the first block of chapters are about conceptual and rationale issues related to SS and new industrial policy.

Chapter 2 is written by Dominique Foray, one of the godfathers of the SS approach. In it, Foray clarifies the fundamentals of SS—its "sector nonneutral" character, its rationale and the role of the entrepreneurial discovery process, the optimal level of concentration, and the continuous nature of the process.

Chapter 3, by Yevgeny Kuznetsov and Charles Sabel, analyzes the key feature of the new open economy industrial policy, which can also be described as the process (evolutionary) approach. Its key features are its experimental character based on diagnostic (problem-solving) monitoring of a relevant project portfolio. Unlike the European Union's approach outlined by Foray, which is focused on the question of "what," this approach is more concerned with the issues of "how" or the institutional design for policy. The authors introduce the notion of a "Schumpeterian development agency" as key to this approach.

The second block of chapters brings the implementation issues of SS into focus in the context of two developed parts of the European Union (Scandinavia and Germany), contrasted with the less-developed regions of Southern Europe.

Chapter 4, by Bjoern Asheim, Markus Grillitsch, and Michaela Trippl, focuses on how competitive advantage through SS can be promoted based on the industry-specific modes of innovation and knowledge bases. They show how in high-income Scandinavian economies, companies, and regions are building competitive advantages based not only on science, technology, and innovation (STI mode), but also on experience (doing-using-interacting or DUI mode). Scandinavian regions have developed their SS strategies applying this broad perspective on innovation, which is well adapted to their regional and industrial specificities.

In Chapter 5, Henning Kroll explores the involvement of German regions in the European Union's SS agenda. He shows that the degree of their participation is not only determined by their capacities for SS policy, but also by political expedience. He finds that three important aspects matter most for the uptake of SS policies: economic size, multilevel governance framework, and political culture.

In Chapter 6, Lena Tsipouri explores the potential of SS in the modernization of the economies of Southern Europe. She investigates the possibility of a long-term impact and shows the varied impact of EU regional policy in the past. Based on a comparative overview of several regions, she demonstrates that regional development policy can restructure the business sector in the medium-to-long term, and build resilient, technologically advanced economies. However, most often it leads to pockets of excellence, which remain isolated. In addition, she documents the inadequate responses of Southern regions to the ex-ante preconditions and how continuous priority is given to the absorption of funding over the "quality" of spending.

The third block of chapters explores the issues of industrial and innovation policies in various non-EU contexts (in USA, China, Korea, Israel, Russia, and Argentina).

In Chapter 7, Charles Wessner and Thomas R. Howell present a major example of successful regional economic development in the United States, "Tech Valley," the nanotechnology cluster based around Albany, New York, which reflects the SS concept. This initiative arose in a cooperative fashion, reflecting long-term, state-level development goals made possible in part by the determination and competency of local development actors at different levels, and also by the presence of shared, cutting-edge facilities. They show that path dependency is not necessarily destiny, but that success rests crucially on cooperation at multiple levels.

In Chapter 8, Justin Yifu Lin presents the key policy features of New Structural Economics, an approach that postulates that the industrial structure of an economy is endogenous to its endowment structure. The key policy issues of this perspective are how to turn the latent comparative advantage industries to the nation's competitive advantages. In this chapter, Lin further develops the approach by outlining five different industrial policies for middle-income economies rooted in the New Structural Economics framework and based on the industry's distance to the global technological frontier. He outlines the facilitating role of the state in each of these cases.

In Chapter 9, Keun Lee analyzes one of the key questions of SS: in which activities to specialize. He proposes the "cycle time of technologies" as a criterion for SS, which is superior to other approaches. In short-cycle technologies, the dominance of the incumbent is often disrupted, and new technologies represent "windows of opportunity." In this chapter, Lee proposes several strategies for implementing this criterion, which is focused on how public interventions could avoid both targeting and design failures by involving private firms from the beginning.

Chapter 10 by Ksenia Gonchar, Yevgeny Kuznetsov, and Imogen Wade, presents several examples of real-life SS processes in middle-income economies (such as Russia, Israel, and Argentina) with a significant knowledge base but weak institutions. These cases are framed within a three-stage model, which explains growth and structural change from the first mover problem to the issue of collective action or regional cluster coordination problem, to the critical mass problem or how to acquire or build a bundle of highly specialized and interrelated institutions. Their examples show that regional development is usually a by-product of the national or global success of private first movers, but the key challenge is around their clustering. The model and examples show that the policy agenda for advanced and less-developed regions must be designed and implemented differently.

The fourth block is about the role of global value chains (GVCs) in SS. Unfortunately, we have only one chapter to cover this critical dimension of the SS, which also reflects a significant knowledge gap in the understanding of the role of GVCs as mechanisms of technology upgrading and the role of SS-type policies.

In Chapter 11, Louis Brennan and Ruslan Rakhmatullin explore how to transnationalize SS, that is, how innovation policy can help decision makers use GVCs as mechanisms of local technological upgrading. They develop a novel methodology that regions can employ to engage with GVCs built around a three-tier approach. The first tier is about the policy and strategy levels, the second about a focus on cluster-related activities, and the third about project-level activities to support emerging value chains.

The fifth and final block of the book is about the institutional environment and implementation issues for SS. The focus on design and the issues of selecting priorities is important. Yet in the end, the implementation and broader institutional context will determine the effectiveness of new industrial innovation policies, such as SS. As evidence in the book demonstrates, the key challenges of SS concern its implementation in less-developed regions and countries, a focus of the chapters in this block.

In Chapter 12, Erkki Karo, Rainer Kattel, and Aleksandrs Cepilovs explore the institutional preconditions for experimental governance as the basis of SS policies in the context of the Baltic states and the Central European countries. They show that the maturity, or level of development, of national, regional, and sectoral innovation systems regarding actor capabilities and networks determines the depth and quality of SS, and especially of the entrepreneurial discovery processes. The entrepreneurial discovery process has resulted in consciously broad and vague specializations, which will need to be followed by implementation and further selection at a more "granular" level. However, this requires significant policy experimentation (design of novel and flexible policy interventions), which is highly challenging and would require an explicitly flexible approach regarding administrative rules and regulations when implementing the policy.

Chapter 13, by Alasdair Reid and Nikos Maroulis, analyzes the implementation challenges of SS. They explore how SS strategies are being translated into programs, notably regarding the types of instruments applied. The experimental nature of SS policy should also extend into the modes or instruments of its implementation. Based on four country cases (Finland, Scotland, Poland, and Greece) they find new delivery arrangements (open innovation platforms) in developed countries/regions, and a dominance of traditional public agency/management authority models with limited room for innovative and strategic initiatives in less-developed EU countries.

Chapter 14, by Radu Gheorghiu, Liviu Andreescu, Marian Zulean, and Adrian Curaj, is a case study of Romania's SS priority selection, which used a foresight exercise as its "entrepreneurial discovery process." This is an attempt to make the process of priority selection as politically neutral as possible through combined data analytics with broad consultations focused on consensus making. They show that the large-scale but one-off exercise has so far failed to generate an enduring entrepreneurial discovery mechanism. The experimental nature of the process was subsequently circumvented by established policy and political routines. The case well illustrates the strengths and limits of the "depoliticization" approach to priority selection.

Finally, in Chapter 15 Slavo Radosevic summarizes key findings of the volume and outlines key policy messages.

For editors
Slavo Radosevic

ENDNOTES

1. http://ec.europa.eu/invest-in-research/monitoring/knowledge_en.htm
2. http://s3platform.jrc.ec.europa.eu/home
3. The exact figure that will be spent under the label of Smart Specialization (SS) depends on how we define its scope. The estimate of EUR120 billion includes around EUR40 billion of the European Regional Development Fund (ERDF), which is directly aimed toward SS activities (i.e., subject

to the conditionality), and EUR83 billion for the broader support for industrial modernization (i.e., including small- and medium-sized enterprises). An additional EUR110 billion includes funding for a low-carbon economy (only some of which is innovation). The further we move away from direct research and innovation (R&I) expenditure, the less direct is the linkage with the S3 process. So, if we take the very broad definition of S3, the overall figure is EUR250 billion, and it includes EU funding, national cofinancing, and private sector leverage.

REFERENCES

Aghion, P., Boulanger, J., Cohen, E., 2011. Rethinking industrial policy. Breugel Policy Brief. Available from: http://bruegel.org/2011/06/rethinking-industrial-policy/.

Foray, D., Goddard, J., Goenaga Beldarrain, X., Landabaso, M., McCann, P., Morgan, K., Nauwelaers, C., Ortega-Argilés, R., 2012. Guide to research and innovation strategies for smart specialization (RIS 3). European Commission. Available from: http://ec.europa.eu/regional_policy/sources/docgener/presenta/smart_specialisation/smart_ris3_2012.pdf.

Gianelle, C., Kyriakou, D., Cohen, C., Przeor, M. (Eds.), 2016. Implementing Smart Specialisation Strategies. JRC IPTS, Luxembourg, Available from: http://s3platform.jrc.ec.europa.eu/documents/20182/154972/Implementing+Smart+Specialisation+Strategies+A+Handbook/2a0c4f81-3d67-4ef7-97e1-dcbad00e1cc9.

Lin, J.Y., 2012. New structural economics: a framework for rethinking development and policy. World Bank Res. Obs. 26 (2), 193–221.

Mazzucato, M., 2013. The Entrepreneurial State: Debunking the Public Vs. Private Myth in Risk and Innovation. Anthem Press, London.

Oughton, C., Landabaso, M., Morgan, K., 2002. The regional innovation paradox: innovation policy and industrial policy. J. Technol. Trans. 27, 97–110.

Rodrik, D., 2007. One Economics, Many Recipes: Globalization, Institutions, and Economic Growth. Princeton University Press, Princeton, NJ.

Streeck, W., 2014. Buying Time: The Delayed Crisis of Democratic Capitalism. Verso, London.

Chapter 1

Assessing EU Smart Specialization Policy in a Comparative Perspective

Slavo Radosevic
University College London, London, United Kingdom

Chapter Outline

Academic Highlights

- Analyzes the origins and rationales for the emergence of the new industrial and innovation policies and elaborates their key stylized features.
- Develops a comparative analysis of seven contemporary approaches, which belong to a group of new industrial and innovation policies.
- Positions EU smart specialization conceptually as a case of an incomplete new industrial innovation policy in the context of other similar approaches.

Advances in the Theory and Practice of Smart Specialization. http://dx.doi.org/10.1016/B978-0-12-804137-6.00001-2
1

Policy Highlights

- Outlines the policy implications of the seven emerging approaches of new industrial and innovation policies.
- Elaborates the key challenges of EU innovation policy within the context of similar approaches.

INTRODUCTION

This chapter aims to set the scene for the contributions in this volume, as well as highlight the major issues related to contemporary industrial policies and smart specialization (SS) in particular. The key point of departure is that SS is considered as a type of new industrial and innovation policy, which shares similarities with other approaches, but also has its unique features.

The 2008 Global Financial Crisis (GFC) shook up the firmly held belief among policy makers in developed economies in "free market" policies, as the crisis itself required extensive state intervention in the financial system, including rescuing and nationalizing the major banks. The current situation calls for a reexamination of past policy approaches within their historical context, and a conceptualization of the emerging approaches. However, the GFC is not the only trigger to the revival of industrial policy. Climate change as the biggest market failure in history (Stern, 2006) shows that *laisezz faire*–led technology trajectories do not guarantee the emergence of technologies that can help reduce global warming. Moreover, the rise of China (Heilmann and Shih, 2013) and the related premature deindustrialization of the developing world (Rodrik, 2016) demonstrate the importance of industrial policy as a mechanism to counteract this trend.

Industrial policy is a much politicized and overloaded term, one that is often reduced to the idea of "infant industry" through foreign trade protection. In the last 30–40 years, industrial policy has changed in nature and has been practiced in forms that are not usually associated with the established notion of industrial policy (Rodrik, 2004). It has been widely implemented through innovation, regional, and FDI policy, and its area of application shifted from foreign trade and protection to domestic regulatory and support systems in a relatively open trade and FDI context. In fact, we have seen a convergence of innovation policies globally, which are at the core of new industrial policies. With respect to that, the term industrial policy should be understood here in its very broad meaning encompassing innovation, FDI, and regional policies. Crespi et al. (2014) use the term *productive development policies*, which possibly better reflect the issues that this book addresses. To avoid identifying with the old type of vertical industrial policies, and also to differentiate new industrial policy from conventional horizontal innovation policies, we label it as *industrial innovation policy*. We do not consider it as an oxymoron, but rather a fair reflection of a merger of innovation and industrial policy. Its focus is neither industries as sectors defined by products, nor broadly defined innovation capabilities outside their industry application.

In the next session, we discuss background issues, including the rationale and specificity of industrial policies, Section, "A Brief Historical Reminder" discusses what preceded the emergence of new industrial policies (NIP). Section, "Key Features of New Industrial Policies: A Stylized Picture" discusses the major stylized features of NIP. Section, "New Approaches to Industrial Policy" compares the following seven approaches characterizing the contemporary landscape of new industrial policy: binding constraints to growth; product space method; new structural economics; neo-Schumpeterian approach; Schumpeterian approach; process (evolutionary) view of industrial policy, and EU smart specialization policy. Section, "Challenges of Smart Specialization" elaborates the key challenges for the EU of SS policy. The chapter ends with Section, "Conclusions".

Rationales and Framework for Industrial Policy

The justification for industrial policies lays in the insufficiency of market mechanisms to allocate and coordinate economic activities in a way that ensures productivity growth and improves social welfare (Aghion et al., 2011a; Bator, 1958). The market failure is usually discussed in the context of remedy, which is government intervention (Krueger, 1990). So, the crux of the debate on industrial policy is the costs and benefits of market versus government failures. A conventional view is that it is always better to tolerate market failures than government failures (Krueger 1990). Contrary to this are views that industrial policy lies behind many of the success stories (Amsden, 1989; Rodrik, 2006; Wade, 1990). Far too often the debate on market versus states is model driven rather than empirical. Besides, these issues are framed as polar and ignore the importance of commons or intermediate organizational forms in between states and market (Ostrom, 1990). From an innovation policy perspective, industry commons are R&D, engineering, and manufacturing capabilities that are of a collective nature and area-specific (Berger, 2015; Pisano and Shih, 2009). Moreover, conventional economic discourse does not consider a variety of institutional factors, such as mechanisms of private–public interactions that can reduce government failures (Chang, 1994). In a nutshell, the discussion is too often general and ignores the specificities of different industrial and innovation policies and instruments.

It is important to bear in mind that both market and government failures are fraught with information problems (Chang 1994; Stiglitz and Greenwald, 2014). Market failures are affected by the issues of market power, and government failures by self-seeking bureaucrats while both are affected by negative externalities (Buigues and Sekkat, 2009). The argument about market failure is centered on the issue of appropriability, that is, the lack of incentives for an innovator to embark on a costly and risky innovation project given how easily its proprietary knowledge can "spill" over to others. In addition to market failures, there are coordination failures among firms and nonmarket institutions or system failures (OECD, 1998). So, we consider appropriability and coordination failures as the two core rationales for industrial and innovation policy.

Summarizing a voluminous literature on the rationales and framing of innovation and industrial policies (Berger, 2015; Crespi et al., 2014; Radosevic, 2012) we conclude that:

- Both market and government failures are reflection of endemic imperfect information, bounded rationality, and knowledge transfer problems;
- There is no priori better governance solution, be it a market, government, or other; rather, the best solution depends on the context;
- A government/market dichotomy is not very helpful to guide policy, as any policy can be designed and implemented in the context of various other stakeholders.

Why are Industrial and Innovation Policies "Hard"?

Industrial and innovation policy is an area where economists disagree on its definition, scope, and object, while holding adamant views on the issue. The discussion earlier helps us understand why industrial and innovation policies are hard to design and implement. The three major factors mentioned earlier that make industrial and innovation policies or "productive development policies" (PDP) difficult to implement and design are all succinctly summarized by Crespi et al. (2014).

First, the problems of industrial and innovation (I&I) policies are not known ex-ante. Even when problems are defined, generic solutions are difficult to agree on, while specific policy instruments will be most often country or region specific. This indeterminacy of industrial (innovation or regional) policy makes its design and implementation a search process (Crespi et al., 2014, p 322). So, from the outset these policies require the policy process to be organized as a "policy discovery process."

Second, industry and innovation policies deliver results after many years, often much longer than electoral cycles. The multiyear frameworks within which the EU regional policies are implemented also stretch beyond electoral periods. This feature makes the political economy of I&I and regional policies very different from macroeconomic policies, where short-term political considerations play a much stronger role.

Third, I&I policies require technical, operational, and political (TOP) capabilities to implement program routines, manage funds, and secure political support. However, these capabilities are usually scattered across a larger number of actors and stakeholders, which are not often available (Crespi et al., 2014, pp. 321–324). The knowledge and technical skills requirements for I&I policies are demanding, often beyond the competencies in the public sector. They require collaboration with the private sector, which often has a better in-depth understanding of the issues involved. They also require cooperation across several public agencies or bodies, which is not always easy to achieve. So, unlike implementing macroeconomic policy, I&I policies are by definition interministerial, intersectoral, and multistakeholder in nature.

Fourth, like all other policies, I&I policies are prone to capture and rent-seeking, even though their "carrots" and "sticks" are less clear than with some other policies.

Finally, given these complexities of design and implementation, I&I policies require developed institutional capabilities that go well beyond those required for macroeconomic policies. Some of these capabilities are the outcome of different historically rooted roles of the state and business in various economies and cannot be built by a small team of "modernizers."

A BRIEF HISTORICAL REMINDER

The current revival of industrial policy or mainstreaming of innovation policy cannot be understood outside its historical context. Hence, in this section, we briefly overview the genealogy of industrial policy or the sequence of stages leading to its revival.

The import substitution (IS) consensus of the 1950–70s represents the last wave of industrial policies to which the current revival can be compared. The IS is usually referred to as the "old industrial policies," which were based among others on the assumption that technology can be developed equally well in a protected environment (Radosevic, 1999; Chapter 2).

These strategies ran increasingly into problems due to limited domestic markets, insufficient competitive pressures, the tendency to overdiversify production, and an antiexport bias of the IS macroregime (Crespi et al., 2014; Radosevic, 1999; Ramos, 2000). We consider IS industrial policies as pivotal examples of policies during 1950–70s, but they were by no means the only type. East Asia and Japan had their versions of industrial policies, with the stronger role of performance requirements. The former Eastern Bloc could be considered as having an extreme form of an IS regime. The more developed world had its version of IS through a Colbertist type of industrial policy[1] and a range of national champions projects and sectors with very different outcomes.

The Washington Consensus (WC) era represents the period between 1980–90s and early 2000s up to the 2008 GFC. It was a radical shift in the global political economy when compared to the import substitution period of 1950–70s. This policy philosophy represented a reaction to the failures of the state in attempting to correct those of the market. This period accounts for a shift toward a greater role for markets and a limited role of the state. Its features are well known and are summarized in Williamson (1990, 1999).

The assessment of this period is that WC-based policies in their original form failed to deliver on their promises. In particular, these policies initially neglected institutions completely. Then the so-called "second-generation" reforms were introduced, which were heavily institutional in nature. The focus of this so-called Augmented WC was in "getting institutions right." This policy coincided with a period of "rediscovering" institutions in economics, although the term "institutions" has been and still is used as a placeholder (Nelson, 2006), that is, like the notion of "total factor productivity" in growth. Rodrik (2006a) summarizes the

"Augmented WC" policies, which were a paradigmatic example of "free market" policies: part of a shift toward a neoliberal economic policy philosophy that was a characteristic of the OECD or the more developed world.

A 2005 World Bank "mea culpa" study lists the disappointments, which, according to the WC, could not have occurred. In this period, the growth of China and Vietnam took place, which—although a pleasant surprise—should not have happened according to the WC. From an international political economic perspective, we are currently in the period of post-WC (or confusion) (Naim, 1999; Rodrik, 2006a). One of the features of this period is the revival of industrial policy (Wade, 2012). However, we still lack a clear understanding of the conceptual character of new industrial policies. Radosevic (2012) is an example of a developed conceptual characterization of the so-called post-WC industrial and innovation policies. Milberg et al. (2014) is probably the most articulate characterization of industrial policies in the context of globalization. They explicitly contrast import substitution, export-oriented, and vertically-specialized industrialization. In this chapter, we depict seven approaches to industrial and innovation policy, which we describe as "new industrial policies." These share several common features, which are quite distinctive compared to the old type of industrial policies.

KEY FEATURES OF NEW INDUSTRIAL POLICIES: A STYLIZED PICTURE

The current policy landscape is changing, and no single coherent political philosophy dominates. Nevertheless, debates can be situated within the triangle of three philosophies. The first is "big push" and old-style "picking winners" policies, including different versions of Colbertist industrial policies (for a critique of French and European policies of this type, see Cohen and Lorenzi, 2000). The "picking winners" policies operate as a kind of "straw man" in the discussions about industrial policy. This is mainly because the institutional conditions and context for the old type of industrial policy have changed dramatically in Europe and globally, which makes a critique of any of the old types of industrial policy irrelevant. The second area is the structural reforms and horizontal policies, which still dominate the policy practice but have lost their intellectual dominance and can be considered as the "old man." Third, "new industrial policies" are a novel player on the policy landscape and may be regarded as the "new man."

New industrial policies (NIP) share, as a major common point of departure, the idea that the "ultimate" constraints to growth are unknown, and these constraints need to be "discovered" through the process through which an understanding of these limitations emerges. The premise of the new industrial policies is that policy makers cannot know what the right policy interventions are and need to set up a process to "discover" them (Crespi et al., 2014, p. 28).

Unlike the old-style industrial policies, new industrial policies recognize that the government does not possess all the necessary information to make the right decisions. Equally, firms do not have perfect foresight about the opportunities and constraints that they are facing in the long-term. In fact, all views are partial, and no actor possesses a panoramic view of an industry. Industrial policy is primarily a process characterized by the establishment of search networks or "cooperative public and private sector efforts that anticipate technological change and its effects rather than a priori defined targets (Kuznetsov and Sabel, 2006; Sabel, 2005; Wilson and Furtado, 2006[2]). The target objectives may be achieved in a variety of ways, which makes these policies strategic.

The actual implementation is more critical than the ex-ante rational design of policies. Because of the need to learn from specific and local conditions, "there is a strong element of indeterminacy in strategic policies, by definition, in contrast to market failure policies which, ideally, should be able to calculate the welfare effects of each intervention. As the outcome is not known in advance—only the strategic objectives—the implementation is more important than the initial design. The policy process becomes a learning activity in itself" (Radosevic, 1997, p. 192).

As the policy outcomes are inherently unknowable ex-ante, it is important to get the policy process right. How we design a setting in which private and public actors come together to solve problems in the productive sphere is the main issue (Rodrik, 2007). A good institutional design will enable industrial policy to happen as a discovery process—one in which firms and the government learns about the underlying costs and opportunities and engages in strategic coordination (ibid.).

To be effective, new industrial policy requires a "rich" institutional context but also new forms of governance. What this means is that an institutionally "rich" system of government-business relations, and of self-organizing mechanisms within business and industry, is the best way to correct both government and market failures. In addition, NIP in their idealized form requires so-called "experimentalist governance." Sabel and Zeitlin (2011, p. 17) define this as "a recursive process of provisional goal setting and revision based on learning from the comparison of alternative approaches to advancing them in different contexts," (p. 19). This approach recognizes that in complex situations of strategic uncertainty, as in cases of NIP, a traditional principal–agent relationship falls apart. Instead, governance arrangements that are polyarchical, and goals and metrics relying on agents' experiences, are the most effective solution.

Given that no actor has a panoramic view of reality, the traditional weberian bureaucracy approach would fail miserably. Hence, an NIP situation requires Schumpeterian bureaucracy for which policy itself is a discovery process. However, Schumpeterian bureaucracy can only be effective if the institutional precondition for experimentalist governance exists: primarily, developed forms of "nonmarket articulation of market" or rich networks of business and consumer associations in communication with government bodies. Very often, this undeveloped gray area between business and government is a much bigger bottleneck to industrial policy than the administrative capacities of government. The issue boils down to how to build an institutional setting for "embedded autonomy" (Evans, 1985) or a situation in which the state has autonomy but is equally enmeshed in rich knowledge networks with the private sector, through which it can enter into dialog about growth challenges. As Rodrik (2004) points out, the institutional setting that balances autonomy and embeddedness is far more important than the specifics of individual policy instruments.

Given the various imperfections of institutional settings for industrial policy, the aim is to formulate policies that match institutional capacities. As pointed out by Rodrik (2007, p. 113), "a first-best policy in the wrong institutional setting will do considerably less good than a second-best policy in an appropriate institutional setting."

In states with weak institutional capabilities, policy overreach is a real possibility. The capacity to coordinate actions across public sector agencies and to effectively engage in collaboration with private sector actors is essential to a new industrial policy. If these capabilities are absent, "the focus ought to be not on policy 'best practice' but on policy 'best matches' with institutional capabilities" (Crespi et al., 2014, p. 29).

An additional challenge is realizing "embedded autonomy" in a globalized context, which is much harder than in a context with clearly delineated national spaces. The issue is "openness" versus "autonomy" and, in the framework of a globalized economic environment, about where the border lies. The globalization of the 1990 and 2000s has blurred the boundaries between domestic and foreign economic spaces. Examples of this are IPR, foreign access to national R&D programs, and national versus international regulations and standards. In addition, equity and nonequity linkages in marketing, finance, production, and other business activities have blurred the boundary between the domestic and foreign determinants of technology transfer. So the possibilities for influencing technology transfer at the "borders" have been reduced, and consequently, there has been a policy shift toward domestic or intraregional regulations that make use of increasing production, market, and other linkages (Radosevic, 1999).

We outlined earlier the main conceptual features of the emerging new industrial policy thinking and practice. We cannot cover here in greater detail all their characteristics, but in stylized form new industrial and innovation policies can be summarized as follows:

- Focused on innovation and technology upgrading in an intersectoral context, where industry boundaries are not defined through products, but rather "sectors" and where "activities" correspond to "capabilities;"
- "Smart" because they recognize that the ultimate limits to growth and the relevant solutions are not known ex-ante;
- "Market friendly" because they show respect for comparative advantages and export transformation;
- Oriented toward both horizontal and vertical policy instruments, a dichotomy, which is considered operationally not very useful;
- Assuming either explicitly or implicitly some elements of experimentalist governance;
- Guided by the perceptions of not only market failure, but also system failure;

- Centered around the private sector and innovation ecosystem actors;
- Global value chains are considered as significant potential levers of technology upgrading.

These stylized features reflect the variety of emerging approaches rather than one specific approach. In the next section, we depict seven distinct approaches, which all share some of the aforementioned stylized features of new industrial policy.

NEW APPROACHES TO INDUSTRIAL POLICY

New industrial policies (NIP) are a set of emerging analytical approaches by countries and regions, which try to support active diversification and technology upgrading. Their rise should be seen in the context of the perceived limits of structural reforms and horizontal (generic) innovation policies as the only policies to promote technology upgrading and structural change, especially in the post-2008 period.

We consider the following approaches[3] as the new industrial policies:

- Binding constraints to growth: Rodrik et al.; McKinsey et al.
- Product space method: Hausman and Hidalgo
- New structural economics: Justin Jifu Lin et al.
- Neo-Schumpeterian approach: Keun Lee
- Schumpeterian approach: Aghion et al.
- Process (evolutionary) view of industrial policy: Sabel, Kuznetsov, Teubal et al.
- Smart specialization policies: Foray et al.

These are distinctive methodological approaches in selecting priorities and identifying the key policy aims. They differ widely regarding their normative as opposed to analytical features and degrees to which they articulate them. However, they all share the following three common departing points:

1. *No single agent (be it government, its agencies, firms, or R&D organizations) has a panoramic view of the economy.* All opinions are partial, hence the constraints on growth or new promising specializations are not known ex-ante. With respect to that, all NIP approaches are smart, as they recognize the inability of policy and market actors to have perfect foresight.
2. *The key feature of NIP is getting the policy process such that it can lead to the "discovery" of new specializations.* A key feature is not focusing on the policy outcomes, that is, on specializations or diversifications as these are inherently unknowable ex-ante, but on the design of "discovery processes."
3. *Policy making is an endogenous variable in the process of discovery, coordination, and implementation of industrial policy, which facilitates the process of self-discovery by agents.* Policy uses market-friendly instruments but given a variety of institutional contexts and distances of countries in relation to the technology frontier, policy mixes are mixtures of first and second best solutions. In other words, "one size does not fit all" is the pervading policy principle.

Binding Constraints to Growth: Rodrik et al.; McKinsey Global Institute

The growth diagnostics framework developed by Hausmann et al. (2005) assumes that there are many reasons why an economy does not grow. However, only some of these constraints are so important that they hinder growth significantly. For that purpose, they have developed a top-down approach, which aims to diagnose potential constraints that impede the growth process (Hausmann et al., 2005). It purports to unveil the areas where there might be high-payoff interventions regarding growth. The binding constraints model is based on the logic that growth is dependent on private investment (rate of return). If private investments are low, then this is either due to low returns on economic activity, the high cost of finance, or both. Accordingly, there are three classes of variables, which must be considered when investigating the reasons why there is a low rate of private investments. The first class of variables is related to low social returns (geography, poor human capital, bad infrastructure). The second class of variables is related to low appropriability represented through government failures (corruption, taxes, crime, the judicial system, political stability, uncertain economic policies, regulations) and market failures (information failure, coordination failure). The third class of variables is related to the cost of finance, which may be a result of poor access to international finance (country risk, credit rating) or to poor local finance (poor intermediation, access to and cost of finance, and low domestic savings).

This approach and methodology are useful to analyze the binding constraints to firms" growth. However, countries usually have more than a single binding constraint, which hampers its growth. It is unclear whether removing the major binding constraint will necessarily have a greater effect than gradually reducing many constraints (Rodríguez, 2005). Moreover, the method is focused on physical investments, which may not be the most important driver of growth (Agosin et al., 2009; Felipe and Usui, 2008), although problems with investments are a symptom of broader problems in the economy (Hausmann et al., 2008).

A parallel to this macrobased approach is a microbased one developed by McKinsey Global Institute in a series of projects over the 1990s and early 2000s to identify binding constraints [Lewis, 2004; Palmade, 2005 and a series of studies, which are available on the McKinsey Global Institute website (www. mckinsey.com/mgi/)]. McKinsey has developed a methodology that explores the causes of low productivity at the level of individual industries where data are not easily available. With respect to that, binding constraints that need to be discovered are not only country—but also industry-specific. Their evidence shows that very often constraints are located in nontechnological issues like organization or policy-induced distortions, while the productivity gap is concentrated in nonindustry sectors, such as retail. Their approach is very useful in detecting sectors of high and low productivity, as well as the most important reasons for these differences. They persuasively show that factors that hinder productivity are not generic economy-wide factors, but specific industry weaknesses, some of which are very often related to vested interests. This approach does not have a clear view regarding industrial policy, but it does show a link between special interests and anticompetitive behavior. By focusing on the demand side and consumer interest, it is an useful antidote to industrial policy's strong focus on the supply side.

Like other NIP approaches, the "binding constraints" approach starts from the same assumption that ultimate constraints need to be "discovered," that is, they are not known in advance. The procedure of discovery is quite different in Rodrik et al.'s macrobased approach versus McKinsey's microbased approach. However, once binding constraints are removed, both these approaches assume that firms will grow, that is, there are no other constraints to growth related to the institutional system, etc.

Product Space and Export Product Complexity (Hausmann and Hidalgo): Trade-Based Specializations (Diversification) Approach

The product space approach is based on the stylized fact that countries tend to have productive structures similar to that of their richer neighbors. Accordingly, firms in the existing sectors have knowledge that is helpful for successful upgrading/diversification to adjacent sectors in the product space. So, within this framework, two considerations are critical: the notion of relatedness or proximity between products and the quality or value embedded in a country's exports. The approach is to measure the sophistication of the tradable products using income level as the weighting factor. This allows categorizing relationships between the export industries, as well as evaluating the export profile of a country at a given time. The richer countries will export more complex products, that is, products that are less ubiquitous due to the complex knowledge required for its production.

This conceptual approach emerged initially in a paper by Lall et al. (2006), who developed a measure for sophistication of export goods based on the per capita income of the countries exporting them. They show that more sophisticated products embody greater capabilities and more advanced technologies, which can serve as proxies of the technology upgrading of economies. Hausmann et al. (2007) have developed a similar measure of product sophistication where they show that countries with more sophisticated export baskets tend to grow faster. Hidalgo and Hausmann (2009) propose a new measure of export sophistication or complexity. Products are more complex when fewer countries competitively export them, and these countries have dense export baskets, with many products. A country's export complexity is measured by its Economic Complexity Index (ECI): the average complexity of the basket products that it exports competitively. The ECI aims to capture the underlying productive capabilities that countries accumulate (Hausmann et al., 2014). Felipe et al. (2012) use Hidalgo and Hausmann (2009) methodology and computed measures of product and country complexity for 124 countries, showing that the export shares of the most complex products increase with income, while exports of the less complex products decrease with income.

The limitations of the product space method are largely technical. First, trade data are only a proxy for the productive structure of an economy, and in some cases, can substantially deviate from actual sectoral contributions to GDP. Nontraded products and sectors involve relevant, productive capabilities, which are not directly visible in export data. Second, a single trade code may lump together items requiring different skills sets, thus overlooking differences in product quality. Thus, countries that export similar products may, in fact, have very different productive capabilities (Crespi et al., 2014). Third, differences in market structure across countries make export performance a better or worse estimate of productive capacities depending on trade openness, domestic market size, and other related factors. Fourth, the potential importance of services exports in fostering economic growth is not accounted for. Finally, trade data may not reflect actual value added of final exports due to geographically dispersed assembly industries (e.g., the Mexican *maquila* system), which could overstate the actual productive capacities of a country. The fragmentation of global value chains (GVCs) distorts the picture of so-called assembler economies, which show a sophisticated export basket but are de facto engaged in low-complexity assembly of high-tech goods (e.g., Hungary and Malaysia) (Schteingart, 2015). As a result, among the top 20 countries in the Atlas of Economic Complexity (Hausmann et al., 2014) we find four Central and East European countries (Czech Republic, Hungary, Slovenia, and Slovakia), whereby Hungary is ranked ahead of the United States. This obviously confuses products with the underlying capabilities. In a GVC fragmented world, what matters is not the final product, but the actual tasks that are involved in their production (Baldwin, 2016). However, the biggest drawback of the method is that it cannot capture improvements that stem from process innovations or quality upgrading.

Both the product space method and its regional version (Neffke et al., 2011) assume that the proximity of products, as measured by the frequency with which they are coproduced by individual countries/plants— signals similarity in the underlying capabilities. Namely, it is assumed that products, which are close to each other in terms of industry classification, have similar underlying capabilities. However, in both cases, technology upgrading is reduced to product variety and ignores process innovation or quality upgrading. Producing the same products at a higher quality is an equally important path of technology upgrading (Crespi et al., 2014, p.294). For example, Dulleck et al. (2005) show that quality upgrading is a critical dividing line between successful technology upgrading of Central European countries and the low-quality trap of Romania, Bulgaria, and partly the Baltic states. Similar products may have entirely different underlying capabilities or skills levels, which are reflected in their quality. Of course, different qualities of the same product can be treated as altogether different goods (ibid.). Furthermore, quality upgrading may be an opportunity to move to unrelated products (for this see Crespi et al., 2014, who have a case study of Leonisa).

In short, relatedness or horizontal upgrading is only one dimension of technology upgrading, one, which is inextricably linked to vertical or quality upgrading as depicted later.

Nevertheless, the product space analysis of export complexity is a useful first approximation of areas of a country's or region's latent comparative advantages (Fortunato et al., 2015; Crespi et al., 2014, p. 283). Based on the product space method, it may seem logical that policies should support the shift toward areas of proximate opportunities. Its direct policy implication is that there are no short cuts in technology upgrading and that path dependency is inevitable. However, some countries have demonstrated that "short cuts" are possible, especially in the periods of "windows of opportunities" or fast structural changes (Lee, 2013, for the case of Korea). Moreover, Crespi et al. (2014) cite the example of Ireland, which has chosen to specialize in ICT, pharma, financial services, and other services (technical support, consumer services, and consulting). While two of these sectors were already present in the country, the other two were entirely new (ibid., p. 258). Finally, the authors of this approach (Hidalgo et al., 2007) are aware that pursuing only proximate opportunities may have limited effects and that policies to promote large jumps would be more desirable. New structural economics explicitly takes on these issues when considering differences in the income levels of countries, which should be regarded as "reference" (leading dragons) or sources of technological knowledge (Section, "New Structural Economics").

New Structural Economics

Like the product space method, new structural economics (NSE) is also a trade-based approach to specialization. However, NSE focuses on the economic structure and structural change as drivers of technology upgrading (Lin, 2012). It assumes that countries' comparative advantages emerge from the evolving potential of a country's endowment structure. In this process, the economy relies on the market for the allocation mechanism at any stage of development, but the state plays a facilitating role in the process of upgrading (Lin, 2012). The mechanism that drives this process is a recycling of comparative advantages from more advanced to less developed economies via outward FDI and trade. With respect to this, NSE follows the "flying geese" theory of development (Akamatsu, 1962; Ozawa, 2005), where growth and integration are merged into one conceptual framework to make a kind of "tandem" theory of growth.

The main messages of the new structural economics are the following (Lin, 2012):

1. A sector-targeted industrial policy is essential to achieve dynamic structural change and rapid, sustained growth in an economy.
2. Most industrial policies fail because they target industries that are not compatible with the country's comparative advantage.

3. A successful industrial policy should target industries that are the country's latent comparative advantages.
4. Historical experiences show that successful countries' industrial policies, in general, targeted industries in countries with a similar endowment structure and somewhat higher per capita income.
5. The Growth Identification and Facilitation Framework (GIFF), based on NSE, is a new and effective way to target latent comparative advantage industries and to support their growth.

Latent comparative advantage refers to an industry that has low factor costs of production but too high transaction costs to be competitive in domestic and international markets. Firms will be viable, and the sectors will be competitive once the government helps the firms overcome coordination and externality issues to reduce risk and transaction costs. For countries with a similar endowment structure, the forerunners' successful and dynamic industrial development provides a blueprint for the latecomers' industrial policies. The "sunset" industries in leading countries will become the latent comparative advantage of the latecomers. With respect to that, there is a similarity between the NSE and product space approaches whereby less developed countries should target industries of their richer neighbors. However, NSE is much more specific in how to go about this, while the product space approach is confined to the "what" but not the "how."

There is a sharp contrast in industrial policy between NSE and the approach of Transition Economics (TE) (see Berglof et al, 2015). NSE rationalizes a gradualist approach to trade liberalization and a temporary protection to industries that are inconsistent with "comparative advantages defying" industries built in the past. Contrary to this, TE does not see value in maintaining and subsidizing currently inefficient industries. NSE holds that governments need to support industry-specific infrastructures, which are consistent with current or potential (latent) comparative advantages: hence, only broad horizontal policies are insufficient. TE is skeptical toward any vertical policies. NSE advises a "dual track approach" and "second best policies," of which TE is again distrustful. Finally, NSE recognizes the role of pioneer firms in the process of industrial upgrading and firm heterogeneity, which makes it similar to (neo)-Schumpeterian economics, as we will discuss later.

The NSE is theorizing largely based on China's experience over the last 30 years. This approach is well-developed, with an elaborate and detailed methodology. It has been applied in several countries (Lin and Treichel, 2011). The GIFF operationalizes key insights of NSE based on current and latent comparative advantages as criteria for specialization choices. Based on this approach, Lin in Chapter 8 extends his original approach by applying it not only to catching-up industries but also to others, including leading-edge industries. In that respect, we could say that NSE has become more Schumpeterian in its approach.

The Neo-Schumpeterian Approach of Keun Lee

This approach is epitomized in the research and seminal contribution of Lee (2013), which represent theorizing largely based on Korean and Taiwanese experiences. The key feature of the neo-Schumpeterian approach is that policies should depend on the distance of the country from the technology frontier. In Lee's neo-Schumpeterian interpretation, countries cannot catch up by directly emulating or replicating the practices of the forerunning economies, but by taking a different path. This approach contrasts with the product space approach where catching-up countries should target areas of specialization of their richer neighbors or actively transfer activities in which their richer neighbors are losing comparative advantages. In a neo-Schumpeterian perspective, catch-up is chasing a moving target and a strategy of emulating or following the technology leader may not be suitable once countries come closer to the technology frontier. With respect to that, the neo-Schumpeterian approach is relevant for middle-income countries moving toward the technology frontier, while the NSE approach is more useful to low-income economies moving to middle-income.

The neo-Schumpeterian approach is market friendly, and like other NIP approaches aims to "discover" areas of specialization. What makes the neo-Schumpeterian approach a NIP is that specialization choices are not obvious, but historically contingent on "windows of opportunity." These are periods and areas of fast technical change where incumbents have not been able to accumulate significant technological advantages. In these periods and industries, leaders are unable to create cumulative technology advantages, which lower the barriers to entry and create an open window of opportunities to latecomers. Therefore, latecomers need to specialize in "short cycle technology-based sectors" in which old knowledge quickly depreciates, and new knowledge tends to emerge more often. A proxy that Lee uses for these sectors is a mean citation lag in patent citations. Areas where patents cite more recent patents are deemed to be short cycle technology (SCT) areas. Targeting a SCT area is contrary to the product space methodology, which recommends specializing in long cycle technologies, dominated by rich countries and where barriers to entry are higher (Lee, 2013). Hence, in both cases diversification matters, but in the neo-Schumpeterian approach the short cycle technologies are important. Similar to the product space method, the neo-Schumpeterian approach is much more articulated about which areas countries should specialize in (what), rather than on how to organize this process (how).

The Schumpeterian Approach of Aghion et al.

Schumpeterian growth theory is the formalized framework to analyze key aspects of innovation-led growth (Aghion, 2004; Aghion and Howitt, 1992). With respect to that, Schumpeterian theory shares similarities with the neo-Schumpeterian approach, which also recognizes that the distance (proximity) to the technology frontier matters for technology choices.

Schumpeterian theory derives innovation and imitation behavior "endogenously from the profit-maximization problem facing a prospective innovator." It assumes that faster growth implies a higher rate of firm turnover because this process of creative destruction allows new innovators to enter the market and for former innovators to exit. The Schumpeterian perspective recognizes the heterogeneity of firms by distinguishing between incumbents and new entrants and between young and old firms. The core of creative destruction is the replacement of inefficient incumbents by more productive new entrants. Hence, the importance of different views on competition depending on whether the sectors are "creative destructive" or "creative accumulating."[4]

The perspective's significant feature is that the determinants of a country's performance will vary with its proximity to the technological frontier (Aghion et al., 2015). The more advanced countries rely on frontier innovation, which in turn requires more creative destruction. A country behind the technology frontier will grow based on imitation, and its institutional setup will reflect differences in the growth drivers when compared to the global technology leaders. This approach enables us to explore what kinds of policy changes are needed to sustain convergence as a country approaches the technology frontier.

Two major policy implications of Schumpeterian growth theory are, first, the idea that growth-enhancing policies or institutions vary with a country's level of technological development; and second, the idea that the distribution of firm sizes and firm dynamics are endogenous variables shaped by the institutional context. The interaction of institutions or policies with technological variables means that countries at different distances from technology frontier require diverse growth-promoting institutions (policies) (Aghion et al., 2011b). In countries behind the technology frontier, growth is driven by technological imitation, and their policy design should be different from that of countries operating at the technology frontier. For example, the importance of openness, property rights, the nature of the financial system, or level of education differs between technology leaders and followers. The closer countries are to the technology frontier, the more their institutional features should be conducive to "creative destruction." The more they are behind the frontier, the more they should be conducive to "creative accumulation."

Schumpeterian models show the importance of market structure and competition for innovation-led growth. As long as sectoral policies can ensure a sufficient degree of market competition, they are compatible with Schumpeterian policies, especially in high-growth activities. Therefore, vertical policies are welcome when: (1) the government chooses to pick activities, not particular firms; (2) the criteria underlying the selection of activities are clear and verifiable; and (3) the vertical interventions are properly governed (Aghion et al., 2015). A Schumpeterian approach favors procompetition industrial policy and shows that a sectoral policy can be effective if it promotes competition. The second justification for a vertical policy is that potential knowledge spillovers induced by projects with large-scale spillovers are significant. An example of this latter type of policy can be found in Eliasson (2010) who analyzes the Swedish defense sector. In a dynamic context, the difference between private and social returns to the same activities is so large that *laissez-faire* is an inferior option.

The Schumpeterian approach recognizes that vertical targeting is necessary but gives priority to horizontal targeting, such as basic and applied research, higher education, and labor mobility. For example, at the EU level, vertical targeting would be more growth promoting than vertical targeting at the country level, where there may not be market competition due to a limited local market. As long as vertical policies at the country level are promoting market competition or are focused on sectors with a higher degree of product market competition, they are effective.

Aghion and Akcigit (2015) refer to the activist role of the state as the "strategic state" or the "smart state." This role is highly warranted in the EU context, where states need to combine austerity with growth-enhancing policies. The indiscriminate (Keynesian) public spending has limited effects or is not feasible. The governments also need to focus public investments on a small number of growth-enhancing areas and sectors. This shift requires changes in the governance structures of specific public sectors or structural reforms to be compatible with growth. So, the Schumpeterian approach recognizes that innovation policy measures alone are insufficient. Innovation policies usually need to be accompanied by structural reforms. The uniqueness of the Schumpeterian approach is that it considers the issue of technology innovation in the broader institutional context of other economic policies.

The implication of Schumpeterian perspective is that successful innovation is not solely a matter of adequate innovation policy. Innovation policy measures, which do not consider product and labor market regulations, have limited effects. This proposition comes from empirical evidence within the Schumpeterian approach. For example, subsidies for IT adoption alone will not suffice unless there are complementary measures that can facilitate its adoption, such as improving skills and reregulating labor and product markets. Innovation policy measures alone do not suffice unless accompanied by tax reform to encourage entrepreneurship or supply of skilled labor. Aghion and Akcigit (2015) argue that structural reforms play a fundamental role in speeding up the IT diffusion, and that complementarity between product and labor markets matter.

The integration of industrial/innovation policy with structural reforms is critical to overcome the disjointed nature of these two policy areas. When structural reforms ideas are considered within the context of technology accumulation, policy conclusions often turn out to be qualitatively different. For example, innovation performance requires organizational learning and accumulation of knowledge, which in turn need stable and longer-lasting labor relations. Hence, the currently fashionable recommendation to make labor markets more flexible has a down side of reducing labor productivity (Kleinknecht and Naastepad, 2005). Flexibility improves employment, but it also reduces trust, loyalty, and commitment of personnel, which help stop a firm's technological knowledge "leaking out" to competitors (Kleinknecht, 1998). Easier hiring and firing and shorter job tenure are discouraging training and "learning by doing," which in turn weaken the accumulation of firm-specific and "tacit" knowledge. An excessively flexible labor market undermines incremental learning and the building up of firm-specific knowledge trajectories (Vergeer and Kleinknecht, 2014).

Hence, structural reforms should be a part and parcel of innovation policy measures. Their content should differ depending on the technological area and development of the country or region. The novelty of the Schumpeterian approach is that it considers institutional variables in interaction with technology variables. So, flexible labor markets, product market deregulation, standards policy, specific sectoral regulatory regimes, and other issues always need to be judged as adequate or inadequate in relation to technological opportunities and the nature of technological change (incremental vs. radical; cumulative vs. disruptive).

Process (Evolutionary) View of Innovation (Industrial) Policy

The process (evolutionary) view is exemplified in the NIP "corner" of the World Bank. Key studies outlining this approach include Kuznetsov and Sabel (2011), Dutz and Kuznetsov (2014), Sabel et al. (2013), Teubal (1997), and Avnimelech and Teubal (2008). Furthermore, Crespi et al. (2014) are partly applying this approach to Latin America.

The key insight of the process view is that "the exact nature of the problems faced by the street level bureaucrats frontline worker in the public sector is not known in advance" (Sabel and Zeitlin, 2010). From this, it follows that policy goals cannot be defined clearly ex-ante, which in turn requires "search networks" to be established. This proposition stems from the assumption also shared by other NIP approaches that no one has a panoramic view of the economy; all points of view are partial. Accordingly, there is no principal–agent: "You can't specify the precise goals or the means for achieving them all at once, ex-ante, and therefore goals need to be redefined, and the means for achieving them, by detecting bottlenecks or errors, and then searching out and eliminating their causes" (ibid., p. 12.).

The epistemological basis of this perspective is based on the notion of experimental governance. Unlike the new public management approach, experimentalist governance does not rest on a principal–agent relationship, but describes the emergence of policy as a process based on a "recursive learning mechanism and dynamic accountability through peer review" (Sabel and Zeitlin, 2010). This means that principals recognize their limited knowledge of the implementation context and define policy objectives as an iterative process in cooperation with agents.

Stemming from this, policy governance rests on four principles (Sabel and Zeitlin, 2011). First, policy goals are established in interaction with the affected stakeholders. Second, stakeholders have a significant degree of autonomy in pursuing different programs or projects ideally through a portfolio of projects or programs. This enables them to adjust funding as the situation evolves. Third, their performance is monitored through a system of "diagnostic monitoring," which discovers unforeseen events in the portfolio of projects and tries to correct them or use them as new opportunities, rather than through expost evaluations on a project-by-project basis. Fourth, the goals, metrics, and decision-making procedures are reviewed in the light of new problems and possibilities.

This approach assumes that even in very disadvantaged countries or regions there are pockets of vitality (some good firms or public organizations, highly skilled professionals, departments, etc.), which are "stuck" in low-growth traps. It is possible to use pockets of excellence that work in a specific country to improve those pockets that do not. The short-term aim is humble: to accelerate what already exists, starting from pockets of excellence in the private and public sectors. The long-term goal is to create a "critical mass" of capabilities and interactions, which can be enlarged and may have a macroeconomic effect. For an analysis of this approach, see Chapter 10.

In "experimentalist governance," there is no clear separation between policy design and implementation. Learning takes place in the process of the application during which capabilities are upgraded, and policy design adapts. In a similar vein, Andrews et al. (2012) have independently developed the problem driven iterative adaptation method (PDIA). Both approaches, PDIA and experimentalist governance, are very relevant for industrial and innovation policy, where "often the exact nature of the problems and the best way to address them are not known ex-ante" (Crespi et al., 2014). Crespi et al. (2014) have merged both approaches into a so-called EFA Cycle framework (experimentation–feedback loops–adaptation), which begins with experimentation—as with Sabel and Zeitlin (2011)—and ends with adaptation, as in Pritchett et al. (2013). They define *experimentation* as a space in which different approaches to solving a given problem are allowed and their results systematically evaluated. *Feedback loops* are necessary for the process to figure out which approaches are workable and which are not. The final activity is to *adapt* policy to a particular institutional context.

EU Smart Specialization Approach

We consider SS as the EU's version of new industrial policy. It is epitomized in Knowledge for Growth Policy brief written by an expert group led by Foray et al. (2009). As this policy brief appeared, we note an emerging industry of academic papers, which discuss issues related to the design and implementation of this policy perspective[5]. In the EU context, its novelty lies in an explicit prioritization and selectivity, as well as in a departure (at least nominally) from the only high-tech approach to EU innovation policy (McCann and Ortega-Argilés, 2015).

This approach is probably the most elaborate and ambitious formulation of new industrial innovation policy (Foray et al., 2011). Smart specialization strategies (S3) serve as preconditions or "ex-ante conditionalities" for the use of the EU Structural Funds 2014-20 in the area of R&D, innovation, and ICT. The sheer scale of investment projects (EUR250 billion in 2014–20 period) selected based on the S3 logic makes it also worthwhile to study.

The SS aims to reconcile two logics: vertical (not horizontal) prioritization with dynamism, entry and competition, and entrepreneurship. Central to this approach is policy design and the so-called entrepreneurial discovery process (EDP). EDP is about finding suitable niches, which match regions' latent comparative advantages. In this approach, neither sectors, nor individual firms are prioritized; rather, new activities (domains) are given prominence. The process aims to generate structural change through the inclusive process of stakeholder involvement in the EDP.

Regarding the EDP, the key feature of the SS process, an S3 is different from mission-oriented programs, which are usually based on top-down decision making. In deciding on priorities, stakeholders need to have a global perspective on their potential competitive advantages and a willingness to cooperate to create a critical mass of RDI activities that may generate structural change and growth.

SS is designed as a linear process, which consists of the following stages (Foray et al., 2012):

Step 1: Analysis of regional potential for innovation-driven differentiation
Step 2: RIS 3 design and governance—ensuring participation and ownership
Step 3: Elaboration of an overall vision for the future of the region
Step 4: Selection of priorities for RIS3 + definition of objectives
Step 5: Definition of a coherent policy mix, roadmaps, and action plan
Step 6: Integration of monitoring and evaluation mechanisms

The notion of "entrepreneurial discovery" upon which the SS approach is based stems from Hayekian economics, which considers the use of existing knowledge as the crucial problem in economics. Hayek relies on Polanyi's idea of tacit knowledge to argue that knowledge is always perceived through cognitive frameworks, which differ among individuals. Accordingly, understanding a region's latent comparative advantages depends as much on objective information as on the subjective assessment of stakeholders. In a Hayekian perspective, the market is considered as the only mechanism where different views of entrepreneurial opportunities can coexist in free competition. By invoking EDP, SS seems to be a Hayekian approach, but equally, by inviting nonmarket actors into the SS process and invoking a kind of collectivist entrepreneurial insight, it is a broader perspective. The EDP is about addressing uncertainty through the collective "discovery" process. Within a Hayekian or Austrian economics perspective, entrepreneuship takes place based on tacit insights of individual entrepreneurs. However, EDP also involves firms, research-technology organizations, policy bodies, and NGOs. Thus, EDP extends the idea of the discovery process to nonmarket actors. Broadening the discovery process is resolved by treating all actors in the EDP as "entrepreneurs." For example, the idea of Schumpeterian, as opposed to Weberian, bureaucracy is concomitant to this idea, as well as to the concept of the entrepreneurial state (Mazzucato, 2013). However, the jump from individual to collectivist insights or "discoveries" is not a trivial issue.

Given the differences in the cognitive and interpretive frameworks of actors, the EDP of SS can be critiqued as based on the faulty epistemological assumption that knowledge is something out there to be "discovered" (Hodgson, 1999). As Hodgson (1999) argues, all knowledge depends on preconceptions and prior conceptual frameworks that in principle are not out there to be "discovered" and cannot be established simply by reason and fact. However, we should recognize both the team-based character of tacit knowledge, and the idea that social groups can share cognitive and interpretative frameworks. Therefore, by recognizing social and not only the individual nature of knowledge, different stakeholder groups may develop their specific tacit understanding of entrepreneurial opportunities. In addition, the analysis and subsequent learning that accompany EDP can change individuals' views. We must, however, recognize that there are limits to this convergence process. The practice of SS shows that the jump from individual to collective "discovery" is extremely difficult to achieve, particularly in less developed regions and countries.

Understanding the domains of latent comparative advantage often involves tacit knowledge, which cannot be easily subject to the deliberation of various committees. The tacit nature of entrepreneurial opportunities poses limits to the EDP of SS. The more ideas on priority areas that are far-fetched or implausible, the harder it will be to agree on priorities. To avoid disparate and often conflicting views on entrepreneurial opportunities, stakeholders may go for the lowest common denominator, that is, for technology domains that are far too broad to be considered "discoveries" of entrepreneurial opportunities. Moreover, the "depth" of consensus on SS technology priority areas may vary widely depending on the institutional context of SS policy or the extent to which stakeholders interact with each other.

Given the uncertainties about entrepreneurial opportunities, SS inevitably requires some form of experimentalist governance. With respect to that, the linear nature of the SS process seems to be a design fault that needs to be corrected. Moreover, the SS handbook (Foray et al., 2012) points to the continuous nature of EDP, which is hard to reconcile with the linearly designed model. The emerging practical experiences of SS suggest that implementation cannot evolve separately after the design stage without provoking change in the initial design or priorities. The interactions between stages call for more pilot projects, which allow for learning and changes in the initial design along with implementation. Equally, the needed governance cannot be hierarchical and exclusively target-driven, but would need to bring all stakeholders into the process of direct deliberations and the governance system should modify the targets based on peer review-type mechanisms (Sabel, 2005).

Summary

The table here summarizes the key features of the new industrial innovation policies on two critical dimensions, *the method for selecting policy priorities*, and the *role of policy in its implementation*.

	The method for discovering specializations (What?)	Role of policy (How?)
Binding constraints to growth	Typified path (Rodrik et al.) or in-depth analysis (McKinsey)	Sector-specific regulatory regimes and macro measures
Product space method	Proximity in product space based on income	Imitative policies of neighbors in product space or ambiguous about policy direction
New structural economics approach	Sunset relocations from "reference" (leading dragon) economies	Active and facilitating role of the state which varies by the nature of comparative advantages
Neo-Schumpeterian approach	Identify areas of "short cycle technologies," that is, of high technological opportunities and low barriers to entry	Facilitating role of the state by coordinating the process of discovery of areas of short cycle technologies and subsequently promoting them
Schumpeterian approach	Differentiated innovation or imitation choices depending on distance to technology frontier	Sector-specific choices in conjunction with other micro policies
Process (evolutionary) view	Iterative peer review-based process	Policy is actively shaping implementation and design through "diagnostic monitoring." It requires a Schumpeterian development agency
EU smart specialization approach	Entrepreneurial discovery process	Formal preconditions and milestones to validate the process

In what concerns the methods, which are used to "discover" priorities, we can discern those approaches, which are codified or structured, as opposed to those that do not have a detailed blueprint on how to go about analyzing and selecting priorities. Binding constraints to growth in both versions (Rodrik et al. and McKinsey) have developed different types of methodological blueprints on identifying key constraints to growth. Moreover, the product space method and NSE in its original version, as well as the neo-Schumpeterian approach, have developed diagnostic approaches concerning how to go about selecting specialization priorities. EU smart specialization also has a very formalized and structured approach, which continues to be further developed.[6] The Schumpeterian approach has the most elaborate background growth theory, but does not yet have a "readymade" blueprint. The process (evolutionary) view considers the process of iterative peer review as the primary method and in that respect, lacks a "manual" for how to discover specializations.

The role of policies in implementing the "discovered" areas of specializations is the least articulated in the product space method and binding constraints approach. It is assumed that the both approaches give straightforward policy implications, but the issue of implementation is not explicitly articulated. The NSE, Schumpeterian, and neo-Schumpeterian approaches explicitly recognize the important, facilitating, and active role of the state, although the scope of state involvement differs. However, in all three approaches policies should be technology-specific rather than generic. The EU's SS has developed a formalized process, which explicitly requires compliance with ex-ante criteria by regional and national governments for the SS process to be valid. The process (evolutionary) view is the most explicit about the institutional requirements for implementing effective specialization. It considers a diagnostic Schumpeterian development agency and diagnostic monitoring procedure as the key institutional preconditions.

CHALLENGES OF SMART SPECIALIZATION

The evidence on implementation suggests that the logic of SS works pretty well in the context of the most developed EU countries and regions (McCann and Ortega-Argilés, 2015; Chapters 4, 5, and 13).[7] However, these are not the regions and countries that are the major recipients of Structural Funds for which SS is the ex-ante conditionality. Thus, in that respect, we share the view of McCann and Ortega-Argilés (2015) about this internal contradiction of SS. However, we do not perceive the issues of (un)related diversification to be the major weakness of the SS in its application to peripheral regions. Instead, we find that the greatest challenges are in the following four areas. First, SS in less developed countries and regions does not reflect country-specific challenges and drivers of technology upgrading. These issues are key to the product space, Schumpeterian, neo-Schumpeterian, and NSE approaches. Formally, the EDP should accommodate a search for country-specific drivers and areas of specialization. Instead, we observe an excessively R&D-driven process. Second, SS strategies are too often inward-oriented, which is expected given that the issue of GVCs as levers of regional technology upgrading has been ignored in the initial design of the SS methodology. This aspect is strongly present in NSE and implicit in the product space method. Third, the institutional capacity for SS policies is considered as unproblematic although the evidence (Chapter 13) suggests that implementation issues are equally if not more important than the EDP. Institutional capacities are closely related to the issues of implementation. This dimension is strongly present in the process (evolutionary) approach and neo-Schumpeterian focus on policy mix. We now address each of these challenges in more depth.

Does SS Reflect Country/Region-Specific Challenges and Drivers of Technology Upgrading?

The innovation process in catching-up economies is based on the adoption and incremental improvement of existing technologies, rather than on investments in R&D. The innovation policy of these economies often ignores this crucial fact and instead focuses excessively only on R&D-based innovations (Radosevic, 2016).

SS does not explicitly recognize country/region-specific challenges and the drivers of technology upgrading. The EDP approach of Foray et al. (2012) is seen as a mechanism that can accommodate different technology upgrading challenges. However, this is only true formally, not in practice, where R&D and STI models of technology upgrading prevail. We think that any new approach should be much more explicit regarding the differences in technology upgrading challenges across EU28 regions. Otherwise, we will get an excessively high-tech approach and copying of the "best practice" approaches, as exemplified by different Silicon Valley inspired plans in the less developed EU regions and countries. This issue seems much more important than the place-based versus sector-based contradiction that has been the concern of the regional economics literature.

The EDP should ensure that SS strategies reflect country- and region-specific drivers of technology upgrading, which would then lead to different policy approaches. What we observe in practice is the lack of differentiation in approaches to SS and an excessive R&D or high-tech focus. The supply-side RDI measures dominate, while demand-led innovation programs are neglected. This will lead to successful centers of excellence in less developed EU regions but with similar structural weaknesses regarding RDI gaps and with weak or no local impact.

Less developed EU economies and regions correctly perceive the S3-related funding as a unique opportunity to jumpstart and breed a "science-based" sector, by providing broad financial support for commercial R&D. However, creating "pockets of R&D excellence" is the easier part of the story. Enlarging and linking them with the rest of economy is much more challenging. With respect to that, Israel's experience is of great relevance, as it illustrates a very successful high-tech sector that has nevertheless not been able to generate spillovers and economy-wide productivity growth (Trajtenberg, 2015). In addition to R&D, there is a much stronger need in less developed regions to support the primary sources of innovation, which are found in non-R&D activities, such as design, engineering, technology transfer, quality and process improvements, etc. In developed regions, the challenge is to link up S&T Innovation (STI) with the doing-using (DUI) mode of innovation (Chapter 4).

Inward Orientation and Weak Transnationalization of SS

SS strategies are too often inward-oriented. Given the dominance of global value chains in the growth and modernization of less developed regions, it is of the utmost importance to take this dimension of SS much more explicitly on board. Finally, the major tension that we observe today is among the place-based supporting activities, such as clusters and the GVC as levers of modernization (Baldwin, 2016).

SS strategies should be the key to technology upgrading, but the issue is how can the local production stage of GVC become its building block? (Radosevic and Stancova, 2015). One view is that GVCs are the key to technology upgrading. The argument is that in a globalized context, it does not make much sense to build local clusters; instead, being plugged into a GVC is sufficient. An alternative view is that a country or region should link up only when they can benefit from the linkages. Therefore, regions should first build endogenous technological capability and only then link up. These are mutually exclusive views, both with significant trade-offs.

The successful examples of the coupling between GVC and local industry and technology capacities are rare. Often cited examples are the Irish National Linkages Program (NLP) and the Singaporean local industry-upgrading program (Chapter 10). Beside these high-profile success stories, there are a variety of programs with different degrees of success. For example, Crespi et al. (2014) describes a Malaysian program as an example of both failure and success (pp. 270–271). Benacek (2010) also describes the case of CzechInvest, the strategic promotion agency in Czech industrial restructuring.

For now, we are unable to offer a policy toolbox to decision makers. This dimension has been ignored in the *SS Handbook*, and there have been recent attempts to further develop it (Primi, 2014; Radosevic and Stancova, 2015; Chapter 11). Moreover, UNIDO and the German Society for International Cooperation (GIZ) have integrated an analysis of GVCs as part of an evidence-based industry policy analysis (http://www.equip-project.org/).

Institutional Capacity for SS Policies

The institutional capacity for SS policies is considered unproblematic, at least if we are to judge based on the SS methodology (Foray et al., 2012). On the other hand, both SS approaches, as well as the place-based regional approach, strongly highlight the importance of an inclusive SS process, which should bring all stakeholders on board. This is by definition the issue of institutional capacity. However, it does not offer much on what should be done when vested interests prevail or when the institutional capacity for SS is simply not in place. For example, Foray and Goenaga (2013, p. 3) rightly point out that the challenge for SS is how to follow the vertical logic of prioritization "while avoiding the government failures usually associated with the top-down and centralized bureaucratic processes of technology choices and selection."

Among new industrial and innovation policy approaches, only the process (evolutionary) view integrates these issues through the notion of experimentalist governance (Sabel and Zeitlin, 2011). Our argument is that if SS is to be effective, both these questions—institutional context and selection of priorities—would need to be brought into the SS discourse and be part of SS design. The fragmentation of the institutional infrastructure for innovation—the lack of institutionalized links both between R&D and the business sector and among RDI organizations, represents a real constraint on endogenous growth and development (Kuznetsov and Teubal, 2011).

Effective industrial policy requires both developed policy capabilities and a rich network of public–private interactions. As demonstrated in a seminal work by Evans (1985), one of these factors alone does not suffice. Policy capabilities without the capacity to engage in dialogue with the private sector are insufficient. A competent and autonomous bureaucracy that lacks a rich information exchange with the private sector will not be able to engage in policy activities in which sector-specific knowledge is critical. On the other hand, good communications with the private sector but limited policy capabilities are also not enough.

In the absence of sufficient autonomy of the public administration, innovation and industrial policy programs can be prone to "government capture" by the private sector. In short, SS requires the capacity to overcome trade-offs of "embedded autonomy" (Evans, 1985), that is, the public sector should have a detailed understanding of the specific technology and market context but not be captured by particular interests.[8] A formal consultation process where the public sector listens to the private sector may not be sufficient for the former to obtain useful information and to apply the policy effectively. On the other hand, the private sector may misuse this interaction for rent seeking rather than information sharing so that the outcome is the unequal exchange of rents rather than of information and knowledge (Crespi et al., 2014).

Although a high degree of "embedded autonomy" is a desirable precondition for effective industrial and innovation policies, it is unrealistic to expect that it can often be met. In fact, the degree to which "embedded autonomy" is required may vary across different types of innovation programs. As Crespi et al. (2014) point out, "the modality of interaction with the private sector depends on the kind of policy it is meant to support." In addition, countries and regions have different degrees of "embedded autonomy" due to policy legacies and path dependencies (Chapter 10). These can vary from a context where the public sector enjoys considerable independence from the private sector (as in South Korea) to one where social consensus is embedded, as in Ireland (Crespi et al., 2014). Within this range, we find a variety of situations with very diverse degrees of propensity and public sector capacity to interact with the private sector. For example, only some actors within the state sector or region can interact.

Furthermore, the public and private sectors themselves may not be well-organized. The public sector may not be organized in a way that it can interact with industry. In that case, private sector-led institutions can play a mediating role in public–private interactions. In addition, the private sector may be very poorly organized so that the public sector needs to improve private-private coordination. Business associations may poorly represent real stakeholders, or they may be weak in inducing its members to commit resources and abide by the association's rules and decisions (Crespi et al., 2014). If newly emerging sectors play a significant role in SS, then we may expect them to have inadequate representation and low visibility, which puts the onus on the public sector to improve its visibility.

The absence or presence of coordination capabilities within the public or private sectors will determine the appropriateness of specific policy types. Horizontal policies will be more appropriate as compared to vertical when public–private coordination is weak. Moreover, single agency based policies will be preferred when intrapublic sector coordination is undeveloped. In a nutshell, policy design should be tailored to the coordination capacities in innovation policy. Instead of going for "best practice" policies, it is advisable to aim for "the best matches" between capabilities and policies (Crespi et al., 2014, p. 347). As Crespi et al. (2014) point out trying to emulate best practices can often lead to tasks that may widely exceed public sector capabilities. This is what we often find in many less developed regions (Chapters 10, 12, and 13).

What are the potential solutions in cases where public sector organizations are not conducive to the complex coordination required by innovation policy (Crespi et al., 2014)? For example, the public sector may operate under very rigid rules, which prevents it from engaging in the entrepreneurial discovery process. This may necessitate some public agencies operating under flexible rules or even under the rules of the private sector. Also, private sector should be involved in the governance structure of public agencies. In other cases, public agencies may need a separate remuneration system as the only way to attract highly skilled personnel. In some cases, these agencies should be established by law to give them organizational stability and the freedom to convene and engage the private sector.

When public–public sector coordination is weak, specialized interministerial cabinets and high-level task forces are necessary. When an organization in charge of the policy is weak, it should be made to purchase services of other agencies via a dedicated budget (Crespi et al., 2014; see also Hausmann et al. (2008) for a relevant illustrative example about South Africa). The bottom line is that we may expect pockets of administrative excellence for SS policy to exist. If they do not exist, it is imperative that they be created or be part of the ex-ante conditionality for the disbursement of funds.

The Challenge of Implementation

As the SS process moves from design to implementation, the new challenges are being crystallized. We distinguish between challenges caused by the need to fit a new conceptual idea to the reality of the EU's economic and administrative constraints (and the issues of implementation failures, which are endemic to the transfer of policy models).

SS Strategies Between New Industrial Policy and Political and Administrative Requirements

The design of the EU's smart specialization policy as depicted in the RIS3 Guide is a compromise between different policy requirements and objectives (Chapter 12). Compromises are usually inevitable in policy design and implementation, but if they dominate they can lead to much less effective policy. In the EU SS context, we can note the following four contextual and administrative factors, which represent a challenge for the SS policy.

First, SS is by definition a kind of experimentalist policy, as would be expected given the importance of EDP in its design. However, this inevitably clashes with the rigid administrative nature of the EU funding programs, which need to be cost effective and cannot be easily squared with the requirements for selectivity, learning, and trial and errors. The application of SS would require a Schumpeterian bureaucracy that is best nurtured through autonomous public agencies with the freedom to make their rules (Chapter 3).

Second, the experimentalist nature of SS clashes with the political pressure for fast absorption of EU funds, which reduces the potential influence of SS to meet impact and absorption targets.

Third, while the RIS3 Guide introduces EDP, in practice the process itself is seen more as a strategic planning exercise (Chapter 12).

Finally, in several less developed EU regions and countries, SS is the only growth policy in a macroeconomic context that is predominantly driven by austerity policies. Hence, the opportunities for matching local funds in many countries and regions are pretty meager, which reduces the potential of SS as a growth policy.

Implementation Failures and SS

In less developed EU regions and countries, SS strategies have initiated a significant change in innovation policy whose real effects remain uncertain. There is some indication that SS is perceived as a "game to be played." However, once funds are available, we can expect small changes, as local innovation ecosystems will accommodate instruments to their liking. This is the scenario of "isomorphic mimicry" where national or regional stakeholders can maintain legitimacy through imitating the process of entrepreneurial discovery but without actually making any functional changes. This phenomenon is quite widespread in the context of development aid; the EU structural funds inevitably carry some of these features (Pritchett et al., 2013). On the other hand, it may be the case that requirements for successful implementation are simply not yet in place in the EU's less developed regions, which are being pushed "too hard too soon, thereby creating a situation of premature load bearing in which stresses exceed capability" (Pritchett et al., 2013, p. 16). Given how new SS is and the still limited knowledge about its implementation challenges (see Chapter 13 for valuable insights), we still do not fully understand how far policy capabilities in SS are the root cause of the difficulties in implementing SS. To be more specific, we are still unclear as to whether the major issues are technical, operational, or political capabilities.[9] All three types of capabilities are necessary for an effective innovation policy. For example, Romania's Foresight Program represents a case of a technically very successful program but whose final effects are undermined by political interference or weak political capabilities (Chapter 14). This example shows that the policy capacity cannot be reduced to technical capabilities and that political and organizational constraints are equally important.

CONCLUSIONS

In this chapter, we have "positioned" SS in the landscape of emerging approaches to new industrial innovation policy (NIP). These approaches have emerged independently, but we argue that they nevertheless share several common features characterizing them as new "industrial innovation policies." They have all developed as a response to the inadequacies of *laissez-faire* and structural reforms as the only mechanism to generate growth and structural change. Moreover, they are a response to the problems of the old type of industrial policies, as well as the insufficiencies of only horizontal innovation policies. A common idea to all new industrial innovation policy approaches is that the ultimate constraints to growth are unknown. All seven approaches try to address the issues related to choosing specializations, as well as to the challenges of technology upgrading and innovation-based growth. Unlike old industrial policies, they are concerned with the difficulties in identifying specialization choices and in organizing the process or methodology through which these options can be selected. By recognizing the limits of governments *and* the private sector to make informed choices, they can all be considered "smart."

Each of these approaches has its unique strengths and weaknesses, but they inevitably address different issues within the industry/innovation policy area and offer diverse solutions. The binding constraints to growth approach aims to discover specific constraints to growth from either a macro or micro perspective. The product space method explores the desirable areas of trade-based specialization in a global context. New structural economics has the same concern but sees the solution in a tandem-based trade specialization by identifying latent comparative advantages. Lee's neo-Schumpeterian approach finds desirable areas of specialization in technological areas in the opposite direction–in the areas of new "windows of opportunities" where technology leaders have not yet accumulated technological advantages. The Schumpeterian approach explores the importance of market structure and competition for innovation-led growth and shows that vertical industrial policy can be growth enhancing while also promoting competition. The process (evolutionary) view of industrial policy sees policy as a "discovery process," and is based on the discourse of experimentalist governance. This approach can therefore identify which institutional features are required for workable industrial/innovation policies. The core of the EU smart specialization approach is the "entrepreneurial discovery process," which engages all stakeholders in exploring potential entrepreneurial opportunities or domains of specializations that are then supported by publicly funded programs and projects.

Within this landscape, we have focused largely on the EU smart specialization approach, which is the biggest ongoing innovation policy experiment in the EU, if not in the world. Our conclusion is that SS represents a case of "incomplete" new industrial innovation policy. It shares with the other six approaches compared here the idea that no individual stakeholder has a complete view of reality, and this justifies the entrepreneurial discovery process (EDP). There is evidence that the benefits of the EDP in terms of its process and participatory effects (Kroll, 2015; Paliokaitė et al., 2016) are quite positive. Moreover, in its policy practice more than in a normative sense, it follows experimentalist governance principles as a way to reconcile the sometimes huge differences between the policy capacities of countries/regions and the SS strategies as an ex-ante conditionality for the use of structural funds (Chapter 13). However, the SS approach also suffers from several significant deficiencies, which keep it from being an effective mechanism of structural change and technology upgrading.

First, it neglects global value chains as levers of place-based growth, and this volume provides some further suggestions for changes in this respect. Second, the SS guidelines do not explicitly consider the differences in drivers of growth across regions and countries. Third, the institutional context and the institutional capacities required for the SS process are assumed as given. Fourth, implementation of SS is caught in between the requirements stemming from the experimentalist nature of SS policy, and the political and administrative requirements of implementing the policy (Chapter 13).

ACKNOWLEDGMENTS

I am highly indebted to Ricardo Crescenzi for very thorough comments and suggestions on longer version of this chapter. I am also grateful to Jan Larosse, Krysztof Piech, and my coauthors of this volume, in particular Imogen Wade and Liviu Andreescu, for insightful comments and suggestions on earlier versions of this chapter. However, all remaining errors remain entirely my responsibility.

ENDNOTES

1. Colbert was a 17th century French Finance Minister who advocated strong state intervention under King Louis XIV.
2. Wilson, S., Furtado, J., 2006. Industrial Policy and Development. CEPAL Rev. 89.
3. Unlike Foray (2015), we do not include mission-oriented policies in NIP (Foray et al., 2012), as we consider that they do not meet the criteria of being new industrial policies. We also do not include the "entrepreneurial state" perspective of Mazzucato (2013), which focuses largely on the R&D role of the state. In conceptual terms, both these perspectives on the state and industrial

policy are de facto not new; rather, they are the rediscovery of the old truth about the relevance of the state but in a new technological and neoliberal context. Finally, we do not include Romer (1994) idea on self-organizing industry investment boards, which is quintessentially a new industrial policy idea but remains an interesting though speculative conceptual idea.
4. "Creative destruction" sectors are characterized by high technological opportunities, low appropriability, and low cumulativeness of technological knowledge; while "creative accumulation" sectors are characterized by high appropriability and cumulativeness of technological knowledge (Malerba, 2004).
5. For some of these papers, see the IPTS website http://s3platform.jrc.ec.europa.eu/knowledge-repository and the rising number of academic journal papers including thematic issues and edited books.
6. https://consultation.onlines3.eu/
7. As pointed out to me by Ricardo Crescenzi, this is in line with what has been shown with respect to cohesion policy in general: better performing regions or regions with better socioeconomic conditions and a balanced mix of territorial policies or with higher absorptive capacity are those that benefit more from the policy.
8. See OECD Recommendation of the Council on effective public investment across levels of government, 2014, p. 18.
9. Technical capabilities are capabilities to implement and evaluate individual policy instruments or policy mixes. Operational capabilities are managerial capabilities to fund and run innovation agencies and other innovation policy bodies. Political capabilities are capabilities to secure political support to accomplish the mission and safeguard against political capture (Crespi et al., 2014).

REFERENCES

Aghion, P., Akcigit, U., Howitt, P., 2015. Lessons from Schumpeterian Growth Theory. Am. Econ. Rev. 105 (5), 94–99.
Aghion, P., Akcigit, U., 2015. Innovation and Growth: The Schumpeterian Perspective, Draft Survey for discussion, COEURE Coordination Action, June 11, 2015. Available from: https://phuenermund.files.wordpress.com/2015/06/aghion-akcigit-innovation-and-growth-draft-for-discussion-june-2015-updated.pdf.
Aghion, P., Boulanger, J., Cohen, E., 2011. Rethinking Industrial Policy, Breugel Policy Brief, June, Issue 04. Available from: http://bruegel.org/2011/06/rethinking-industrial-policy/.
Aghion, P., Harmgart, H., Weisshaar, N., 2011b. Fostering growth in CEE countries: a country-tailored approach to growth policy. In: Radosevic, S., Kaderabkova, A. (Eds.), Challenges for European Innovation Policy: Cohesion and Excellence From a Schumpeterian Perspective. Edward Elgar Publishers, Cheltenham.
Aghion, P., 2004. Growth and development: s Schumpeterian approach. Ann. Econ. Finance 5, 1–25.
Aghion, P., Howitt, P., 1992. A model of growth through creative destruction. Econometrica 60 (2), 323–351.
Agosin, M., Fernández-Arias, E., Jaramillo, F. (Eds.), 2009. Growing Pains: Binding Constraints to Productive Investment in Latin America. Inter-American Development Bank, Washington, DC.
Akamatsu, K., 1962. A historical pattern of economic growth in developing countries. J. Dev. Econ. 1 (1), 3–25.
Amsden, A.H., 1989. Asia's Next Giant: South Korea and Late Industrialization. Oxford University Press, New York, NY; Oxford.
Andrews, M., Pritchett, L., Woolcock, M., 2012. Escaping Capability Traps through Problem Driven Iterative Adaptation (PDIA), Working Paper, No. 299, Center for global Development, Washington, DC.

Avnimelech, G., Teubal, M., 2008. Evolutionary targeting. J. Evol. Econ. 18 (2), 151–166.

Bator, F., 1958. The anatomy of market failures. Q. J. Econ. 72, 351–379.

Baldwin, R., 2016. The Great Convergence: Information Technology and the New Globalization. Harvard University Press, Cambridge, MA.

Benacek, V., 2010. Is the Czech economy a success story? The case of CzechInvest: the strategic promotion agency in Czech industrial restructuring, ECLAC, Series Commercio International 101, Division of International Trade and Integration, UN, Santiago. Available from: http://repositorio.cepal.org/bitstream/handle/11362/4445/1/S2009416_en.pdf.

Berger, S., 2015. Making in America: From Innovation to Market. The MIT Press, Cambridge, MA.

Berglof, E., Lin, J.Y., Radosevic, S., 2015. Transition economics meet new structural economics. J. Econ. Policy Reform 18 (2), 89–95.

Buigues, P.-A., Sekkat, K., 2009. Industrial Policy in Europe, Japan and the USA: Amounts, Mechanisms and Effectiveness. Palgrave Macmillan, London.

Chang, H.-J., 1994. The Political Economy of Industrial Policy. Macmillan, London and Basingstoke.

Cohen, E., Lorenzi, J.H., 2000. Politiques Industrielles Pour L'Europe. La Documentation Française, Paris.

Crespi, G., Fernandez Arias, G., Stein, E., 2014. Rethinking Productive Development: Sound Policies and Institutions for Economic Transformation. Inter-American Development Bank and Palgrave Macmillan, New York, NY.

Dulleck, U., Foster, N., Stehrer, R., Woerz, J., 2005. Dimensions of quality upgrading. Econ. Transit. 13 (1), 51–76.

Dutz, M.A., Kuznetsov, Y. (Eds.), 2014. Making Innovation Policy Work: Learning Form Experimentation. OECD and World Bank, Paris.

Eliasson, G., 2010. Advanced Public Procurement as Industrial Policy: The Aircraft Industry as a Technical University. Springer, Heidelberg.

Evans, Peter, 1985. Embedded Autonomy: States and Industrial Transformation. Princeton University Press, New Jersey.

Felipe, J., Kumar, U., Abdon, A., Bacate, M., 2012. Product complexity and economic development. Struct. Change Econ. Dyn. 23, 36–68.

Felipe, J., Usui, N., 2008. Rethinking the Growth Diagnostics Approach: Questions from the Practitioners, ADB Economics Working Paper Series No. 132, Asian Development Bank. Available from: https://www.adb.org/sites/default/files/publication/28230/economics-wp132.pdf.

Foray, D., 2015. On the policy space of smart specialization strategies, Presentations at the Second Workshop in preparation for this volume, Bucharest, 12–13 November 2015; and ERSA Lecture, March 4, 2016, DG for Regional and Urban Policy.

Foray, D., David, P.A., Hall, B.H., 2009. Smart Specialization: The Concept Knowledge, Economists Policy Brief no. Available from: http://ec.europa.eu/invest-in-research/pdf/download_en/kfg_policy_brief_no9.pdf.

Foray, D., Goenaga, X., 2013. The Goals of Smart Specialization, IPTS Policy Brief, No. 01/2013, Seville. Available from: http://ftp.jrc.es/EURdoc/JRC82213.pdf.

Foray, D., David, P.A., Hall, B.H., 2011. Smart specialization: from academic idea to political instrument: the surprising career of a concept and the difficulties involved in its implementation, École Polytechnique Fédérale de Lausanne, MTEI Working Paper 2011, no. 1. Available from: https://infoscience.epfl.ch/record/170252/files/MTEI-WP-2011-001-Foray_David_Hall.pdf.

Foray, D., Goddard, J., Goenaga Beldarrain, X., Landabaso, M., McCann, P., Morgan, K., Nauwelaers, C., Ortega-Argilés, R., 2012. Guide to research and innovation strategies for smart specialization (RIS 3), European Commission, Brussels. Available from: http://ec.europa.eu/regional_policy/sources/docgener/presenta/smart_specialisation/smart_ris3_2012.pdf.

Hausmann, R., Hidalgo, C.A., et al., 2014. Atlas of Economic Complexity: Mapping Paths to Prosperity. MIT Press, Cambridge, MA.

Hausmann, R., Rodrik, D., Velasco, A., 2008. Growth Diagnostic. In: Serra, N., Stiglitz, J.E. (Eds.), The Washington Consensus Reconsidered: Towards a New Global Governance. Oxford University Press, Oxford.

Hausmann, R., Hwang, J., Rodrik, D., 2007. What you export matters. J. Econ. Growth 12, 1–25.

Hausmann, R., Rodrik, D., Velasco, A., 2005. Growth Diagnostics, The John F. Kennedy School of Government, Harvard University. Available from: http://citeseerx.ist.psu.edu/viewdoc/download?doi=10.1.1.446.2212&rep=rep1&type=pdf.

Heilmann, S., Shih, L., 2013. The Rise of Industrial Policy in China, 1978–2012, Harvard-Yenching Institute Working Paper Series. Available from: http://www.harvard-yenching.org/sites/harvard-yenching.org/files/featurefiles/Sebastian%20Heilmann%20and%20Lea%20Shih_The%20Rise%20of%20Industrial%20Policy%20in%20China%201978-2012.pdf.

Hidalgo, C.A., Hausmann, R., 2009. The building blocks of economic complexity. Proc. Natl. Acad. Sci. USA 106 (26), 10570–10575.

Hidalgo, C.A., et al., 2007. The product space conditions the development of nations. Science 317, 482–487.

Hodgson, G., 1999. Economics and Utopia: Why the Learning Economy is not the End of History. Routledge, London.

Kleinknecht, A., Naastepad, C.W.M., 2005. The Netherlands: Failure of a Neo-Classical Policy Agenda. Eur. Plan. Stud. 13 (8), 1193–1203.

Kleinknecht, A., 1998. Is labour market flexibility harmful to innovation? Camb. J. Econ. 22 (3), 387–396.

Kroll, H., 2015. Efforts to Implement Smart Specialization in Practice - Leading Unlike Horses to the Water. Euro. Plan. Stud. 23 (10), 2079–2098.

Krueger, A., 1990. Government Failures in Development. J. Econ. Perspect. 4 (3), 9–23.

Kuznetsov, Y., Sabel, C., 2011. New Open Economy Industrial Policy: Making Choices without Picking Winners, World Bank PREM Notes, Economic Policy No. 161, September 2011. Available from: https://openknowledge.worldbank.org/handle/10986/11057.

Kuznetsov, Y., Sabel, C., 2006. Global Mobility of Talent from a Perspective of New Industrial Policy: Open Migration Chains and Diaspora Networks, World Bank, Mimeo. Available from: https://www.wider.unu.edu/sites/default/files/rp2006-144.pdf.

Kuznetsov, Y., Teubal, M., 2011. Sequencing public interventions to support techno entrepreneurship. In: Paper Prepared for a Conference, Challenges and Policies for Promoting and Sustaining Inclusive Growth. 24-25 March, 2011, Paris.

Lall, S., Weiss, J., Zhang, J., 2006. The "sophistication" of exports: a new trade measure. World Dev. 34 (2), 222–237.

Lee, K., 2013. Schumpeterian Analysis of Economic Catch-Up: Knowledge: Path-Creation and the Middle Income Trap. Cambridge University Press, New York.

Lewis, W.W., 2004. The Power of Productivity: Wealth, Poverty, and the Threat to Global Stability. University of Chicago Press, Chicago.

Lin, J.Y., 2012. New structural economics: a framework for rethinking development and policy. World Bank Res. Obs. 26 (2), 193–221.

Lin, J.Y., Treichel, V., 2011. Applying the Growth Identification and Facilitation Framework: the Case of Nigeria, World Bank Policy Research Working Paper No. 5776. Available from: https://ssrn.com/abstract=1915868.

Malerba, Franco, 2004. Sectoral systems of innovation: basic concepts. In: Malerba, F. (Ed.), Sectoral Systems of Innovation Concepts, Issues and Analyses of Six Major Sectors in Europe. Cambridge University Press, Cambridge, UK.

Mazzucato, M., 2013. The Entrepreneurial State: Debunking the Public vs. Private Myth in Risk and Innovation. Anthem Press, London.

McCann, P., Ortega-Argilés, R., 2015. Smart specialization, regional growth and applications to European Union Cohesion Policy. Reg. Stud. 49 (8), 1291–1302.

Milberg, W., Jiang, X., Gereffi, G., 2014. Industrial policy in the era of vertically specialized industrialization, in Transforming Economies: Making Industrial Policy Work for Growth, Jobs and Development. In: Salazar-Xirinachs, J.M., Nübler, I., Kozul-Wright, R. (Eds.), International Labour Office (ILO), Geneva, pp. 151–178. Available from: http://dukespace.lib.duke.edu/dspace/handle/10161/11422.

Naim, M., 1999. Fads and fashion in economic reforms: Washington consensus or Washington confusion? Working Draft of a Paper Prepared for the IMF Conference on Second Generation Reforms, Washington, DC. Available from: https://www.imf.org/external/pubs/ft/seminar/1999/reforms/Naim.HTM.

Neffke, F., Henning, M., Boschma, R., 2011. How do regions diversify over time? industry relatedness and the development of new growth paths in regions. Econ. Geogr. 87 (3), 237–265.

Nelson, R.R., 2006. What Makes an Economy Productive and Progressive? What are the Needed Institutions?, Paper presented at the Inaugural Vernon W. Ruttan Lecture on Science and Development Policy, University of Minnesota. Available from: http://www.sssup.it/UploadDocs/5694_2006_24.pdf.

OECD., 1998. Special Issue on "New Rationale and Approaches in Technology and Innovation Policy", Featuring papers from a Conference jointly organized by the OECD and the Austrian Government, Vienna, 30–31 May 1997, No. 22.

Ostrom, E., 1990. Governing the Commons: The Evolution of Institutions for Collective Action. Cambridge University Press, Cambridge.

Ozawa, T., 2005. Institutions, Industrial Upgrading, and Economic Performance in Japan: The "Flying-Geese" Paradigm of Catch-up Growth. Edward Elgar, Northampton, MA.

Palmade, V., 2005. Industry level analysis: the way to identify the binding constraints to economic growth, World Bank Policy Research Working Paper 3551. Available from: http://documents.worldbank.org/curated/en/958281468780904432/pdf/wps3551.pdf.

Paliokaitė, A., Martinaitis, Z., Sarpong, D., 2016. Implementing smart specialization roadmaps in Lithuania: lost in translation? Technol. Forecast. Soc. Change 110, 143–152.

Pisano, P.G., Shih, W.C., 2009. Restoring America Competitiveness, Harvard Business Review, July-August, pp. 114–125.

Primi, A., 2014. Production Transformation Policy Reviews: a policy assessment and guidance tool for knowledge sharing and peer learning, OECD Development Centre, OECD Initiative for GVCs, Production Transformation and Development.

Pritchett, L., Woolcock, M., Andrews, M., 2013. Looking like a state: techniques of persistent failure in state capability for implementation. J. Dev. Stud. 49 (1), 1–18.

Radosevic, S., 2016. Upgrading technology in Central and Eastern European economies, IZA World of Labor 2016, March 2017. Available from: http://wol.iza.org/articles/upgrading-technology-in-central-and-eastern-european-economies/long.

Radosevic, S., Stancova, K.C., 2015. Internationalising smart specialization: assessment and issues in the case of EU New Member States. J. Knowledge Econ. 6, 1–31. Available from: https://link.springer.com/article/10.1007/s13132-015-0339-3.

Radosevic, S., 2012. Innovation policy studies between theory and practice: a literature review based analysis. STI Policy Rev. 3 (1), 1–45.

Radosevic, S., 1999. International Technology Transfer and Catch-Up in Economic Development. Edward Elgar, Cheltenham.

Radosevic, S., 1997. Strategic policies for growth in post-socialism: theory and evidence based on Baltic States. Econ. Syst. 21 (2), 165–196.

Ramos, J., 2000. Policy directions for the New Economic Model in Latin America. World Dev. 28 (9), 1703–1717.

Rodríguez, F., 2005. Comment on Hausmann and Rodrik. Available from: http://citeseerx.ist.psu. edu/viewdoc/download?doi=10.1.1.372.284&rep=rep1&type=pdf.

Rodrik, D., 2016. Premature deindustrialization. J. Econ. Growth 21, 1–33.

Rodrik, D., 2007. One Economics, Many Recipes: Globalization, Institutions, and Economic Growth. Princeton University Press, Princeton, NJ.

Rodrik, D., 2006a. Goodbye Washington Consensus, hello Washington Confusion? A review of the World Bank's economic growth in the 1990s: learning from a decade of reform. J. Econ. Lit. 44 (4), 973–987.

Rodrik, D., 2006. Industrial Development: Stylized Facts and Policies, John F. Kennedy School of Government, Working Paper; Cambridge, MA: Harvard University. Available from: http:// drodrik.scholar.harvard.edu/files/dani-rodrik/files/industrial-development.pdf.

Rodrik, D., 2004. Industrial Policy for the Twenty-First Century, Harvard University, John F. Kennedy School of Government. Available from: https://www.sss.ias.edu/files/pdfs/Rodrik/ Research/industrial-policy-twenty-first-century.pdf.

Romer, P., 1994. Implementing a national technology strategy With self-organizing industry investment boards, brookings papers. Microeconomics 2 (2), 345–399.

Sabel, C.F., Fernández-Arias, E., Hausmann, R., Clare, A.R., Stein, E., 2013. Export Pioneers in Latin America. Inter-American Development Bank, David Rockefeller Center for Latin American Studies, Harvard University, Cambridge, MA.

Sabel, C.F., Zeitlin, J., 2011. Experimentalist governance. In: Levi-Faur, D. (Ed.), The Oxford Handbook of Governance. Oxford University Press, Oxford.

Sabel, C.F., Zeitlin, J. (Eds.), 2010. Experimentalist Governance in the European Union: Towards a New Architecture. Oxford University Press, Oxford.

Sabel, C.F., 2005. Bootstrapping Development: Rethinking the Role of Public Intervention in Promoting Growth. In: Paper presented at the Protestant Ethic and Spirit of Capitalism Conference. October 8–10 2004, Cornell University, Ithaca, New York. Available from: http:// www2.law.columbia.edu/sabel/papers/bootstrapping%20deve%20send5.pdf.

Schteingart, D., 2015. Productive structure, composition of export, technological capabilities and economic development: does what countries export absolutely matter? Paper presented at GLOBELICS 13th International Conference. 23–25 September 2015, Havana, Cuba.

Stern, N., 2006. Stern Review on The Economics of Climate Change. HM Treasury, London.

Stiglitz, J.E., Greenwald, B.C., 2014. Creating a Learning Society. A New Approach to Growth, Development, and Social Progress. Columbia University Press, New York.

Teubal, M., 1997. A catalytic and evolutionary approach to horizontal technology policies (HTPs). Res. Policy 25 (8), 1161–1188.

Trajtenberg, M., 2015. Innovation Policy for Development: an Overview. Tel Aviv University, NBER and CEPR. Paper prepared for the LAEBA 2005 Second Annual Meeting, Buenos Aires, Argentina (Mimeo).

Vergeer, R., Kleinknecht, A., 2014. Do labour market reforms reduce labour productivity growth? A panel data analysis of 20 OECD countries (1960-2004). Int. Labour Rev. 153 (3), 365–393.

Wade, R.H., 2012. Return of industrial policy? Int. Rev. Appl. Econ. 26 (2), 223–239.

Wade, R.H., 1990. Governing the Market: Economic Theory and the Role of Government in East Asian Industrialization. Princeton University Press, Princeton.

Williamson, J., 1999. What Should the Bank Think About the Washington Consensus, Background Paper to the World Bank''s World Development Report 2000, July.

Williamson, J., 1990. What Washington means by policy reform. In: Williamson, J. (Ed.), Latin American Adjustment: How Much has Happened? Institute for International Economics, Washington DC.

Wilson, S., Furtado, J., 2006. Industrial Policy and Development. CEPAL Review, 89.

FURTHER READING

Crescenzi, R. Giua, M., 2014. The EU Cohesion Policy in Context: Regional Growth and the Influence of Agricultural and Rural Development Policies, LEQS Paper No. 85. Available from: https://ssrn.com/abstract=2542244.

Foray, D., Mowery, D.C., Nelson, R.R., 2012. Public R&D and social challenges: What lessons from mission R&D programs? Res. Policy 41, 1697–1702.

Fortunato, P., Razo, C., Vrolijk, K., 2015. Operationalizing The Product Space: A Road Map to Export Diversification, Discussion Paper No. 219, United Nations Conference on Trade and Development (UNCTAD). Available from: http://unctad.org/en/PublicationsLibrary/osgdp20151_en.pdf.

Moises, N., 1999. Fads and Fashion in Economic Reforms: Washington Consensus or Washington Confusion? Working Draft of a Paper Prepared for the IMF Conference on Second Generation Reforms, Washington, DC. Available from: https://www.imf.org/external/pubs/ft/seminar/1999/reforms/Naim.HTM.

Radosevic, S., 2009. Policies for promoting technological catching up: towards post-Washington approach. J. Inst. Econ. 1 (1), 23–52.

World Bank, 2005. Economic Growth in the 1990s: Learning From a Decade of Reform. World Bank, Washington, DC.

Chapter 2

The Economic Fundamentals of Smart Specialization Strategies

Dominique Foray
Federal Institute of Technology in Lausanne, Lausanne, Switzerland

Chapter Outline

Academic Highlights

- This chapter explains and clarifies the nature of smart specialization strategies as a "sector-nonneutral" innovation policy.
- It discusses the rationale for specialization in the area of R&D and innovation, and identifies the conditions that would make such a process of specialization "smart".
- It emphasizes the importance of the entrepreneurial discovery process, provides an analytical view of this process of information discovery, and highlights its social value.

Policy Highlights

- In the area of R&D and innovation, the logic of critical mass and physical agglomeration is intact as a determinant of R&D productivity and creativity. Most regions, however, cannot reach a critical mass in any sector. They need therefore to specialize. However, specialization is a delicate game and the conditions for and processes of a "smart" specialization are important.

Advances in the Theory and Practice of Smart Specialization. http://dx.doi.org/10.1016/B978-0-12-804137-6.00002-4

- Policy should aim to avoid specialization at sectoral level. Specialization should represent an opportunity to concentrate resources on modes of transformation of sectors or of establishing new ones. Smart specialization targets the development of transformative activities at a degree of granularity finer than the sector level.
- The aim is to shift from the omniscient planner paradigm to the self-discovery paradigm. This shift is based on the fact that the *ex-ante* knowledge—needed to make decisions—is necessarily incomplete.
- The flexibility and the ability to change the current strategy are key points if new options and opportunities are to be continuously observed, assessed, and perhaps exploited. This is why evaluation and monitoring represent other critical elements at any stage of the strategy.

INTRODUCTION

In most regions, policy makers are struggling with the issue of structural changes—how to modernize a huge but not very dynamic agro-food sector; how to help SMEs move forward in the age of industry 4.0; how to establish a new industry at the intersection of renewable energy, and new materials and nanoscience; how to leverage the growth potential of the new technological revolution and drive needed modernization, and diversification of the regional economy? Driving structural changes—more precisely, *positive* structural changes in the form of modernization, diversification, and new industries—is key. Structural changes allow for the basis of future competitiveness and innovation, and help to create new jobs that will help young people to retain the option of staying and working in their own regions.

This chapter aims to articulate a coherent vision of the policy approach that is evoked by the term "smart specialization strategy," and to explore and elaborate the requirements and implications that are consistent with that conceptualization. In the subsequent sections, it discusses the shift from the logic of horizontal policy to smart specialization strategy; summarizes its main principles in terms of rationale and design; and finally, provides an in-depth analysis of the process of entrepreneurial discovery.

FROM HORIZONTAL POLICIES TO RIS3[1]

The last decades of regional innovation policy in Europe have shown that positive structural changes are very difficult to achieve. During these decades, sector-neutral (or horizontal) policies dominated the policy process at regional level in the European Union. A *sector-neutral* policy is a policy that addresses problems that are common to any company and other innovation actors across sectors and fields. Such a policy aims at improving general conditions and fixing generic problems and market failures. There were exceptions, of course, but horizontal policy (or sector-neutral policy) was the main logic underlying resource allocation in the framework of regional and cohesion policy.

Horizontal policies are good policies! First, they are likely to improve important components of the regional system of innovation. Second, they minimize the risks inherent in any policy that selects projects according to preferred fields (Trajtenberg, 2012). Indeed, this sort of policy has the potential to stimulate structural changes through various mechanisms, such as diversification in firms, spin-offs and start-ups, mobility of people, and networking (Boschma and Frenken, 2011).

Although sector-neutral policy was likely to work in the case of top regions, it did not work in the case of transition and less advanced regions (Chapter 6). Most of the less developed regions and transition regions failed to improve the knowledge gap in relation to the top regions. In a few cases when regions managed to improve the knowledge gap to a certain extent, they had difficulties to translate this achievement into real economic convergence. This usually happens when improvement in the knowledge gap is mostly a public sector component, with very little effect on innovation capacities within the private sector (Veugelers, 2010). There is no such thing as a quasimagical effect of public research improvement, certainly not in the form of knowledge spillovers.

Why do we observe such a differentiated impact of horizontal policies among regions with different levels of development? Innovation requires not only general framework conditions—*the basics have to be right*, but also specific capabilities and resources. In top regions, these capabilities are provided by industrial associations, large companies, universities, and public research organizations, through spillovers of research, training, and diffusion of technologies to suppliers. These spillovers constitute the complementary capabilities that most SMEs can draw on even if they have not contributed to their provision (Berger, 2013). However, in the other regions, these sources of complementary capabilities have dried up or have never existed and large holes in the industrial ecosystems have appeared. In the words of Berger (2013), p. 20, *"firms are home alone."* She convincingly argues that *"even start-ups with great innovation and generous funding cannot do it all in house. They need suppliers, qualified workers and engineers, expertise beyond their own."* In many cases, the ecosystem is too poor to provide all these capabilities.

In less advanced and transition regions, regional innovation policy therefore needs to go beyond horizontal measures and address the whole set of capabilities required to innovate in *specific* sectors and emerging fields. This reflects what Hausmann and Rodrik (2006), p. 24 wrote: *"The idea that the government can disengage from specific policies and just focus on general framework conditions in a sector neutral way is an illusion based on the disregard for the specificity and complexity of the requisite publicly provided inputs and capabilities."*

A smart specialization strategy—like few other policies—offers guidelines and principles for governments to reengage in specific policies to promote innovation, and structural changes in specific domains.

Of course, such a policy has a very different logic than the horizontal policy previously described. We can call it "nonneutral" (or vertical). It is a very different policy simply because varied activities require dissimilar things. Supporting biotechnology development for fisheries will require the provision of capabilities in terms of research, suppliers, and services that are very different from those needed to support the development of advanced manufacturing technologies for the footwear industry or the development of ICT for tourism. Such a policy has to deal with the complexity and specificity of each activity and this has a cost. This is *haute couture* rather than *ready-to-wear*. A horizontal policy, such as R&D tax credit is *ready-to-wear* in that it has a cost but is relatively easy to implement. Providing the specific capabilities for a particular emerging activity is tailored and more expensive, therefore *haute couture*.

Many economists are skeptical about the government's capabilities to address such complexity because this requires a detailed understanding of the spillovers and the innovation complementarities involved (Matsuyama, 1997; Klette and Moen, 1999). While I partly share such scepticism (Aghion et al., 2009), the concept of smart specialization is an invitation not to give up, but to recognize the difficulty of the policy process and provide tools and guidelines to overcome these difficulties. This is, in a certain sense, also the agenda of the so-called "new industrial policy."

THE TWO FACETS OF SMART SPECIALIZATION STRATEGIES

The simple intellectual project of smart specialization strategies is that regions will build the capabilities that they need to achieve their own structural changes. A smart specialization strategy thus has two facets (Foray et al., 2009) are as follows:

1. forming capabilities in a few strategic domains;
2. driving structural changes.

Of course, it is always possible to import all the factors of structural changes. One can modernize a tourism sector simply by outsourcing the development and application of ICT solutions to companies that are not based in a region, and this can be a good sectoral policy. However, this is not a smart specialization policy. A smart specialization policy addresses not only structural changes but also the formation of local capabilities to drive these changes. Moreover, it is the function of the entrepreneurial discovery process (see further) to generate enough information for the government to decide where it might be really worthwhile to have a smart specialization where there are potential and opportunities, and where in some other domains a "simple" sectoral policy might be enough because there is no hope of building the capabilities locally needed to transform the sector.

In this picture, the specific properties of general purpose technologies (GPT) play an important role (Bresnahan, 2010; Bresnahan and Trajtenberg, 1995).

Central features of a GPT are horizontal propagation throughout the economy and the complementarity between the invention of the GPT and the development of applications that are related to specific sectors. Most often, GPTs do not offer the complete innovative outcome, but the recombination of GPTs with complementary technologies enables the creation of new innovative solutions. Expressed in economists' language, the invention of a GPT extends the frontier of invention possibilities for the whole economy, while application development changes the production function of one particular sector. Myriads of economically important innovations result, therefore, from the "coinvention" of applications. Moreover, the dynamics of a GPT may be spatially distributed between regions specialized in basic inventions and regions investing in specific application domains which are related to the existing structures.

The GPT framework suggests, therefore strategies that can be pursued advantageously both by regions that are at the scientific and technological frontier, and by those that are less advanced. While the *leader regions*[2] invest in the invention of a GPT or the combination of different GPTs (such as bioinformatics), *follower regions* are often better advised to invest in the *"coinvention of applications"* that is, the development of the applications of a GPT in one or several important domains of the regional economy.

There is, therefore, an important theoretical relationship between smart specialization as a process of diversification and modernization of economic structures and the potential of opportunities offered by such GPTs in *any* region. For sure, smart specialization and its subsequent structural changes can occur through other kinds of innovation dynamics, but the dynamics of GPTs provide crucial opportunities for regions at any level of development to develop new activities and generate structural changes.

MAIN PRINCIPLES OF RIS3

The most concise presentation of a RIS3 might be based on the very simple and usual questions: why, (on) what, how, and when. This section discusses the answers to these four questions to clarify both the goals and the process of a RIS3.

Why?

As the goal of a RIS3 is to form capabilities to achieve specific (sector-nonneutral) goals in terms of structural changes, there are two arguments supporting a specialization logic. There is, on the one hand, the argument of critical mass/agglomeration, and, on the other hand, the argument of the political feasibility of addressing specific capabilities and infrastructures in many different domains or areas.

The formation of capabilities for a specific domain or a specific objective in terms of R&D and innovation cannot be dissociated from the problem of reaching a critical mass of actors and assets in the considered domain. Indeed, the logic of scale, scope, and physical agglomeration as a key determinant for creativity and R&D productivity is intact.

That is so because, first, there are important indivisibilities in R&D at macrolevel: conducting R&D requires a wide range of infrastructure and services, the availability of adequate human resources, and financial institutions and markets. All of these will materialize only if enough R&D is conducted to justify the emergence of the required infrastructure (Trajtenberg, 2002).

Second, innovation is strongly determined by social interactions, informal communication, and serendipity. Therefore, the greater the size of the agglomeration, the greater the potential for knowledge recombination based on local communication, chance meetings, and social relationships (Jaffe, 2015).

The empirical economics of R&D and innovation has produced fundamental results showing how scale, scope, and spillovers are important determinants of R&D productivity. Therefore, critical mass and relational density strongly influence the efficiency and productivity of R&D and other innovation-related activities. Countries or regions with a large agglomeration have an advantage over places with smaller scale and size.

However, most regions cannot reach critical agglomeration in any domain, in every industry. Instead of doing a little bit of everything, choices need to be made. A regional economy needs to specialize in certain domains or fields where it thinks it can position itself as a global leader in the near future.

Such an obvious size-based rationale for specialization is reinforced by another rationale about political feasibility. As already said, RIS3 is a difficult policy because it has to address the specificity and complexity of inputs, capabilities, and coordination in any domain of interest. It is therefore clear that a local government cannot address all potential specific capabilities and infrastructure needs for all new activities. This implies that choices need to be made between different emerging activities or opportunities. As asserted by Hausmann and Rodrik (2006), "*it is not that choices are desirable, they are simply inevitable.*"

There is therefore a double-rationale—critical mass and political feasibility—to justify a specialization strategy. Yet specialization is a dangerous game because it can also mean monoculture, uniformization, and a tendency to be locked into an obsolete technology. There is therefore a need to find a smart way to specialize.

While there is a diversity of approaches to designing and implementing a RIS3, a few principles are central to transforming a somewhat dangerous game into a productive approach to building capabilities for innovation and structural changes.

On What?

The first principle is obvious. Priorities and choices are not made at sectoral level. A typical RIS3 question or arbitrage will not sound like: "*should we focus on textile or chemical engineering, tourism or ICT?*" Sectoral priorities would be irrelevant, because you might find segments and activities that are very dynamic and innovative in each of these sectors, so there would be no reason to exclude them from the strategy. It would be irrelevant too—a distortion—to support all firms in an industry just because they are part of a selected sector. What a RIS3 needs to support are companies and research committed to a project for the transformation of a sector or a project for establishing a new one. Thus, RIS3 is not about selecting sectors, but rather about selecting activities aimed at transforming sectors or establishing new ones. We can call this level "transformative activities"—a midgrained level of granularity that is situated between the microlevel of individual units and the macrolevel of sectors and industries.

How?

By definition, such modes of transformation are not known *ex-ante*. The so-called "beyond principal agent (PA) governance" principle (Sabel, 2004) is relevant here. In the PA governance perspective, the government decides what to do and sets the appropriate incentives for firms to execute the plan. Let us assume now the government does not possess *ex-ante* the knowledge about what to do and, as such, cannot apply the standard PA logic. "*What if, as I and many others assume, there are no principals ... with the robust and panoramic knowledge needed for this directive role?*" (Sabel, 2004, p. 3). The fundamental point here is the Hayekian argument that the knowledge about what to do is not obvious. It is a knowledge "of time and place;" this is localized knowledge which is dispersed, decentralized, or divided. Above all, the *ex-ante* knowledge is incomplete. There is always potential for discovery and surprise about what to do as concrete processes of exploration are undertaken (Kirzner, 1997). The strategic decisions should thus be informed by a discovery process about opportunities, constraints, and challenges. Future priorities, potential specialization domains, and the critical path within each domain towards structural changes need to be discovered through an interactive and decentralized process involving all innovation actors in the regional economy. As such, the process of entrepreneurial discovery is characterized by a strong learning dimension. The social value of a discovery is that it informs the whole system in which a particular domain of R&D, innovation, and structural change are likely to create new opportunities (Hirshleifer, 1971). The second part of this chapter is devoted to an extensive presentation of the so-called process of entrepreneurial discovery.

When?

The answer is very simple: at any time as the process is endless. RIS3 is a policy with an experimental dimension. A few bets are placed on various domains. They are rather risky. This is different from a standard policy where the bets are safe and sure (think, for instance, of the standard R&D tax credit instrument). In a RIS3, choices have to be made and this is by definition a risky venture. Yet the good news is that it is a living document. Things change; new potential and opportunities may appear and, at our level of "transformative activity," novel priority areas are likely to be identified later in the process. In such a case, they need to be integrated into the RIS3 while the activities that failed need to be excluded from the strategy.

The principle of an endless strategy is central. It is absolutely healthy for the policy process to comprise the option that the strategy can be revised at any time according to the feedback from first experiences as well as the emerging new opportunities and potential. However, such a principle needs to be coupled with something perhaps less popular in the policy circle: an exit clause after an appropriate period of time so that new priorities or projects can be funded. What Trajtenberg (2015) calls a "self-destruct mechanism" is a key principle. Such a clause should not be applied to the priority as a whole, but rather to the projects that make the priorities concrete as they become mature and, as such, are no longer "new."

THE PROCESS OF ENTREPRENEURIAL DISCOVERY

Identifying priority areas and forming capabilities in these areas are at the core of the RIS3. This is a key process and it is critical for a region to do it on its own. There is no recipe or standard method but a few principles should be considered so as to build transparent and robust means for nominating those activities that show promise from more R&D and other resources.

Conceptualizing the Discovery Process

The discovery information which will be used as a sound base for building a RIS3 is structured by the goals of the considered policy. Such information consists of a compound event are as follows:

- Does domain A represent a strategic domain to drive structural changes in the region? The answer is given by probability $P(A)$.
- Can A be exploited successfully given the current state of capabilities and potential in the region? The response is given by the probability $P(ap)$.

It is clear that the answer to the second question (the discovery of pap) implies concrete investments to support exploratory projects, platforms, and networks to learn about the strategic domain and its potential of development in terms of critical mass and structural changes. It is obviously at this level that discovery and surprise elements will be the most important.

The social value of a process of entrepreneurial discovery is essentially this informational value, which allows the state to answer the two questions mentioned earlier and therefore to make decisions at two levels—what domains, and what processes and projects in each of the selected domains? The process of entrepreneurial discovery also informs firms about opportunities in the various domains.

Companies—most often large companies—can internalize the process of entrepreneurial discovery. They are looking for new strategic domains and ways to explore them concretely. However, the difference between a process of entrepreneurial discovery internalized in a company, and a process of entrepreneurial discovery embedded in a public policy is obvious. In the former case, the social value of the process will be lower than in the latter. Typically, the company will disclose information on P(A), certainly not on P(ap).

When the process of entrepreneurial discovery is supported by a policy, it is critical that the informational value of the process be maximized. The companies which are supported in joining the entrepreneurial discovery process must accept and conform to these rules of information and audit.

Describing the Phases of the Process

Let us describe this process as involving the following steps:

1. The starting point in this process involves the analysis of the structures of the regional economy to identify potential and opportunities. Such analysis is based on a mixture of knowledge. On the one hand, there is a need to provide a sound analysis of regional assets—based on indicators like sectoral productivity, capacity to compete, patent and industry specialization, critical mass, extra-regional networks, and partnerships (Eichler et al., 2015). These are key statistics to identify potential and opportunities in the regional economy. However, such formal analysis needs to be combined with a more contextual knowledge and with insider expertise about facts and issues that are less visible in the statistics. This latter kind of knowledge includes finding out whether there is a strong technical university, and if so in what domains; in which domains are large companies operating; and what kind of global value chains are positioned in the region. Finally, mega-trends (grand challenges) as well as the current development and propagation of the new GPTs need to be taken into consideration.

2. This combination of different types of knowledge and analysis should form the basis for dialogue and interactions between the government and the stakeholders. From this process, priority areas will emerge—a certain number of potential domains of specialization. However, the process does not stop here.

3. It also includes making the action plans that will put these priorities into practice very concrete. Such action plans involve investments in exploratory projects and platforms, and the empowerment of potential leaders who can stimulate collective actions. Phase C is crucially about supporting exploratory projects within each priority domain and providing coordination mechanisms (platforms, networks, etc.) to generate and realize potential synergies and agglomeration effects.

4. Subsequently, the government will support the emerging transformative activities that appear very promising in terms of future innovations, spillovers, and potential to transform the existing structures *and* those which have scale or agglomeration economies or exhibit the characteristics of coordination failures (Rodrik, 2004). The policy process needs to manage the transition from the entrepreneurial discovery phase to the growth of a new transformative activity.

Steps 1, 2, and 3 earlier form the whole process of entrepreneurial discovery, which again does not stop at step 2 (the moment of identifying priorities). At any step, evaluation and monitoring provide possibilities for iteration and feedback.

The Morphology of Priority Areas

Priority areas need to be quite narrow, or at least not too broad. In an area that is too broad—one called "energy," for example—the 12 or 15 projects that are selected and supported are scattered and dispersed. Connections, synergies, and spillovers will hardly happen and critical mass will not emerge. In a narrower priority area, the same number of projects will be more connected, providing potential scale, scope, and spillover effects. Some platforms will be "general-purpose" and the markets for specialized inputs (skills and services) will become thick.

There is, of course, a political rationale underlying the need for broad areas but this is not the right way to proceed because, at the end of the day, the region will not get what a RIS3 is supposed to deliver.

Government Capabilities

What has been described above is a "beautiful theory." However, the concrete process of entrepreneurial discovery is particularly demanding in terms of policy-making capability and monitoring competences. Smart specialization strategies will not succeed if policy-making capabilities at regional level do not reach a high-level of competence and commitment. While this issue cannot be developed further in this chapter due to lack of space, a few key authors are addressing it critically [see in particular, Morgan (2013, 2016) and McCann (2015)].

IS THERE A RIS3 TRAP?

One type of risk is often discussed in connection with RIS3. It involves the notion of incrementalism: regions are locked into trajectories of minor innovation in which they adapt without being able to set the conditions for generating fundamental breakthroughs. This arguably does not constitute a real issue here. In the realm of innovation, there is not only one game in town, in the sense of fundamental invention in a few key enabling technologies that would be generated in a few top places while the rest of the world can wait before adopting them. If innovation were a global public good, perhaps RIS3 would not make any sense: *"once a piece of knowledge is invented it is not necessary to invent it again"* (Dasgupta, 1992, p. 3). But this is not the case. There are an infinite number of potential innovations, which are context-, sector-, and region-specific, and which will never be invented in Silicon Valley!

This means that, for many regions, the point is not inventing at the frontier but rather generating innovation complementarities in existing sectors. These types of complementarities are perhaps less exciting and flashy, but they ultimately represent the key to economy-wide growth in regional economies. Based on a strong RIS3, a secondary region becomes capable of allocating R&D and other inputs in critical domains so as to lever the growth potential of the prevalent GPT invented elsewhere.

CONCLUSIONS

The novelty of smart specialization resides not so much in the goal of the policy but, rather, in its process and design. This novelty is, of course, not "absolute." It has been inspired by Hausmann and Rodrik (2003), and Rodrik (2004) as well as few others.[3]

As such, the smart specialization literature is fully a part of the new industrial policy agenda (Chapter 15), which includes approaches sharing the same kind of "policy design thinking" to avoid the usual mistakes which are likely to happen when a government is engaged in sector-nonneutral policies [see for instance Aghion et al. (2011); Aghion (2012); Aghion and Akcigit (2015) on industrial policy; Foray et al. (2012) on mission-oriented policy; Hausmann and Rodrik (2003, 2006) and Rodrik (2004, 2007, 2014) on development policy; Trajtenberg (2002, 2012) and the foreword in Foray (2015) on high-tech policy; Lin (2012), on new structural economics; as well as Berglof et al. (2015)].

All these contributions try to solve the key problem of finding a balance between the need to provide governments with the policy goal and tools to make strategic decisions about the direction (not only the rate) of inventive activities and the need to preserve and even enhance decentralized entrepreneurial dynamics as the main engine for innovation. However, in most of these contributions, scholars do not go very much further than recommending the coupling of vertical/sectoral policy and competition policy (see Chapter 15, for an in-depth discussion on this issue). Notable exceptions are many papers by Hausmann and Rodrik and by Rodrik alone, as well as the smart specialization literature. Indeed, the design principles and the entrepreneurial discovery process presented earlier do represent significant progress in this agenda.

John Enos (1995) is one of several inspirational people behind RIS3 ideas. He wrote in the 1990s that countries and regions *"should put more effort into choosing, in detail and for the future, the direction of R&D—on what products, what processes, into what markets.*" Furthermore, he mentioned two reasons to support this argument are as follows:

1. If they do not do it, others will do it for them.
2. The knowledge and experience acquired in choosing the right direction—what we call "entrepreneurial discovery"—will be very valuable in carrying out the subsequent stage of product and process innovations.

This is perhaps the main lesson of the first years of RIS3 in the policy landscape of the EU: the entrepreneurial discovery process does have a cost but it also generates many benefits. As such, it represents a great opportunity to learn about potential and opportunities. It is therefore central for building a regional strategy for future competitiveness.

ACKNOWLEDGMENTS

I would like to thank all participants of the workshops in Bucharest for their comments on the preliminary drafts of this chapter and I am grateful to Slavo Radosevic for his detailed comments and suggestions on the first draft.

ENDNOTES

1. Research and innovation strategies for smart specialization.
2. We distinguish between "leader regions" that master the technological frontier, "follower regions" that are able to catch up to a leader region, and "laggards" who struggle to build up absorptive capacities to apply advanced technologies.
3. Only intellectual influences in terms of policy design are considered here. Regional studies on innovation systems do represent, of course, another important inspiration.

REFERENCES

Aghion, P., 2012. Innovation process and policy: what do we learn from new growth theory? In: Lerner, J., Stern, S. (Eds.), The Rate and Direction of Inventive Activity Revisited. The University of Chicago Press, Chicago.

Aghion, P., Akcigit, U., 2015. Innovation and growth: the Schumpeterian perspective, COEURE. Available from http://www.coeure.eu/wp-content/uploads/Innovation-and-Growth.pdf.

Aghion, P., David, P.A., Foray, D., 2009. Science, technology and innovation for economic growth: linking policy research and practice in "STIG Systems". Res. Policy 38, 681–693.

Aghion, P., Boulanger, J., Cohen, E., 2011. Rethinking industrial policy, Bruegel Policy Brief 04/2011.

Berger, S., 2013. Making in America. MIT Press, Boston.

Berglof, E., Foray, D., Landesmann, M., Lin, J.Y., Campos, M., Sanfey, P., Radosevic, S., Volchkova, N., 2015. Transition economics meets new structural economics. J. Econ. Policy Reform 18, 191–220.

Boschma, R., Frenken, K., 2011. Technological relatedness and regional branching. In: Bathelt, H., Feldman, M.P., Kogler, D.F. (Eds.), Dynamic geographies of knowledge creation and innovation. Routledge, London.

Bresnahan, T., 2010. General purpose technologies, in Handbook in Economics of Innovation, vol. 2, eds. B. Hall and N. Rosenberg, Amsterdam, North-Holland Elsevier.

Bresnahan, T., Trajtenberg, M., 1995. General purpose technologies: engines of growth. J. Econom. 65, 83–108.

Dasgupta, P., 1992. The economic theory of technology policy: an introduction. In: Dasgupta, P., Stoneman, P. (Eds.), Economic Policy and Technological Performance. Cambridge University Press, Cambridge.

Eichler, M., Wagner, A., Peters, M., 2015. Smart specialisation: diagnosing the potential of regions. BAK Basel Economics AG, Basel.

Enos, J., 1995. In pursuit of science and technology in Sub-Saharian Africa. Routledge, London, UNU/INTECH.

Foray, D., 2015. Smart specialisation: opportunities and challenges for regional innovation policy. Routledge, London & New York, NY.

Foray, D., David, P.A., Hall, B., 2009. Smart specialisation: the concept, in Knowledge for growth: prospects for science, technology and innovation, Report EUR 24047, European Union.

Foray, D., Mowery, D.C., Nelson, R.R., 2012. Public R&D and social challenges: what lessons from mission R&D programs? Res. Policy 41, 1697–1792.

Hausmann, R., Rodrik, D., 2003. Economic development as self-discovery. J. Dev. Econ. 72, 603–633.

Hausmann, R., Rodrik., D., 2006. Doomed to choose: industrial policy as predicament, Blue Sky Seminar, Center for International Development, Harvard University. Available from: https://www.hks.harvard.edu/index.php/content/download/69495/1250790/version/1/file/hausmann_doomed_0609.pdf.

Hirshleifer, J., 1971. The private and social value of information and the reward to inventive activity. Am. Econ. Rev. 61, 561–574.

Jaffe, A., 2015. Science and innovation in small countries: speculation and research agenda. Asia Pac. J. Account. Econ. 22, 4–12.

Kirzner, I., 1997. Entrepreneurial discovery and the competitive market process: an Austrian approach. J. Econ. Lit. 35, 60–85.

Klette, J., Moen, J., 1999. From growth theory to technology policy: coordination problems in theory and practice. Nordic J. Polit. Econ. 25, 53–74.

Lin, J.Y., 2012. New Structural Economics, Washington DC, The World Bank.

Matsuyama, K., 1997. Economic development as coordination problem. In: Aoki, M., Kim, H.-K., Okuno-Fujiwara, M. (Eds.), The Role of Government in East Asian Economic Development. Clarendon Press, Oxford.

McCann, P., 2015. The Regional and Urban Policy of the European Union: Cohesion, Results-orientation and Smart Specialisation. Edward Elgar, Cheltenham.

Morgan, K., 2013. The regional State in the Era of Smart Specialisation. Ekonomiaz 83, 103–125.

Morgan, K., 2016. Nurturing novelty: regional innovation policy in the age of smart specialisation, Environment and Planning C: Government and Policy first online.

Rodrik, D., 2004. Industrial Policy for the Twenty-First Century, CEPR, Discussion paper Series, no.4767, November 2004. Available from: https://www.sss.ias.edu/files/pdfs/Rodrik/Research/industrial-policy-twenty-first-century.pdf.

Rodrik, D., 2007. Normalizing Industrial Policy, paper prepared for the Commission on Growth and Development, World Bank Working Paper no. 3. Available from: http://siteresources.worldbank.org/EXTPREMNET/Resources/489960-1338997241035/Growth_Commission_Working_Paper_3_Normalizing_Industrial_Policy.pdf.

Rodrik, D., 2014. Green Industrial Policy. Oxford Rev. Econ. Policy 30, 469–491.

Sabel, C., 2004. Beyond principal-agent governance: experimentalist organizations, learning and accountability. WRR—Wetenschappelijke Raad Voor Het Regeringsbeleid, Amsterdam.

Trajtenberg, M., 2002. Government support for commercial R&D: lessons from the Israeli experience. Jaffe, A.B., Lerner, J., Stern, S. (Eds.), Innovation Policy and the Economy, vol. 2, The MIT Press, Boston.

Trajtenberg, M., 2012. Can the Nelson-arrow paradigm still be the Beacon of Innovation Policy? In: Lerner, J., Stern, S. (Eds.), The Rate and Direction of Inventive Activity Revisited. The University of Chicago Press, Chicago.

Trajtenberg, M., 2015. Foreword. In: Foray, D. (Ed.), Smart Specialisation. Opportunities and challenges for regional innovation policy. Routledge, London & New York, NY.

Veugelers, R., 2010. Assessing the potential for knowledge-based development in transition countries, Bruegel Working Paper 01. Available from: http://bruegel.org/wp-content/uploads/imported/publications/100531-PC-_Transition_economies.pdf.

Chapter 3

Managing Self-Discovery: Diagnostic Monitoring of a Portfolio of Projects and Programs

Yevgeny Kuznetsov*, Charles Sabel**
*Migration Policy Institute and The World Bank, Washington, DC, United States;
**Columbia Law School, Columbia University, New York City, NY, United States

Chapter Outline

Academic Highlights

Our two key policy concepts are:
- *Heterogeneity (discretionary differences) of institutions*: it is almost always possible to find some that are working. The issue is using the ones that work to improve those that do not.

Advances in the Theory and Practice of Smart Specialization. http://dx.doi.org/10.1016/B978-0-12-804137-6.00003-6
51

- *Diagnostic or problem-solving monitoring*: the systematic evaluation of the portfolio of projects to detect errors as each of the specific projects evolves and to correct the problems (including the weeding out of inefficient projects) in light of implementation experience and other new information.

Policy Highlights

This chapter shifts the debate about state activism in supporting globally competitive industries from a choice of "picking/dropping winners" to a process of step-by-step transformation of the private and public sectors.

- In such a experimental search, the new industrial policy creates its own context for efficient design and implementation through diagnostic (or problem-solving monitoring)—a procedure to reveal errors and correct them.

INTRODUCTION

The smart specialization (SS) (RIS3) program of the European Commission (EC) is certainly an ambitious experiment. The scale of this effort and its underlying conceptual and policy base call for a reexamination and further development of the RIS3 approach, which is only starting to be formulated in a more systematic manner.

RIS3' perspective on regional development is yet another attempt to put in practice a Hayekian (and, more generally, Austrian) approach to economic policy, which makes trial-and-error experimentation, with attendant error detection and correction [referred to as "self-discovery" in an influential work by Rodrik and Hausmann (2003)], the central challenge of the RIS3 institutional design and implementation. Little thought, however, has been invested so far in examining how exactly such a trial-and-error experimentation should and could be conceived institutionally beyond conventional shibboleths about the need for evaluation. However, the evaluation of outcomes is backward looking, and thus tends to assign guilt for revealed mistakes. In contrast, what is required is *forward-looking identification* of the key issues to resolve, of unavoidable errors of the implementation process, and of remedial measures to address them. Consequently, the key conceptual idea of this chapter is that of *diagnostic (problem-solving) monitoring*. While standard monitoring and evaluation focuses on whether one does "things right," diagnostic monitoring asks whether one is doing "the right thing."

The focus of this chapter is on emerging countries and regions. Although the recent crisis demonstrated that the whole world (not least the United States) is developing, and nearly all economies experiment and make mistakes, the growth episodes we focus on are characterized by a particularly high level of experimentation in discovering new domains of economic activity. The examples we rely upon span from Ireland and Taiwan (China) in the 1960s and 1970s to India and Chile today. The structure of the chapter is as follows. The section "Project

Portfolio and Framework Program as Two Key Conceptual Units of the New Industrial Policy" provides a succinct primer on the new open economy industrial policy. It posits a portfolio of real sector projects and a framework program (portfolio of related public programs) as two central units of the open economy industrial policy. The section dwells on the organizational dimension of self-discovery by introducing the notion of a Schumpeterian development agency (SDA), an agency with the capability and the motivation to experiment, make mistakes, and correct them. The section, "Diagnostic (Problem-Solving) Monitoring Versus Conventional (Accounting) Monitoring" introduces the key notion of diagnostic or problem-solving monitoring, a forward-looking procedure to detect and correct problems and mistakes. Diagnostic monitoring is contrasted with and compared to conventional (accounting) monitoring. The section, "Establishing a Schumpeterian (Diagnostic Monitoring) Segment in RIS3 Practice" provides recommendations for the European Union by proposing a diagnostic monitoring segment into RIS3 practice; in other words, a Schumpeterian embryo within the European Commission administrative machinery. Our discussion of the Debt Management Trust Fund (TF) of the World Bank—a Schumpeterian embryo with explicit diagnostic monitoring procedures—provides an inspiringly realistic benchmark for such a proposal. The section, "Conclusions: Turning Obstacles Into Variables" offers brief conclusions.

PROJECT PORTFOLIO AND FRAMEWORK PROGRAM AS TWO KEY CONCEPTUAL UNITS OF THE NEW INDUSTRIAL POLICY[1]

A key question of the open economy industrial policy is how policy makers can set priorities. In other words, how can policy makers provide public inputs that are customized and bundled to suit the needs of particular domains of some economic activity, but not others? This chapter starts from the premise that policy makers invariably make mistakes, both intentional and unintentional. That requires a shift of focus from a *one-time* choice of winners (sectors, industries, firms, and other organizations) to a *process* of error detection and error correction of such choices (with corresponding attention paid to governance). As a second premise, we take obstacles to reach informed and accountable choice (such as influence of entrenched interests, low capabilities of public sector, etc.) as endogenous variables, or objects of analysis in themselves. Three of them are particularly important:

- *Power of vested interests.* Entrenched interests are likely to derail the search from the provision of public goods toward self-dealing and rent seeking. In particular, the disengagement of the public sector proves to be much more difficult than its engagement, even in successful and promising cases of industrial policy.
- *A necessarily partial view of the economy.* No actor has a panoramic view of the economy or complete knowledge of the distortions that the public sector

is supposed to correct. In today's fast changing economy, neither economists and public officials nor private actors know where the relevant market failures are.

- *Weak capabilities of governments and other economic agents to undertake industrial policy tasks.* In low-income economies in particular, public support for the connections with the world economy can become self-defeating due to nonexistent capabilities. The issue is how to generate such capabilities.

The shift from a one-time choice to a process where obstacles represent endogenous rather than exogenous variables occurs by positing *a real sector project* (and related project portfolio) as a key unit of both action and reflection on the action. Such a project is an investment; a set of activities that are at once finite (i.e., with clear objectives and resources) and malleable (i.e., amenable to adjustment: both objectives and resources are supposed to be provisional and are expected to change). In contrast, in vertical industrial policy, the central unit of action is *strategy*; an exercise in informed imagination whose weight derives from an elaborate approval process. In horizontal industrial policy, the action unit is *a regulatory action* of a (well-functioning) public sector organization, particularly a court. Courts are capable of both assuring and maintaining an "even playing field," as well as restraining their own powers and prerogatives. Both vertical and horizontal industrial policy approaches, for all their apparent differences and contrasts, have proved to be problematic in practice.

It takes time to change an adopted and approved public document, so consensual strategies tend to become obsolete and irrelevant right from the start: they fail to guide action. Likewise, horizontal industrial policy—deregulation initiatives creating an open competitive environment—also proved to be problematic. It is predicated on the assumption of an efficient government focused on the delivery of public goods. Yet what if the public sector is dysfunctional, or at least in part dysfunctional? A typical situation that exists for many, if not a majority of, emerging economies. In that case, the Washington Consensus recipe is to reform it. This is, of course, a long-term undertaking. In the meantime, the vested interests of the dysfunctional public sector thwart horizontal industrial policy efforts in the same way they undermine sectoral (vertical industrial) policy.

By contrast, placing the focus on a project is at once a humble (in the short run) and an ambitious (in the long run) undertaking. In the short term, one relies on the institution of a *project manager*, an individual who demonstrates practical acumen, creativity, and tenacity, even when the environment around him/her is highly problematic. The project manager is the very institution that experiments, makes mistakes, and learns from them (captains of voyages of discovery are one example). Given sophisticated capabilities to design and implement projects, the latter can be arranged in portfolios managed by agencies with specialized capabilities. A type of agency best suited to experiment and perform collaborative search is an *autonomous entity with a mandate to experiment by assembling a portfolio of projects* and carefully monitoring the portfolio, yet remaining accountable for the results of the experimentation. Following Kuznetsov (2009), let us call this kind of agency Schumpeterian Development Agency (SDA). An SDA that manages such a portfolio tends to have an incentive structure, which induces it, or at least permits it, to establish both capabilities and the motivation and discipline to experiment. Examples include project portfolios managed by venture capital (VC) funds, self-discovery agencies, such as DARPA and the like. They manage *portfolios of projects*; there is a common theme and strategy behind the portfolio, even though the strategy may be implicit.

Evidence for the new open economy industrial policy understood as a search for new domains, or, more generally, for capacity-enhancing connections to the world economy through the management of project portfolios, comes from small open economies, such as Taiwan (China), Ireland, or Chile. Taiwan (China) achieved this through the formation of a VC program—an embryonic SDA—that allowed Taiwanese (Chinese)-born engineers, trained both at home and abroad, to deploy their skills in start-up firms, whose activities complemented and facilitated the reorganization of US leaders in the computer and semiconductor industry. VC—still slowly diffusing within the advanced economies and virtually unknown in developing ones outside of Taiwan (China) and Israel—thus effectively became an instrument for orienting and reorienting the direction of development of the national economy in rapidly shifting and highly demanding markets. Ireland created an analogous method for identifying and developing growth-enhancing connections from the 1950s tax exemptions (later reductions) to the corporate profits tax attracted subsidiaries of multinational corporations from promising sectors, such as chemicals, pharmaceuticals, and software.

If Taiwan (China) used VC to connect its expatriate engineers to each other and to world markets, Ireland employed selective FDI. The result in both cases was cumulative capacity building. In Taiwan (China), we saw this in the creation and evolution of firms. In Ireland, we found it principally in the growing responsibilities of managers who rose through the professional networks of particular sectors, at least until the mid-1990s. The chief vehicle of learning— for selecting the most promising collaborators from among those attracted by the incentives, and working with them to ensure incremental improvement of local supply networks, infrastructure, education, and similar—was the state body called the Industrial Development Authority (IDA) (since 1994, called IDA Ireland). Later, from the late 1980s, as domestic firms became more important, the main learning mechanism was Enterprise Ireland. These two SDAs had an explicit mandate to search by experiment. IDA's attention to the systemic or economywide implications of its collaboration with groups of firms can be illustrated by two examples: the way it tracked and reacted to indications of possible skill shortages and the effort directed at supplier development (Box 3.1). Thus, between 1977 and 1979 the agency negotiated agreements with electronics firms that, together, would create demand for some 600 electrical engineers per year, about 4 times the number that Irish universities and regional colleges were then graduating. As it takes between 2 and 5 years to educate technicians and engineers, there was a need for a short-term remedy and a plan for a long-term expansion of the education system. The short-term solution was to convert science graduates to electronics qualifications via 1-year courses; the longer-term solution was to expand existing courses and add new ones. The rapid response of the Higher Education Authority provided reassurance to subsequent investors that Ireland could provide the skills needed and contributed to a renewal of the university and technical training systems.

A typical project in a portfolio is a collaborative program that seeks to alleviate specific constraints, such as skill shortage or lack of qualified suppliers for electronic firms, as in the case of IDA. A project in the new industrial policy portfolio can be a private firm, incubated in collaboration with private partners. For instance, Fundación Chile, an autonomous private–public agency with a modest endowment, acquired the necessary technology, free of charge, from specialist public agencies in the United States in the crisis year of 1982. The Fundación then founded one firm to produce smelts, another to develop hatching and ranching technology for Chilean waters, and a third for smoking fish, creating a foundation for the salmon cluster. Crucially, as the technologies it sought to commercialize became more complex, the Fundación went from seeding firms on its own to coventuring with external partners.

How to scale up diverse but fragile microlevel new industrial policy episodes to the national level? A key problem is the gap between microinnovations and improvements in macroconditions. Incremental changes can lead in principle to wide and abiding transformations. However, deep constraints can remain binding if *microchanges do not achieve a critical mass*. To lessen the risk of such limited outcomes, framework programs provide an environment for microlevel changes to enable continuity and scaling up. They create coherent portfolios out of unrelated programs and initiatives, that is, they are turning "stand-alone" projects into portfolios. The Irish Linkage Promotion program (Box 3.1) and the Taiwanese VC initiative are two examples.

By the end of the 1970s, Taiwan (China) had already developed significant R&D capabilities, such as the Industrial Technology Research Institute (ITRI) and the Electronic Technology Research Institute (ETRI). Yet transforming technology into new firms proved difficult. The large Hinschu Science Park, opened in 1980, was unable to find tenants despite aggressive efforts to lure multinationals. The program started with the efforts of a Minister-without-Portfolio and his influential allies, who convinced the Ministry of Finance to introduce legislation to create, develop, and regulate VC in Taiwan (China), including comprehensive tax incentives and financial assistance. Institutions, such as a Seed Fund, provided matching capital contributions to private VC funds. Two American-style venture funds, H&Q Asia Pacific and Walden International Investment Group, were created and managed by US-educated

> **BOX 3.1 Framework Program: Irish Linkage Promotion Restructures SME Programs**
>
> In the wake of a highly successful FDI program, Ireland faced the challenge of deepening FDI involvement and leveraging the technology then being used to develop an indigenous technological capability. In response, IDA took a calculated risk by bringing together a group of MNCs and potential suppliers through a systematic search process, which came to be known as the National Linkage Promotion program (1987–92). The key problem in developing potential suppliers is the one that is "doomed to choose" among potential suppliers simply because developing large numbers of them is wasteful.
>
> The three main groups involved in the program were:
>
> *Government*: It provided the political imperative and charged various state agencies with supporting the program and cooperating. Budget lines were established, and the Department of Industry took a close interest in the program's operation and effectiveness. Input at this level was essential in maintaining political visibility and support for the program. A total of eight agencies contributed staff and assistance, in part to help SMEs navigate the bureaucracy when seeking the best and most appropriate assistance.
>
> *Industry*: Primarily MNCs (through FDI). The principal sector targeted was electronics, as it was the largest and most dynamic, and had the greatest propensity to source locally. Industry cooperation was sought, and the MNCs, through the Federation of Electronic Industries, contributed to program costs in the first 2 years.
>
> *SMEs*: A rigorous assessment procedure was used to select participating companies. It included an analysis of existing or potential capabilities against perceived supply opportunities, a detailed examination of financial management, and an assessment of existing management and of the firms' potential.
>
> An essential part of the program was the development by Linkage executives of close relationships with key MNCs. Due to the number of agencies involved in the program, a well-balanced and multifaceted team of experts in management, business development, technical issues, accounting, and banking was the key to success.

Chinese living overseas who received invitations to relocate to Taiwan (China). Once the first venture funds proved successful, domestic banks and large companies created their own VC funds. As those funds started to pay off, even the conservative family groups decided to invest in VC funds and information technology businesses. By the late 1980s, when companies, such as Acer and the returnee company Microtek, were publicly listed on the Taiwan (China) Stock Exchange, the VC industry in Taiwan (China) took off.

A search network to identify successive constraints and then people or institutions that can help mitigate these constraints. A search network consisting initially of key, dynamic, and forward-looking members of the Taiwan (China) government and leading overseas Chinese engineers in Silicon Valley was central to the emergence of the VC industry. This network did not have a blueprint, yet it did have a role model (Silicon Valley) and a clear idea of "what to do next." By defining each subsequent step along the road, the network became wider and eventually incorporated skeptics and opponents.

As the Taiwanese (Chinese) and Irish examples illustrate, framework programs have three distinct features that distinguish them from typical government policies. First, they *start from existing institutions and programs and reshape them*. By linking better performing segments of private and public sectors, they alleviate existing institutional constraints and come up with new solutions. They link exceptions from a general rule allowing them to institutionalize their agendas. Both the Taiwanese VC program and the Irish linkage efforts were initially viewed with skepticism; yet, drawing on existing organizations and programs, the champions created sustained dynamics (in backward linkages with VC development) and won skeptics over.

Second, *they start at the organizational periphery and are therefore less susceptible to rent seeking*. Public programs and policies have three constituencies: users/clients, public sector bureaucrats, and politicians. All three rely on government programs as a source of rent seeking: visible political payoffs for politicians, kickbacks for public sector servants, and subsidies to maintain the current business practices for users. However, by design framework programs do not have large budgets of their own: they rely on other programs. In economic parlance, the motivational effect is transformation from *rents to quasi rents*; *rents contingent on performance and effort*. Framework programs start small and require little public money, yet substantial effort to establish. For that reason, as the Taiwan (China) example illustrated, these programs have not been taken seriously by established interests. They were contingent on the articulation of quasi rents (which by definition require creativity and effort), rather than the simple capture of rents.

Third, by linking better performing segments of an existing institutional framework and searching for out-of-the-box solutions to familiar problems, *the institutional framework too is reshaped*. There appeared to be no institutional space for the VC industry in Taiwan (China) in the 1980s, so tight was the grip of established large agents (large firms and banks). The institutional framework for VC industry and the industry itself emerged simultaneously, in a dynamic virtuous cycle.

A new private sector, which learns to innovate by connecting to the world economy, and a new public sector capable of providing complementary public inputs for private sector search develop together: they are two sides of the same collaborative process. This process of the simultaneous emergence of embryos of Schumpeterian private and public sector begins even if the government is overall weak or incoherent, and many firms are rent seeking, as the public and private sectors are highly heterogeneous: there are (nearly always) positive variations of performance, dynamic exceptions from a general (mediocre) rule. In the self-discovery parlance, entrepreneurial self-discovery is predicated on public sector self-discovery and vice versa. Triggering and, more importantly, sustaining this process of collaborative mutual self-discovery is the key objective of the new open economy industrial policy (Table 3.1).

TABLE 3.1 Three Generations of Industrial Policy

	Vertical industrial policy: *backward linkages*	Horizontal industrial policy: *market failures*	Open economy industrial policy: *missing connections*
Incentives for private agents	Rents (in the form of infant industry protection or other price distortions)	Subsidies (when private returns are believed to be lower than social returns)	Quasi rents: rent opportunities that are contingent on one's effort and/or performance
How *capabilities* of private agents are believed to be enhanced	Rents are invested in firm-level learning	Background conditions are improved: improvement of investment climate	To capture the rent opportunities, the firm and the government jointly engage in root cause analysis: identification of bottlenecks to progressively relax the binding constraints
Focus	*Microlevel* and sectoral (picking winners)	*National level*: institutional infrastructure: financial markets and regulatory environment (backing winners)	*Mezzolevel*: connections between agents (matching winners)
Main conceptual axis	(Assumed strong) *government capabilities* enable and monitor firm-level learning	*Background conditions* to mitigate market failures and distortions; assuring balance of macroaggregations and eliminating, in the aggregate, the many microimpediments to growth	*Search network*: to identify successive constraints and then people or institutions that help mitigate (in part) the difficulties associated with these constraints
Key institution to design and implement policies	*Strategy*: an overarching document to guide decisions	*Strong government capabilities*: to assure relevant background conditions	*Portfolio of (related) projects*: to design, experiment, and make it grow *Framework program*: portfolio of (related) public programs

(Continued)

TABLE 3.1 Three Generations of Industrial Policy (*cont.*)

	Vertical industrial policy: *backward linkages*	Horizontal industrial policy: *market failures*	Open economy industrial policy: *missing connections*
How the coordination problem is resolved	*Bureaucratic coordination*: Coordination council (working group) as a means of coordination Often they become cartels of established interests		Project-based coordination ad-hoc collaborative consortia: to design and make grow relevant project portfolios
Sequencing of policies and programs	*Reliance on strategy* of industrial transformation and reforms		Working with the willing: bootstrapping of changes from micro- to mezzo- and then macrolevel
Main problem	State capture: development of capabilities gets subverted by entrenched interests	Absence of a link between macrochanges and increase in micropotential	Gap between microinnovations and improvements in macroconditions; deep constraints remain binding; microchanges do not necessarily achieve critical mass
Examples	Infant industry protection	Reduction of regulatory burden; creation of VC funds	Supplier development program; development of VC networks

VC, Venture capital.

Note that individual SS experiences judged most successful, such as that of the Basque Country (Przeor, 2016), tap both into the existing project implementation experience and local reform frameworks. For example, Metropoli 30 is a private–public regional reform institution established in the Basque country in 1990 to initiate regional transformation and reform. Technalia is a public organization with an active private sector board established in 2000; it triggered, eventually, a reform of regional R&D organizations.

Table 3.1 summarizes and juxtaposes three generations of industrial policy: vertical (picking winners), horizontal (assuring adequate background conditions or backing winners), and new (open economy) policy (searching for relevant connections or matching winners).

DIAGNOSTIC (PROBLEM-SOLVING) MONITORING VERSUS CONVENTIONAL (ACCOUNTING) MONITORING

As learning and experimentation are central, the governance procedure needed to ensure that the open economy industrial policy achieves its goals is *diagnostic or problem-solving monitoring*: the systematic evaluation of the portfolio of projects to detect errors as each of the specific projects evolves and to correct the problems (including the weeding out of inefficient projects) in light of implementation experience and other new information.

More specifically, conventional monitoring refers to the determination that a goal has been met or a rule followed, and to the distribution of rewards if behavior meets expectations or the imposition of penalties, if it does not. Thus, monitoring in the conventional view plays a key part in applying incentive systems by which principals, who fix goals and rules, guide the behavior of the agents charged with meeting these requirements. The goal of diagnostic monitoring, in contrast, is to determine why goals were not met (or exceeded), or why behavior deviated from rules. Instead of assuming that agents failed to meet expectations because they were insufficiently or improperly motivated, it assumes that the agents acted as they did either because they lack the capacity (such as the training, the support from other functions, etc.) to achieve the targets, or that the targets and rules are misspecified, and are in need of revision. Put another way, where conventional monitoring assumes that principals know what needs to be done and how to do it—and the only open question is the best method for motivating compliance with their plans—diagnostic monitoring assumes that principals can err in specifying means and ends, and that careful attention to the problems agents face and the accommodations they devise can provide important clues about such error and confusion. Yet diagnostic monitoring does not exclude the possibility that agents fail in their responsibility. Thus, under diagnostic monitoring the initial responses to underperformance are analyzing the problem and providing support to remedy it.

To introduce elements of diagnostic monitoring, one can put in place, for example, *project selection reviews*, which would consist of two or three members with an appropriate mixture of expertise. In a 2-day site visit, the team would review the documentation of the project and discuss its status with the stakeholders, including not just the relevant firms and service providers, but also actors in a position to judge the performance of both. These actors can be, for instance, selected customers and suppliers to the firms or participants in training and capacity-building programs.

In this procedure, *the central governing body is a deliberation council* and the focus is on three questions:

- Did the deliberation council initially include all those with the relevant capacities and interests and, if not, was its membership modified so that it eventually did?
- Did the discussion of possible projects canvas plausible alternatives, and was the final choice well motivated?

- Has the project met its milestones and, if not, is there a clear understanding of why that has not happened and a corresponding adjustment of the project's goals and timetable?

As an illustration of a specific response to these three questions, let us consider three very different examples. The first two examples are business sector organizations (Fundación Chile and public biotechnology initiatives in India), which have introduced a routinized system of monitoring and evaluation that regularly reviews the progress of each undertaking, brings problems to the surface early, and where possible organizes technical support to overcome them. The third and the most intriguing example—the World Bank Debt Management TF—has endeavored to do the same within the conventional public sector management.

Fundación Chile

In Fundación Chile, staff members, hired on the basis of demonstrated technical knowledge and familiarity with the markets and business practices in a particular sector, apply for internal grants to develop a case for launching a new venture. The best of these preliminary plans can be used to apply for a second, longer-term grant to develop a business plan for a new venture, typically in partnership with outsiders. They can apply for further grants until the proto-venture becomes a candidate for seed capital and enters the familiar sequence of VC financing. At every stage, projects are benchmarked against internal and external alternatives, and the resulting start-ups are the institutionalized expression of the searches triggered by that benchmarking. In turn, the start-ups relax constraints on the formation of the clusters whose growth propels the Chilean economy. The Fundación Chile version of diagnostic monitoring is far from error proof: for example, it failed to introduce vaccines to prevent the propagation of fish disease that devastated the salmon cluster. However so far, at least, the transparency inherent in the broad and continual benchmarking of projects at every stage has also functioned as an effective governance mechanism, ensuring that public funds are indeed directed toward public purposes, as best as these can be defined at any given moment.

Public Policy Initiatives in Biotechnology in India

India has developed a series of policy initiatives over the past 5 years to adapt available biotechnologies to local needs in healthcare, agriculture, industry, and the environment, as well as to commercialize resulting products at broadly affordable prices. This "accelerated technology absorption framework program" includes six complementary elements: translational research (determining how generally proven technologies must be adapted to local context, and validating the effectiveness of the contextualization), further training for qualified researchers, regulatory reforms, establishing global consortia to connect Indian firms and researchers to advanced developments, formation of public–private partnerships, broadly interpreted, and special-purpose vehicles for effective project management. Of interest here are two public–private programs: the Small Business Innovation Research Initiative (SBIRI) and Biotechnology Industry Partnership Program (BIPP).[2] The programs' success has been to support successful indigenous development, in collaboration with a global public–private partnership, of the first oral rotavirus vaccine to significantly reduce child mortality from diarrhea. In developing the vaccine, an Indian company for the first time brought the vaccine to phase III trials, and in this connection India conducted its first community clinical trial directly through doctors and clinics, marking a substantial step forward in the country's capacity to meet global regulatory requirements under conditions that both develop national technical capacities and help assure the suitability of products for domestic use.

It is clear that, building on the milestones that life science firms typically set themselves, and the regimes they engender for exchanging information with each other, the selection process is more probing and informative than is usual in normal private sector applications for public support. *Both the SBIRI and BIPP programs thus send expert teams to visit applicant firms to assess their capacities and plans.* Once firms have been selected for support, separate teams, whose membership differs from the group making the initial assessment, make periodic visits to monitor progress during the course of the project. These visits are surely more searching and revealing than the desk reviews that are customary in such situations. In addition, given the rapid developments in biotechnology globally, and the broad range of their initiatives, SBIRI and BIPP monitor not only the progress of sponsored firms toward their goals, but whether *other* firms, in India or elsewhere, have also met program milestones. If they have met them, SBIRI and BIPP check how the overall research and development strategy should be redirected to avoid duplication of efforts and build immediately on what has been achieved.

Debt Management at the World Bank

As a last example of a shift in the direction of monitoring-intensive development policy, consider the (co)management of country debt that has emerged at the World Bank over the last decade. Broadly speaking, two sets of developments demonstrate just how hard to predict—how uncertain—key factors affecting debt management have become, and are likely to remain. First, successive financial crises revealed that the risk of the various components of a country's debt portfolio could change rapidly and unpredictably. In some countries (Argentina, Brazil, Indonesia, and Russia), the currency exposure proved to be a key determinant of an increase in debt. In others, the public sector became responsible for implicit contingent liability related to banks (Turkey, Korea, or Thailand) or other parts of the private sector, aggravating existing vulnerabilities in the debt portfolio with a similar negative impact on the overall debt level and the government's budget. In low-income countries, changes in real effective exchange rates, often caused by unfavorable commodity price trends, aggravated debt service problems (World Bank and IMF, 2009).

The second set of developments concerns public–private partnerships in infrastructure development, a significant component of the World Bank's activity. As public–private partnerships, often at the subnational level, became more important to infrastructure projects, it also became clear that prudence required "proactive" management of contingent liabilities associated with complex projects. Given the uncertainty of on-the-ground outcomes, it also became apparent that proactive management in turn depended on ongoing exchange and monitoring, with special attention to the links between contractual undertaking and debt/fiscal management or, more generally, between the local context and the macroeconomy (to combine the partial view of the various actors into a quasi-panoramic view for key decision makers, such as the Minister of Finance and Prime Minister) (Kuznetsov et al., 2011).

The first step in the process that emerged out of these overlapping concerns and experiences is a diagnostic review that determines which legislation, institutions, and debt management operations and misconnections among them are impeding successful management at various points in the whole debt cycle. The goal of this diagnosis is to identify key weaknesses in the debt management system, without assigning blame (even if bad performers are identified), and to provide support services, customized to the requirement revealed by the diagnosis, to help remedy the problems. Making this diagnosis typically takes 2 weeks of intensive consultations with relevant institutions and staff (3–4 weeks if premission and postmission time is included). Provisional results are discussed at high levels. The diagnosis is then codified in a reform plan, which lists actions—including the provision of capacity-building services—to correct key weaknesses, assign responsibilities and budget, establish milestones and deadlines, and specify outcome and output indicators to measure success. Capacity-building services can include training for the client's debt managers in, among other things, the use of specialized instruments, such as the Debt Management Performance Assessment (DEMPA) tool[3]; elaboration of medium-term debt management strategies produced by experts from the World Bank or IMF, but, as the established lingo of development professionals goes, "fully owned" by domestic authorities; and follow-up on implementation of reforms. The DEMPA tool helps client countries detect shortfalls and constraints, and helps them overcome any detected obstacles. At a minimum, the tool helps clients meet debt management performance objectives; at best, its use can lead to increased borrowing capacity and thus to an increase in the resources available to promote growth and poverty reduction.

Typically, there will be another full diagnostic review of debt management performance after 3 years. In the interval between these full-dress reviews, there will be periodic examinations of performance and revisions of the diagnostics tool as circumstances change, not least in response to the ongoing interventions. Note that a policy directed toward institutional capacity building through intensive monitoring emerges in a domain—debt management—where conventional incentives (conditionality) should be most effective. The outcome of inadequate debt management for a vulnerable country is likely to be a debt crisis, with loss of control of the national fate. When national actors do lose control, they are incentivized to regain it by meeting certain conditions. Put more bluntly, conditionality is a reform through high-powered incentives: meet the conditions, get a big reward; fail to do so, suffer a large penalty. Conditionality should be at its most effective when the stakes are highest, when failure is ruinous and success restores substantial freedom of action to the vulnerable actor.

We should expect debt management to consist of a detailed statement of what targets must be met and of the results of (not) meeting them. However, as we just saw, we actually find something quite different. The emergence of such an elaborate system of monitoring and capacity building that we observe in the debt management area—much of it financed by special-purpose TFs that increase the flexibility of operations by putting it outside the jurisdiction of many normal World Bank governance procedures—amounts to the practical recognition that conditionality does not work even where it should be most effective.

The example of the debt management procedures and Debt Management TF is crucial for our argument for at least two reasons. First, it shows how an experimental embryo can emerge within the top-down public sector, and hence how the two logics of monitoring—conventional and diagnostic—can coexist and even complement each other. Second, it demonstrates an alternative route to the emergence of capacity-enhancing experimentation stemming from weak capabilities. The usual domain of SDAs is cutting-edge innovation, with its attendant pervasive uncertainty. For instance, Jordan and Koinis (2013) demonstrate how experimentation with a project portfolio and elements of diagnostic monitoring emerge as the almost default option in a paragon of experimentation, DARPA (an organizational unit of the US Department of Defense, so another case of complementarity between the two contrasting organizational logics). The Debt Management TF, in contrast, deals with unusually weak capabilities, rather than unusually uncertain technological challenges. Most of its clients are in Africa and careful experimentation to enhance their capacity (capacity-enhancing experimentation) is the only realistic way to proceed. The other option (waiting until the institutional capabilities of the client improve) is plainly not an option given the urgency of the debt burden.

As Table 3.2 summarizes, the "why" of diagnostic monitoring and the "what" of conventional monitoring are best thought of as complementary. They may be procedurally similar, such as using benchmarking, but the meaning of the procedures remains starkly different. In conventional monitoring, benchmarking is a comparison of formal indicators, such as world league tables of performance. However, macrolevel indicators and league tables, for instance, the

TABLE 3.2 Diagnostic (Problem-Solving) Versus Conventional (Accounting) Monitoring

	Conventional	Diagnostic
Key question	What (is the gap between performance target and outcome)?	Why (is there a gap)?
Users who benefit from monitoring	External to the process (e.g., funding agencies)	Participants in the process (e.g., project managers)
Relevant expertise	General (task management)	Specialized expertise: new knowledge is created in the process
Information-gathering procedures	Focus on formal indicators of performance Performance reports	Focus on site visits Technical meetings of diverse experts
Risk management procedure of project and programs	Ex-ante (before the project/program begins): through elaborate indicator-based risk rating of projects, both at the design and implementation stages	Endogenous: "just in time" error detection and correction
Overall perspective	Backward looking: to assign guilt (of bad performance)	Forward looking: to detect and correct problems
Benchmarking	Of formal indicators (e.g., outcome and output indicators) Optional information-gathering tool	Key question is which benchmark is relevant for a portfolio in a given context Key management tool
Implementation experience of real sector projects	Implicit in application and selection criteria	There is no substitute for implementation experience

competitiveness rankings of countries portray developing economies precisely as what they are not: as homogenous wholes. In diagnostic monitoring, in contrast, the point of benchmarking is to reveal the relevant heterogeneity and the key question is which benchmark is relevant for a portfolio in a given context.

Problem-solving monitoring examines the implementation experience of a project. In contrast, the basic conceptual unit of the RIS3 perspective is strategy. To generate the project implementation experience in RIS3 cases, one first needs to translate and transform a strategy into a portfolio of real sector projects, that is, create a "proof of concept" for the strategy (in terms of the bootstrapping model of Chapter 10, this is the initiating impulse stage). Next, one needs to test this proof of concept by implementing the portfolio of first mover projects (the first mover stage). The translation of a strategy into projects will be dwelled upon in the next section.

ESTABLISHING A SCHUMPETERIAN (DIAGNOSTIC MONITORING) SEGMENT IN RIS3 PRACTICE

The three episodes of diagnostic monitoring discussed in this chapter were performed by (embryos of) Schumpeterian public sector agencies in India and Chile (not countries with the strongest institutional capabilities), and in the World Bank, a paragon of top-down, principal-agent bureaucracy. Our tentative conclusion is that Schumpeterian embryos and diagnostic monitoring procedures can emerge both in contexts with relatively weak institutional capabilities and in a top-down Weberian bureaucracy; quite a reassuring statement for EU bureaucracy in general and for the RIRIS3 process in particular. Sanguine as it is, the conclusion underlines the central issue of public sector capability to deliver relevant public goods and the need for reform to enhance this capability. As already noted, new public and private sector agencies emerge together as two sides of a collaborative process. Research that has been sponsored in connection with RIS3 shows clearly that the results of individual operations or projects depend on the overall quality of regional institutions; weak institutions increase the chances of failure (Rodriguez-Pose et al., 2014).

So to improve outcomes, RIS3 would need to help reform weak regional institutions, while regional reform strategies will have to be place based, such as development strategies. Furthermore, before or during the setting up of the process for identifying and diagnostically monitoring projects, a related process for reforming regional institutions should also be activated. We are not talking about a comprehensive reform, but about a strategy of "engagement with the willing": even in regions with generally weak institutions, there are actors that perform better than others and many that can improve. The aim, therefore, should be to identify the high performers and the rapid improvers, get them involved in selecting and diagnostically monitoring projects, and then use their successes to create both pressure and support for further reforms. Such dynamics of reform—humble initially, yet ambitious in hindsight—are precisely what happened in our two earlier examples of place-based development, VC in Taiwan (China) and FDI in Ireland. In contrast, even when RIS3 experiences explicitly focus on generating real sector projects—as in the pilots in the Vanguard initiative in Italy (Vanguard Initiative, 2016) and the project development labs in Eastern Macedonia and Thrace in Greece (Przeor, 2016)—they are not always accompanied by regional reform strategies to trigger the bootstrapping dynamics. Consequently, there is a risk of continuing "business as usual" only with novel and fancy headings.

More specifically, our analysis entails the following implications for RIS3 practice.

Bringing in the Issue of Public Sector Coordination and Reform: RIS3 as a Framework Program

The notion of a framework program was introduced in the section "Project Portfolio and Framework Program as Two Key Conceptual Units of the New Industrial Policy" as a central coordinating device of the open industrial policy: a framework that at once scales up and institutionalizes portfolios of microreforms, and creates a coherent public effort on the basis of disparate public support programs (see Box 3.1 for illustration). In this perspective, each individual regional RIS3 case (e.g., the Croatia SS initiative) should be a framework program tapping into, leveraging, refocusing, and reforming the multitude of existing public sector efforts. The umbrella SS initiative at a European level—the portfolio of individual RIS3 experiments—thus becomes a "framework of frameworks."

For instance, one can turn the project development labs in Eastern Macedonia and Thrace in Greece into project implementation labs, which would identify bottlenecks in regional public goods (human capital and higher education, logistics, and collective institutions, such as design centers), design, and help put into effect reform strategies to implement them. Again, that means that RIS3 should not be just a bottom-up exercise, but a combination of bottom-up, top-down, and "inside–out" dynamics, which proceeds horizontally, from the organizational periphery (good exceptions) to the organizational mainstream).

A Proposal for Diagnostic Monitoring Pilots for (Self-Selected) RIS3 Experiences

While leaving the overall architecture of RIS3 monitoring intact, one can introduce a modest incremental change: institute a diagnostic monitoring pilot for advanced RIS3 cases where the implementation experience of relevant projects (i.e., related to new domains identified by the SS strategy) already exists. More specifically, one can propose two pilots. The first pilot would take place in an advanced setting, where there are both project portfolios and framework programs to build upon (e.g., the Basque country RIS in Spain exists both as project portfolios and as framework programs to regional organizations, Metropoli and Technalia). The second pilot would be carried out in a less-developed setting, for example, Croatia's RIS.

To put it differently, the overall architecture would remain that of a conventional (accounting) monitoring, yet more sophisticated RIS3 clients would be given an option (and the attendant support) to engage in diagnostic (problem-solving) monitoring of the projects they are developing. This is a two-track approach: rely on the established procedures, while introducing novelty by engaging with "the willing," with dynamic exceptions from the general rule. Such an approach is humble and ambitious at the same time: modest in the short term because the proposed change is small and marginal, and yet simultaneously ambitious in the long run because, if the micropilots are allowed to continue and scale up, they promise to dramatically reform the established procedures.

A Proposal for a Two-Track Selection of New RIS3 Cases

Consistent with the two-track approach, we propose an alternative: a portfolio-focused methodology (consisting of four steps) of RIS3 selection for funding:

Step 1. Planting the seeds: ad-hoc creation of initial portfolios of possibilities and real sector projects

An assumption is that there are some existing leaders with an urge to act and develop what is emerging in the region. This is an *initiating impulse*, both in terms of provisional actions and of a tentative vision and strategy to be corrected subsequently.

Step 2. Creating a portfolio of collaborative real sector projects: choice of collaborators

This is a central step through which a provisional portfolio of projects becomes institutionalized, with the choice of collaborators for the execution of projects becoming the central issue. A few procedures have emerged to facilitate such a choice. For instance, one procedure is a two-stage, facilitated selection process for collaborative projects in a new domain for a country. In the first stage of the process, applications from stakeholders are assessed against the selection criteria established by a selection board, which then recommends which applicants proceed to stage two. At stage two, the selection board should seek to identify synergies among applicants to ensure that the best combinations of participants and support are identified for each consortium application. This process may involve an independent facilitator to broker between applicants in negotiating arrangements for forming a single-project consortium.

Step 3. Growing a portfolio of collaborative projects: diagnostic (problem-solving) monitoring

Details of this step have been discussed earlier [section, "Diagnostic (Problem-Solving) Monitoring Versus Conventional (Accounting) Monitoring"]. This step also includes benchmarking a portfolio of projects and possibilities. The benchmarking here does not consist of strategies or formal indicators (conventional league tables of performance are irrelevant), but a comparison of project experience. Benchmarking is useful to the extent that it sheds new light on that experience. More pragmatically and cynically, it helps to minimize unavoidable surprises, particularly nasty ones. In contrast, in the current RIS3 guide, all business procedures, such as benchmarking, focus on formal indicators (http://RIS3platform.jrc.ec.europa.eu/regional-benchmarking).

Step 4. Transforming promise into process: triggering a process of creating a shared vision of the future

This stage is about involving all stakeholders by celebrating success, that is, turning success stories into role models for others to follow. Moreover, it also incorporates public outreach, that is, turning multiple visions into a single shared one.

The key idea behind this methodology is the simultaneous development and growth of: (1) projects, (2) possibilities and related strategies, and (3) reforming public institutions involved in the implementation of projects and strategies. This represents a "triple bootstrapping." In other words, the idea is to create an embryo of SDA in the current RIS3 practice, a proverbial Trojan horse. By focusing on a portfolio of projects in operation, this funding window will initiate and enhance an embryo of new Schumpeterian public and private sectors. The set of management procedures under the existing and proposed new funding windows will be quite different, even if they share the same title. Whereas benchmarking under the existing funding window consists of strategies and plans performed on the basis of formal indicators, under a Schumpeterian window it is rather about examining the project portfolios and related management practices of relevant agencies, so that experiences and management practices of paragon regional development agencies would come to light.

CONCLUSIONS: TURNING OBSTACLES INTO VARIABLES

This chapter shifts the debate about state activism in supporting globally competitive industries from a choice of "picking/dropping winners" to a process of step-by-step transformation of the private and public sectors. In such a process, the new industrial policy creates its own context for efficient design and implementation in three ways. First, the shifting the focus of analysis and institutional design from the private sector to a new public sector capable of providing customized and flexible public goods enables private agents to compete globally. In other words, new public and private sectors emerge simultaneously. The key concept here is heterogeneity (discretionary differences) of institutions: it is almost always possible to find some that are working. The issue is using the ones that work to improve those that do not. This hypothesis assumes that there are always opportunities for development in a given economy, and that some actors, private and public, begin to take advantage of them.

Second, the shifting the debate from the "what" and the "why" of industrial policy to the "how," that is, to the institutional design of relevant institutions, at the limit, such design represents a management issue. Hence, this leads to the conception of new industrial policy as a "reflection action" and as a (continuous) management of the triple heterogeneity (of projects, strategies, and institutions).

Third, and as a result of the last point, the new industrial policy creates its own context for efficient design and implementation by *turning obstacles* (such as *corrupt and dysfunctional governments, clientelistic networks, etc.*)

into variables. Errors and entrenched interests subverting the public good are assumed as normal and, in fact, are invited to be spoken out. *Error-proof institutions are replaced by continuous error detection and correction.* In this view, a developing economy resembles a vast, continuously improving, Toyota-style production system, in which it is presumed that no actor can have a sufficient panoramic view of operations to be able to identify obstacles *ex-ante* (thus rendering vertical industrial policy naïve and unrealistic). The chief problem for the policy and the policy maker is devising search networks (with corresponding governance mechanisms to check opportunism) to detect and help facilitate the relaxation of constraints to growth as they emerge.

Regarding the RIS3 experience, the chapter endeavors to add value to the thinking on SS practice in three ways. First, by shifting the emphasis from strategy (vision) to project (action); an investment with certain risks and returns. More specifically, the unit of experimentation is a project portfolio, and the central procedure of capacity-enhancing experimentation is diagnostic monitoring. Diagnostic (or problem-solving) monitoring is the systematic evaluation of a portfolio of projects to detect errors. Each of the specific activities involved evolves and corrects the problems (including weeding out the activities deemed inefficient) in light of implementation experience and other new information. More specifically, conventional monitoring refers to the determination that a goal has been met or a rule followed, and to the distribution of rewards if behavior meets expectations or the imposition of penalties, if it does not. Thus, monitoring in the conventional view plays a key part in applying incentive systems by which principals, who fix goals and rules, guide the behavior of the agents charged with meeting these requirements. The goal of diagnostic monitoring, in contrast, is to determine *why* goals were not met (or exceeded), or why behavior deviated from rules.

The chapter's second contribution to SS is to illuminate the notion of SDAs, namely, those entities that experiment with project portfolios, make errors but employ procedures to monitor these project portfolios, and correct the errors. Examples in the area of regional development include Scottish Enterprise and the IDA. A Japanese proverb: "vision without action is a dream, action without vision is a nightmare," is an apt call for a balance between action (design and implementation of a project portfolio) and vision (elaboration of a shared strategy). In SDAs, the priority is on informed action. Although in SDAs the vision part is secondary to the actual project experience, it nonetheless remains important and takes two forms: benchmarking of relevant experiences and shared vision exercises as pragmatic tools to generate or enhance collective action. In stark contrast to the practice of SDAs, the RIS3 practice emphasizes vision and strategies, rather than projects.

Third, the chapter provided specific suggestions with respect to the current EU SS procedures. In addition to (rather than instead of) the existing funding window, which emphasizes funding on the basis of promises of a neat strategy, we suggest a new pilot funding window that would be based on actual implementation experiences of an ongoing project portfolio.

ENDNOTES

1. Parts of this section closely follow Kuznetsov and Sabel (2011).
2. The Indian example is based on K. Vijayaraghavan and Mark A. Dutz, *Biotechnology Innovation for Inclusive Growth: A Policy Study of Initiatives to Foster Accelerated Technology Absorption for more Affordable Development in India* (Dutz et al., 2014).
3. See http://web.worldbank.org/WBSITE/EXTERNAL/TOPICS/EXTDEBTDEPT/0,,content MDK:21707750~menuPK:64166739~pagePK:64166689~piPK:64166646~theSite PK:469043,00.html

REFERENCES

Dutz, M., Kuznetsov, Y., Lasagabster, E., Pilat, D. (Eds.), 2014. Making Innovation Policy Work: Learning from Experimentation. OECD and World Bank, Paris.

Jordan, L.S., Koinis, K., 2013. Flexible delivery: organizations that can fail and still succeed. Competitive Industries Note 3, 1–4. Available from: http://documents.worldbank.org/curated/en/592641468278746843/pdf/826610BRI0Comp00Box379873B00PUBLIC0.pdf.

Kuznetsov, Y., 2009. Which Way From Rent-Seeking? Schumpeterian vs. Weberian Public Sector. World Bank, Mimeo, Washington, DC.

Kuznetsov, Y., Sabel, C., 2011. New open economy industrial policy: making choices without picking winners. Prem Note 161, World Bank. Available from: https://openknowledge.worldbank.org/handle/10986/11057.

Kuznetsov, Y., Moreno-Lopez, P., Sabel, C., Mandri-Perrott, C., 2011. Tools for institutional diagnostics of growth: counter-intuitive lessons from debt management. Presentation to PRMED, World Bank, December 7, 2011.

Przeor, M., 2016. Research and innovation strategies for smart specialisation (RIRIS3) in the EU. Presentation for the World Bank, March 25, 2016.

Rodriguez-Pose, A., Di Cataldo, M., Rainoldi, A., 2014. The role of government institutions for smart specialisation and regional development. JRC-IPTS Working Papers JRC88935. Institute for Prospective Technological Studies, Joint Research Centre. Available from: https://ideas.repec.org/p/ipt/iptwpa/jrc88935.html.

Rodrik, D., Hausmann, R., 2003. Economic development as self-discovery. Working Paper. Available from: http://j.mp/1gP3ylk.

Vanguard Initiative, 2016. Matchmaking Event Report. Available upon request.

World Bank, IMF, 2009. Developing a medium-term debt management strategy (MTDS)—guidance note for country authorities. Available from: http://siteresources.worldbank.org/INTDEBTDEPT/Resources/468980-1238442914363/MTDSGudianceNoteCA.pdf.

Chapter 4

Smart Specialization as an Innovation-Driven Strategy for Economic Diversification: Examples From Scandinavian Regions

Bjørn Asheim*,**, Markus Grillitsch**, Michaela Trippl†
*University of Stavanger, Stavanger, Norway; **Lund University, Lund, Sweden; †University of Vienna, Vienna, Austria

Chapter Outline

Academic Highlights

- Smart specialization means:
  - Diversified specialization into areas of existing or potential competitive advantage, which differentiates a region/nation from others.
  - Smart identification of these areas through a process of entrepreneurial discovery, in which all actors are mobilized to be able to discover domains for securing existing and future competitiveness (individual entrepreneurs, firms, universities, technology transfer offices, public development agencies, etc.).

Advances in the Theory and Practice of Smart Specialization. http://dx.doi.org/10.1016/B978-0-12-804137-6.00004-8

- Competitive advantage through smart specialization can be promoted in all types of industries but based on the industry specific modes of innovation and knowledge bases:
  - Firms innovate based on research (STI—science technology innovation) and experience (DUI—doing using interacting).
  - Analytical, synthetic, and symbolic knowledge drive innovation activities of firms.
- This allows for varied strategies of smart specialization, including:
  - Building the absorptive capacity of DUI based firms by increasing their research-based competence (introducing analytical knowledge).
  - Combining unrelated knowledge bases to move into new related and unrelated industries.
  - Combining related knowledge bases to move into unrelated industries.
  - Moving into high-value added niches by introducing symbolic knowledge in traditional sectors.

Policy Highlights

- Scandinavian cases represent regions with highly developed economies, good governance, and strong institutions yet exhibit important differences in their:
  - Knowledge infrastructure
  - Industrial structure
  - Innovation policy
- All three regions have developed their smart specialization strategies based on a thorough analysis of their innovation capacity and with an increasing focus on new path development by exploiting unique assets and responding to global challenges.
- The different preconditions are reflected in the smart specialization strategies and ways in which the three regions aim to achieve their objectives:
  - Taking into account industry specific modes of innovation and knowledge bases (although sometimes only implicitly).
  - Adapting strategies to regional and industrial specificities.
- This corroborates the importance of applying a broad perspective on innovation policy and the relevance of the knowledge-based approach.

INTRODUCTION: SMART SPECIALIZATION—PRESENTATION AND CLARIFICATION

Smart specialization is probably the single largest attempt ever of an orchestrated, supranational innovation strategy to boost economic growth through economic diversification. It has been launched by the European Commission, and is a strategic approach to an industrial policy for national and regional economic development, pursuing a high road strategy of innovation-based competition as the sustainable alternative to a downward spiral of cost competition (i.e., the low road strategy), which dominates in the majority of regions in Southern and Eastern Europe (Milberg and Houston, 2005). As such, smart specialization represents a new industrial policy that aims to promote new path development and economic diversification, going beyond "just" a regional innovation strategy more narrowly defined (Chapter 1). Furthermore, for the first time in the EU, smart specialization provides a policy framework or platform for promoting and implementing a broad-based innovation policy. This is of critical and strategic importance given the failure of the linear, research and development (R&D)-based innovation policy in the EU following the Lisbon Declaration 2000 that set a goal of allocating 3% of GDP to R&D. The rationale was that this should transform the EU into the most competitive region in the world, but the outcome was very different. Thus, it is of great importance that smart specialization is fully and correctly understood, not the least because the choice of key words (i.e., "specialization" and "entrepreneurial discovery") may lead policy makers and practitioners to make false interpretations and draw wrong conclusions (Asheim, 2014).

Smart specialization is not about "specialization" as known from previous regional development strategies, that is, a Porter-like cluster strategy, but about *diversified* specialization. What this means is that countries should identify areas or "domains" as the smart specialization literature prefers to call it—of existing and/or potential competitive advantage, where they can specialize in a different way compared to other countries and regions. A smart specialization strategy implies maximizing the knowledge-based development potential of any country or region, with a strong or weak R&I system or with a high-tech or low-tech industrial structure. Countries and regions should diversify their economies primarily based on existing strengths and capabilities by moving into related or unrelated sectors.

"Smart" in the smart specialization approach refers to the way these domains of competitive advantage should be identified, which is through what is called "entrepreneurial discovery." However, the emphasis here is not on the role of traditional entrepreneurs, resulting in a policy focus only on firm formation as an individual entrepreneurial project. As underlined in the writings on smart specialization, "entrepreneurial" should be understood broadly to encompass all actors (including individual entrepreneurs), organizations (including firms and universities through intrapreneurship, knowledge-based entrepreneurship, and spin-offs), and agencies (technology transfer offices and public development agencies) that have the capacity to discover domains for securing existing and future competitiveness. Perhaps, Van der Ven et al. (1999) describes "the entrepreneur" as one type of leadership along the "innovation journey" comes close to what is meant by entrepreneurial discovery in the smart specialization approach. The authors talk about the entrepreneur as a role likely to be played by a core network of interacting actors from the national innovation system, comprising a limited number of firms, universities, public research organizations, and government institutions (Van der Ven et al., 1999), which should also include, especially in small countries, nonlocal actors in cooperating transnationally and interregionally. Such a broad interpretation of "entrepreneurial discovery" avoids the pitfall of ignoring the systemic nature of innovation. The systems approach to innovation policies also highlights the role of government in driving innovation, as well as the balance between exploration and exploitation (Asheim and Gertler, 2005; Asheim et al., 2011b, 2016).

In the following section, the theoretical framework of the smart specialization approach for economic diversification is laid out; emphasizing how new path development can be pursued within the framework of a broad-based innovation policy. This builds on the *knowledge base* approach, which was key to the constructing regional advantage (CRA) strategy (Asheim et al., 2006, 2011a). The knowledge-based approach argues that economic diversification and innovation-based competition can be achieved in all industries or sectors yet in different ways, depending on industry-specific modes of innovation and knowledge bases. Section, "The Cases: Scandinavian Regions" illustrates how smart specialization strategies have been designed and implemented in three Scandinavian regions, using the theoretical framework to inform the analysis. Section, "Conclusions: Comparative Perspectives on Smart Specialization Strategies in Scandinavian Regions" offers some comparative conclusions discussing whether the strategies will result in diversified specialization, and whether one can corroborate the relevance of the theoretical framework to guide the design and implementation of a smart specialization strategy for economic diversification.

NEW PATH DEVELOPMENT FOR ECONOMIC DIVERSIFICATION

There is strong agreement that innovation is the key factor promoting economic diversification and increased competitiveness in a globalizing knowledge economy. Competition based on innovation implies choosing the high road strategy, which is the only sustainable alternative for developed, high-cost regional, and national economies, as well as for the future of developing economies (Milberg and Houston, 2005). For a long time, such a strategy was considered the same as promoting high-tech, R&D-intensive industries in accordance with the linear view of innovation. Increasingly, researchers and policy makers have realized that a broader and more comprehensive view on innovation as interactive learning has to be applied to retain and develop competitiveness in the context of heterogeneous countries and regions of Europe at very different stages of economic development. Thus, it is fundamentally important to avoid "one size fits all" policies, given the diversity of regional economies and innovation systems (Tödtling and Trippl, 2005). All drivers of innovation—both supply- and demand-side [user, market, demand (social innovation)], as well as employee-driven innovation—have to be integrated into an overall approach to innovation policy, as R&D intensity is not the same as innovation capacity. Knowledge is a far broader concept than R&D. This requires a differentiated knowledge base approach, distinguishing between analytical, synthetic, and symbolic knowledge (Asheim, 2007; Asheim and Gertler, 2005); as well as a broad view on innovation including both R&D-based [Science, Technology, Innovation (STI)] and experience-based [doing, using, interacting (DUI)] innovation (Lorenz and Lundvall, 2006).

Knowledge processes have become increasingly complex in the globalizing knowledge economy. The binary view of knowledge as either codified (i.e., knowledge that has been stored in certain media and can be readily transmitted to others) or tacit (i.e., knowledge that is difficult to transfer to another person by means of writing down or verbalizing it) becomes too simplistic to accommodate this increased complexity and to provide an adequate understanding of knowledge creation, learning, and innovation. Thus, there is a need to go beyond this simple dichotomy. One way of doing this is to distinguish between "synthetic," "analytical," and "symbolic" types of knowledge bases, which partly transcends the tacit-codified dichotomy by arguing that the two forms of knowledge always coexist, but in different combinations; and by emphasizing that, while all types of economic activity can be innovative, the modes of innovation differ, transcending the high tech-low tech dichotomy (Asheim, 2007). As this threefold distinction refers to ideal-types, most activities are in practice comprised of more than one knowledge base. However, one knowledge base will represent the critical knowledge input which the knowledge creation and innovation processes cannot do without. New combinations of knowledge bases seem to become increasingly important as the sources of new path development.

An analytical knowledge base refers to economic activities where scientific knowledge relying on formal models and codification is highly important. Examples are biotechnology and nanotechnology. University-industry links and the respective networks are, in this case, more important than in the other types of knowledge bases. Knowledge inputs and outputs are more often codified than in the other types of knowledge bases. Consequently, the workforce more often needs some research experience or university training. Knowledge creation in the form of scientific discoveries and (generic) technological inventions is more important than in the other knowledge types, and, thus, innovations are science-driven. Often, inventions lead to patents and licensing activities. Knowledge is applied in the form of new products or processes, and there are more radical innovations than in the other knowledge types. An important route of knowledge application is the new firms and spin-off companies, which are formed on the basis of radically new inventions or products.

A synthetic knowledge base refers to economic activities where innovation takes place mainly through the application or novel combinations of existing knowledge. Often, this occurs in response to the need to solve specific problems when customers and suppliers interact. Thus, innovations are user, market, and demand driven. Industry examples include plant engineering, specialized advanced industrial machinery, and shipbuilding. University-industry links are also important for this knowledge base, but more in the field of applied R&D than in basic research. Tacit knowledge is more important than in the analytical type, in particular because knowledge often results from experience gained at the workplace, and through learning by doing, using, and interacting. Compared to the analytical knowledge base, more concrete know-how, craft, and practical skills are required. They are provided by technical universities, polytechnics, or by on-job training. Overall, this leads to a rather incremental way of innovation, dominated by the modification of existing products and processes.

Symbolic knowledge is related to the creation of meaning and desire, as well as aesthetic attributes of products, such as designs, images, and symbols, and to their economic use. The increasing significance of this intangible type of knowledge has been noted by OECD (2013), which mentions, for example, design as a new source of growth that is part of firms" knowledge-based capital. Other examples include the dynamic development of cultural production, such as media (film making, publishing, and music), advertising, design, brands, and fashion. In cultural production, the input is aesthetic rather than cognitive. This demands rather specialized capabilities in symbol interpretation and creativity. This type of knowledge is often narrowly tied to a deep understanding of the habits and norms and the "everyday culture" of specific social groupings. Due to the cultural embeddedness of interpretations, this type of knowledge base is characterized by a distinctive tacit component and is usually highly context-specific. The acquisition of essential creative, imaginative, and interpretive skills is less tied to formal qualifications and university degrees than to practice in various stages of the creative process. However, this knowledge base has also become increasingly knowledge intensive.

When designing and implementing a "smart specialization-informed innovation strategy" for industrial and economic diversification, it is necessary to go beyond considering how to secure "path extension," which has been the main goal of traditional innovation policies. Path extension mainly results in incremental product and process innovations in existing industries and technological trajectories. While this can secure competitiveness and growth in the short- and medium-term, in the long-term these industries run the risk of path exhaustion, that is, depleting the capacity for renewal. Path renewal takes place when existing local firms move into different but related industries through regional branching or unrelated knowledge base combinations (Asheim et al., 2011a). New path creation represents the most wide-ranging change in a regional economy. It includes the establishment of new firms in novel sectors, or firms that introduce new products, processes, and/or business models in the regional economy. Path creation is most often R&D driven and can either be the result of knowledge-based entrepreneurial discovery (university spin-offs through commercialization of research results) or proactive national innovation policy aimed at promoting new path development, as is the goal of VINNOVA's (Swedish Governmental Agency for Innovation Systems) Centre of Expertise Programmes (Coenen et al., 2017).

The main problem of traditional industries with respect to promoting new path development (path renewal) and making them more innovative and competitive is a low level of education and competence and a lack of investment in

R&D. This implies that these firms and industries have a low absorptive capacity, which limits their capability of accessing, acquiring, and applying new and often external knowledge, of making use of new production equipment and penetrating new markets, especially international ones. It also handicaps them in approaching universities to make their knowledge more research-based and/or informed, which would extend their mode of innovation to the STI type. What is needed is to build the absorptive capacity of DUI-based firms by increasing their research-based competence (Isaksen and Nilsson, 2013). This is an important strategy to upgrade traditional industries, as research has demonstrated that combining DUI and STI makes firms perform better by utilizing both analytical and synthetic knowledge bases (Lorenz and Lundvall, 2006).

Such upgrading can take place through unrelated knowledge base combinations leading to new related industries. We maintain that this has been overlooked and represents an unexplored potential for new path development. Empirical illustrations of unrelated knowledge base combinations resulting in new path development would be traditional textile and shoe industries moving into technical textiles by adding nanotechnology (analytical knowledge base) to the traditional (synthetic) knowledge base of the industry; the food industry (synthetic knowledge) producing functional food using biotechnology (analytical knowledge); or the development of new media industry by combining unrelated symbolic knowledge with the analytical/synthetic knowledge bases of the existing ICT industry.

Another strategy to upgrade traditional industries is to move into high value-added niches. This strategy can be realized most efficiently by mobilizing the symbolic knowledge base, often in combination with synthetic knowledge, and applying a platform approach, that is, one transcending traditional sectors, in the concrete design and implementation. This would normally imply that the firms continue to rely on the DUI mode of innovation, but are able to climb the value-added ladder by introducing new products that have a strong element of symbolic knowledge so as to achieve product differentiation. The end-result would be unique products at the high-end of the global market in sectors, such as food and tourism.

One example of the power of exploiting the symbolic knowledge base to create a unique product as a distinct luxury good in the high-quality market of smoked salmon is the Swiss Balik salmon. It achieves 2–3 times higher prices and value-added than comparable Norwegian smoked salmon, even if the basic raw material (farmed Norwegian salmon) is the same. The difference is the marketing of the product: Balik salmon is sold in Caviar House outlets—not Fine Food stores—at airports to achieve exclusivity, and the accompanying story that it is made with a recipe from a Russian tsar and washed in water from Swiss mountain rivers. This example of a market-related innovation using symbolic knowledge demonstrates the value-creating potential of such innovations.

Examples of upgrading strategies in tourism are the Ice Hotel in Northern Sweden with 30,000 guests every season (November–April) and The Santa

Claus Village in Rovaniemi, in Northern Finland, which attracts visitors by advertising the possibility of crossing the "magical" Arctic Circle in reindeer-drawn sledges.

Some of the ideas of the smart specialization approach are—as already mentioned—derived from the constructed regional advantage (CRA) approach coming out of work by an expert group appointed by the EU Commission's DG Research (Asheim et al., 2006, 2011a). The main message of the CRA approach is to promote competitive advantage for diversified specialization through an innovation-based product differentiation creating unique products, building on the view that this can be achieved in all types of industries, yet based on the industry-specific modes of innovation and knowledge bases. Thus, the CRA approach represented a broad-based innovation policy. This makes the approach instrumental in designing and implementing an innovation-based policy for promoting diversified specialization. Moreover, as the aim of CRA was to inform the development of *regional* innovation strategies, it constituted an explicit spatial, *place-based* approach. Thus, we are inclined to maintain that the smart specialization approach has something to gain from the CRA approach (Asheim et al., 2011a; Boschma, 2014), which may help it become a more powerful policy tool for promoting new path development in regions.

The CRA approach implies that competitive advantage has to be constructed on the basis of the uniqueness of firms' and regions' capabilities (Asheim et al., 2006). As an important initial strategy for new path development, regions and countries should base their competitive strategy on industries in which they have traditionally been doing well. The existing industrial structure will, in most regions, represent the main source of new path development to secure future competitiveness (Boschma, 2015). In the following three cases, we look at the main differences in the regions, the key driving factors, and the policy options with respect to diversified specialization, as well as the resulting new path development.

THE CASES: SCANDINAVIAN REGIONS

This paper draws on three empirical studies of Scandinavian regions: the North Denmark Region (NDR), Scania in Southern Sweden, and Møre og Romsdal in North Western Norway. The two latter instances are case studies developed as part of a FP7 research project on "smart specialization for regional innovation;" the first is an expert assessment of NDR's work on smart specialization undertaken by one of the authors on behalf of DG Regio. While to outsiders Scandinavia may look very homogenous, the regions are quite different with respect to innovation capacity and industrial structure. Møre og Romsdal is a moderate innovator, relying heavily on an experience-based or DUI mode of innovation, while both NDR and Scania are innovation leaders, according to the European Scoreboard. Scania in particular has a strong R&D performance, and has formed, together with some other advanced, leading regions in Europe, what they call "the Vanguard Initiative for New Growth by smart specialization." In each of the cases, we look at "innovation and diversification potential," as well as "strategies and policies for new path development." Taken together, the comparative analyses of these regions will hopefully give insights into how a smart specialization strategy can be designed and implemented in three highly developed regions in coordinated market economies characterized by close cooperation between the private and public sectors, good governance, and strong institutions nationally and regionally. At the same time, the regions also represent contrasting cases with respect to innovation capacity and innovation policy.

North Denmark Region[1]

NDR is a region with a rich resource endowment. Among European regions, it has positioned itself as an innovation leader. The region is organizationally thick with good governance, strong institutions, and a population of 580,000. Denmark has a well-developed and coordinated national research and innovation policy, with good connectedness between the national and regional levels. Thus, it has fulfilled the ex-ante conditionalities for designing and implementing a smart specialization strategy.

Denmark is one of the best performing economies in the EU and ranks high on various international innovation and competitiveness rankings. It is also one of the top performers in Europe with respect to the share of GDP allocated to R&D, only behind Finland and Sweden. Denmark is one of the few countries that managed to fulfill the EU's 3% target for R&D as a percentage of GDP.

Innovation and Diversification Potential

NDR is a well performing region that has rapidly improved its competitive advantage. According to the European Regional Innovation Scoreboard, since 2014 NDR has belonged to the group of European regional innovation leaders, a position it also held in 2010. The region performs well with respect to R&D expenditures in the business sector, SME in-house innovation activities, as well as in product and process innovations introduced by SMEs. Poor performance is found in non-R&D innovation expenditures and European Patent Office applications, while the performance on other indicators is average. Quite logically, the most innovative regions, which are characterized as innovation leaders, are typically found in the most innovative countries (in addition to Denmark, Sweden, Finland, Germany, and Switzerland). In the benchmarking tool, which is available on the smart specialization platform website, the regions which NDR could use for benchmarking purposes are Southern Sweden (the region of Scania, which is another case in this chapter) and the Central Denmark region, with which NDR already cooperates closely.

The region's industrial structure represents in many ways a dual structure. On one hand, one finds the traditionally dominating industries, which are either large, process-based firms (such as those in the production of cement), or smaller firms (often SMEs) that depend on an experience-based mode of innovation. In the NDR context, such firms can be found in the food, construction, maritime, and tourism sectors. On the other hand, there are research- and knowledge-intensive, mostly emergent, sectors, which are based on commercializing research results from Aalborg University and are described as "regional front technologies" in the regional innovation and development plan.

A key to making traditional industries more innovative and competitive is to strengthen the absorptive capacity of firms relying on an experience-based mode of innovation (synthetic knowledge base) by increasing their R&D competences (analytical knowledge base). Examples of this would be for the food industry to start producing functional food directed at the growing market of obesity and other life style diseases in collaboration with medical and biotechnology research at Aalborg University; or for the maritime sector to link up with the research on intelligent transport systems, logistics, and ICT at the university, a collaboration already underway.

Another path to upgrade traditional industries is to move into high value-added niches. This is a strategy that can be most efficiently realized by mobilizing symbolic, intangible knowledge (branding, design, fashion), combined with a platform approach to achieve product differentiation. In NDR there is, for example, potential in combining food (gastronomy) with nature and culture to produce a tourist product that can be customized to the preferences of demanding international customers and thus create a high level of value added.

However, the general low educational and competence level in the region's traditional SMEs, and a lack of investment in R&D, represent the greatest threats to such upgrading paths due to the firms' low absorptive capacity. A low absorptive capacity will have a negative impact on firms' potential to become more innovative and to link up with national and international collaborators, for example, in global value chains and innovation and production networks. Together with the problems of attracting and retaining highly qualified people, especially graduates of Aalborg University, this challenge must be overcome as part of a successful smart specialization strategy.

The other part of the dual industrial structure of the NDR is the research- and knowledge-intensive, mostly emergent, sectors, which are based on the regional front technologies within energy, health and life science, and transportation (including logistics and the maritime sector). These all areas represent strong research milieus at Aalborg University. In addition, ICT should be added to these regional front technologies as it has been and remains both a research stronghold and an important industrial sector (although not as important as before). ICT is also a general-purpose technology that can increase productivity in other sectors. These technologies are found in firms, which are part of regional clusters and networks. In some of these areas, such as medical technology, energy efficiency and embedded software, wireless communication, and sustainable energy (especially connected to windmills), the university's research is world leading.

Applying an R&D-based strategy is a very costly development and differentiating strategy, with a high failure rate yet yielding positive results in new firm growth and job generation in the long-term. However, given the strong research base in key technologies, which can address future societal challenges regionally, nationally, and globally; this research capacity and access to the best knowledge internationally should, of course, be exploited in an optimal way. In addition, the front technologies represent a combination of analytical/scientific and synthetic/engineering R&D-based knowledge (e.g., medical technology), which brings them closer to being exploited (commercialized) than "pure" analytical knowledge, such as biotechnology. The traditional focus on an R&D-based strategy, manifested in a strong national science and technology policy in Denmark, represents an important asset in implementing such a strategy, especially as the regional front technologies are also part of national prioritized technologies. If the available national funding for developing these technologies is mobilized together with accessible EU funding through Horizon 2020 and other relevant programs in a smart way, a considerable amount of funding should be available for commercializing these technologies, leading to new firm formation, generation of highly qualified jobs, and the attraction of Foreign Direct Investment, especially R&D units from international corporations. The latter can take advantage of connecting up to the university's leading research milieus and of the accessibility to the highly qualified labor force graduating from Aalborg University. In many ways, these resources are so far only marginally exploited in the region.

Strategies and Policies for New Path Development

NDR has selected the following "growth areas" to be prioritized as a basis for diversified specialization through its smart specialization strategy (Fig. 4.1).

An optimal situation for regions is when regional strongholds, either traditionally or based on research strengths at the regional universities, are found within the same areas, which are prioritized nationally. NDR seems to be in such an optimal situation, as the strong areas selected by the Growth Forum North Denmark Region correspond to the nationally prioritized sectors. This puts NDR in a very favorable position for designing an efficient smart specialization strategy.

In the existing regional innovation and development strategy, the North Denmark Region has classified sectors in focus areas of clusters (ICT, food, construction industry, health and life science, and the maritime sector) and networks (tourism and energy). Moreover, as referred earlier the so-called regional front technologies are also identified in energy (sustainable energy, such as wind, hydrogen, wave, and biofuel), health and life science (medical technology, social innovation), and transport (intelligent transport systems including logistics). The regional innovation and development plan also proposes, with

FIGURE 4.1 **Selected growth areas of the NDR's smart specialization strategy.** Maritime industry, energy, climate, ITC, health and welfare, foods, and tourism represent growth areas with considerable regional potential (and therefore implemented in the strategy as supported clusters). Water, bio, and environment, and creative businesses and design are national growth areas with limited growth potential. Construction and housing is a regional strength position, which we chose to include in the analysis and subsequently in the strategy (Smart City).

reference to food and tourism, the application of a platform approach based on combining knowledge, including intangible knowledge.

Both in national plans and in the regional innovation and development plan, we find strategies for dealing with the problems connected to the low educational and competence level and the lack of R&D investment in many Danish firms, especially in SMEs in traditional industries. Nationally, we see mobility plans, that is, subsidizing the hiring of academic work force in firms not previously employing this category of workers, as well as financial support for SMEs to acquire research-based knowledge through collaboration with universities. Regionally, we find a focus on firm-oriented competence development and continued education, as well as the matchmaking institution where Aalborg University plays a key role.

One way to increase the development and exploitation rate of the front technologies is to make public procurement for innovation (PPI) a central instrument. The areas of health and welfare are confronted with huge societal challenges generally due to societal aging, which requires these sectors to operate in a smarter way. More specifically, the building of the new university hospital in the region close to the university offers a big opportunity for using PPI to support the development of these technologies. In fact, all the front technologies (energy, health and life science, transport/logistics, and ICT) could be stimulated by effective use of PPI. As the public sector is the large, critical, and demanding customer in this area, and the region has the main responsibility for health, the region has a unique opportunity to influence the development and exploitation of these front technologies.

However, successfully promoting new path development, either in the form of path renewal (regional branching based on related variety or unrelated combinations of knowledge bases) or new path creation based on commercialization of research-based knowledge, will require concrete and specific action lines. Regionally, what seems to be lacking is a higher capacity of formulating specific and concrete action lines, due to difficulties in the decision-making "Growth Forum." All municipalities in the region are represented there and have found it hard to agree on the kind of tough choices leading to prioritizations, which are needed to successfully implement a smart specialization strategy. This is a major challenge in the process of designing and implementing a productive smart specialization strategy for regional development in NDR.

Scania (Skåne), Southern Sweden[2]

Scania is a wealthy and highly innovative region with approximately 1.2 million inhabitants situated in the southern-most part of Sweden. Compared to other European regions, Scania performs well in terms of unemployment, GDP per capita, competitiveness, and quality of governance.

Innovation and Diversification Potential

The wider Southern Sweden region has been classified as an "innovation leader" in the Regional Innovation Scoreboard 2014. A study by the OECD (2012) found that Scania is one of the most innovation-intensive regions within the OECD, performing the role of a "knowledge and technology hub." Key strengths include high R&D expenditures in the business sector (reflecting the presence of research-intensive firms in the region), a large share of population with tertiary education, and a strong endowment of human resources in science and technology. This points to a highly developed analytical knowledge base and the prevalence of the STI mode of innovation. The DUI innovation mode seems to be less important (when measured by "non-R&D innovation expenditures"). This score, however, follows a general pattern of other Swedish regions. Moreover, the region's SMEs have strong in-house innovation capabilities, collaborate intensively with external partners, and perform well when it comes to introducing product and process innovations. A weakness of Southern Sweden seems to be the exploitation and commercialization of its strong R&D assets and the knowledge generated regionally. The capacity to generate radical innovation (measured by sales of new-to-market and new-to-firm innovations) appears to be rather low.

Scania hosts an organizationally thick and diversified regional innovation system and thus exhibits excellent potential for economic diversification through new path development. Since the 2008 financial crisis, the region has undergone some structural change. Manufacturing industries have somewhat declined and employment has shifted toward the service sector and knowledge-intensive activities. The region's industrial structure is characterized by a high degree of heterogeneity with many sectors contributing to total employment. Among the most important are the food, packaging, life science, ICT, moving media, and clean tech industries, reflecting the presence of all three types of knowledge bases (analytical, synthetic, and symbolic) and offering potential for new path development based on combinations of knowledge bases.

Scania is also well endowed with knowledge-generating organizations, further enhancing opportunities for path renewal and new path creation. Both Lund University (one of the most prestigious and largest universities in Scandinavia with strengths in science, technology, and medicine) and Malmö University College (particularly strong in design, media, and culture) play an active role in shaping regional innovation and diversification dynamics. Lund University has been involved in the establishment of facilities, such as Ideon Science Park, Medicon Village, MAX IV, and ESS (European Spallation Source). New path creation in sectors, such as ICT and biotechnology in Scania would not have been possible without the competences provided by Lund University. It has also played an important role in path renewal and upgrading of traditional sectors, contributing to the rise of functional food activities, which reflect a combination of analytical and synthetic knowledge bases, in Scania. In general, Lund University contributes to regional development through the establishment of spin-off companies, by performing joint research with firms, by participating in intermediary organizations and networks, and by providing consultancy support and advice in different technological areas. Malmö University College has played a major role in the transformation of the city of Malmö. It has contributed to the emergence of a new media cluster (reflecting path renewal based on a combination of analytic/synthetic and symbolic knowledge bases) by providing skilled labor and collaborating in joint projects with firms.

A striking feature of the regional innovation system is the large number (around 100) of public, quasi-public, and private business and innovation support organizations. Firms (and other stakeholders) located in the region thus benefit from a plentiful offer in terms of networking opportunities, counseling activities, and so on. There is, however, also a negative side. Many support organizations present in the region have overlapping functions and compete for funds and attention from entrepreneurs, as well as other actors (Zukauskaite and Moodysson, 2014). There is a lack of cooperation and coordination among the support organizations, resulting in a fragmented innovation support system.

Actions have only recently been taken to improve the situation with the establishment of a coordination body.

Strategies and Policy Priorities for New Path Development

Innovation policy ranks high on the policy agenda in Scania. Over the past 10 years or so, regional authorities have adopted an innovation-driven regional development approach. In 2011, a new strategy [International Innovation Strategy for Skåne (IISS) 2012–20]) was launched, largely building on the rationale of smart specialization. Based on a thorough analysis of strengths and weaknesses of Scania's regional innovation system, the strategy was developed primarily by the "Research and Innovation Council in Skåne" (FIRS), a body founded in 2010 consisting of representatives from Region Skåne, the universities, municipalities, and key industrial sectors. Thus, the strategy is evidence-based and the result of a collective, participatory process where a wide variety of stakeholders have been included. The selection of policy priorities in the IISS can be seen as the outcome of a highly inclusive process, based on intensive discussions and collaboration among key regional stakeholders.

Three main focus areas (prioritized areas) are identified in the IISS: smart sustainable cities, smart materials, and personal health. These are all broad areas targeting global challenges, with a clear focus on combining regional strengths. For each focus area, a platform has been created. Platform coordinators employed by Region Skåne are in charge of encouraging collaboration between various actors in their respective platforms.

The chosen priorities reflect Scania's heterogeneous regional industrial structure and research strengths. They are broad enough to encompass many important sectors present in the region. Smart sustainable cities, smart materials, and personal health are platforms where different sectors can intersect to create new solutions and identify activities leading to new path development. Most likely, this broad way of selecting priority areas would not have been possible in a region with more specialized economic structures, reflecting the consideration of place-specific factors in the case of Scania.

The IISS also explicitly aims to increase the region's international connectedness and, consequently, a key feature of the IISS is its strong international dimension. The new innovation strategy aims to foster international cooperation and strengthen the region's position in knowledge networks by developing bridging organizations and global strategic alliances. It covers a stronger emphasis on collaboration within the Öresund cross-border region and expresses the intention of opening up the selected innovation arenas to nonlocal actors on a global scale. Thus, the IISS represents a move beyond inward-looking policies, toward greater outward orientation, focusing on external linkages, international collaboration, and wider reaching knowledge networks.

The IISS covers several other novel elements. It reflects the adoption of a broad approach to innovation, including service innovation, as well as public sector innovation. It thus goes beyond previous policies, which mainly focused on promoting research-based innovation, exploiting the strengths in the knowledge generation subsystem. The IISS indeed shows an evolution from research commercialization as the main policy target toward a more systemic approach to innovation. Furthermore, a shift has taken place from a traditional view of clusters based on a sector logic toward an approach focusing on interindustry crossovers, combining knowledge bases, and bringing actors with different backgrounds together in innovation activities through "open innovation arenas." In turn, these arenas are organized in platforms with two or more arenas, which are broadening the variety of actors who can collaborate (Fig. 4.2).

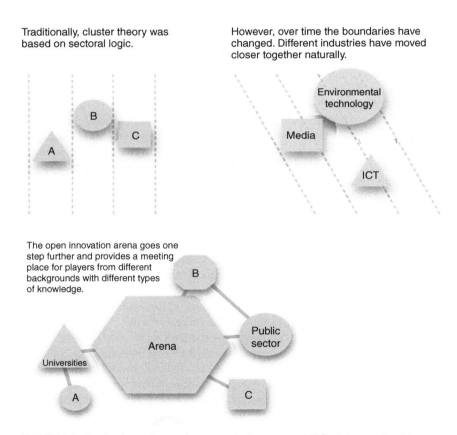

FIGURE 4.2 Logic of open innovation arenas in the context of Skåne's international innovation strategy. It moves beyond the sectoral logic of the cluster theory toward an open space where actors from different backgrounds and with various types of knowledge can meet. *(Söderström, P., Ekdahl, N., Lindbom, M., et al. 2012. Developing New Innovative Areas and Creative Environments. FIRS/SIS, Malmö.)*

The IISS is seen as an overarching strategy to which policies in the whole region should be aligned and related. On a practical level, Region Skåne is doing this by relating its "Regional Development Plan for 2030" to the innovation strategy, acknowledging the IISS as a "central tool in the work (for strengthening the innovative capacity in Scania)" (Region Skåne, 2014, p. 24). In addition, there are units working very closely on the innovation strategy within the regional administration. One example is the entrepreneurship unit working with the Sounding Board for Innovation in Scania, where a wide variety of innovation relevant actors are brought together.

The governance structure has been an important determinant of how the region has engaged in developing the IISS. The highest elected regional governance body, Region Skåne, carries formal responsibility for regional development issues. The political mandate for dealing with these issues was added to Region Skåne's primary responsibilities (mainly health care and public transport) in the late 1990s. However, at the same time, Region Skåne lacks resources for large-scale budgetary commitments.

This has led to Region Skåne approaching regional development and questions regarding regional innovation capacity as a coordinator in the regional innovation system, rather than taking on large funding commitments and acting as a big investor. To aid this, Region Skåne has conducted several studies on the regional economic structure in general and innovation activities in particular, for example, through functional analyses of the regional innovation system. These identified issues with a fragmented system containing many supporting organizations, and a lack of service innovation support and support to companies in later phases of development. Thus, coordination and systemic leadership has been a key task for Region Skåne during the last five years. The establishment of two public–private coordination bodies, namely the research and innovation council (responsible for the development of the region's smart specialization strategy) and the sounding board of innovation (in charge of increasing the level of coordination between the large number of supporting organizations), has played an important role in this regard.

The IISS is without any doubts a "new generation policy strategy," containing many elements of the emerging smart specialization paradigm. It is an evidence-based and place-based policy, building on a thorough analysis of Scania's innovation capacity and aiming to promote innovation and industrial renewal by exploiting unique assets and responding to global challenges. Policy priorities have been selected in a participatory, inclusive way, involving a large variety of key stakeholders in Scania. The IISS has a strong international orientation and reflects a move from a narrow, R&D-based view toward a much broader understanding of innovation. The smart specialization practices in Scania have been a source of inspiration for the development of the national innovation strategy and the policy development processes regionally. The design of the IISS also has the potential to become a role model for other European regions.

Møre og Romsdal, North Western Norway[3]

This section builds on a case study of the Møre og Romsdal region in North-Western Norway with a population of 265,000. It is an illustration of a specialized and relatively peripheral region with a competitive manufacturing industry building largely on a synthetic knowledge base and a DUI mode of innovation. However, the landscape is changing, meaning that firms must make continuous efforts to remain competitive in existing fields and to venture into new fields.

The case is highly interesting due to the region's outstanding economic and export performance, despite its low ranking on common innovation indicators. On one hand, it represents a perfect case for advocating a broad perspective on innovation and knowledge bases as the foundation of firms' and regions' competitiveness. On the other hand, this case allows us to unveil the potential for renewal in regions that are not blessed with a high degree of related and unrelated variety or with strong universities conducting basic research.

Innovation and Diversification Potential

Møre og Romsdal is one of the global hubs in the maritime industry where leading firms, such as Ulstein and Rolls Royce are located. Regional ship owners control 40% of the world's most advanced offshore fleet. The maritime cluster is one of only a few worldwide in which all actors of the value chain are represented. Input–output analyses have shown that the cluster exhibits high regional connectedness, as well as national and international linkages (Møreforsking, 2014). In terms of employment and value creation, the maritime industry is most important in Møre og Romsdal. Besides a high degree of vertical and horizontal integration, the maritime industry therefore also benefits from a thick labor market.

The maritime industry can be described as a traditional manufacturing industry that relies largely on a synthetic knowledge base. In other words, the workforce has a high level of experience-based, tacit knowledge in the field of engineering. Learning and innovation is supported by a high level of trust regionally, which allows for informal and quick communication between the various actors in the regional cluster. Furthermore, interaction and learning also occurs to a high degree between the management and employees thanks to flat hierarchies and the Scandinavian model of learning work organizations (Lorenz and Lundvall, 2006). The maritime industry benefits from university colleges and applied research institutes, which have adapted their educational programs, as well as R&D activities to the needs of the industry. R&D is mainly applied and support in testing and application development. The maritime industry is organized in a cluster, the Global Centre of Expertise "Blue Maritime," a category in Innovation Norway's industrial cluster program reserved for the internationally most competitive clusters.

The combination of strong experience-based engineering knowledge, an institutional environment that fosters knowledge exchange and learning between and within organizations of the cluster, as well as tight collaboration between the industry and higher educational institutes explains the high speed of incremental innovation that has substantially contributed to the cluster's leading position.

However, the maritime industry is currently facing tremendous challenges due to the dramatic fall in oil prices since the second half of 2014. The fall in oil prices has strained profits for the more demanding, technologically complex, and costly offshore exploration and exploitation activities. This represents a big challenge for the Norwegian economy overall, and the maritime industry in particular, which delivers specialized equipment and provides services to offshore installations off the coast of Western and Northern Norway. Furthermore, due to the previously high profit margins and restricted supply of labor, the wages are very high in the traditional industries thereby reducing the incentives to explore new economic opportunities.

Besides the maritime and oil and gas industries, Møre og Romsdal has a specialization in the marine and furniture industries. The marine industry has substantial future potential. Møre og Romsdal has a long tradition in fishery, which contributes to the strong regional export performance equally as much as the sales of manufacturing goods. However, the marine industry has changed. Due to high labor costs, firms have invested significantly in process innovations that reduce the required labor input through automation and robotization. In that regard, synergies between the maritime and marine industries have appeared. In fact, the rough fishing conditions have put high requirements on ships and fishing equipment, creating the sophisticated demand that spurs innovation and competitiveness (Porter, 1998).

Due to the increasing cost pressures in traditional fishery, firms have begun to venture into biomarine. Biomarine describes the inflow of biotechnology into traditional marine activities that leads to new functional foods (e.g., healthy oils), health and pharmaceutical products, or flavors. Besides, traditional fishery is complemented by aquaculture, that is, the farming of salmon, cod, and halibut. Due to these new developments, the marine industry has expanded steadily since 2000 and the market is expected to grow significantly in future.

The renewal of the marine industry challenges the regional knowledge infrastructure specialized on experience-based engineering knowledge. The further development of the biomarine sector, in contrast, requires strong analytical, science-based competencies. However, until this year, when the Norwegian University of Science and Technology in Trondheim merged with Aalesund University College, the region had no university; only the university college in Molde had university status for logistics. Furthermore, R&D expenditures per capita are far below national average and only a small minority of researchers in Møre og Romsdal have a doctoral degree. This weakness is problematic not only for biomarine, but also for increasing the knowledge intensity of maritime and other industries.

The strong linkages of actors in the regional innovation system are further promoted through several cluster initiatives financed by Innovation Norway and the Research Council of Norway. The Norwegian cluster program operates on three levels: (1) the Arena program targets emerging clusters; (2) well-established, economically strong, and export-oriented clusters can apply to the Norwegian Centre of Expertise program; and (3) the Global Centre of Expertise (GCE) program stimulates strongly developed clusters with a leading position in global value chains. The GCE Blue Maritime cluster in Møre og Romsdal was one of the first two GCEs in Norway. In addition, three Arena clusters support the marine industry (Legasea), the furniture industry (Norwegian Rooms), as well as activities in logistics, material, and production technologies (iKuben). Regional entrepreneurs show strong ownership of and lead these cluster initiatives.

Strategies and Policy Priorities for New Path Development

The significant drop in oil prices has shaken the industrial basis of Møre og Romsdal and put economic diversification at the top of the regional policy agenda. In light of being a highly specialized and rather peripheral region, the region focuses on three main strategic priorities relating to: (1) broadening the vision to capture potential new development paths; (2) upgrading and adapting the knowledge base of the existing industry through a combination of regional investments and strategies to access complementary extraregional sources; and (3) seeking opportunities for cross-fertilization between regional industries and clusters.

Regional stakeholders agree that their core assets are access to the ocean, high competencies in dealing with difficult maritime operations, and strong environmental standards. Building on these assets, their vision is for their region to be a global leader in the environmentally sustainable exploitation of the ocean space. The vision thus captures current specializations but opens the way for a large variety of related activities concerning, for instance, subsea operations, renewable energies, advanced maritime operations, marine, and transport. The vision underlines the importance of developing generic competencies in material technologies, robotization and automatization, visualization, bioeconomy, biotechnology, logistics, and design (Fig. 4.3). In Møre og Romsdal, the vision is shared by firms, higher educational institutes, and regional policy makers.

Semiperipheral and specialized regions potentially find it easier to develop a broadly accepted vision compared to major agglomerations because fewer stakeholder groups and agendas need to be coordinated. Nevertheless, even a small region, like Møre og Romsdal has a variety of actor groups, which are associated with different institutional contexts and potentially conflicting interests. This includes a fragmented municipal structure, potential tensions between homegrown firms and multinational cooperations with headquarters abroad, as well as diverging needs and development stages of the industries present in the region. Hence, institutional variety exists even in small regions and requires

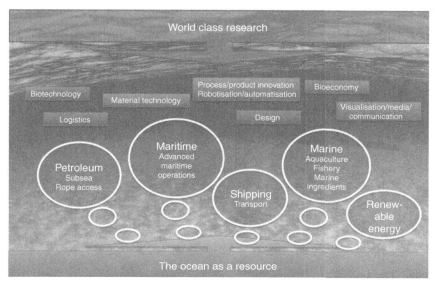

FIGURE 4.3   Selected growth areas in the regional development strategy of Møre og Romsdal. The ocean as resource provides the basis for the key sectors (petroleum, maritime, shipping, marine, renewable energy) to be developed. Upgrading of R&D capacities, as well as firm competencies in generic technologies (biotechnology, logistic, material technology, robotization and automatization, design, bioeconomy, visualisation/media/communication) are key elements to achieve competitive advantage in the core sectors.

processes of coordination and negotiation of interest. In Møre og Romsdal, these processes are supported by a strong local identity and trust among people who grew up in the region. Furthermore, we find that locals are represented in managing positions of the multinational firms, thereby acting as translators of cultures and regional ambassadors. In addition, several cross-cutting institutional arrangements, such as the Aalesund Knowledge Park ensure coordination between industries. It is this "institutional connectedness" that strongly supports the aligning of interests, development of a shared vision, and coordinated action (Grillitsch, 2016; Grillitsch and Asheim, 2017).

The second key strategic element is upgrading and adapting the regional knowledge base: strong efforts have been undertaken here to enhance research capabilities in the private and public sectors. This has translated into a higher share of staff with a PhD, industry-sponsored professorships, and a successful application of the Aalesund University College to the "Centre for Research driven Innovation" program. The latter promotes research collaboration with industry, in this case mainly the maritime industry, focusing on strategic and targeted basic research, as well as advanced applied research. This application was done in partnership with the Norwegian University of Science and Technology. This will potentially increase the access to basic (analytical knowledge) and applied (synthetic knowledge) research for firms regionally.

However, given the narrow knowledge base and peripheral location of Møre og Romsdal, new path development also relies heavily on accessing extraregional resources and knowledge. This regional limitation and hence the need to search beyond regional boundaries is widely appreciated in the region. The GCE Blue Maritime defines scouting for knowledge globally as a core activity. The higher education and research institutes aim to establish national and international linkages. Leading firms in the region collaborate with nonlocal partners to bring in complementary knowledge (mainly analytical and symbolic knowledge).

Besides seeking to upgrade and adapt the regional knowledge base, one priority also lies in creating synergies between existing regional clusters. In particular, cross-fertilization is promoted by an organization called Aalesund Knowledge Park, which coordinates the GCE Blue Maritime and the Legasea Arena cluster, as well as an offshore wind project and a program to support start-ups. As already mentioned, synergies exist between the maritime and marine industries. Furthermore, the furniture cluster initiative Norwegian Rooms focuses on branding (i.e., using symbolic knowledge), which can potentially also contribute to enhancing value creation in the other industries. Good potential is also seen in the promotion of generic competencies related to, for instance, material and production technology or logistics (promoted by the iKuben cluster).

However, a closer investigation of the potential synergies has also shown that the clusters are in different growth stages and face varying challenges. For this reason, the main strategy of the maritime industry is to diversify into related sectors, such as renewable energy, where the technological competencies can be reused. In contrast, the marine industry emphasizes national and international linkages to renowned research organizations and firms. The focus lies on identifying niches in which Møre og Romsdal has a competitive edge in global markets, rather than diversifying from an existing position of global leadership. The challenges of the furniture industry are different and pivot around building competitive advantage through design, the creation of symbolic value, and innovation in production processes.

CONCLUSIONS: COMPARATIVE PERSPECTIVES ON SMART SPECIALIZATION STRATEGIES IN SCANDINAVIAN REGIONS

There are similarities and differences between the three cases, making them interesting to compare when discussing smart specialization as a strategy for economic diversification. All three regions are Scandinavian, which makes them good representatives of highly developed economies with good governance and strong institutions. On the other hand, only two of the regions, NDR and Scania, are part of the EU, where the implementation of a smart specialization strategy is compulsory. In contrast, Norway is not a member of the EU so does not have this requirement. However, Møre og Romsdal, as well as other regions in Norway have chosen to use smart specialization to guide and inform their work on counties" R&D and development plans. Moreover, the regions differ in their innovation capacity and industrial structure. Møre og Romsdal is only a moderate innovator, relying heavily on an experience-based or DUI mode of innovation, while both NDR and Scania are innovation leaders according to the European Scoreboard.

Besides, when it comes to innovation policies at national and regional levels, there are interesting contrasts between the three countries. Sweden has always ranked as one of the countries with the highest level of R&D expenditures; Denmark is becoming one of the leaders, while Norway has relatively modest spending on R&D. This reflects partly the different industrial structures in the three countries, but partly also a lower prioritization of R&D and innovation in Norwegian industrial policy. Sweden has a long tradition of publicly funded, 10-year programs for building competence considered to be of strategic importance for the future competitiveness of Swedish industry (e.g., generic technologies, such as ICT, electronics, and biotech). As the Centre of Expertise (CoE) programs aim to create new path development, they have a strong focus on exploration, that is, new research-based knowledge, and are consequently university owned, even while the close link between exploration and exploitation is always underlined (thus the reference to the CoEs as "strong research and innovation milieus"). This is why OECD has described Sweden as the most resilient economy in Europe (OECD, 2013).

The innovation systems approach has traditionally held a strong position in Sweden's innovation policy. The "strong research and innovation milieus" mentioned earlier are an example of a regional innovation systems strategy. In Norway, one finds strong sectoral, national innovation systems around the dominating industries (oil and gas, maritime, marine, and process industry), while the absence of research-based regional universities—in contrast to Sweden—has resulted in a void of regional innovation systems. This has partly been substituted by strong clusters, which use the Norwegian University of Science and Technology as the main exploration hub. The region of Møre og Romsdal may represent a change in this situation toward an emerging regional innovation system through the merger of the regional university-level college and the national technical university. Denmark, on the other hand, has not used an innovation systems approach but has relied more on a linear model, putting strong efforts into supporting basic research at the expense of exploitation. This has resulted in a lower level of innovation than what could be expected from the relatively high R&D spending. NDR's rank as an innovation leader reflects the level of R&D spending, which does not necessarily translate into comparable strong innovation performance. Thus, one finds neither regional innovation systems in Danish regions, nor strong clusters as in Norway. The result may be a less efficient implementation of smart specialization strategies due to the absence of strong intermediaries.

All three regions were well prepared for taking on board the smart specialization perspective. The three regions applied a similar logic about how to promote innovation and economic growth in their previous R&D and development plans. Nevertheless, NDR (in part) and Møre og Romsdal, especially, placed greater emphasis on path extension, and thus less on new path development, which is the core of smart specialization. The introduction of a smart specialization strategy seems to have strengthened the focus on new path development.

The regions' strategies build on a thorough analysis of their innovation capacity and aim to promote innovation and new path development by exploiting unique assets and responding to global challenges. The regions have opted for rather broad visions as guidance for achieving diversified specialization. Scania has chosen smart sustainable cities, smart materials, and personal health as their priority areas. Møre og Romsdal focuses on the ocean space, combining strengths in the maritime and marine sectors. The region of NDR has a more sectoral prioritization in which "front technologies" play an important role. The differences in industrial structure and innovation capacity are reflected in the ways they aim to reach their goals. Scania in particular, and partly also NDR, can rely more on the R&D capacity of their regional universities, while Møre og Romsdal still has to depend on and develop its experience-based mode of innovation. Thus, the cases also provide a good illustration and confirmation of the need to apply a broad-based innovation policy, which smart specialization encourages by emphasizing those countries and regions should diversify their economies starting with existing strengths. The cases illustrated here also confirm the relevance of a knowledge-based approach in designing and implementing smart specialization strategies. This approach is an important instrument in demonstrating how innovation-based diversification can be achieved in various sectors with different knowledge bases and modes of innovation. Thus, it also shows how a policy that goes beyond old "one size fits all" models can be applied to accommodate the needs and potential of heterogeneous European regions.

ENDNOTES

1. This section builds on the following report: Asheim (2014)
2. This section builds on the following report: Trippl et al. (2015)
3. This section is based on the following book chapter: Asheim and Gertler (2005)

REFERENCES

Asheim, B.T., 2007. Differentiated knowledge bases and varieties of regional innovation systems. Innov.—Eur. J. Soc. Sci. Res. 20 (3), 223–241.

Asheim, B.T., 2014. North Denmark Region RIS3. An expert assessment on behalf of DG Regional and Urban Policy, EU Commission, Aalborg.

Asheim, B.T., Gertler, M., 2005. The Geography of Innovation: Regional Innovation Systems. In: Fagerberg, J., Mowery, D., Nelson, R. (Eds.), The Oxford Handbook of Innovation. Oxford University Press, Oxford, pp. 291–317.

Asheim, B.T., et al. 2006. Constructing regional advantage: principles–perspectives–policies. Final report from DG Research Expert Group on "Constructing Regional Advantage." DG Research, European Commission, Brussels.

Asheim, B.T., Boschma, R., Cooke, P., 2011a. Constructing pegional advantage: platform policies based on related variety and differentiated knowledge bases. Regional Studies 45 (7), 893–904.

Asheim, B.T., Oughton, C., Lawton Smith, H., 2011b. Regional innovation systems: theory, empirics and policy. Regional Studies 45 (7), 875–891.

Asheim, B.T., Grillitsch, M., Trippl, M., 2016. Regional innovation systems: past–presence–future. In: Doloreux, D., Shearmur, R., Carrincazeaux, C. (Eds.), Handbook on the Geography of Innovation. Edward Elgar, Cheltenham.

Boschma, R., 2014. Constructing regional advantage and smart specialisation: comparison of two European policy concepts. Ital. J. Reg. Sci. 13 (1), 51–65.

Boschma, R., 2015. Towards an evolutionary perspective on regional resilience. Reg. Stud. 49 (5), 733–751.

Coenen, L., Asheim, B.T., Bugge, M., Herstad, S., 2017. Advancing regional innovation systems: what does evolutionary economic geography bring to the policy table? Environ. Plann. C. 35 (4), 600–620.

Grillitsch, M., 2016. Institutions, smart specialisation dynamics and policy. Environ. Plann. C 34, 22–37.

Grillitsch, M., Asheim, B.T., 2017. Cluster policy: renewal through the integration of institutional variety. In: Hassink, R., Fornahl, D. (Eds.), Cluster Policies From a Cluster Life Cycle Perspective. Edward Elgar, Cheltenham.

Isaksen, A., Nilsson, M., 2013. Combining innovation policy: linking scientific and practical knowledge in innovation systems. Eur. Plann. Stud. 21 (12), 1919–1936.

Lorenz, E., Lundvall, B.-Å. (Eds.), 2006. How Europe's Economies Learn: Coordinating Competing Models. Oxford University Press, Oxford.

Milberg, W., Houston, E., 2005. The high road and low road to international competitiveness: extending the Neo-Schumpeterian trade model beyond technology. Int. Rev. Appl. Econ. 19 (2), 137–162.

Møreforsking, 2014. GCE BLUE Maritime, Klyngeanalysen 2014. Molde/Ålesund.

OECD, 2012. OECD Territorial Reviews: Skane, Sweden. OECD, Paris.

OECD, 2013. OECD Reviews of Innovation Policy: Sweden. OECD, Paris.

Porter, M., 1998. Clusters and the new economics of competition. Harv. Bus. Rev. 76, 77–90.

Region Skåne, 2014. The Open Skåne 2030, Skåne's Regional Development Strategy.

Tödtling, F., Trippl, M., 2005. One size fits all? Towards a differentiated regional innovation policy approach. Res. Policy 34, 1203–1219.

Trippl, M., Miörner, J., Zukauskaite, E., 2015. Smart Specialisation for Regional Innovation – Final Report, Scania, Sweden. CIRCLE, Lund University.

Van der Ven, A., et al., 1999. The Innovation Journey. Oxford University Press, New York, NY.

Zukauskaite, E., Moodysson, J., 2014. Support Organizations in the Regional Innovation System of Skåne. FIRS, Lund.

FURTHER READING

Asheim, B.T., Grillitsch, M., 2015. Smart specialisation: sources for new path development in a peripheral manufacturing region. In: Strand, Ø., Nesset, E., Yndestad, H. (Eds.), Fragmentering Eller Mobilisering? Regional Utvikling I Nordvest. Fjordantologien 2015, Forlag1.

Chapter 5

Smart Specialization Policy in an Economically Well-Developed, Multilevel Governance System

Henning Kroll
Fraunhofer Institute for Systems and Innovation Research ISI, Karlsruhe, Germany

Chapter Outline

Academic Highlights

- Whether smart specialization is considered in practice does not only depend on capacities but, primarily, on political considerations.
- Three main aspects matter for the uptake of smart specialization policies: economic size, multilevel governance framework, and political culture.
- German regions have not fully taken advantage of the new policy agenda as the relation between needed effort and expected benefit was not favorable.

Policy Highlights

- Specificities of governance frameworks and political cultures need to be taken into account before smart specialization policies are locally promoted.

Advances in the Theory and Practice of Smart Specialization. http://dx.doi.org/10.1016/B978-0-12-804137-6.00005-X

- Misconceptions can be overcome through active exchanges between agenda promoters and local policy makers to identify feasible options.
- Smart specialization policies harbor the potential to reorient existing policies in the face of the new challenges confronting Germany's economy.

INTRODUCTION

In general terms, smart specialization has been discussed as a new type of industrial policy that, if applied and implemented successfully, will improve performance and productivity in quite different types of regional economies (Foray, 2014; Foray et al., 2012). Not uncommonly for economics-driven policy (Geels, 2010; Perez, 2013), it builds on the assumption that policy making can be considered a translation of academic insights into economic and societal practice (Laranja et al., 2008). Against this background, the most commonly recognized obstacles to successful implementation are institutional frameworks (Rodríguez-Pose, 2013), administrative capacity (Kroll, 2015a,b; Lodge and Wegrich, 2014; Moore, 1995; Morgan, 1997), as well as the commitment to good governance (Acemoglu and Robinson, 2000; Farole et al., 2011; Rodríguez-Pose et al., 2014).

When considering regions' response to the RIS3 ex-ante conditionality (JRC-IPTS, 2015) in these terms, however, the situation in Germany must appear as a paradox. Undoubtedly, its national institutional framework is robust, both human and professional capacities in regional administrations are substantial, and neither the country, as such, nor its regions, have been found lacking in good governance in international comparisons (Charron et al., 2013). Overall, the country does not encounter many of the more fundamental institutional and governance barriers that have been highlighted as obvious obstacles to strategic industrial policy making in other countries (Kroll, 2015a,b; Rodríguez-Pose, 2013) (Chapters 6, 12, and 14). Still, the political uptake of smart specialization has in most cases been less than enthusiastic, turning Germany into a persistent "white spot" on the current map of RIS3-inspired policies.

Quite evidently, many regions have only engaged, with the concept reluctantly and under external pressure and delivered strategies barely exceeding minimum requirements. Furthermore, some engaged external consultants to write strategies for them or, in a scarcely veiled move, to resubmit existing strategy papers (Kroll et al., 2014). At the same time, there are some regions that have indeed actively engaged in both the policy process and local "processes of entrepreneurial discovery," using the *ex-ante conditionality* as an opportunity to clarify existing strategies, broaden existing processes of consultation, and methodologically develop their intervention logic further (Kroll and Stahlecker, 2014).

To understand this seeming "German paradox," it is important to recognize and acknowledge that policy is a societal system. It is distinct from academia and consulting, as well as from the economic or industrial sectors; moreover, policy is situated in both factual and institutional contexts yet also has an inner dynamic of its own (Edler and James, 2015; Metcalfe, 1994). For many years, this point has been recognized and developed in political science (Cohen et al., 1972; Kingdon, 1984), to be later taken up in innovation system studies that identified policy as an autonomous, active player in the overall coevolution of innovation systems (Flanagan et al., 2011; Kuhlmann and Arnold, 2001; Martin, 2010). Clearly, therefore, the translation of concepts into policy practice (or its absence) cannot be understood comprehensively only in terms of institutions, capacities, and the absence of good governance alone. Rather, it should be understood as also including the partial take up of external inspiration by a separate system following its own internal logics, both political and administrative (Radosevic, 2012).

Against this background, the present chapter will seek to address three main issues, adding rigor and conceptual clarity to recent case study-based findings on the uptake of smart specialization in the German context (Kroll et al., 2016). First, why have so many German regions decided to engage so little? Second, which characteristics were decisive in triggering selected others to become exceptions from the general rule? Third, how has the latter group of regions benefited from efforts related to the smart specialization agenda?

The chapter answers these questions by placing three aspects at the center of the analysis. First, the economic potential of a strategy's reference area that determines both factual options, and, indirectly, the redistributive pressure on regional governments (Boschma et al., 2012; Iacobucci, 2014) (Chapter 12). Second, the governance framework determining the tasks allocated to that government in a multilevel, multiactor setting (Kuhlmann, 2001), the complexity of its internal operations, and the role of EU funding in the administrative process. In short, the question here is whether a regional-level agency with a clear mandate for RIS3-type policies exists (Barca, 2009; Charles et al., 2004; Kroll, 2015a). Third, the general political culture determining the willingness of governments to actively drive entrepreneurial processes of discovery (Amable, 2003; Cernat, 2006; Hall and Soskice, 2001; Mazzucato, 2013) or, more generally, to consider externally proposed policy guidelines as an opportunity rather than a hassle (Chapter 6).

The rest of the chapter is structured as follows. The subsequent section conceptually outlines why these dimensions are decisive in addressing the main issues relevant here. Subsequently, an empirical section describes the German situation in general, and analyzes two positive cases. Finally, the chapter draws some policy conclusions.

CONCEPTUAL BACKGROUND

Clarity and Ambiguity of Smart Specialization

When introduced as a new approach, the smart specialization concept built upon the recognition that Europe, as a whole, lagged behind the United States in terms of productivity, as Member States' industrial policies had failed to transform the economic structure of the Union in a suitable manner. On this general level, Foray et al. (2011), McCann and Ortega-Argilés (2014) and others concluded that the problem lay less with the sectoral composition of the European economies as such (i.e., too few high-tech industries), and rather with the way in which different types of industrial sectors, both high-tech and traditional, operated internally. More precisely, these authors underlined that an entrepreneurial dynamic of recombination and discovery of new domains was lacking in many fields and would, in the future, have to be nurtured by a new type of industrial policy.

With a view to policy implementation, this in principle succinct finding raises two challenges. First, it leaves open how and to what extent the state or public actors can or should engage in processes of discovery that, at least as conceptual desiderata, have been defined as "entrepreneurial." Second, it sticks to a conception of policy as a translator of academic recommendations into practice. In essence, this presupposes that there is one single "translator" able to execute this new industrial policy under its remit.

Had the execution of the concept remained in the realm of industrial policy, that is, the European Commission Directorate-General for Industry and the responsible Member States' authorities, both might have been comparatively easily accommodated. Practically, however, the concept was made a guiding notion in European Regional Policy, thus excluding some relevant national-level actors from implementation, while, at the same time, involving others with different competences and mandates outside of industrial policy *per se* (Foray et al., 2011; Kroll, 2015a). Conceptually, it became intertwined with the notion of "place-based policies" (Barca, 2009), turning what was initially a national-level, productivity-oriented concept for industrial policy into one spanning a much broader range of regional-level objectives, including socioeconomic well-being and, in some polities, even redistribution (Foray et al., 2012; Kroll et al., 2016). On that basis, work on a consistent and shared regionalized concept of smart specialization remains underway (Boschma, 2014; Capello and Kroll, 2016; Foray, 2016) and is far from complete.

At the same time, smart specialization became a politicized and outcome-oriented agenda, as the European Commission had to live up to its self-set target of the ex-ante conditionality (Gianelle et al., 2016; Gianelle and Kleibrink, 2015; Kroll, 2015a). While in Foray's early writings, entrepreneurial discovery processes (EDP) were to be supported as aims in themselves, with constantly shifting and evolving domains at their core (Foray et al., 2009), the European Commission's ex-ante conditionality now called for the clear identification and delineation of investment priorities at the regional level, as guidance for the coming support period (European Commission, 2013). As these periods last more than 7 years, this approach appears to resemble—or at least to move towards—the type of strategic planning that smart specialization should, in principle, seek to avoid (Boschma, 2014).

In brief, the role of smart specialization in Europe's multilevel, multiactor governance system has become simultaneously more limited and more diverse. More limited, as the task was now clearly assigned to those political authorities responsible for European Structural and Investment Funds (ESIF); more diverse, as the mandate, agenda, and capacities of these ESIF management authorities could hardly differ more strongly among the different Member States.

Against this background, three main dimensions must form part of a conceptual framework seeking to explain the likelihood of an active uptake of smart specialization policies in specific regions.

Variation in the Economic Potential of Regions or Nations

Differences with a view to economic capacities in a strategy's reference area (be it regional or national) are important as they determine the respective government's overall options and justifiable political room for maneuver (Chapters 6 and 12).

One aspect of this is the question to what extent regions should actually specialize, that is, focus their investment on a limited number of fields. As meaningful specialized investment presupposes critical mass, economically larger regions can and should sustain more fields of specialization than smaller ones (Boschma and Iammarino, 2009; Cooke, 2016, 2012). In consequence, smaller regions have to make more rigorous choices if they want to achieve global excellence in something, while larger regions can seek to actively build regionalized systems of "related variety" (Frenken et al., 2007). While larger regions can thus support complementary, potentially networkable and mutually reinforcing domains, smaller regions will have to seek this variety in global value chains, not through complex local specialization. Moreover, larger polities have more stakeholders who lobby against the loss of established claims which, in the short-run, may be relevant and legitimate, for example, with a view to employment (Boschma, 2014; Iacobucci, 2014). Hence, taking "tough," future-oriented decisions, as the RIS3 guide commands (Foray et al., 2012), can be quite complex in larger regions and may not simply be the "common sense" choices (Foray et al., 2012).

A second aspect is the issue to what extent entrepreneurial processes of discovery are already prevalent among the region's industrial players. If that is the case, policy makers and public actors have a lesser—or at least a different—role to play in triggering and sustaining them (Kroll and Stahlecker, 2014). All being well, there will naturally be a lesser role for an entrepreneurial state (Landabaso, 2014). Moreover, if local firms excel at launching their own, successful EDPs, a much stronger case can be made for seedbed-type horizontal policies to support emerging niches (Markard and Truffer, 2008) and it will be much harder to argue that a prescient state is needed to tell the industrial sector in which direction to go (Kroll, 2015a). Legitimately, moreover, the regional electorate will neither expect, nor necessarily support, political interference, with what is broadly considered a functional system (Kroll et al., 2014; Kroll and Stahlecker, 2014), in particular if such intervention were to come with additional, still to be financed, public expenses.

Where the local industrial system has been unable to generate such processes through horizontal funding (Oughton et al., 2002), the argument of Foray et al. (2009), Coffano and Foray (2014), Landabaso (2012, 2014) and others becomes more compelling. Where local firms do not produce visions and systemic activities (Landabaso, 1997), local research organizations, associations, clusters, or even the state itself may be needed to set relevant impulses around which business creates new pathways of development (Foray et al., 2012). At the same time, the regional electorate will be more open to see public investment happen and this type of region will be more likely to cofinance most related expenses from substantive European allocations (Kroll, 2015a).

Variation in the Regional Governance Set-Up and Multilevel Context

Differences with respect to a region's governance set-up and multilevel governance context are important as they determine its government's capability for administrative action.

A first aspect of interest is multilevel governance (Hooghe and Marks, 2001; Kuhlmann, 2001). As research has shown, different policy actors may play similar roles in varying contexts and vice versa (Aghion et al., 2009; Flanagan et al., 2011). In more concrete terms, many European regions, including the German Länder, are not responsible for industrial policy on their own; in more positive terms, they can take a strategic national industrial policy for granted. If support for new entrepreneurial discovery and emerging domains is already provided for, in part through elaborate systems and through substantial financial volume at the national level (BMBF, 2014), different questions arise regarding the best policy mix and philosophy for the use of European funding at the regional level.

A second dimension concerns the structural complexity of, and the information failures in, the regional administration. A common fallacy is to assume that "governments" are somehow single actors, capable of and interested in targeted action, as long as basic conditions of good institutions, sufficient capacity, and good intentions are fulfilled (Geels, 2010; Laranja et al., 2008). In reality, however, many regional governments are complex structures in which capacities are fragmented across different remits, agendas abound, interagency communication is limited and policy makers interpret existing rules in different ways (Lawson, 2003). Hence, the coordinative capacity of "the government" is limited and fragmented (Kroll, 2015a) internally as well as externally, with respect to its capacity to change structures in the "real economy" (Landabaso, 2012).

A final aspect is related to the budgetary role of ESIF, the policy area to which "smart specialization" applies. Unless policy makers mentally extend the concept of smart specialization to further areas of science, innovation, and industrial policy under their remit (which so far is not common), regional administrators will determine the intensity of their response to RIS3-related requirements based on the budgetary relevance of the policy area in question (Niskanen, 1994). In economically more developed regions, however, the role of ESIF allocations in regional innovation policy is very limited and, consequently, so is the interest of regional administrations to adopt their political framework and/or strategies (Kroll et al., 2014).

Variation in the Political Culture of Relevant Regional-Level Polities

Differences with a view to a region's political culture are important as they determine their governments' inclination to allow stakeholder participation as well as to actively explore and pursue economically given opportunities under conditions of uncertainty (Arnstein, 1969; Hausman and Rodrik, 2003; Wanna and Forster, 1996).

One aspect of interest is government's prior experience with participation-based strategy processes as a tool to guide policy intervention (Arnstein, 1969; Bohle and Greskovits, 2012) (Chapter 12). Quite obviously, such a culture was less than perfectly developed in many peripheral regions during the last support period (2007–13) (Chapter 6) and even in well-developed economies (Kroll and Stahlecker, 2014) (Chapter 4). While at the national and European level, discussions about participatory, challenge-driven innovation policy have emerged, been debated in the academic sphere (Daimer et al., 2012; Lindner et al., 2015) and been translated into manifold national strategy documents (e.g., BMBF, 2014), much less has happened regionally. On the other hand, some regions pursued elaborate participatory exercises long before the RIS3 effort (Kroll and Stahlecker, 2014).

A second aspect is particular regional governments' general tendency to subscribe to proactive policy rationales or to consider themselves as experimental policy makers in the sense of an entrepreneurial public sector (Kingdon, 1984; Landabaso, 2014; Mazzucato, 2013). In reality, many governments in successful regions are caught between a conviction that "hands-off," market-oriented policies will be the best possible way to support well-running regional economies and inherent risk aversion prompted by their being subject to regular reviews by courts of auditors and financial ministries with a less than Schumpeterian understanding of proofs of efficacy (Chapter 12).

A final relevant aspect is governments' inclination to respond positively to external requirements or suggestions from higher political levels. In federal systems, with somewhat unclear principal-agent structures, this tendency is often not very pronounced, since regional governments define themselves through their independence and ability to take strategic choices as and when they see fit. As Schmidt (2004) argued for the national level, polities used to being at the nexus of power and coordination tend to respond neither enthusiastically, nor always adequately to external interventions. Hence, new policy concepts "prescribed from above" may, even in those regions, be regarded with skepticism. This can happen despite the fact that such polities had in the past pursued, under different names and designations, policies very similar to what we call "smart specialization" today (Kroll and Stahlecker, 2014).

A GUIDING FRAMEWORK FOR ANALYSIS

In the following, we seek to establish an empirical basis for assessing why so many regions have not engaged in the RIS3 process (e.g., JRC-IPTS, 2015) while, at the same time, pointing out why exceptions occurred.

As outlined earlier, the case studies will make reference to the following key dimensions:

- economic potential, size of and entrepreneurial dynamics in relevant economy;
- governance framework, sharing of tasks, complexity, and role of EU funding;
- and political culture, overall experience, entrepreneurialism and decisions.

Regarding the positive exceptions, we additionally try to establish how these regions have profited from the RIS3 process—even though, for them as well as for other regions, the RIS3 agenda was not novel.

To that end, the case studies will explore the following three dimensions of change:

- changes with respect to the actual EDP in the region;
- change in the governance system;
- and changes in political culture.

In the following, this chapter will address these aspects making concrete reference as far as possible to both the majority of nonengaging Länder as well as, separately, to two specific cases that may arguably have benefited in different ways. Insights are based on document analysis and interviews with various stakeholders which were mostly identified in the studies quoted. The interpretation of these interviews rests entirely with the author.

A SEEMING GERMAN PARADOX—BACKGROUND

Evidently, the main issues addressed by the smart specialization concept (lack of productivity and lack of industrial performance) were less pressing in Germany than in parts of Southern and Eastern Europe (Reid et al., 2012) (Chapter 6).

Many regions in the latter Member States struggled with even the first step of building a basic institutional framework for consultation processes, which in more than one case ran counter to long-established (and still cherished) traditions of centralized governance (Chapter 12) (Kroll, 2015a). In Germany's federal system, in contrast, processes of stakeholder consultation and decentralized strategic governance are common. By and large, all responsible authorities command sufficient technical capacity to pursue both efforts professionally (Kroll and Stahlecker, 2014).

Moreover, many of Germany's Länder had pursued strategy-driven regional innovation policies for more than a decade, so that policy makers at all the levels had inevitably become acquainted with the concept to some extent. While interregional competition between German Länder may have caused some duplication, it has certainly also created a general openness towards investment into specific regional areas of strength (Kulicke and Kroll, 2006). Additionally, active industrial and technology policies have been pursued by various Western German regions for decades, not least prompted by the aim to overcome structural challenges and sector-specific crises (Kroll and Meyborg, 2014). Since reunification, similar traditions of regional capacity building through targeted governance have been more or less successfully taken up in Eastern Germany (Kroll, 2012; Zenker and Kroll, 2014).

Finally, there is a substantial track record of regional innovation strategies that predates the RIS3 agenda by close to a decade. In 2006, 7 out of 16 Länder had published innovation strategies, while only two had explicitly abstained from doing so. In other Länder, partial strategies had been developed and/or strategically-oriented policies remained implicitly based on earlier strategies from the 1990s. While not necessarily well-documented, these partial and/or historic outlines ascertained a continuous and stable orientation of regional science, innovation, and economic policy (Kulicke and Kroll, 2006).

Expectedly, therefore, many Land governments' first reaction to the announcement of the RIS3 ex-ante conditionality was skepticism (Kroll et al., 2016). In particular, those that did not receive high allocations from the ESIF budget did not perceive any need to change proven policies significantly. While many did not necessarily oppose the agenda's objectives as such, they would, at the same time, argue that Germany was more or less meeting these criteria already. In particular, the detailed RIS3 guidelines were greeted with reservation, as many did not see how following standardized prescriptions "by the book" could improve their activities. Contrary to the concept's original intention, some started to fear that RIS3 might lead to an undue formalization and harmonization of existing approaches (Kroll et al., 2014).

Acknowledging these preoccupations, the European Commission reacted with a broad-based communication effort, in which German regions, among others, were invited to act as best practice examples. The Director General at that time made clear that *"many German regions already possess many of the capacities needed"* and should simply *"uphold, update, and further develop existing processes"* (Deffaa, 2012). While many regions' policy makers continued to lament the approaches' *"unduly academic nature"* (Kroll et al., 2014), the overall opinion regarding the RIS3 agenda began to gradually improve (Kroll and Stahlecker, 2014). For a moment, it therefore seemed that German regions, like those of other countries, would gradually join the process. Two years later, however, we have to conclude that the refusal of many regions to do so has remained robust. Apart from submitting minimum standard strategy documents, their active engagement with the overall process has remained negligible.

CASE STUDIES

Skeptical Regions (Standard Cases)

Background Situation

In Germany, in particular Western Germany, critical mass and preexisting entrepreneurial dynamics are not usually inhibiting factors. Nonetheless, certain differences can obviously be observed. While most regions' economic potential is substantial and diverse enough to justify claims for related variety, few of them display more than three to four major areas of international excellence. In most of these, EDPs are actively pursued by companies large and small, not uncommonly involving a vivid system of intermediaries and public research agencies.

Concerning governance, all German Länder are part of a complex federal-regional sharing of tasks that is defined by the constitution and has been established for decades. In the field of innovation and technology policy, a major share of the budget to support areas of international strength under an overarching strategy (BMBF, 2014) rests with the federal government. According to these national investment priorities, many lead projects that result from successful processes of entrepreneurial discovery in Germany's regions could be financed without major regional contributions. For example, "Leading-edge Clusters" support market-oriented projects with up to EUR8 million annually for up to 5 years (BMBF, 2015), while the federal government's new "Research Campus" support line funds strategic, precompetitive research consortia with up to EUR2 million annually for up to 15 years. In that way, the German federal government acts as an important scene-setter for regional level policy which has, against this background, often resorted to horizontal approaches for the broader industrial basis rather than a few lighthouse consortia. Second, the governance structures in German Länder are complex.

Responsibilities are usually distributed across at least three authorities (Ministry of the economy, Ministry of science, and the state chancellery). Each of these bodies can have more than 100 employees in several departments and, naturally, a diverse set of particular interests. In these set-ups, effective coordination commonly constitutes a substantial challenge. Finally, ESIF funding does not usually play a substantial role in regional science and innovation policy in German regions. While it can often be a relevant source of funding for a particular set of business support measures, the German constitution also gives all Länder complete authority over higher education—involving much more substantial, although in part less flexible budgets. In absolute terms, moreover, European funding is fairly limited. In five Western Länder, European Regional

Development Fund (ERDF) allocations remain below EUR50 per inhabitant—compared to typically around EUR1,000 in Poland or Portugal. Northern Länder and the Saarland receive between EUR100 and EUR200. Even in Eastern Germany, allocations rarely exceed EUR500 per inhabitant (Eurostat, 2016; Inforegio, 2016). Commonly, therefore, European Regional Policy neither wins elections, nor inspires administrations.

As for political culture, German Länders' experiences of participation-based strategies is mixed. In general terms, of course, Germany is a long-established democracy and compound polity (Chapter 12) with a long track record of participative approaches in many policy fields. On the other hand, this has not necessarily always been most prominently the case in research and technology policy. Furthermore, consultations with regional experts and stakeholders have in many cases been informal and of an ad-hoc, business-club nature, typically engaging with the "usual suspects" rather than following a sustained formalized approach in line with the concept of a truly engaged public sector, as envisaged in the RIS3 guidelines. In addition, the tendency to proactively engage in regional technology policy is mixed. Some regions, like Bavaria and North Rhine-Westphalia (NRW), tend to follow a proactive approach, whereas a majority of the rest, such as Hessen or Baden-Württemberg, strongly lean towards hand-off policies. Finally, Germany is characterized by a long tradition of decentralized governance and strong regional identity (with the obvious exception of the early 20th century). Up to today, therefore, German Länder prefer to see themselves as autonomous polities that do not have to directly follow any third party's instructions or prescriptions—and do not much appreciate to be confronted with external ex-ante conditionalities.

Potential Impact

Given all these criteria, the potential economic impact of RIS3 strategy processes remains nonobvious in most cases. In strong regions, like Bavaria or Baden-Württemberg, there is, factually, a limited need to pursue the type of concentrated specialization that the European Commission has tended to recommend. Concerning their potential contributions to a European division of tasks (Foray, 2009), many German Länder can sustain a notable number of regional "specializations." Moreover, EDPs are functioning well within most of Germany's regional economies, so that no direct political intervention is needed to initiate them. Finally, it is clear that, with the limited amount of funding available, no substantial incentives could be provided to that end. Certainly, however, there is differentiation. Some Eastern Länder are indeed struggling to find a suitable balance between specialization and diversification, between modern technologies and traditional industries, for example, in the wake of the collapse of the solar industry. So far, few specific regional discourses have been developed to address these issues. From a factual perspective, therefore, RIS3 processes are less than relevant in some regions—and have not been pursued, while for others they offer obvious opportunity—and have been pursued.

As for governance, all Länder are part of the same multilevel governance system, yet profit from it to different degrees. Leading Länder like Bavaria or Baden-Württemberg, which already attract a lot of national-level excellence funding (which they can then top up) naturally have to worry less about designing their stand-alone, proactive industrial policies. Others—due to lack of local capacity— have less access to national funds and so have to prepare their own ground. Arguably, many regions have not directly engaged with localized strategy building, as they consider excellent lighthouse projects as their part in a larger national endeavor, more than a regional decision alone. Instead, many regional governments see their main role as that of providing a seedbed through broad-based support for all regional companies, that is, also for those that have no access to national funding and/or are active outside the current focal areas of interest.

In what concerns the question of structural complexity, the division of tasks within many regional administrations is deep-rooted and often cherished. The larger the administration, the more complex the problem becomes. Quite often, RIS3 processes were developed within single units, and by that very fact stood from the outset little chance of affecting the momentum of a much larger administration, even if formally passed at cabinet level. In administrations that chose a legalistic approach, for example, by outsourcing ex-ante compliance to consultants, little difference was made. In those which established a broad-based coordination process or in which the remit for RIS3 was less fragmented from the outset, one of the results was often a temporary improvement in communication. Finally, the degree of coordinative effort also depends on the budget involved. Evidently, no large regional administration will embark on a substantial restructuring of internal processes for a budget of EUR 10–25 million per year. When dealing with larger budgets, the interest of regional authorities was typically stronger, more broad-based, and the resulting coordinative efforts turned out to be both more pronounced and more lasting.

With respect to political culture, one has to—in the majority of cases—think of changes that occurred in pockets and niches rather than prevalently. Irrespective of the exact aspect in question (be it participation or new concepts of priority areas), much depended on the specific administrators tasked with the RIS3 process. Typically, some degree of interest and active engagement developed at the level of project officers and was, to a certain extent, shared in higher echelons of the administration. Thus, efforts to conceptually improve or simply change approaches to policy making and implementation, which would at other times not have been granted resources, gained further legitimacy and achieved some results with respect to program design. On the downside, less open administrations decided to outsource the process to consultants wholly or in part, thus foregoing the opportunity to trigger new considerations in-house. In some cases, the initially adverse reception of the ex-ante conditionality persisted until today, preventing all meaningful change. In others, limited engagement with the RIS3 agenda spurred reflection on some relevant issues only, without really changing the overall culture.

In a nutshell, many German regions did not engage with RIS3 because (1) *economically*, there was factually no need for action; (2) *administratively*, the means required were not justified in the light of the potential benefit; and (3) *politically*, they were simply not interested. Those that deviated from these three baseline conditions became typically more actively engaged, as illustrated with two specific examples below.

North Rhine-Westphalia

Among Germany's federal states, NRW in the north-west of the country is particular in subsuming some of the country's most prosperous and most deprived areas, both urban and rural, under the roof of one government. With its close to 18 million population, the federal state is larger than many EU Member States. It displays substantial economic diversity in many fields, ranging from its legacy as Germany's former centre of coal and heavy industry to modern high-tech corporations of international renown (Kroll and Meyborg, 2014). Evidently, it can make multiple contributions to a European division of tasks (2009), so that a narrowing down of policy support in specific fields is, from that perspective, not really needed. Furthermore, the region undoubtedly possesses sufficient critical mass in different fields to sustain a system of "related variety" at the regional level. Processes of entrepreneurial discovery are fairly dynamic in some industries yet remain lagging in others. In some of NRW's declining sub-regions, EDPs are characterized by persistent lock-ins. To a certain extent, this can be attributed to an insufficient transformation of mindsets in regions that are still characterized by traditional industries (Kroll and Meyborg, 2014).

With respect to governance, key players in the region profit to a notable extent from an integration into the national-level framework of innovation policy. However, the region is not necessarily dependent on these investments in conducting a successful innovation policy, as it also has its own means for strategic investments given the overall robust nature of the regional economy (Kroll and Meyborg, 2014). Moreover, the region has had to develop different types of regionally specific policies through the years, as the transformation-related challenges it was facing could typically not be well addressed through nation-wide policies alone.

Due to the region's large size in terms of geography, economy, and population, the resulting administrative challenges are complex and the region has developed over time one of the largest administrations in Germany. In terms of staff and budget spent for administrative efforts, it would arguably be sufficient to govern a small Member State (Kroll and Meyborg, 2014). Consequently, the state is characterized by a corresponding level of complexity and internal diversity of agendas between different ministries, which leads to substantial challenges with regard to interagency coordination and communication. Before reunification, NRW was Germany's key recipient of European Structural Funding, due to the substantial transformation-related challenges it was facing. Over the years, it has developed substantial administrative capacity in dealing with this type of support policy and in integrating it into its own regional support effort (Kroll and Meyborg, 2014). The amount of available ERDF funding per inhabitant (EUR 68) is rather low in both national and international comparative terms. However, the absolute budget of more than EUR 1.2 billion (Inforegio, 2016) remains sizeable—large enough to attract substantial administrative interest.

In terms of participative culture, NRW comes close to a model. During the decline of its old industries in the 1980s and 1990s, its social democratic governments established inclusive processes of debate as well as decision making that have left an imprint on the region's political culture to this day. Dealing with regional challenges in a way that involves economic as well as social partners, both incumbents and newcomers, is a deeply rooted feature of local economic culture. It represents the positive counterpart to the earlier mentioned lock-ins that still exist in some areas. Likewise, public entrepreneurialism, in terms of supporting new industrial domains when old ones fall into decline, remains an issue that NRW has been dealing with since the 1970s and that is in no way alien to the local political culture (Kroll and Stahlecker, 2014). Having turned from an economic powerhouse to a recipient of compensation funds on both national and European levels, the regional government tends to be more open to engage in external discussions about policy options than the average German region. At the same time, the "state-like" character of the regional administration comes not only with notable self-confidence, but also with trust in their own, proven policy approaches. Like other German regions, it may thus be open to persuasion but its inclination to respond to external pressure is below average.

In the course of the RIS3 process, NRW took up and modified its own strategy process, one that had already been initiated some time before the agreement on the ex-ante conditionality. For implementation, it could draw on a well-established system of regional cluster policy that had been developed under earlier support periods (Koschatzky et al., 2017). Hence, local ownership of the strategy process as well as of the potential tools for implementation was high from the beginning. More problematic was the fact that, within the large regional administration, ministries tend to clearly delineate their remit. Moreover, the ministry responsible for RIS3, although dealing with innovation, was not the same as the one responsible for the administration of structural funds. Consequently, intensive processes of consultation had to be launched so that the ministries could align their respective strategies with each other, not necessarily integrating the support effort, but forming a more cohesive approach. In the end, a solution was found by integrating three regional strategies into one overall document: the "research strategy," the "lead-market strategy," and the "technology transfer strategy." This unified strategy, due to prior consultations, was free of contradictions (Kroll and Stahlecker, 2014). Moreover, the process for the "lead-market strategy" was the last to start and could be completed conceptually in light of the smart specialization agenda and thus acknowledge the RIS3 guidelines. In the coming years, the nature of (financially sizeable) competitive calls to support activities spurred by existing clusters will be adapted according to the RIS3 provisions (Kroll and Meyborg, 2014). With this instrument, NRW has a powerful tool at hand to make a difference to regional processes of entrepreneurial discovery, not only by injecting funding, "with a RIS3 mindset," but also by triggering activities among existing entrepreneurially-minded consortia and clusters.

In summary, the effect on the EDPs will likely be notable, as the new lead market domains will affect the orientation of existing, well-functioning policies. At the same time, they will contribute to a rejuvenation that NRW's participative culture, in which traditional players are still strong, regularly needs. Arguably, the integration with this direct translation mechanism is the most positive effect of NRW's RIS3 effort (Koschatzky et al., 2017). At the governance level, some progress has been made because the ex-ante conditionality has prompted coordinative efforts across directorates and ministries that would otherwise not have occurred (Kroll and Meyborg, 2014). This ensured the formal coherence of the overall economic strategy of the regional government. Nonetheless, the rather piecemeal nature of the final document, which still visibly consists of three strategies, cannot be denied.

Finally, not much could be changed in terms of political culture. On the upside, a lot was already well-established; on the downside, the process was too short to break path-dependencies in mindsets, even within the ESIF managing authorities (Kroll and Meyborg, 2014). Nonetheless, the government's conceptual openness prompted the adoption of a "lead-market approach" that, in line with smart specialization, turns away from a myopic technology-push perspective towards one that considers the potential and perspective economic utility of technology deployment in different sectors (Kroll and Stahlecker, 2014).

Saxony

Unlike NRW, the Free State of Saxony only joined the Federal Republic in 1990. From the time of its political (re-)constitution in the current form, it has been the focus of very successful policy efforts to enable economic transformation. Following the downfall of the planned economy in the German Democratic Republic, critical mass in competitive industrial structures as well as their ability to entrepreneurially identify new business opportunities were lost in all prior areas of excellence, with the notable exception of a still highly qualified human capital base. In the following two decades, continuous government policy supported the establishment of new foci of excellence, e.g. in information technology, while at the same time actively promoting the reuptake of prior strengths, for example, in machine-building (Kroll, 2012). Throughout this period, a concentration of large-scale efforts on certain key areas has been characteristic of regional industrial policy, without ever denying the utility and need for horizontal policies in the field of low-volume grants that help to structurally transform the outdated SME sector. Twenty years later, Saxony displays critical mass in some areas of global relevance but, being much smaller than

NRW with only 4 million inhabitants, it also has a far more limited number of such areas. Likewise, the ability to entrepreneurially identify new business opportunities (EDPs) has been restored in many fields, making the region Eastern Germany's prime example of robust economic transformation (Kroll, 2012). For parts of its still fragmented and traditional SME sector, however, the picture is less than clear. Arguably, the greatest need for new external triggers to entrepreneurial discovery may therefore lie outside the region's already thriving fields of excellence.

In governance, Saxony has substantially profited from national-level investment in its transformation effort, be it in the set-up of public research institutions or, later, for the support of leading-edge clusters around them and the region's top universities (Kroll, 2012). In short, the region's potential contributions to a European division of tasks (Foray, 2009) were, to no small extent, already built based on national sources. Often, the regional government prepared and negotiated such lead investments politically and complemented them with its own funds. In its use of European Structural Funding, however, it focused primarily on supporting those midrange firms that could not be put on the radar of the federal government (Kroll, 2012).

Organizational complexity in the regional administration is, to the contrary, rather limited. Following reunification, the complete regional administration was set up a new meaning that it is organizationally still relatively new and free of the remnants and inconsistencies that older administrations typically display. In addition, it is overall far smaller than its counterpart in NRW, in line with the size of the region. Overall, most RIS3 relevant responsibilities are subsumed under the remit of two directorates within one ministry, and this ministry's coordination with other local agencies works comparatively well (Kroll et al., 2016). In general, the Saxon regional administration is one of the most efficient and professional within the nation. European funding and national-level cross-subsidies, finally, have been constitutive for regional innovation policy throughout the process of economic reconstruction (Kroll, 2012). Hardly any regional-level innovation policy has ever been launched without a decisive contribution from European funding, and the level of European investment per inhabitant is, at more than EUR500 per capita, comparatively high. Hence, the effective administration and deployment of the region's more than EUR2 billion ERDF funds is a key issue within the regional administration up to cabinet level (Inforegio, 2016).

Concerning political culture, Saxony has a well-developed participative culture, yet of a rather different nature to that in NRW. In past decades, its governments were exclusively conservative and strived for a process of technology-driven capacity building rather than one of accommodation of the social impact of economic change following the downfall of traditional industries, as in NRW. Arguably, moreover, the participatory efforts in recent years could have been more coordinated and extended to a broader base of stakeholders. Evidence to this effect is provided by the absence of a formal regional innovation strategy between 1992 and 2013 (Kroll, 2012). With a view to their inclination to actively engineer economic transformation through priority setting, Saxon policy makers would likely argue that their task was one of adding momentum to entrepreneurial undertakings with proven promise, rather than one of transforming an existing economy. A general conservative conviction to let the market determine the orientation of low- to mid-scale projects went along with a decisive commitment to courageously invest quite notable amounts of public money in well-selected large-scale projects. Thus, the political culture was characterized by a balanced double strategy (Kroll, 2012). Against this backdrop, most notable is the conceptual openness of several high-level decision makers in the responsible authorities once it became obvious that the former level of national and European subsidies would not be sustainable during the 2014–2020 support period. In an effort called the "regional ERDF strategy," a broad-based consultation was initiated—once more before the ex-ante conditionality was imposed externally. Regional policy makers attended several peer review meetings with the European Commission, actively discussed and sought to become a RIS3 best practice case in both strategy design and monitoring. This led to a broad-based, well-organized consultation process among multiple stakeholders (Kroll et al., 2016).

As a result, Saxony has arguably developed one of the best strategy documents within the German context, making direct reference to notions, such as cross-innovation and linking investment in technologies to their likely economic effects in certain sectors, as well as the main socioeconomic challenges that they may help address (SMWA, 2013). In implementation, however, the picture is somewhat less clear: the bulk of funding will, in the coming support period, continue to be allocated through horizontal measures. Consequently, much will depend on the discretionary decisions of evaluators and project officers in the local support bank. Legally, the commitment of future funding to the various "cross-innovation" domains identified in the strategy remains rather weak and flexible (SMWA, 2015).

Consequently, the direct impact of local RIS3 efforts on the processes of entrepreneurial discovery will likely be less substantial than in NRW as established instruments of implementation, like NRW's cluster policy, remain absent (Koschatzky et al., 2017). Nonetheless, it could have some effects on the deployment of existing, horizontal support instruments, even if those are more likely to materialize in weaker areas of the regional economy rather than in strongholds of European relevance. On the other hand, the strategic effort of drafting a regional innovation strategy was certainly useful to legitimize the regional government's recent major investments in key areas of competence, for example, EUR200 million in the ICT field.[1] As in prior decades, the rationale to undertake them, which consists of smart specialization-type considerations, now has a clear point of reference in the formal regional innovation strategy (SMWA, 2013). Apparently, therefore, Saxony stays committed to its proven double strategy of targeted public investment and horizontal policies.

With respect to the regional governance system, the strategy process certainly set a positive impulse, as it did in many other contexts. However, as most structures were already fairly effective and used to a strategic, evidence-based approach, little substantial improvement occurred. Instead, prior experiences from the Saxon case may have, in the context of the RIS3 peer review activities, inspired policy making elsewhere. The region's political culture, finally, has been more positively affected than in the case of NRW. Indeed, prior policy making had been characterized by a strong evidence-based approach, based on the commissioning of regular reports on several aspects of the regional economy (unique for the country in scale), on an above average number of program-level evaluations, and on large-scale, transparent monitoring (Kroll, 2012). However, it was also characterized by informality and ad-hoc decisions; without an external impulse, the planned "ERDF strategy" process might have been insufficient to break with that habit in a substantial manner (Kroll et al., 2016). Furthermore, the active engagement in the RIS3 process in cooperation with the European Commission mobilized extra funds that allowed some administrative units to commit time and effort to conceptual considerations and to the development of a well-elaborated regional innovation strategy. Arguably, this is the most distinctive benefit of the RIS3 process in the Saxon case.

To conclude, it is notable that while NRW is a more or less unique case, other positive examples displaying characteristics similar to that of Saxony can be found in Eastern Germany, for example, Saxony-Anhalt and Thuringia (Kroll and Stahlecker, 2014). In general, these Länder, just like Saxony, have made significant advances in conceptually defining investment priorities as interfaces of sectors and technologies, just as the smart specialization approach requires. Arguably, moreover, they have partly realized more lasting adaptations in the field of consultation and governance.

SUMMARY AND DISCUSSION

Overall, this chapter finds that the seeming "German paradox" regarding smart specialization policy is, compared to other economies (Chapter 6), due to the following factors: first, a less urgent need for immediate transformative change; second, transaction costs resulting from the constant task of reconciling interests in large and complex administrations (Chapter 12); and, finally, a certain lack of openness to engage with external recommendations from third parties (Chapter 14). Moreover, German regions, just as several Nordic ones (Chapter 4), may have a propensity to accept path extension as a suitable model.

Consequently, exceptions from the rule of limited and reluctant engagement are typically found where the situation deviates with respect to one or more of the earlier mentioned dimensions. Despite the overall positive situation in the national economy, most Eastern as well as several Western Länder continue to face a more urgent need for transformative change; in addition, given their limited size, they could indeed benefit from an improved interregional division of tasks as outlined by Foray (2009). Likewise, not all regional administrations are in the described sense over-complex. For other regions, European funding is sufficiently important to trigger coordination efforts despite notable obstacles. Finally, not all German regional policy makers are equally hesitant to take on board recommendations from third parties, in particular when they themselves have identified a persistent need for economic change in their region. Table 5.1 summarizes this situation for both "standard" regions showing comparatively little interest, and for our two case studies, which have become more proactively engaged.

With a view to the resulting impact, this chapter finds that, even in more fertile environments, the most obvious changes remain in the area of local governance and political culture, a finding also identified under different circumstances in other chapters in this book (Chapters 4 and 6). As in those cases, however, it remains unknown to what extent path-dependencies can be broken (Chapter 12) or whether they will remain temporary (Chapters 6 and 14). For the moment, however, several new and robust coordination for a have been established and administrators interested in conceptual considerations have been enabled to contribute to midterm visions for regional policy. The latter might otherwise have been neither as clearly consolidated, nor brought to the attention of high-level decision makers at cabinet level. If and when actual processes of entrepreneurial discovery will be affected remains for now an open question, a point also noted in other chapters of this book. However, the RIS3 process starts off from a much better basis than elsewhere (Chapter 12) (Kroll, 2015a, b).

As for implementation, hopes rest with existing cluster organizations and policies, which, unlike in some Nordic countries (Chapter 4), appear well-positioned as interlocutors between technological innovation and industrial development. Together with the numerous steering and working groups set up to accompany RIS3 strategy building, there seems to be a reasonable basis for path development. Overall, it appears more likely that RIS3 based policies can sustainably address relevant tasks in some German regions—in contrast to countries in crisis where such tasks may be simply too daunting (Chapter 6).

Even if, for now, the impact of the RIS3 process has mostly remained centered on governance and policy culture, one can hope that some aspect of these transformations will be lasting. Whether subsequently we will see actual impacts at the level of regional economies will become clearer over the coming decade.

POLICY CONCLUSIONS

In conclusion, this chapter strongly cautions not to impose smart specialization policies without being sensitive to the national or regional context, or even lecture on these policies in an overly generalist manner. In principle, smart specialization is a general paradigm that comes with important, albeit generic,

TABLE 5.1 Starting Conditions for and Impact of Smart Specialization Policy in German Regions

	"Usual cases"	North Rhine-Westphalia	Saxony
Starting conditions			
Economic potential			
Critical mass	Often strong enough	Given in many fields (broad industrial base)	Given in some fields (focused industrial base)
Business-based EDP	Often present	Partially present (lock-in issues)	Present in key sectors (yet not beyond)
Governance			
Multilevel context	National funding dominant	National funding relevant	National funding relevant
Organizational complexity	Rather high (with exceptions)	Very high	Comparatively limited
Role of EU funding	Limited, often not decisive for regional policy mix	Relevant, but also substantial regional efforts	Decisive, key basis of regional innovation policy
Political culture			
Participative culture	Midrange	Strong	Midrange
Public entrepreneurialism	Low	Strong	Midrange
Conceptual openness	Limited	Midrange	High
Changes/impact			
Dynamics of EDP in the region (however triggered)	Limited/negligible	Notable	Relevant
Regional governance system (effectiveness/coherence)	Limited/negligible	Relevant	Some
Political culture (entrepreneurialism)	In pockets only (experimental actions)	Some	Notable

recommendations that must be interpreted in a specific framework of application, by those understanding this context. European-level policy should enable this sensitivity, in particular by better taking into account local histories and administrative contingencies. Furthermore, the chapter shows that the take-up of any similarly inspired policy, that is, one focused on enabling bottom-up processes of discovery, depends on local ownership. As the administrative implementation of this new spirit encounters obstacles even in polities with substantial capacities, policy makers have to be convinced of the benefit that such action harbors for them.

Therefore, after the initial "stick" of the ex-ante conditionality, which was certainly a needed approach, European policy makers should now expressly move to a more "carrot"-oriented approach in communication and practice, triggering the voluntary take-up of locally owned strategies. As the German cases illustrate, off-the-shelf smart specialization policies face a real danger of repeating the Washington Consensus-type fallacies of external advisers seeking to impose recommendations without sufficiently taking into an account local history and complexity and without communicating their core notions adequately. Any smart specialization policy thus pursued is bound to alienate those meant to eventually own it—and hence bound to fail. Consequently, future efforts to drive the actual implementation of smart specialization inspired policies should be based on regular exchanges between policy makers, experts and, not least, entrepreneurs and businesspeople where all parties can contribute their specific knowledge. With the European Commission's RIS3 platform and regular workshops, an important step has been taken in this direction.

Perhaps more importantly, the German case also illustrates that initial misconceptions can be constructively overcome through active engagement on both sides and a mutual willingness to reconcile the conceptual with the feasible. As a reasonable policy paradigm, the smart specialization concept harbors the potential to rejuvenate and reorient existing policy practice in the face of the new, global challenges confronting Germany's currently successful economy as much as other countries. If well-communicated, it can provide grounds for a more effective, stakeholder-driven approach to innovation policy.

ENDNOTE

1. https://www.bmbf.de/de/deutschland-staerkt-mikroelektronikforschung-605.html

REFERENCES

Acemoglu, D., Robinson, J.A., 2000. Political losers as a barrier to economic development. Am. Econ. Rev. 90 (2), 126–130.

Aghion, P., David, P.A., Foray, D., 2009. 'Science, technology and innovation for economic growth: linking policy research and practice in "STIG Systems". Res. Policy 38, 681–693.

Amable, B., 2003. The diversity of modern capitalism. Oxford University Press, Oxford.

Arnstein, S.R., 1969. A ladder of citizen participation. J. Am. Inst. Plann. 35, 216–224.

Barca, F., 2009. An agenda for a reformed cohesion policy: a place-based approach to meeting European union challenges and expectations, Available from: http://www.europarl.europa.eu/meetdocs/2009_2014/documents/regi/dv/barca_report_/barca_report_en.pdf

BMBF, 2014. The new high-tech strategy, innovations for Germany, Berlin: BMBF, Available from: http://www.hightech-strategie.de/de/The-new-High-Tech-Strategy-390.php

BMBF, 2015. Deutschlands Spitzencluster/Germany's Leading-Edge Clusters, Berlin: BMBF.

Bohle, D., Greskovits, B., 2012. Capitalist Diversity on Europe's Periphery. Cornell University Press, Ithaca.

Boschma, R., 2014. Constructing regional advantage and Smart specialisation: comparison of two European policy concepts, Scienze Regionali. Ital. J. Reg. Sci. 13, 51–68.

Boschma, R., Iammarino, S., 2009. Related variety, trade linkages, and regional growth in Italy. Econ. Geo. 85, 289–311.

Boschma, R., Minondo, A., Navarro, M., 2012. Related variety and regional growth in Spain Papers. Reg. Sci. 91, 241–256.

Capello, R., Kroll, H., 2016. From theory to practice in smart specialization strategy: emerging limits and possible future trajectories. Eur. Plan. Stud. 24, 1393–1406.

Cernat, L., 2006. Europeanization, Varieties of Capitalism and Economic Performance in Central and Eastern Europe. Palgrave Macmillan, New York, NY.

Charles, D., Perry, B., Benneworth, P. (Eds.), 2004. Towards a Multi-Level Science Policy: Regional Science Policy in a European Context. Regional Studies Association, Seaford.

Charron, N., Dijkstra, L., Lapuente, V., 2013. Regional Governance Matters: Quality of Government within European Union Member States. Reg. Stud. 48, 68–90.

Coffano, M., Foray, D., 2014. The centrality of entrepreneurial discovery in building and implementing a smart specialisation strategy, Scienze Regionali. Ital. J. Regional Sci. 13, 33–50.

Cohen, M.D., March, J.G., Olsen, J.P., 1972. A Garbage Can Model of Organizational Choice. Adm. Sci. Q. 17, 1–25.

Cooke, P., 2012. Complex Adaptive Innovation Systems: Relatedness and Transversality in the Evolving Region. Routledge, London.

Cooke, P., 2016. Four minutes to four years: the advantage of recombinant over specialized innovation—RIS3 versus "smartspec". Eur. Plan. Stud. 24, 1494–1510.

Daimer, S., Hufnagl, M., Warnke, P., 2012: Challenge-oriented policy-making and innovation systems theory: reconsidering systemic instruments, in Innovation system revisited - Experiences from 40 years of Fraunhofer ISI research, 217–234, Stuttgart: Fraunhofer Verlag

Deffaa, W., 2012. We count on the innovative potential of the regions: interview with Dr. Walter Deffaa, Director General DG Regional and Urban Policy, European Commission.(in German).

Edler, J., James, A., 2015. Understanding the emergence of new science and technology policies: Policy entrepreneurship, agenda setting and the development of the European Framework Programme. Res. Policy 44, 1252–1265.

European Commission, 2013. Regulation (EU) No 1303/2013 of the European Parliament and the Council of December 17, 2013 laying down common provisions on the ERDF, the ESF, the CF, the EARFD, and the EMFF and laying down general provisions on the ERDF, the ESF, the CF, and the EMFF and repealing Council Regulation (EC) No 1083/2006. Available from: http://eur-lex.europa.eu/legal-content/en/TXT/?uri=celex%3A32013R1303

Eurostat, 2016. Database. Available from: http://ec.europa.eu/eurostat/data/database

Farole, T., Rodríguez-Pose, A., Storper, M., 2011. Cohesion policy in the European Union: growth, geography, institutions. J. Common Mark. Stud. 49 (5), 1089–1111.

Flanagan, K., Uyarra, E., Laranja, M., 2011. Reconceptualising the "policy mix" for innovation. Res. Policy 40, 702–713.

Foray, D., 2009. Understanding smart specialisation. In: Pontikakis, D., Kyriakou, D., Van Bavel, R. (Eds.), The Questions of R&D Specialisation: Perspectives and Policy Implications. European Commission/JRC, Seville, pp. 14–24.

Foray, D., 2014. Smart Specialisation: Opportunities and Challenges for Regional Innovations Policy. Routledge, London.

Foray, D., 2016. On the policy space of smart specialization strategies. Eur. Plan. Stud. 24, 1428–1437.

Foray, D., David, P. A., Hall., B.H., 2009. Smart specialisation—the concept, knowledge economists policy brief no.8, June, 9. Brussels: European Commission, Available from: http://ec.europa.eu/invest-in-research/pdf/download_en/kfg_policy_brief_no9.pdf

Foray, D., David, P.A., Hall., B.H., 2011. Smart specialization—from academic idea to political instrument: the surprising career of a concept and the difficulties involved in its implementation, MTEI-WORKING PAPER-2011-001, Lausanne: École Polytechnique Federale de Lausanne, Available from: https://infoscience.epfl.ch/record/170252/files/MTEI-WP-2011-001-Foray_David_Hall.pdf

Foray, D., Goddard, J., Goenaga, X., Landabaso, M., McCann, P., Morgan, K., Nauwelaers, C. Ortega-Artilés, R., 2012. Guide to research and innovation strategies for smart specialisation (RIS3). European Commission, Smart Specialisation Platform. Available from: http://s3platform.jrc.ec.europa.eu/c/document_library/get_file?uuid=a39fd20b-9fbc-402b-be8c-b51d03450946&groupId=10157

Frenken, K., Van Oort, F., Verburg, T., 2007. Related variety, unrelated variety and regional economic growth. Reg. Stud. 41, 685–697.

Geels, F.W., 2010. Ontologies, socio-technical transitions (to sustainability), and the multilevel perspective. Res. Policy 39, 495–510.

Gianelle, C., Kleibrink, A., 2015. Monitoring mechanisms for smart specialisation strategies, S3 policy brief series no. 13/2015, Available from: http://s3platform.jrc.ec.europa.eu/documents/10157/eb795374-55f6-4034-a408-2df585f9b926

Gianelle, C., Kleibrink, A., Doussineau, M., 2016. Monitoring innovation and territorial development in Europe: emergent strategic management. Eur. Plan. Stud. 24 (8), 1438–1458.

Hall, P.A., Soskice, D., 2001. Varieties of Capitalism: The Institutional Foundations of Comparative Advantage. Oxford University Press, Oxford.

Hausman, R., Rodrik, D., 2003. Economic development as self-discovery. J. Dev. Econ. 72 (2), 603–633.

Hooghe, L., Marks, G., 2001. Multi-level Governance and European Integration. Rowman & Littlefield, Lanham, MD.

Iacobucci, D., 2014. Designing and implementing a smart specialisation strategy at regional level: Some open questions, Scienze Regionali. Ital. J. Reg. Sci. 13 (1), 107–126.

Inforegio, 2016. Regional Policy—European Commission; Regional policy in your country. Available from: http://ec.europa.eu/regional_policy/index_en.cfm

JRC-IPTS, 2015. Registered countries and regions in the S3 platform, Available from: http://s3platform.jrc.ec.europa.eu/s3-platform-registered-regions

Kingdon, J., 1984. Agendas, alternatives and public policies. Longman, New York.

Koschatzky, K., Kroll, H., Schnabl, E., Stahlecker, T., 2017. Cluster policy adjustments in the context of smart specialisation? Impressions from Germany. Edward Elgar, Cheltenham & Northampton.

Kroll, H., 2012. Regional Innovation Monitor Plus, Regional Innovation Report Saxony. Technopolis Belgium, Brüssel.

Kroll, H., 2015a. Efforts to implement smart specialization in practice—leading unlike horses to the water. Eur. Plan. Stud. 23 (10), 2079–2098.

Kroll, H., 2015. Weaknesses and opportunities of RIS3-type policies, seven theses, Available from: http://www.isi.fraunhofer.de/isi-wAssets/docs/p/de/publikationen/Thesenpapier_RIS3.pdf

Kroll, H., Meyborg, M., 2014. Regional Innovation Monitor Plus, Regional Innovation Report North Rhine-Westphalia. Technopolis Belgium, Brüssel.

Kroll, H., Stahlecker, T., 2014. Prozess und Auswirkungen der Entwicklung von "Strategien intelligenter Spezialisierung" in deutschen Ländern, Studien zum deutschen Innovations system 14-2015, Available from: http://www.efi.de/fileadmin/Innovationsstudien_2015/ StuDIS_14_2015.pdf

Kroll, H., Muller, E., Schnabl, E., Zenker, A., 2014. From smart concept to challenging practice— how European regions deal with the commission's request for novel innovation strategies, Working Paper Policy and Regions No. R2/2014, Karlsruhe: Fraunhofer ISI.

Kroll, H., Böke, I., Schiller, D., Stahlecker, T., 2016. Bringing Owls to Athens? The Transformative Potential of RIS3 for Innovation Policy in Germany's federal states. Eur. Plan. Stud. 24, 1459–1477.

Kuhlmann, S., 2001. Future governance of innovation policy in Europe—three scenarios. Res. Policy 30, 953–976.

Kuhlmann, S., Arnold, E., 2001. RCN in the Norwegian Research and Innovation System. (Rep. No. 12 Background Report). Royal Norwegian Ministry for Education, Research and Church Affairs, Oslo.

Kulicke, M., Kroll, H., 2006. Analyse der Innovationsstrategien der 16 Länder im Vergleich zur Hightech-Strategie der Bundesregierung. Fraunhofer ISI, Karlsruhe.

Landabaso, M., 1997. The promotion of innovation in regional policy: proposals for a regional innovation strategy. Entrep. Reg. Dev. 9, 1–24.

Landabaso, M., 2012. What public policies can and cannot do for regional development. In: Cooke, P., Parrilli, M.D., Curbelo, J.L. (Eds.), Innovation, Global Challenge and Territorial Resilience. Edward Elgar, Cheltenham, pp. 364–381.

Landabaso, M., 2014. Time for the real economy: the need for new forms of public entrepreneurship, Scienze Regionali. Ital. J. Reg. Sci. 13, 127–140.

Laranja, M., Uyarra, E., Flanagan, K., 2008. Policies for science, technology and innovation: translating rationales into regional policies in a multi-level setting. Res. Policy 37, 823–835.

Lawson, T., 2003. Institutionalism: on the need to firm up notions of social structure and the human subject. J. Econ. (37), 175–207.

Lindner, R., Daimer, S., Beckert, B., Heyen, N., Koehler, J., Warnke, P., Wydra, S., Teufel, B., 2015. Addressing orientation failure: conceptual thoughts on how to integrate directionality in the systems of innovation heuristic. Paper presented at the 2015 Annual Conference of the EU-SPRI Forum. Available from: http://euspri-helsinki2015.org/abstracts/pdf/6C1_EU–SPRI_ Helsinki_2015_Innovation_System_Framework_Lindner.pdf

Lodge, M., Wegrich, K., 2014. Administrative capacities. In: Hertie School of Governance (Ed.), The Governance Report 2014. Oxford University Press, Oxford, pp. 27–48.

Markard, J., Truffer, B., 2008. Technological innovation systems and the multi-level perspective: towards an integrated framework. Res. Policy 37, 596–615.

Martin, B., 2010. Science policy research—having an impact on policy? Office of health economics seminar briefing no.7, December 2010.

Mazzucato, M., 2013. The entrepreneurial state: debunking public vs. private sector myths. Anthem Press, London & New York.

McCann, P., Ortega-Argilés, R., 2014. The role of the smart specialisation agenda in a reformed EU cohesion policy, Scienze Regionali. Ital. J. Reg. Sci. 13, 15–32.

Metcalfe, J., 1994. Evolutionary economics and technology policy. Econ. J. 104, 931–944.

Moore, M., 1995. Institution building as a development assistance method: a review of literature and ideas. In: Bennedich, C. (Ed.), SIDA Evaluation Report. Swedish International Development Authority, Stockholm.

Morgan, K., 1997. The learning region: institutions, innovation and regional renewal. Reg. Stud. 31 (5), 491–503.

Niskanen, W., 1994. Bureaucracy and Public Economics. Edward Elgar, Cheltenham.

Oughton, C., Landabaso, M., Morgan, K., 2002. The regional innovation paradox: innovation policy and industrial policy. J. Technol. Transf. 27, 97–110.

Perez, C., 2013. Innovation systems and policy: not only for the rich? Working Papers in Technology Governance and Economic Dynamics no. 42, Tallinn University of Technology, Tallinn.

Radosevic, S., 2012. Innovation policy studies between theory and practice: a literature review based analysis. STI Policy Rev. 3, 1–45.

Reid, A., Komninos, N., Sanchez, J., Tsanakas, P., 2012. RIS3 National Assessment: Greece. Smart specialisation as a Means to foster economic renewal. Report to European Commission, DG Regional Policy, Brussels: European Commission.

Rodríguez-Pose, A., 2013. Do institutions matter for regional development? Reg. Stud. 47, 1034–1047.

Rodríguez-Pose, A., di Cataldo, M., Rainoldi, A., 2014. The Role of government institutions for smart specialisation and regional development, JRC Technical Reports. S3 Policy Brief Series No. 04/2014.(Luxembourg: Publications Office of the European Union).

Schmidt, V.A., 2004. Europeanization of national democracies: the differential impact on simple and compound polities. Politique Europeénne 13, 115–142.

SMWA, 2013. Innovationsstrategie des Freistaates Sachsen, Dresden: Sächsisches Staatsministerium für Wirtschaft und Arbeit.

SMWA, 2015. Innovationsstrategie des Freistaates Sachsen, Available from: www.innovations strategie.sachsen.de

Wanna, J., Forster, J. (Eds.), 1996. Entrepreneurial Management in the Public Sector. Macmillan, Melbourne.

Zenker, A., Kroll, H., 2014. Regional Innovation Monitor Plus, Regional Innovation Report Saxony-Anhalt. Technopolis Belgium, Brüssel.

Chapter 6

Innovation Policy in Southern Europe: Smart Specialization Versus Path Dependence

Lena J. Tsipouri
National and Kapodistrian University of Athens, Athens, Greece

Chapter Outline

Academic Highlights

- Average gross domestic product per capita between Northern and Southern Europe converged only during boom years and diverged during the 2008 crisis.
- Exceptional cases confirm that regional development can in the medium-to-long term succeed in restructuring business and building resilient, technologically advanced economies.
- Increased funding on R&D ubiquitously improved scientific infrastructure and output in less-favored regions.
- Absorption of funding proved a priority that can turn into resisting change.

Advances in the Theory and Practice of Smart Specialization. http://dx.doi.org/10.1016/B978-0-12-804137-6.00006-1
125

Policy Highlights

- Policies need to selectively follow lessons from successful regions; there are no general rules.
- Smart specialization may make a difference compared to past regional strategies, but southern regions may not respond adequately to the institutional innovation of the ex-ante conditionalities.
- Potentially inadequate compliance with RIS3 will create new challenges for the way forward in the next programming period.
- A key policy issue is to investigate the best way to commercialize knowledge generated in the scientific Pockets of Excellence built over the past years in Southern Europe.

INTRODUCTION

The aim of this chapter is to explore the extent to which the recent shift of regional development policy based on the concept of research and innovation (R&I) strategies for smart specialization (RIS3) can be expected to make a difference in modernizing the economies of Southern Europe (SE). Evidence is used from Portugal, Greece, a large part of Spain, and the Italian Mezzogiorno (namely the regions Abruzzi, Campania, Basilicata, Calabria, Molise, Puglia, and the islands of Sicily and Sardinia). Together with Ireland in the past, this area comprised, until the 2004 enlargement, the less-favored regions (LFRs) of the European Union.[1] These countries/regions share two characteristics that make them a fairly homogenous group with highly distinctive features compared to the original Member States.

1. *They are hard to classify in a global context*: They are neither resilient innovative and sustainable economies nor middle-income countries in the classic sense of the term (Eichengreen et al., 2013). Per capita gross domestic products (GDP) in these countries rank from 36th to 46th globally,[2] but their sectoral composition is typically low/medium tech, their R&D capabilities are uneven and mostly anchored in the public sector, and they classify as moderate innovators.[3] Their growth is episodic, occasionally overperforming, then again underperforming compared to the EU average.
2. *They experience both the benefits and the drawbacks of less-advanced countries belonging to a rich Union*: Thanks to their EU membership, SE regions have access to a large and rich market, which (at the time of their accession) they hoped would provide them with export opportunities; hence economies of scale and scope. The flipside of the access to the large market was the facilitation of import penetration from their more competitive trade partners. On a positive note, they can benefit from the transfer of transborder regional development funding.

To make up for the uneven consequences of free trade postulated by New Economic Geography and New Trade Theory, the European Union adopted a cohesion policy, whereby the less-prosperous regions receive aid from the European budget. These transfers have been a major (occasionally, the only) funding source of the development policy for SE regions, as they grew to about a third of the EU budget. In selected years and specific regions, they make up to 2% of their GDP, creating new opportunities for public and private investments. The way policies were designed to absorb these funds has evolved over the years:

- Initially the funds were mainly spent on physical infrastructure.
- After the first few years of development planning in Europe, the globally accumulated evidence that sustainable productivity increases and international competitiveness can only be achieved through investments in technology (Fagerberg and Verspagen, 2002) inspired the European Commission to encourage LFRs to channel more funds into R&D and innovation.

The governance model has also evolved over the years and changed fundamentally since the adoption of the subsidiarity principle in 1992.[4] The hands-on approach of the Commission was reduced to negotiations in planning, monitoring, and evaluation, while the degrees of freedom of national and regional governments in the implementation phase increased. Recommendations, including the emphasis on research, technological development, and innovation (RTDI) investments and prioritization, were considered but could not be enforced until the introduction of ex-ante conditionalities in 2014 in the context of RIS3.

Before 2004, the main beneficiaries of cohesion funding were Ireland and the southern countries/regions studied here. Ireland excelled, converged, and became the second richest Member State, and was resilient enough to cope with the banking crisis and resume spectacular growth again in 2015. Conversely, as pointed out previously, in the SE countries/regions progress in terms of per capita GDP and productivity growth was sporadic and convergence throughout the 21st century moderate. The different results in the North (Ireland) and the South raise questions about the appropriateness of EU regional development policies, as well as about SE's potential inherent characteristics hampering success. Specifically, was the policy of favoring RTDI investments inappropriate? Should it be abandoned in the future in favor of other types of investment? Was the policy's implementation inadequate because of path dependence? What would be the appropriate implementation and monitoring mechanisms? Will RIS3 compensate for past failures?

The following sections give an overview of the increasing relevance of RTDI in EU cohesion policies and some indications of the impact of this shift. As there is no counterfactual analysis for SE, the indications come from the literature and trends in RTDI inputs/output of R&D, innovation, and GDP growth. For a better understanding of the issue, four case studies are used to examine different policy features and outcomes. We conclude with remarks on the differences between RIS3 and past strategies, highlighting some thoughts on the potential longer-term impact of the new strategy in SE.

THE PRE-RIS3 ERA

Until the 2014–20 programming period, the regional development policy was characterized by increased funding, shifts in priorities, and controversial evaluation conclusions.

Evolution of EU Regional Development Policy

Regional development policy was first adopted in 1974. Competitiveness and innovation gained momentum in regional development planning only in the 1990s through the Regional Innovation and Technology Transfer Strategies (RITTS) and the Regional Innovation Strategies (RIS). While launched independently, the two initiatives shared a vision that European regions needed incentives and guidance to channel their funding toward coordinated, long-term interventions with the ambition to create a momentum for agglomeration economies, interactions, and spillovers that would close the technology gap of lagging regions.

Since 1994, over 30 regions have received support under similar exercises (called RIS Plus and RIS 2). Many adopted the idea enthusiastically, partly because they were willing to learn and experiment, and partly because the funding was competitive and not part of their preallocated quota. Over the years, the methodology crystallized to include regional consensus building, a SWOT analysis, and the definition of a strategic framework and Action Plan. The expectation was that the innovation strategies would lead to more effective planning of the operational programs and the early consensus would contribute to a better implementation process, higher absorptive capacity, and new partnerships, forming sustainable networks and clusters.

Besides the visibly positive influence on building technology transfer infrastructure, the evaluations of these initial programs indicate success in triggering strategic thinking, including regional dialogue (Charles et al., 2000), placing innovation high on the regional policy agenda where it remained long after the project ended (Socintec/INNO, 2005), and competence building (Charles et al., 2000; Socintec/INNO, 2005). However, not all of the high ambitions were met; when they were, it was with varying success. The RITTS evaluation not only stressed that it was an ambitious program, containing several complementary objectives, which together have proved to be beyond the reach of most regions; but also that RITTS came at the right moment to influence the evolution of the regional development policy. The degree of success achieved has been shown to depend mainly on the appropriateness of management practices in the process (Charles et al., 2000).

A rather clear pattern of RTDI design becoming more strategic then emerged when the mainstream structural funds (SF) pushed toward adopting explicit strategies and shifting funds to dedicated RTDI or competitiveness operational programs. A 2005 report suggests that in all the Objective 1 zones,[5] an average planned spending of 4.9% from total available SF was dedicated to RTDI,

TABLE 6.1 European Structural Funds (SFs) Spent on Research, Technological Development, and Innovation (RTDI), 1988–2020

Programming period	Total SF (%)	Value (billion euros)
1988–93	4	2
1994–99	7.6	7
2000–06	11	21.5
2007–13	25	86
2014–20	45	166

Note: This is a slightly more capacious definition of RTDI, broader than elsewhere in this book and includes not only R&D and information and communication technology (ICT), but also investments in small- and medium-sized enterprises (SMEs) and low carbon. Research and innovation (R&I) (TO1) alone accounts for 12% of the cohesion policy. DGRTDI budgets have also witnessed a similar significant increase over this same period [totaling 77 billion euros for 2014–20 (before European Fund for Strategic Investment, EFSI)]. See: Healy et al. (2016, p. 5).
Source: Data for 1988–2013 adapted from Healy, A., Morgan, K., Nauwelaers, C., 2016. Regions as laboratories: what have we learned from twenty years of regional innovation policy in Europe? School of Geography and Planning Paper, Cardiff University, Wales, United Kingdom; data for 2014–20 from Open Data Portal. Available from: https://cohesiondata.ec.europa.eu

compared to 9.8% in the already more competitive Objective 2[6] areas of Western Europe (Technopolis, 2006). Hence, the push for regional innovation strategies slowed from 2007 because the notion was already embedded in the mainstream operation of the European Union's cohesion policy, but while strategic thinking was dominant it was still not mandatory, or at least with no strings attached.

This evolution toward an increasing emphasis on RTDI is reflected in the absolute amount of SF spent, as well as in their share of the total regional development budget (Table 6.1).

National and regional authorities could use the support offered for planning, but were not obliged to strictly follow their own strategic plans and concentrate resources. When the time came to select between absorption and compliance with the strategy, the former prevailed, undermining in certain cases the credibility of the resulting strategies and the trust and willingness of the business sector to be involved in future strategy building. Over time, the strategy messages were diluted because of:

- the lack of systematic evaluations feeding back into new policies,
- the internal satisfaction because funds were coming from abroad,
- the repeating mistakes, and
- the political message to primarily pursue absorption.

One may argue that the first attempts did not fulfill their ambitions because, while formal rules were appropriate (the description of policy design requirements), informal ones did not change because there was no local agreement or enforcement designed for their implementation (linking RIS to the main funding flows).[7]

In reaction to these repeated gaps between strategy and implementation, the European Structural Investment Funds (ESIF) planning adopted the ex-ante conditionality of RIS3 in the 2014–20 programming; a significant change of governance rules in the evolution of regional innovation strategies.

Evaluation of EU Regional Development Policy

The rationale of European intervention is balanced economic growth and development in the Union. Several studies have identified convergence during the 1990s (Faíñaa and López-Rodríguez, 2004; Leonardi, 2006; Stephan et al., 2005), in particular for the most developed among LFRs, suggesting in certain cases a problem of intercountry convergence achieved at the cost of intracountry cohesion (Cappelen et al., 2002; Marzinotto, 2012; Rodríguez-Pose and Fratesi, 2002). Other studies claim that real convergence occurred only initially (Cuadrado-Roura and Mancha, 2005), while structural interventions were ineffective later (Ederveen et al., 2006). Rodríguez-Pose and Fratesi (2002) and Sterlacchini (2008) explain the precarious convergence through the distribution of resources, which favored infrastructure rather than human resources development. Still others emphasize that it is the regulatory framework that needs to be further improved to make intervention more effective (Bachtler and Gorzelak, 2007), and only a radical restructuring of cohesion policies can address the European Union's challenges (Barca, 2009; Farole et al., 2011).

Institutional maturity (Bache and Jones 2000; Ederveen et al., 2002; Hooghe, 1996; Smyrl, 1997) and the potential for local networking (Ansell et al., 1997; Faludi, 2006) were introduced after the first evaluations as key variables determining the potential for convergence. Part of the debate over the latter is the potential for exploiting agglomeration economies and the particular role of cluster policy (Nathan and Overman, 2013). Later, this was contested by the additional emphasis on exploiting the potential of joining global value chains (Rodríguez-Pose and Fratesi, 2002), rather than sticking to the benefits of clusters. However, the difficulty is that peripheral regions find it extremely difficult to capture a share of regional value from wider production chains whose scope and locus of control are largely beyond their reach (Benneworth and Hospers, 2007; Vang et al., 2007; Yeung, 2000). Eichengreen et al. (2013) see Spain, Portugal, and Greece as having difficulties in climbing the product quality ladder and in exporting high-tech products, which caused them to fall into the middle-income trap and experience severe growth slowdown.

This brief review of the literature suggests that the cohesion policy has indeed met its convergence target only in specific periods of time and/or some of the LFRs. The (linear model–based) hope that RTDI support would be the silver bullet leading to long-term competitiveness by eliciting the same forces of growth as in the technologically advanced countries proved to be an illusion.

A Success Story: Scientific Pockets of Excellence

When it became clear that research organizations alone would not drive growth, a new set of interventions was designed to link research organizations with the business sector. Clusters, networks, regions of excellence, and similar initiatives that worked effectively in technologically advanced regions did not produce the expected results in LFRs. The competent and excellent research teams networked internationally because local incentives were never as generous or interesting as international collaborations. In many cases, scientific teams have been increasingly detached from local production.

Recent research has identified several *Pockets of Scientific Excellence* (PoEs) in universities in SE (both in LFRs and transition regions). However, universities in cohesion regions are only able to excel in a tiny number of scientific fields (Bonaccorsi, 2016). The limited range of excellence may imply the need for a higher concentration of resources compared to regions where higher-education institutions (HEIs) excel in a broader number of fields. Concentration and links to the local economy need to coevolve to make a difference. The challenge for policy, knowing that PoEs exist, is not only to identify, but also to support them with concentrated funds and ensure their connection to the local economy. Resistance from other research teams in this concentration will be inevitable.

GROWTH AND COMPETITIVENESS IN SOUTHERN EUROPE

Three of the four SE countries and the Italian regions of Mezzogiorno have seen their GDP and productivity increase after 1980, along with simultaneous considerable improvement in their R&D capabilities. Unfortunately, many regions have started to lag in terms of GDP per capita since the 2008 crisis.

GDP Trends

GDP per capita grew substantially from 1986 until 2000 in all of the southern regions. This period is characterized by significant GDP per capita growth in Spain and Portugal, responding to the initial benefits from their accession and global growth trends.

The trends of GDP per capita since 2000 have been quite diverse (Table 6.2):

1. Southern GDP per capita compared to the EU average started at 64%–81% in 2000 and peaked to 65%–93% in 2008, to decline again after the outbreak of the crisis.
2. From 2000 to 2014, Greece and Spain converged to the EU average, while Portugal almost kept pace and the Mezzogiorno fell further behind.

TABLE 6.2 Southern European (SE) Economic Performance Between 2000 and 2014 (Current Prices)

GDP per capita (euros)	Greece	Italy/ Mezzogiorno	Portugal	Spain	EU average
2000	13.200	21.800/14.523	12.500	15.900	19.600
2008	21.800	27.600/18.473	16.900	24.300	26.000
2014	16.200	26.500/17.574	16.700	22.400	27.500
CAGR 2000–14	3.50%	2.05%/2.08%	2.72%	3.61%	2.75%
CAGR 2000–08	6.81%	3.26%/3.36%	3.96%	5.88%	3.69%
CAGR 2008–14	−5.07%	−0.77%/−0.88%	−0.56%	−1.76%	0.49%

For the calculation of the compound annual growth rate (CAGR), please refer to Endnote 12.
Source: Eurostat, Italstat, and author's calculations.

3. However, the 2008 crisis was a powerful turning point and the start of divergence: Greece, Italy, and Spain converged to the EU average in terms of GDP per capita in current euros until 2008.
4. Greece's performance was extreme, with the highest convergence and divergence rates, while Spain was the southern country with the best performance throughout the period.

Trends in R&D

The emphasis on R&D by the European Commission, combined with the willingness and ability of the research community, led to a very sharp increase of gross expenditure on R&D (GERD) and expenditure by the business enterprise sector (BERD), which started from a very low level in the southern regions. GERD per capita was multiplied by 15 in Portugal, 10 in Greece, 8 in Spain, and almost 2 in Italy. For the Mezzogiorno regions, the rise between 1994 and 2013 was sevenfold in Molisse (starting at the bottom); threefold in Puglia, Calabria, and Campania; and less than twofold in Abruzzo and Basilicata.[8] This funding went primarily to building research infrastructure, which was rudimentary before accession. Research intensity, however, reached only 50% or less of the EU average. The rise of BERD was even more pronounced, but BERD/GDP remains still at 15%–20% of the EU average in Greece and Portugal and less than 50% in Spain (Table 6.3). The Mezzogiorno regions show a very uneven path of BERD growth and range, also between 10% and 20% of the EU average (RIM, 2015). Most of the growth of GERD is funded by the public sector, government, and/or HEIs.

TABLE 6.3 R&D Trends in the Last 20 Years

		European Union	Greece	Spain	Italy[a]	Portugal
GERD per capita (euros)	1986	—	13.4	37.4	123.1	13.5
	2000	351.6	75.55[b]	142.8	218.9	90.4
	2008	479.5	143.2	321.9	323.8	245
	2014	558.4	135.6	273.6	341.7	213.8
GERD/ GDP	1995	—	0.42	0.77	0.94	0.52
	2000	1.79	0.56[b]	0.89	1.01	0.72
	2008	1.85	0.66	1.32	1.16	1.45
	2014	2.03	0.83	1.2	1.29	1.29
BERD per capita (euros)	1986	—	3.8	20.9	71.9	3.5
	2000	227.2	18.5	76.6	109.6	25.1
	2008	303.1	—	176.8	173.4	122.7
	2014	356.6	46.2	143.8	190.3	98.7

BERD, Expenditure by the business enterprise sector; GDP, gross domestic product; GERD, gross expenditure on R&D.
[a]No aggregate data for the Mezzogiorno. Data for individual regions are taken from the Regional Innovation Monitor (RIM).
[b]Missing value. Calculated as the average value of 1999 and 2001.
Source: Data from Eurostat, 2015. Total intramural R&D expenditure (GERD) by sectors of performance. Available from: http://ec.europa.eu/eurostat/web/products-datasets/-/t2020_20

As with GDP, R&D per capita declined after the crisis, but only moderately and may simply be linked to the SF cycle. Research intensity did not decline in Greece because of the significant GDP decline, but it dropped in Spain and Portugal, where the GDP declined to a lower level.

A positive trend not interrupted by the crisis is the improvement of scientific output: the rise of citable documents continued from 1996 to 2014, not only in absolute numbers, but also as a share of Europe and the world (with a small decline in Greece in 2014) (Table 6.4). International collaborations have also continued to increase (Table 6.4). Even in terms of highly cited scientific publications, the three SE countries (there are no regional data) have seen their shares growing and rank at the bottom of the EU15, but ahead of all EU13 (post-2004 accessions) (European Commission, 2016).

The high growth of scientific outputs is observed mostly in social sciences, economics, and humanities. STEM, the basis for innovation, is growing at below average rates, with the exception of computer science.[9] There are several interpretations of this trend: the current structure of the business sector does not create demand for STEM research, hence there is a chicken-and-egg situation of what will take off the ground first; the growth of information and communication technology (ICT) is related to the relatively lower cost of infrastructure and high skill intensity. Start-ups are mostly observed in this domain.

TABLE 6.4 Scientific Output in Greece, Portugal, and Spain (1996–2014)

Greece	Citable documents	Cites per document	International collaboration (%)	Publications of the country as % of Europe	World (%)
1996	4.94	17.10	33.46	1.47	0.44
2000	6.24	20.91	31.59	1.67	0.52
2008	14.89	12.91	36.39	2.61	0.75
2014	15.07	0.56	47.26	2.38	0.64
CAGR (1996–2014)	0.06	−0.17	0.02	0.03	0.02

Spain	Citable documents	Cites per document	International collaboration (%)	Region (%)	World (%)
1996	36.85	21.57	27.67	11.03	3.30
2000	39.81	25.64	28.15	10.75	3.32
2008	69.34	15.68	39.01	12.14	3.49
2014	84.02	0.65	43.90	13.21	3.58
CAGR (1996–2014)	0.05	−0.18	0.03	0.01	0.00

Portugal	Citable documents	Cites per document	International collaboration (%)	Region (%)	World (%)
1996	2.66	17.10	39.62	0.79	0.24
2000	4.04	21.18	39.91	1.07	0.33
2008	11.84	14.04	47.71	2.01	0.58
2014	18.45	0.53	49.89	2.83	0.76
CAGR (1996–2014)	0.11	—	0.01	0.07	0.07

Data for the Italian Mezzogiorno unavailable.
Source: Scimago Journals and Country Rank. Available from: www.scimagojr.com

Trends in Innovation

The ultimate targets of innovation strategies and SF are growth and welfare, which can only be achieved through business innovation. Companies in the southern regions may be innovative, as indicated by the Community Innovation Survey, but their innovations are mainly incremental and nontechnological, very rarely radical ones. Given complexities of innovation metrics and benchmarking are hard (Lundvall and Tomlinson, 2000), we use patents and scoreboard positions to gain some insight into the progress of innovation in SE.

The three southern Member States (again no aggregate evidence on the Mezzogiorno) have improved their international patenting activity considerably, thanks to their low starting points but still having comparatively lower share of patents granted per billion euro GERD (Greece has 42.59, Spain 35.22, Portugal 15.19, and 112.79 of EU28 average). The increases in patents per million inhabitants were faster in the south but remain marginal, with the exception of Spain, which reached almost 30% of the EU average.

Turning to the annual composite Innovation Union Scoreboard Summary Innovation Index[10] (European Commission, 2015), we note a deterioration of the overall innovation performance of Greece (from 69.85% to 65.69% of the EU average), and of Spain (from 76.33% to 69.42%), while Portugal's performance improved (from 70.33% to 72.64% of the EU average).

At the same time, the World Economic Forum data show a systematic decline in the competitiveness ranking of all four SE Member States since the outbreak of the crisis: Greece's Innovation score fell from the 46th position out of 125 countries in 2006–07 to 88th out of 142 countries, and started to catch up again in 2015–16 after the introduction of structural reforms. Similarly, Portugal caught up much faster and ranked 28th out of 140 countries in 2015–16. Spain showed a very similar pattern to Greece, reaching its worst performance in 2010–11, before rising to 37th position of out of 140 countries in 2015–16. Italy's performance is mostly determined by the industrialized northern regions.[11]

CASE STUDIES

Why Case Studies are Important

Macrodata suggest that the 30 years of the current model improved the knowledge infrastructure in all SE regions, but affected long-term performance in only some of them. We selected four cases, two encouraging and two disappointing, to assist us in understanding the different impacts. The selection of the case studies considered the following:

- The selected regions all started adopting regional innovation strategies early.
- Compound average annual growth[12] in purchasing power parity (PPP) over the whole period shows that the GDP per capita growth ranking changes considerably when the pre- and postcrisis periods are separated. Our assumption is that resilience to a crisis is the best signal of effective policies, hence good practices were selected from regions performing well all over the entire period considered (the Basque Country and Norte).

- Conversely, the disappointing performers for the entire period came from Italy and Greece, hence Campania and Central Macedonia were selected.

In addition, the selection factored in the availability of data and references.

The Basque Country: A Promising Case

Economic Structure and Performance

Although the Basque Country is one of the smallest regions in Spain, accounting for less than 5% of the Spanish population, it is a success story in the sense that it started with a GDP per capita very close to the Spanish average and has systematically outperformed both Spain and the EU average. Its growth in the 2000–14 period at 4.11% was the highest in Spain and declined during the crisis by only 1.42% (Eurostat).

It was suggested that this rapid economic growth was initially brought about by the economy's increasing capacity to utilize available resources, rather than achieving higher productivity rates because the economy was relatively well placed to capitalize on industrial policies mobilizing regional assets. However, the practical full deployment of existing capital and human resources in the economy also pointed to the exhaustion of this source of economic growth and the need to embark on a new competitive stage to increase the productivity of resources and avoid the middle-income trap: this was called the innovation phase (Orkestra-Instituto Vasco de Competitividad, 2009).

The policies adopted to face these challenges were apparently successful: measured by the latest territorial and business competitiveness indicators, the level of competitiveness, improved return on assets, and productivity. Many firms are now sound, though there is still a large group of vulnerable firms and firms experiencing losses (Orkestra-Instituto Vasco de Competitividad, 2015). In the last *Regional Innovation Scoreboard 2014*, the Basque region is positioned quite well among all the European regions in the group of innovation followers, alongside one other Spanish region (i.e., Navarre).

A measure of this success can be seen in its positioning today in the first quintile of EU regions in GDP per capita and other key socioeconomic indicators, and its much stronger position than other parts of Spain in the context of the current economic crisis (Valdaliso and Wilson, 2015). This long-term success has attracted the attention of academics and policy makers and the Basque Country has become an international reference point (Morgan, 2016).

Regional Innovation Strategies: Past and Present

The Basque Country region has a strong trajectory in proactive industrial policy (Valdaliso and Wilson, 2015). Regional development strategies started in the 1980s. At that time, the economy was characterized by no inward investments and a weak research infrastructure, so the regional government was determined to: (1) modernize the manufacturing sector and (2) harness the power and resources of the newly founded regional state for economic renewal and social solidarity (Cooke and Morgan, 1998; Healy et al., 2016; Valdaliso and Wilson, 2015). Unable to attract inward investment from abroad, the government was forced to rely on its own indigenous efforts (Cooke and Morgan, 1998) and adopted an endogenous growth model focused on building new capabilities based on accumulated experience. This attitude was somewhat similar to the idea of entrepreneurial discovery.

A research system had to be created from scratch regionally. In the early 1980s, the innovation system of the Basque Country was inexistent, with research intensity below 0.1%. Subsequent R&D and innovation policies helped the region achieve R&D shares of 2.12% of GDP by 2012 (EC, Internal Market). This increase in GERD outperformed both Spain and the EU average from 2000 to 2008, and has only slightly fallen behind in 2010 (RIM). The structure of R&D investment is atypical for the south because 75% of the implementation is directed to companies and private nonprofit institutions. From 2000, the business sector has been the main driver of innovation. Expenditures from higher education (especially since the creation of the university-attached Basque Excellence Centers, BERCs) and from the government (inclusion of health R&D units in the R&D system) also increased.[13]

The first steps addressed the creation of a regional research infrastructure. R&D policy emphasized creating spaces for connection and knowledge exchange with a nonnegligible number of Research Centers of Excellence, Centers for Collaborative Research, a Network of Technological Centers, and four Technology Parks. These and the clusters constitute a strong model based on a triple-helix approach, which gives a central place to interactions.

The government adopted two long-term initiatives. In the 1980s, it helped fashion a new "knowledge transfer system," while in the 1990s it took the lead in creating "cluster associations" to encourage firms to collaborate (Morgan, 2016). Although traditional sectors were the first to create cluster associations, they then spread to a dozen key sectors and came to account for nearly a third of the gross value added and more than a quarter of the total employment in the Basque Country (Etxabe and Valdaliso, 2013; Morgan, 2016). The following three key milestones can be identified:

- 1992: Following a mapping of industrial sectors, instruments were developed to support the development of new associations based on the identified clusters regionally and to support existing ones. Twelve cluster associations now exist.
- 2000: A new framework was developed, emphasizing the cluster associations' strategic planning process to better align cluster logic and regional priorities.
- 2009: A move to extend the policy, beginning a "precluster policy," that is a top-down approach to identifying and developing new clusters (Oyon, 2014). The post-2009 policy came after the stabilization/modernization of the old

industrial sectors; the appropriate time for the region to turn to generating new science-based knowledge (nano- and biosciences). Significant public investments in research infrastructure chose to go ahead with a modernization of the regional governance system. Now the scientific specialization given by the distribution of R&D expenditures also shows relative strengths in bio- and nanosciences, as well as engineering.

Despite the visible success in terms of GDP growth, RTDI inputs, improvement in infrastructure and experimentation, and reexamination and progress of policies, the literature seems divided on the depth and intensity of technology transfer, that is, regarding the ability of the Basque economy to transform into an innovation follower and then a leader. While acknowledging success stories, some criticism remains:

- Science, technology, and innovation policies tended to follow a linear model, with investments skewed toward creating a previously nonexistent research infrastructure (Orkestra-Instituto Vasco de Competitividad, 2009). The region faces some challenges with respect to knowledge infrastructures, as it has built a complex but powerful knowledge system. The challenge is now to reach full-capacity utilization. It is therefore fundamental to assess and evaluate the role of every individual unit of infrastructure regarding its goal and original mission. It is also important to understand whether any individual units of infrastructures are failing, even while the whole knowledge system is well performing (Magro and Navarro, 2012). In a way, some of the deficiencies typical for the southern regions, such as the lack of transformation of research results to innovation and limited interactions within the regional innovation system, could not be (completely) avoided.
- This applies in particular to the new clusters. Bio-, micro-, and nanoscience specializations are a result of recent public efforts made in these fields, while technological engineering represents the traditional trajectory of incumbents. However, nano- and biosciences are not yet integrated into the region's sectoral composition.[14]
- Trends in the performance of research infrastructure are also questionable, as missions become increasingly blurred. Although Cooperative Research Centers were created to conduct basic research, they had to be oriented toward industrial needs, and transferred to the industrial sector directly, even though other specific agents were closer to the market. Furthermore, technology centers themselves have evolved since their inception, from providing technological services to Basque firms (and therefore closer to development activities) to conducting primarily applied research, due to their internationalization through European (mainly) competitive programs and also due to the cuts by both the Spanish central government and regional government. The latter had to translate some of their support funds to finance the new knowledge infrastructures being created.[15]

- More systemic policies, establishing links between the different innovation agents, played only a secondary role (Orkestra-Instituto Vasco de Competitividad, 2009) and were inadequately exploited.
- Governance did not develop alongside the policy success: the participatory view has always been undertaken in the strategy or policy design phase, but not in the implementation or evaluation phases. Implementation is mainly carried out by officials and regional agencies, while evaluation has been top-down and did not follow a participatory process.[16]

Responding to criticism and threats of stagnation or recession after the crisis, the Basque government embraced RIS3 and reinforced its tradition in industrial policy. The vision is to develop the actions required to position the region among Europe's most advanced and competitive regions. It reformed its science, technology, and innovation (STI) governance system, improving coordination, interdepartmental cooperation, and evaluation, which were historically the weak points (Valdaliso and Wilson, 2015). The specialization focus is on biosciences, nanosciences, and alternative energy.

Lessons From the Case Study

The Basque story tells us that, even in regions considered models, competitive pressures continue, and maintaining competitiveness can be as hard as gaining it at the beginning of a new trajectory. This is a success case, owing its achievements both to some characteristics atypical for the south and to its long-term persistent innovation strategies. The lessons can be summarized as follows:

- The region is atypical in the composition of its manufacturing sector and in the large share of R&D performed by companies, as well as in its political situation and the lack of inward investment. Regions with different sectoral specializations may not be able to follow similar paths.
- The significant degree of regional autonomy gives the Basque Country more freedom to act compared to other southern regions.
- There is enormous inertia and resistance to new approaches by the incumbent actors and constituencies of these policies with vested interests. This is a characteristic that the Basque Country shares with other southern regions. However, in this case policy persistence for change helped overcome the path-dependent trajectory of STI policy (Valdaliso and Wilson, 2015).
- The development of STI policies in a context of abundance of resources has led to a very complex and cumbersome system, which is unable to coevolve and adapt to the new context without severe reforms. The initial success story did not save the region from the crisis-triggered challenges, which include difficulties in maintaining the public investment needed for the operation of the dense RTDI and technology transfer public infrastructure, the increasing need for business–academic cooperation, the shift toward new activities that have not borne fruit before the outbreak of the crisis, and, last but not least, internal political tensions (Morgan, 2016).

RTDI strategy and policy in the region can be seen as an evolutionary process, whereby starting from scratch, the government experimented with the linear model and built up research infrastructure in existing sectors, then tried to promote external economies via clusters and expanded infrastructure for technology transfer and new technologies. Some, but not yet all, of these experiments were successful and some of the ambitions fulfilled. In hindsight, it is precisely the capacity to experiment and redesign interventions with a balance between the short and the long term (Orkestra-Instituto Vasco de Competitividad, 2015), rather than follow the "business-as-usual" model, which allowed the Basque Country to recover from two industrial crises in the last decades of the 20th century.

In a nutshell: while the challenges persist, the Basque economy may have advanced to the point where it has largely overcome the "European middle-income trap" and come closer to the resilience exercised in more advanced regions.

Norte: A Promising Case

Economic Structure and Performance

In the 1980s, the Norte region was the most industrialized in Portugal, specializing in labor-intensive, low value–added, traditional industries, with the textile and clothing sector accounting for about 50% of the total manufacturing employment, followed by wood, cork, and metal processing. The metropolitan area of Porto presented a more diversified industrial structure, with important machinery and metal products industries and the presence of R&D-intensive production (Bateira and Ferreira, 2002). Competition from low-cost countries eroded these advantages, reduced GDP, and led many entrepreneurs to divert investments to nontradable sectors, which were profitable and secure (Moreira et al., 2006). At that time, the Norte region had a severe lack of basic infrastructure and the lowest levels of schooling in the country, high drop-out levels, incipient professional training, the lowest rates of secondary and university attendance, and low R&D investment (Charles et al., 2000). This called for a new strategy, which coincided with Portugal's accession to the European Union.

In the period 2000–10, Norte region's GDP nominal growth rate was below the national growth rate, yet slightly higher than the EU27 rate. The Portuguese sovereign crisis broke the trend of Norte's convergence with the EU27 average performance, but the region started outperforming the country average. In the *Regional Competitiveness Index 2013*, Norte ranked third among the seven Portuguese regions (RIM). The present situation shows radical improvements in infrastructure, and the younger workforce is more qualified, creative, and flexible. The region is home to several universities and internationally reputed research institutes (Charles et al., 2000). The most remarkable feature is that, during the present financial crisis, the region demonstrated resilience, with a relatively better economic performance than the rest of the country and a surprising capacity for export growth toward new external markets, mainly in traditional sectors.

Regional Innovation Strategies: Past and Present

The region ranks at a medium–high level within the European context, having moved upward since 2007, to some extent (unlike most southern regions) converging to the EU average during the crisis. The measures recently implemented nationally and regionally have allowed Norte to achieve a better position regarding scientific and technological infrastructure, size of human resources involved in Research and Technological Development (RTD) activities, companies' innovation activities, and innovation support services to firms, among others.[17] This has been achieved thanks to a gradual shift of priorities from "the domination of infrastructure expenditure in the early periods to a more balanced distribution..." (Charles et al., 2000). A combination of modernizing old manufacturing industries (such as wine, footwear, cork, and furniture) and requests for incentives from some industrial groups and entrepreneur associations led to renewed growth and emerging new activities (such as electronics, automobile components, and pharmaceuticals). Tensions accompanied this new policy mix. Traditional firms and industrial associations complained about the lack of support in their modernization efforts, while universities and HEIs were attacked for benefiting from support without increasing their links with the regional economic structure. Recent years have proved such assertions wrong. Traditional industries have become increasingly open to the integration of new technologies. Norte has seen the emergence of an elite of firms that, despite not being statistically dominant, have played an important role in the new regional economy.[18]

As in all of the southern regions, the transformation started with investments in the R&D system supported by the first Community Support Framework,[19] which was channeled to the three public universities, funding new buildings, laboratories, scientific equipment, and industrial parks (Charles et al., 2000). In the first two programming periods, a series of technology centers were created, funded both from national and regional sources, but evaluations indicate that: "Complementarities between enterprises and technological institutions could have been more fully explored, the absence of which undermined the possibility of achieving critical mass ... the ERDF programmes 'fell into the temptation to support each and every investment'" (Charles et al., 2000). Similarly, the first attempts at cluster creation in the 1990s failed because "the government opted to place the public sector in the leading role" (Charles et al., 2000).

Policies have gradually shifted from infrastructure to human resources, enterprise, and innovation. Innovation strategy development started with the regional EU pilots (Santos, 2000), which made only limited steps in concentrating resources. More innovation strategies followed, the most recent of which is the Norte 2020 initiative for the period 2014–20.[20] The first strategies had limited impact but, given that regional governments in Portugal lacked real autonomy, the various RISs were perceived as "a way to influence the establishment of public policy priorities permitting an allocation of funds based on identified regional and industrial needs."[21] The conception of these documents had an important institutional learning effect (Moreira et al., 2006).

The proportion across the successive European Regional Development Fund (ERDF) funding periods varied from 5% of expenditures in 1989–93, to around 7% currently (Charles et al., 2000). This shift was recommended because "SMEs need a customized and interactive innovation policy, managed at a regional level" (Bateira and Ferreira, 2002). Most Portuguese studies have stressed the problems of interaction (Santos and Simões, 2014), and now smart specialization is expected to be the basis for investments more focused on intangible factors of competitiveness.[22]

Regional gross expenditure on R&D (GERD as percentage of GDP) rose from 0.23% to 1.51% in the period 2000–10, and the region ranked second only to the capital in terms of research intensity. Businesses are the main R&D players regionally: in 2010, 46% of R&D expenditure came from activities implemented by businesses. For R&D infrastructure, and compared to other Portuguese regions, Norte now ranks first for number of the RTD units (Santos and Simões, 2014). At the same time, regional universities have improved their positions in both European and international rankings (Charles et al., 2000).

Gradually, innovation policies improved when a national public–private forum to plan clusters was created, which in Norte meant introducing the goals of developing textile, footwear, and wine clusters. The footwear sector is a success case (attributed to the Technology Center for the Footwear Industry) because it succeeded in developing a global strategy based on quality and design (Charles et al., 2000). Emerging clusters in new sectors followed, where firms [spin-offs, small- and medium-sized enterprises (SMEs), and multinationals] worked hand-in-hand with universities and novel ERDF-supported research centers to create poles of excellence (RIM,[23] gives examples in some fields of electronics, cutting-edge machinery and equipment, pharmaceuticals, and automobiles). Their performance varies. The electronics cluster has a high share of the overall cluster activity due to the presence of some multinational companies, while the northern communications cluster could not take off the ground because the main telecommunications operators were located in Lisbon (Moreira et al., 2006). A large health cluster is also under development. This process is still quite new and will need continued support (Charles et al., 2000). The large investments in the pharmaceutical, tire, semiconductor, and wind-energy sectors (Charles et al., 2000) suggest that an economic transformation is under way. In addition, there are some examples of internationally renowned technology transfer organizations and HEIs, which have opened up facilities in the region supporting its ambition to develop into a knowledge-based economy (a "Fraunhofer Institute," MIT Portugal, Carnegie Mellon Portugal, UT Austin Portugal).

The 2007–13 period saw a new strategy supporting two science and technology parks and clusters of ICT activities. As of this writing, the RIS3 preparation indicates that the learning process has been invaluable: Norte prepared its "Regional Strategy 2015," which formed the basis for the Regional Operational Program (ROP) "New Norte" and relied extensively on stakeholder involvement and modern tools for providing the necessary evidence basis for appropriate policy decisions (Charles et al., 2000). The timely and participative process indicates a willingness to really exploit the strategic concept rather than trying to comply with the ex-ante conditionality.

Progress is visible, but this does not suggest that Norte has overcome all challenges typical to the south. More efforts for interaction and shifts in higher value–added activities are needed. If the positive momentum does not continue, the region risks falling behind again, as has happened before.

Lessons From the Case Study

The region of Norte is of interest for two reasons connected with the evolution and success of its policies:

- It was the most prosperous industrialized region in Portugal, fell behind, and regained momentum.
- It was the first region to adopt an innovation strategy as early as the 1990s, benefiting from the RTP pilot, but strategic thinking did not initially succeed; it was only gradually that strategies were translated into an appropriate policy mix.

Over the last 15 years, several exercises were carried out to develop and implement innovation strategies. Some succeeded more than others and impacts improved over time indicating that persistence led to institutional learning and maturity. R&D investments and subsequent systematic improvement in innovation policy could only bear fruit in the last decade, but this is particularly visible in the relative performance of the region during and after the 2008 crisis. In many cases, the region caught up and outperformed the national average in the last years. High BERD and a mix of modernization of traditional sectors and emerging more modern activities are also signs of improvement. The timely and adequate preparation of the RIS3 'Regional Strategy 2015', which formed the basis for the ROP 'New Norte', shows the willingness to really adopt a strategic concept and respect it during implementation. It will hopefully cope with the need to further modernize the economy.

Campania: A Disappointing Case

Economic Structure and Performance

Campania, with a population of 5.8 million, is the second most populous and the most densely populated Italian region. GDP per capita is persistently among the lowest in Italy, while innovation performance is moderate. The fragile regional economy in Campania has been affected greatly by the recent economic crisis. Unemployment was the highest in Italy and well above the national average

(Schrittwieser Consulting, 2014). The industrialization rate is low, while the share of employment in agriculture is higher than in the rest of the country. Campania is one of the regions more oriented toward agrofood production, with an urgent need of modernization (Caiazza and Volpe, 2013), while the innovativeness and export intensity of its clothing industry are mainly positively affected by interactions with suppliers. The impact of participation in trade fairs was found insignificant and did not justify the participation costs (Zucchella and Siano, 2014).

The region has many SMEs operating in traditional sectors, mainly clothing and the agrofood industry. They lack an adequate organizational and financial structure, and most appear impermeable to the diffusion of new technologies and preserve their small size. There is a systemic problem preventing the circulation of knowledge and technical solutions between research and industry. The prevailing models of cooperation are characterized by few players, weak ties, and occasional opportunistic alliances that have proven to insufficiently take advantage of specific opportunities, such as the availability of financial resources from European Programs. There is a high density of manufacturing firms, but the export capability is low and, while there are many researchers, the capacity for innovation is also low (Zollo et al., 2011).

Strengths exist (Akca, 2006), but could not be sufficiently exploited (Zollo et al., 2011). Above-average companies that were resilient enough to successfully outlive the crisis and to overperform are few but well positioned, as they interact with the innovation ecosystem and have a good international reputation (Thomas et al., 2015).

Regional Innovation Strategies: Past and Present

R&D investment is low, but has increased over time thanks to the SF. In 2011, GERD per inhabitant was EUR197 in Campania compared to EUR327 in Italy. R&D intensity has increased from 0.91% in 2000 to 1.31% in 2013, with only a slight decline in 2009–11 (Eurostat). Campania is underindustrialized relative to the rest of Italy, therefore the contribution of BERD to GERD is lower than that of other Italian regions. However, over the period 2002–11 regional BERD per capita grew much more quickly than GERD (69.4% vs. 25.6%), which is attributed to the investments made by large industrial groups, such as Fiat (automobile) and Finmeccanica (aerospace and defense). The share of regional human resources dedicated to S&T and patenting is also very low.[24] According to the results of the *Regional Innovation Scoreboard 2014*, Campania has improved its innovation performance over the years, but it remains a "moderate performer."

Italian regions were late starters with innovation strategies. The first regional government to adopt an Innovation Strategy was Campania (OECD, 2011). It was not until very recently that the regional innovation system started taking shape, but still the most relevant recent initiatives in terms of innovation policy are the creation of the regional R&I network and the redefinition of the governance of the regional innovation system. The regional innovation strategy is based on a key regional programming document published in 2001. The regional strategy has then been updated with the ROP 2000–06, with a Regional Law for the promotion of scientific research in Campania in 2005, and finally with the ROP 2007–13.

The regional strategy has been mainly focused on the creation of 10 regional Competence Centers to reinforce the regional research base. Following the example of other Italian regions, in 2012 the regional administration promoted the creation of *Campania In.Hub*, the regional R&I network coordinated by the regional innovation agency Campania Innovazione. However, it seems that the region is reconsidering the role played by the ERDF-funded "Centri di Competenza," after evaluating their interactions with SMEs, turning those centers unable to collaborate with businesses into real company support centers. In addition, the absorption of the allocated SF funding (under RTDI priorities) is still well below the target.[25]

Now, RIS3 gives special emphasis to innovation. Strengths in the RIS3 include the past efforts of public interventions, namely critical mass of public spending in R&D and specialization in knowledge-intensive sectors, as well as the presence of innovative technology clusters and niches of excellence (biotechnology, aerospace, and automobile). The problem is that these strengths appear disconnected from the productive system, as confirmed by the identification of weaknesses in the SWOT analysis, namely, low investments in ICT, low competitiveness of the production and innovation systems, limited technological process and product innovation, scarcity of researchers in companies, low propensity to cooperate, and limited capacity for patenting (RIS3 Campania).[26] The key points of the current regional innovation strategy refer to the integration of the regional research system to support the conversion of an economic system prevalently based on traditional industries into a knowledge economy. In the government's view, the regional system should be able to better interact with local businesses and to promote technology transfer, stimulate the growth of industrial R&D services, and improve human capital employed in R&D services.[27]

The inability to create interactions between the available infrastructure and local SMEs remains at the heart of the regional weaknesses. Ponsiglione et al. (2012) show using comparative data that: "Campania exhibits an unbalanced structure of innovation dimensions and the major points of weakness are related to the lack of an effective system of links among the actors of innovation" rather than to the lack of actors or funding.

Lessons From the Case Study

Campania was the first Italian region to formally adopt a regional innovation strategy (but this came after pilots in other Member States). Over the years, the strategy has had only one discernible outcome: the increase of publicly funded and publicly performed GERD and the enrichment of the region with public

R&I centers. Neither the strategies, nor the strong emphasis of the ERDF on R&I have changed the composition or behavior of the business sector. Only a few large Italian firms that relocated to Campania have contributed to increasing the BERD. The region suffered disproportionately from the crisis, the weaknesses remain the same, and the RIS3 document is trying to address them identifying practically the same challenges as previously.

Central Macedonia: A Disappointing Case

Economic Structure and Performance

Central Macedonia is a region with a multifaceted history of progress and retrogression: being among the top regions in Greece in terms of share of manufacturing and competitiveness, exceeding the 75% threshold in 2007–13. Unfortunately, the region was so severely hit by the crisis that it slid back during 2014–20. The regional economy did not present the necessary resilience and suffered significant losses during the period of the Greek austerity crisis, capital controls, and liquidity constraints.

The strength of the region is the above average (nationally speaking) manufacturing share and a (comparatively) dense infrastructure. Yet the economy is still weak, composed of SMEs in traditional sectors (food and beverage, textile and clothing, and furniture) and a few large companies in metal production, chemicals, and plastics. Emerging industries and FDI started during the convergence period with medicine and health services, software, international retail chains, business services, and tourism services. Weaknesses include the low share of modern sectors, the attractiveness of neighboring, low-cost Bulgaria for traditional industries seeking to relocate, low technology and R&D investment, and limited achievements of the technology intermediary structures regarding their local cooperation.

In Greece, the central government overshadows regional initiatives. The ROPs of Central Macedonia had to be aligned to national overarching objectives and types of interventions, and the bulk of the funds received by the region was distributed via sectoral programs managed in Athens.

Regional Innovation Strategies: Past and Present

The region of Central Macedonia is rather well positioned in terms of RTDI in the Greek context. Public and higher education R&D expenditures are close to the national average, but, despite the comparatively high share of manufacturing business R&D, expenditures are low. In recent years, the stagnant or even declining shares were attributed mainly to the business sector. BERD as a percentage of GDP and of GERD within the region is 0.12% and 16.5%, respectively. Patenting activities are also marginal.[28]

According to the *Regional Innovation Scoreboard 2014*, the region of Central Macedonia is a moderate innovator, with innovation performance below the EU average. Despite improvements in the last decade, the region still lacks the resources, networks, and measures needed for its growth. There is a good level of non-R&D–based innovation expenditure, which Avranas and Nioras (2011) attribute to the strategies adopted by medium- to low-tech companies to confront competition, overcome the deficiencies of low-skilled personnel, and circumvent their weakness, namely, the inability to invest in R&D. However, it also reflects the nature of the regional economy (heavily based on services, tourism, agrofood, etc.), with sectors that do not normally invest in technological R&D but innovate through design, organizational change, and buying in of technologies and processes. Hence, there may be a "hidden innovation" potential in the regional economy, although the crisis has probably weakened the capacity to invest (Reid et al., 2012).

Compared to the rest of Greece, institutional thickness is advanced, with a large modern university and one of the most successful research centers in the country, which has excellent links to industry, although these links are more international (Sidiropoulos and Tsipouri, 2011). It also has smaller specialized universities, several technology transfer organizations and intermediaries, plus a technology park. Still, none of them has a significant track record of sustainable connections with regional producers. Scientific specialization is only partly reflected in the regional industrial specialization (Reid et al., 2012).

Central Macedonia is one of the regions that started regional planning early, and with a lot of zeal. Innovation planning was of high quality from the beginning, thanks to actors directly involved and strongly committed to progress. RIS Plus resulted in a revised Action Plan compared to RTP, based on accumulated experience, and helped adopt many innovative actions into regional planning mechanisms. An additional innovation strategy is a focus on Thessaloniki, the regional capital, neglecting the periphery (Reid et al., 2012), which was used as a basis for the RIS3. There is no evidence whether the disentanglement of Thessaloniki from the region will have a positive effect or lead to fragmentation.

A series of pilot projects was designed collaboratively and some of them were scaled-up and funded by the ROP (Reid et al., 2012). However, until 2013 most of the regionally promoted activities consisted of building up RTDI infrastructure and raising awareness, as the real support actions and the regulatory framework were decided and implemented by the central government. This deprived the region of the freedom and flexibility needed to consistently implement its Action Plan.

Hence, despite the evolution of regional planning, Central Macedonia had neither the autonomy nor the means to test its plans on the ground, experiment, and amend them. The regional actors participated actively in central calls with variable success. To boost the share of higher-tech industry and knowledge-intensive services, numerous initiatives have been launched, but their implementation has stagnated due to the failure of the stakeholders (including public administration) to embrace the project, mobilize the necessary resources, and create the necessary regulatory environment for the concept to become functional (Avranas and Nioras, 2011). The effort to create a regional innovation system ran out of steam once public funding stopped.[29]

The review of policy directions of ongoing and future R&I policies indicates that R&I policy is a permanent concern in the development programs of Central Macedonia.

Lessons From the Case Study

Central Macedonia is an example of a region that embraced the idea of innovation strategies early and systematically. However, only a few actions of those programmed have been implemented, due to limited funds that were made available for R&I and the actual centralization of R&I policy. The most successful actors link nationally and internationally more than regionally.

The multiple layers of planning have resulted in institutional learning and have attracted the attention of regional actors helping to take advantage of calls and opportunities for funding from the central administration and the European Union. Initially, some impact was generated, but it retrogressed rapidly after the Greek austerity crisis.

Weaknesses during the preparation of RIS3 remained those identified in the 1990s, that is, fragmentation of innovation support activities and lack of coordination at the regional and local levels. Reid et al. (2012) attribute this weak performance to the slow pace of restructuring from low-to-medium technology toward higher-tech manufacturing. By and large:

- At an initial stage, planning took advantage of local strengths and generated a visible impact.
- At a later stage, however, the RIS3 process was insufficient to cope with the challenges of the Greek crisis.

The lack of regional coordination and limited regional autonomy, in addition to the restricted embeddedness of key actors, proved insufficient to ensure continuity. Convergence began but was interrupted. In the current programming period, regional autonomy in Greece has increased. This eliminates one of the past impediments. The challenges are now the responsibility of the region more than previously.

CONCLUSIONS: THE PAST AND FUTURE OF REGIONAL INNOVATION STRATEGIES IN SOUTHERN EUROPE

Expectations from regional development aid range from the highly ambitious, expecting LFRs to change structures and behavior and turn into resilient advanced economies, to limited impact or no change at all. The European LFRs, benefiting from transnational development aid since the 1980s, demonstrate variable impacts. In SE, progress in terms of per capita GDP and productivity growth was visible before the crisis, but then reversed. Overall convergence was moderate. Macrodata, academic literature, and case studies tend to agree that funding, strategies, and behavioral adaptation are all needed to make a difference.

EU policy makers recognized that R&D and, later, innovation are significant driving forces for economic growth in the 1990s; hence the Commission introduced incentives for both public and business expenditures to RD&I. Following this intervention, GERD and BERD per capita increased, but decreased again partially after the crisis. However, R&D intensity improved, indicating that the decline of GDP was higher than that of R&D. PoEs have been created, even if in few regions and academic fields. The increased funding ensured sustainable improvements in scientific output (e.g., publications and citations), but only occasional contributions to economic growth. Explicit innovation strategies for increasing the impact of regional development were first adopted in the late 1990s. In this sense, RIS3 is more of an evolution than revolution of European policies, but it is distinguished from the past because of the administrative innovation of the ex-ante conditionality: strategy adoption and entrepreneurial discovery are a prerequisite for releasing funds.

Evidence from *case studies* suggest that the funding, recommendations, and persistence on RTDI incentives from the European Commission have produced very different results, ranging from almost continuous adaptation to global challenges and convergence to practically no change. In general, infrastructure and institutional capabilities have improved everywhere, but dimensions, such as regional solidarity, degrees of political autonomy, and the existence of a manufacturing sector (even if traditional or declining), play an important role. However, while administrative autonomy, persistent long-term policies, and concentration of resources are important, they are far from sufficient conditions for upgrading the regional economy: external factors are crucial and were found to be stimulating in some cases (e.g., the lack of inward investment in the Basque Country, which paved the way for endogenous growth policies) and inhibiting in others (the easy relocation of manufacturing from Central Macedonia to Bulgaria, where outward investment in certain cases meant complete relocation and not expanding investments). The latter is a crucial point for policy decisions: once PoEs are created, they face opportunities and incentives to link to established productive capabilities in advanced regions: this is a double-edged sword maintaining state-of-the-art knowledge and some funding on the one hand, but limiting the possibility to benefiting the local economy more, on the other.

What does the past tell us about the future? Formal rules for change were introduced early, but could not always change informal rules and local routines. There are both forces for and against change: the latter have been dominant in many SE regions. During the current programming period (or at least its beginning), austerity policies and persistent recessionary forces have diminished national funding resources, so SFs constitute a significant (if not the only) contribution to public RTDI investments. Ministries and agencies, as well as higher education and research centers, have suffered from the fiscal consolidation and they are very likely to be exercising pressures for absorbing funds in a "business-as-usual" way, despite the Commission's firm statement that this should stop. So the two opposed forces of conservatism and experimentation for the future are amplified:

• On the one hand, pressure will be exercised for the survival of companies and agencies under threat by the use of European Structural Investment Funds to alleviate the burden of the austerity budgets.
• On the other, the experience of disillusionment will speak in favor of taking time for appropriate policy design and focus on entrepreneurial discovery.

The first experiences point toward limited concentration again. The strategies posted by SE at the central repository[30] indicate 318 priorities reported; 177 of these priorities were described at a very generic level. Key enabling technologies were mentioned often. In a very few cases there were real examples of smart specialization: aquaculture (among the priority areas for a few regions), sea-linked cosmetic products, the shoe industry, innovative solutions in logistics, and deep-sea mining. Yet these are the exception of regions daring to concentrate, not the rule. Plus, the concept of entrepreneurial discovery cannot work unless local actors collaborate well. This is not always the case and it may be harder when funds are scarce.

At any rate, the current regulation means that the European Commission is now facing a new challenge. After the strategy design and/or an Action Plan is completed and agreed and the process starts, there are no instruments to guide regions away from "business-as-usual": the risk of an unholy alliance of businesses solving their operational problems and public authorities sticking to the priority of absorption is imminent, and may corrupt the entrepreneurial discovery process. In this case, European policy makers will face the dilemma of radical measures of enforcement to bring the derailed process back on track (blocking funding sources and wasting time) or of diluting the RIS3 message. It is not easy to respond to this dilemma. Possible new ideas that are needed include: (1) making taxonomies and approaching regions with varying characteristics (e.g., degree of autonomy, structural composition, stakeholder involvement, and role of external influence) with differentiated policies rather than having a uniform ex-ante conditionality, (2) special treatment for PoEs, and (3) local experimentation and change of interventions rather than too much continuity.

ENDNOTES

1. In fact, it is practically impossible to distinguish the different research, technological development, and innovation (RTDI) data for individual regions, as they have been entering and leaving the different objectives of the European Union [gross domestic product (GDP) per inhabitant less than 75% of the community average, regions that would have been eligible if the threshold of 75% of GDP had been calculated for the European Union at 15 and not at 25, and regions that recently exceeded 75% of the average GDP of the EU15 http://ec.europa.eu/regional_policy/sources/what/future/img/eligibility20142020.pdf]. Some regions have exceeded 75% and then fell behind again after the crisis. In Spain, the North is significantly wealthier than the South. However, for the purposes of looking at Southern Europe (SE), we consider the three countries

as a whole (as they have joined the EU with low GDP per head and significant development challenges) and distinguish regions only in Italy, where the North–South divide is very marked and persistent over time.

2. http://data.worldbank.org/indicator/NY.GDP.PCAP.CD/countries?order=wbapi_data_value_2014%20wbapi_data_value%20wbapi_data_value-last&sort=asc&display=default

3. https://ec.europa.eu/growth/sites/growth/files/infographic-innovation-union-01.png

4. The principle of subsidiarity is defined in Article 5 of the Treaty on European Union. It aims to ensure that decisions are taken as closely as possible to the citizen and that constant checks are made to verify that action at the EU level is justified in light of the possibilities available at the national, regional, or local level. Specifically, it is the principle whereby the European Union does not take action (except in the areas that fall within its exclusive competence), unless it is more effective than action taken at the national, regional, or local level.

5. Regions with GDP per capital lower than 75% of the EU average; most SE regions belong to the Objective 1 zone.

6. The eligibility criteria for Objective 2 regions are virtually identical to the three basic Objective 2 criteria for the 1994–99 period: unemployment rate above the community average, a percentage share of industrial employment exceeding the community average, and a decline in this employment category (http://ec.europa.eu/regional_policy/sources/docoffic/official/regulation/pdf/irfo_en.pdf).

7. In institutionalist terms, the initial Regional Innovation Strategies (RIS) attempts failed to produce institutional change.

8. Data for selected regions from the Regional Innovation Monitor (RIM).

9. Own calculations based on www.scimagojr.com

10. The Summary Innovation Index is composed of the following categories: human resources, research systems, finance and support, firm investments, linkages and entrepreneurship, intellectual assets, innovators, and economic effects.

11. https://www.weforum.org/reports/ and http://www3.weforum.org/docs/gcr/2015-2016/Global_Competitiveness_Report_2015-2016.pdf

12. Compound annual growth rate (CAGR) is calculated as follows: $e^{\beta} - 1$, where β is the estimated regression coefficient of the logarithm of the ratio of the yearly GDP to the baseline GDP (year = 1990), that is, $y_i = \ln\left(GDP_i / GDP_{1990}\right)$, regressed on the number of years passed baseline, that is, $x_i = year_i - 1990$. Had we used a traditional CAGR, the results would be misleading because of the sharp decline in some countries and regions after 2009.

13. https://ec.europa.eu/growth/tools-databases/regional-innovation-monitor/news/rim-plus-presents-outcomes-regional-visit-basque-country

14. https://ec.europa.eu/growth/tools-databases/regional-innovation-monitor/news/rim-plus-presents-outcomes-regional-visit-basque-country

15. https://ec.europa.eu/growth/tools-databases/regional-innovation-monitor/news/rim-plus-presents-outcomes-regional-visit-basque-country

16. https://ec.europa.eu/growth/tools-databases/regional-innovation-monitor/news/rim-plus-presents-outcomes-regional-visit-basque-country

17. https://ec.europa.eu/growth/tools-databases/regional-innovation-monitor/news/regional-innovation-policy-trends-norte-region-portugal

18. http://ec.europa.eu/regional_policy/archive/innovation/innovating/download/avr99/en_innov.pdf

19. This was the name of Integrated Programming in the 1980s and 1990s.

20. https://ec.europa.eu/growth/tools-databases/regional-innovation-monitor/news/regional-innovation-policy-trends-norte-region-portugal

21. http://ec.europa.eu/regional_policy/archive/innovation/innovating/download/avr99/en_innov.pdf
22. https://ec.europa.eu/growth/tools-databases/regional-innovation-monitor/news/regional-innovation-policy-trends-norte-region-portugal
23. https://ec.europa.eu/growth/tools-databases/regional-innovation-monitor/news/regional-innovation-policy-trends-norte-region-portugal
24. https://www.dropbox.com/home/Campania?preview=Campania+-+Internal+Market%2C+Industry%2C+Entrepreneurship+And+Smes+-+European+Commission.html
25. https://ec.europa.eu/growth/tools-databases/regional-innovation-monitor/region/italia/sud/campania
26. http://www.regione.campania.it/assets/documents/por-fesr-2014-2020.pdf
27. https://ec.europa.eu/growth/tools-databases/regional-innovation-monitor/region/italia/sud/campania
28. https://ec.europa.eu/growth/tools-databases/regional-innovation-monitor/region/ellada/voreia-ellada/kentriki-makedonia
29. http://www.gsrt.gr/central.aspx?sId=120I500I126I646I495215
30. http://s3platform.jrc.ec.europa.eu/ (Data November 2016.)

REFERENCES

Akca, H., 2006. Assessment of rural tourism in Turkey using SWOT analysis. J. Appl. Sci. 6, 2837–2839.
Ansell, C.K., Parsons, C.A., Darden, K.A., 1997. Dual networks in European regional development policy. J. Common Market Stud. 35, 347–375.
Avranas, A., Nioras, A., 2011. Regional Innovation Report Kentriki Makedonia. Regional Innovation Monitor project for DG Enterprise of the European Commission. Available from: https://ec.europa.eu/growth/tools-databases/regional-innovation-monitor/sites/default/files/report/makedonia_gr12_rim_regional_innovation_report.pdf.
Bache, I., Jones, R., 2000. Has EU regional policy empowered the regions? A study of Spain and the United Kingdom. Reg. Fed. Stud. 10, 1–20.
Bachtler, J., Gorzelak, G., 2007. Reforming EU cohesion policy: a reappraisal of the performance of the Structural Funds. Pol. Stud. 28, 309–326.
Barca, F., 2009. An agenda for a reformed cohesion policy: a place-based approach to meeting European Union challenges and expectations. Available from: http://www.europarl.europa.eu/meetdocs/2009_2014/documents/regi/dv/barca_report_/barca_report_en.pdf.
Bateira, J., Ferreira, L.V., 2002. Questioning EU cohesion policy in Portugal: a complex systems approach. Eur. Urban Reg. Stud. 9, 297–314.
Benneworth, P., Hospers, G.J., 2007. The new economic geography of old industrial regions: universities as global–local pipelines. Environ. Plan. C 25, 779–802.
Bonaccorsi, A., 2016. Addressing the disenchantment: universities and regional development in peripheral regions. J. Econ. Pol. Reform, 1–28, Available from: http://www.tandfonline.com/doi/full/10.1080/17487870.2016.1212711.
Caiazza, R., Volpe, T., 2013. How Campanian small and medium enterprises (SMEs) can compete in the global agro-food industry. J. Food Prod. Market. 19, 406–412.
Cappelen, A., Castellacci, F., Fagerberg, J., Verspagen, B., 2002. The impact of regional support on growth and convergence in the European Union. J. Common Market Stud. 41 (4), 621–644.
Charles, D.R., Nauwelaers, C., Mouton, B., Bradley, D., 2000. Assessment of the regional innovation and technology transfer strategies and infrastructures (RITTS) scheme. Final Evaluation Report. European Commission, Brussels.

Cooke, P., Morgan, K., 1998. The Associational Economy: Firms, Regions, and Innovation. Oxford University Press, Oxford.

Cuadrado-Roura, J.R., Mancha, T., 2005. Política Económica. Elaboración, Objetivos e Instrumentos, third ed. McGraw-Hill, Madrid.

Ederveen, S.G., Groot, H.L., Nahuis, R., 2002. Fertile soil for structural funds? A panel data analysis of the conditional effectiveness of European regional policy. CPB Netherlands Bureau for Economic Policy Analysis. Discussion paper n. 10.

Ederveen, S., Groot, H.L., Nahuis, R., 2006. Fertile soil for structural funds? A panel data analysis of the conditional effectiveness of European cohesion policy. Kyklos 59, 17–42.

Eichengreen, B., Park, D., Shin, K., 2013. Growth slowdowns redux: avoiding the middle income trap. VOXEU. Available from: http://voxeu.org/article/growth-slowdowns-redux-avoiding-middle-income-trap.

Etxabe, I., Valdaliso, J.M., 2013. Who are the most networked agents within Basque cluster associations? A tentative and exploratory approach to measure structural social capital. The University of the Basque Country. Available from: http://www.reunionesdeestudiosregionales.org/Oviedo2013/htdocs/pdf/p833.pdf.

European Commission, 2015. Innovation Union Scoreboard 2015.

European Commission, 2016. Science, Research and Innovation performance of the EU. Brussels.

Fagerberg, J., Verspagen, B., 2002. Technology-gaps, innovation-diffusion and transformation: an evolutionary approach. Res. Pol. 31, 1291–1304.

Faíñaa, J.A., López-Rodríguez, J., 2004. Regional income convergence and regional policy in the European Union. ERSA Conference Papers (No. ersa04p32). European Regional Science Association. Available from: https://www.econstor.eu/bitstream/10419/116944/1/ERSA2004_032.pdf.

Faludi, A., 2006. From European spatial development to territorial cohesion policy. Reg. Stud. 40 (6), 667–678.

Farole, T., Rodríguez-Pose, A., Storper, M., 2011. Cohesion policy in the European Union: growth, geography, institutions. J. Common Market Stud. 49, 1089–1111.

Healy, A., Morgan, K., Nauwelaers, C., 2016. Regions as laboratories: what have we learned from twenty years of regional innovation policy in Europe? School of Geography and Planning Paper, Cardiff University, Wales, United Kingdom.

Hooghe, L., 1996. Cohesion policy and European integration: building multi-level governance. Oxford University Press, Oxford.

Leonardi, R., 2006. Cohesion in the European Union. Reg. Stud. 40 (02), 155–166.

Lundvall, B.Å., Tomlinson, M., 2000. International benchmarking and national innovation systems. Report for the Portuguese Presidency of the European Union.

Magro, E., Navarro, M., 2012. The role of knowledge infrastructures in regional innovation systems: the case of the Basque Country. Paper presented in the International Conference on Regional Science: the Challenge of Regional Development in a World of Changing Hegemonies: Knowledge, competitiveness And Austerity. Thirty-Eighth Meeting of Regional Studies. AECR, Bilbao. Available from: http://www.aecr.org/web/congresos/2012/Bilbao2012/htdocs/pdf/p518.pdf.

Marzinotto, B., 2012. The growth effects of EU cohesion policy: a meta-analysis. Bruegel Working Paper, 14.

Moreira, A.C., Carneiro, L.F.M., Tavares, M.P.T., 2006. Critical technologies for the North of Portugal in 2015: the case of ITCE sectors—information technologies, communication and electronics. Int. J. Foresight Innov. Pol. 3, 187–206.

Morgan, K., 2016. Collective entrepreneurship: the Basque model of innovation. Eur. Plan. Stud. 24, 1544–1560.

Nathan, M., Overman, H., 2013. Agglomeration, clusters, and industrial policy. Oxford Rev. Econ. Pol. 29, 383–404.

OECD, 2011. Regions and Innovation Policy. Available from: http://www.oecd-ilibrary.org/urban-rural-and-regional-development/regions-and-innovation-policy_9789264097803-en.

Orkestra-Instituto Vasco de Competitividad (España), 2009. II Informe de competitividad del País Vasco: hacia el estadio competitivo de la innovación. Universidad de Deusto, Bilbao.

Orkestra-Instituto Vasco de Competitividad (España), 2015. The Basque Country Competitiveness Report 2015. Productive Transformation in Practice. Basques Institute of Competitiveness, Deusto Foundation, Bilbao. Available from: http://www.orkestra.deusto.es/competitividadcapv/imgs/informes/2015-orkestra-the-basque-country-competitiveness-report.pdf.

Oyon, C., 2014. Strategic cluster policies for new growth shaping strategic partnerships for the transformation of our economies—the evolution of cluster policies in the Basque Country. Available from: http://www.ewi-vlaanderen.be/sites/default/files/bestanden/Cristina%20Oyon_Cluster%20policy%202.0%20in%20BC_EWIFocus_12052014.pdf.

Ponsiglione, C., De Crescenzo, E., Lanzetta, V., Zollo, G., 2012. The analysis of regional innovation systems in Europe: the case of a region with medium-low innovation capability. Fifteenth Uddevella Symposium Entrepreneurship and Innovation Networks. 14–16 June 2012. University of Algarve, Faro, Portugal, pp. 207–225.

Reid, A., Komninos, N., Sanchez, J., Tsanakas, P., 2012. RIS3 national assessment: Greece. Smart Specialisation as a Means to Foster Economic Renewal. A report to the European Commission, DG Regional Policy, Brussels. Available from: http://www.stereaellada.gr/fileadmin/pages/5h_programmatikh/RIS3/RIS3_Greece_National_Assessment_Report_final__February_2013_final_edited_.pdf.

RIM, 2015. Regional Innovation Monitor Plus. Available from: https://ec.europa.eu/growth/tools-databases/regional-innovation-monitor/.

RIS3 Campania. Available from: http://www.regione.campania.it/assets/documents/por-fesr-2014-2020.pdf.

Rodríguez-Pose, A., Fratesi, U., 2002. Unbalanced development strategies and the lack of regional convergence in the EU. Department of Geography and Environment, London School of Economics, London.

Santos, D., 2000. Innovation and territory which strategies to promote regional innovation systems in Portugal? Eur. Urban Reg. Stud. 7, 147–157.

Santos, D., Simões, M.J., 2014. Regional innovation systems in Portugal: a critical evaluation. Invest. Reg. 28, 37–56.

Schrittwieser Consulting, 2014. Analysis of Smart Specialization Strategies in selected Mediterranean coastal regions and countries. Available from: https://creativemedit.files.wordpress.com/2014/10/analysis-of-smart-specialization-strategies-in-selected-mediterranean-coastal-regions-and-countries.pdf.

Sidiropoulos, N., Tsipouri, L., 2011. CERTH/CPERI Benchmarking Report: Fostering Evaluation Competencies in Research. Technology and Innovation in the SEE Region SEE Transnational Cooperation Programme (mimeo).

Smyrl, M.E., 1997. Does European community regional policy empower the regions? Governance 10, 287–309.

Socintec/INNO, 2005. Ex-post evaluation of the RIS, RTTs and RISI ERDF innovative actions for the period 1994-99. Information Report to European Commission (Ref.: E3083). CEC, Luxembourg.

Stephan, A., Happich, M., Geppert, K., 2005. Regional disparities in the European Union: convergence and agglomeration. The Postgraduate Research Programme Working Paper Series No. 4.

Europa-Universität, Viadrina Frankfurt (Oder), Graduiertenkolleg Kapitalmärkte und Finanz-wirtschaft im erweiterten Europa.

Sterlacchini, A., 2008. R&D, higher education and regional growth: uneven linkages among Euro-pean regions. Res. Pol. 37, 1096–1107.

Technopolis, 2006. Strategic evaluation on innovation and the knowledge based economy in relation to the structural and cohesion funds, for the programming period 2007-2013. A Report to the European Commission, DG Regional Policy. Available from: http://ec.europa.eu/regional_policy/sources/docgener/evaluation/pdf/strategic_innov.pdf.

Thomas, A., Passaro, R., Marinangeli, B., 2015. Entrepreneurial behaviors and strategic paths in innovative SMEs: evidence from Italy's Campania region. Glob. Bus. Organ. Excell. 34, 51–62.

Valdaliso, J.M., Wilson, J.R., 2015. Strategies for shaping territorial competitiveness. Routledge, New York, NY.

Vang, J., Chaminade, C., Coenen, L., 2007. Learning from the Bangalore experience: the role of universities in an emerging Regional Innovation System. Centre for Innovation, Research and Competence in the Learning Economy (CIRCLE). Lund University, WP. Available from: http://www.lu.se/lup/publication/61443b24-d348-4e4c-a910-73f6b651ce7a.

Yeung, H.W.C., 2000. Organizing 'the firm' in industrial geography I: networks, institutions and regional development. Progr. Human Geogr. 24 (2), 301–315.

Zollo, G., De Crescenzo, E., Ponsiglione, C., 2011. A gap analysis of regional innovation sys-tems (RIS) with medium-low innovative capabilities: the case of Campania region (Italy). ESU European University Network on Entrepreneurship Conference. University of Seville, Spain, pp. 1–19.

Zucchella, A., Siano, A., 2014. Internationalization and innovation as resources for SME growth in foreign markets: a focus on textile and clothing firms in the Campania Region. Int. Stud. Mgmt. Org. 44, 21–41.

FURTHER READING

European Commission, 2003. Recommendation of 6 May 2003. Off. J. Eur. Union L124. Available from: http://eurlex.europa.eu/JOIndex.do.

Gill, I., Raiser, M., 2012. Golden Growth: Restoring the Lustre of the European Economic Model. World Bank, Washington, Available from: http://www.worldbank.org/en/region/eca/publication/golden-growth.

Rodríguez-Pose, A., Fratesi, U., 2004. Between development and social policies: the impact of European Structural Funds in Objective 1 regions. Reg. Stud. 38, 97–113.

Tomlinson, M., Lundvall, B.Å., 2001. Policy learning through benchmarking national systems of competence building and innovation–learning by comparing. Report for the Advanced Bench-marking Concepts (ABC) Project. European Council, Strasbourg.

Chapter 7

Smart Specialization in the US Context; Lessons From the Growth of the Albany, New York Nanotechnology Cluster

Charles W. Wessner*, Thomas R. Howell**

*Georgetown University, Washington, DC, United States; **Dentons LLP, Washington, DC, United States*

Chapter Outline

Academic Highlights

- The Tech Valley cluster represents a case of limited path dependency.

Advances in the Theory and Practice of Smart Specialization. http://dx.doi.org/10.1016/B978-0-12-804137-6.00007-3
157

- Reflecting the smart specialization concept, the New York nanoinitiative arose in a cooperative fashion, reflecting long-term state level development goals made possible in part by the determination and competency of local development actors.

Policy Highlights

- A major feature of the Tech Valley success is the relative absence of central government funding and support.
- The analysis underscores the importance of multiple levels of cooperation.
- The creation of new institutions—a major new educational institution in the form of the College of Nanoscale Science and Engineering (CNSE)—was a key step.
- A key differentiator was the presence of shared, cutting edge facilities.
- The initiative was grounded in cooperation at multiple levels within the region.

TECH VALLEY—SUSTAINING MOMENTUM

In the past 15 years, a major economic development effort by the state of New York has created "Tech Valley," a research and manufacturing cluster in the upstate Capital Region centered on nanotechnology innovation. This effort has fostered an influx of large- and small-technology-intensive companies and the creation of thousands of high-skill, high-income jobs. The phenomenon known as Tech Valley is significant for a number of reasons, not least of which is that it has seen the reversal of longstanding trends toward outmigration of companies and workers from upstate New York and toward offshoring of US-based high technology manufacturing. In addition, Tech Valley demonstrates how regional economic development can be fostered through long-term public—private partnerships able to generate substantial investments in research and innovation infrastructure. As an initiative of one state, Tech Valley provides valuable best practice lessons for the economic development efforts of other states as well as for the federal government. Under the Obama Administration, the federal government has played an active role in regional cluster development, with a focus on clean energy and manufacturing. Both the state and federal government initiatives represent a long-standing commitment to "place-based" regional development or what is now, in a more refined form, called "Smart Specialization" in Europe.

This chapter describes the recent evolution of federal cluster policies in so far as it puts the development of state-based initiatives in relevant context. The primary focus, however, is on the unique, state-based initiative to develop "Tech Valley" in upstate New York. The term upstate is used to distinguish the North and Western New York from New York City and its environs. The primary focus of this initiative was the Capital Region, that is, the area around Albany, the capital of the state of New York.

The chapter then describes the longstanding efforts of New York State to reverse its economic decline dating back to the 1950s and its decision to focus efforts on nanotechnologies through sustained government, industry, and university collaboration. This sustained development effort is of interest in that it captures a variety of best practice features, including the high level of cooperation, the scale of the investments, the creation of a new institution to carry out research and education in nanoscale technologies, primarily related to the semiconductor industry. These investments were successful in drawing in a major semiconductor manufacturing facility involving billions of dollars in investment, in creating thousands of direct and many more thousands of indirect jobs through the build-out of a supply chain, with ongoing impact on additional employment.

Evolving Federal Regional Policy

In the United States, the federal government has not implemented focused regional economic development programs on a scale commensurate with those of numerous other major industrial countries. With a few exceptions like the 1930s creation of Tennessee Valley Authority, federal regional development assistance has been widely dispersed (geographically and thematically) and distributed in small-scale packets of assistance from many federal entities. Recently, however, this pattern changed. The America COMPETES Act of 2007 established a mandate for the Economic Development Agency (EDA), which assists economically distressed regions by supporting the creation and strengthening of regional innovation clusters. EDA's jobs and innovation accelerator challenge is supporting some of 40 of these regional innovation clusters. The EDA is also participating with other federal agencies in the creation of regional Proof of Concept centers. Similarly, the Department of Energy (DoE) has established regional "energy-innovation hubs" in thematic areas, such as batteries, "green" buildings, and solar energy.

This regional focus of federal investment represents a significant departure from previous more Washington-centric policies. This regional orientation has significantly accelerated in the last years of the Obama Administration with a major emphasis on manufacturing. This reflects a growing sense in the United States that we are able to develop new technology opportunities but only too often are not able to exploit them within the national economy. The initiative also seeks to capture technological development that is not susceptible to low wage competition. Interestingly, it also represents a major effort to learn best practice from other countries, notably the German Fraunhofer Institutes.

The New Manufacturing Initiative

The scale of the Obama Administration's manufacturing initiative is significant. Currently, the Administration is creating what was initially called the National

Network for Manufacturing Innovation (NNMI), a name recently changed to *Manufacturing USA*. The proposed network is to consists of some 15 manufacturing research institutes (with a long-term goal of 40–50 institutes). These government–industry–university partnerships are focused on new promising technologies. The concept is loosely modeled on the German Fraunhofer Institutes. The expectation is that these manufacturing centers will generate regional economic benefits while also supporting the commercialization of promising new technologies, such as 3D printing, new metal alloys, and advanced semiconductor manufacturing.

The institutes created under this policy initiative represent a highly ambitious national effort to address a core national need, that is, to develop and refine new methods of manufacturing, and then disseminate them broadly through a cooperative, regionally-based system. Each manufacturing institute is focused on a new and promising technology opportunity. These include additive manufacturing, digital manufacturing and design, lightweight metal alloys, next generation semiconductor manufacturing, advanced composites, integrated photonics, flexible electronics, next generation fibers and textiles, and "smart manufacturing." The effort to develop and expand the network has drawn on extensive analysis and public engagement in defining needs and design. It involved close consultation with industry and academia to identify promising technologies, followed by regional conferences to publicize the opportunity and refine the technological focus to ensure that the proposed centers would align with industry interest and needs. The actual awards were made through a competitive process that required the participation of multiple institutions, firms, and matching funds. This intensely competitive process brought together substantial coalitions of universities and companies, often working together virtually in natural. Progress has been remarkable, with seven major institutes in place, two forthcoming awards, and plans for six additional institutes scheduled for 2016. The goal is to create a national network of some 15 manufacturing hubs across the United States. At the time this chapter was written (April 2016), the federal government had committed USD 600 million to 8 institutes. This has been matched by over USD 1.2 billion in nonfederal investments from industry, academia, and state governments.

The most recently created institute, established under the auspices of the Department of Defense (DoD) with a consortium led by the Massachusetts Institute of Technology, is focused on the production of fabrics and fibers with exceptional properties. The goal of the consortium is to cooperate in integrating fibers and yarns with integrated circuits, LEDs, solar cells, and other devices to create textiles and fabrics that see, hear, sense, communicate, store energy, monitor health, and change color as needed. The development of this network and its expansion across technologies and regions represents a major accomplishment for the Obama Administration—one that must be sustained for this initiative to have a long-term impact.

The current network, either in place or planned for 2016, includes centers in the following technological areas:

- *America Makes*: Additive Manufacturing, DoD in Youngstown, Ohio (OH);
- *DMDII*: Digital Manufacturing & Design Innovation, DoD in Chicago, Illinois (IL);
- *LIFT*: Lightweight & Modern Metals, DoD in Detroit, Michigan (MI);
- *PowerAmerica*: Power electronics Manufacturing, DoE in Raleigh, North Carolina (NC);
- *IACMI*: Advanced Composites Manufacturing, DoE in Knoxville, Tennessee (TN);
- *Integrated Photonics*: DoD in Rochester, New York
- *Flexible Hybrid Electronics*: DoD in San Jose, California (CA);
- *Smart Manufacturing*: DoE—in solicitation;
- *Revolutionary Fibers & Textiles*: DoD in Boston, Massachusetts (MA).

Needless to say, the results of regional development efforts vary wildly in the United States, as elsewhere. Silicon Valley developed initially through industry–university partnerships, but rapidly took on a momentum of its own. Triangle Park in North Carolina was successful in bringing a much higher level of economic activity to the state, but has not yet achieved the levels of entrepreneurial activity that characterize Silicon Valley. Omaha, Nebraska has had major success in developing its light aircraft industry. The biomedical cluster in Boston has shown remarkable success, whereas the photovoltaic cluster in Northeast Ohio has faced multiple challenges. In all these cases, the role of quality universities, benefiting from visionary leadership, and close cooperation with public research institutions and the private sector have played essential roles in the region's development. Federal support has sometimes been catalytic, but is normally most effective when backed by strong and local public–private commitment. The requirement for private sector and university funding to match federal funding is designed to ensure the commitment of these partners. Thus far, the new institutes have had a very positive local and regional reception. Nonetheless, as with any new initiative, the creation of new institutes, the coordination of multiple partners and agreement on priorities is a challenging process.

A State-Based Initiative

In 2012, President Obama visited New York's "Tech Valley," describing the region's effort as a model for the nation. Notwithstanding this affirmation, interestingly, the federal government's role in Tech Valley has been valuable, even necessary on some regulatory issues, but generally limited in scope and impact. It remains essentially a state-based initiative. Still, some federal contributions have been made. First, the Defense Advanced Research Projects Agency (DARPA) designated SUNY Albany (State University of New York at Albany) as one of four national "focus centers" for semiconductor research. Second, the Department of Transportation funded road improvements which were needed to support the GlobalFoundries wafer fabrication plant in Malta, New York State. Third, the New York Congressional delegation worked to ensure that reviews of wetlands by the Army Corps of Engineers of relevance to the establishment of semiconductor manufacturing operations were completed promptly. In short, elements of the federal government recognized the progress underway in the Capitol Region and in some instances provided regulatory support to its continued development. That said, the initiative is fundamentally a state-based effort spanning almost two decades of sustained investment by state and regional authorities. This independent effort has led to a widespread impression in New York that the state is capable of managing its economic turnaround effort with its own leadership and resources. As such, the "Tech Valley" initiative represents an exceptional example of effective regional innovation policy in the United States.

THE PROBLEM: LONG-TERM ECONOMIC DECLINE

In the first half of the 20th century, upstate New York was one of the most prosperous regions in the United States. It was the site of major innovative manufacturers, such as General Electric, Eastman Kodak, Corning, and IBM, and the region produced a stream of inventions that helped to shape the modern world. It was the home of the nation's oldest polytechnic university, Rensselaer Polytechnic Institute (RPI), and other leading universities. It was a major transportation crossroads, drawing on the Eerie Canal, the rail network, and later the Interstate Highway system. While the region retains these assets today, the broad prosperity that it once enjoyed is a distant memory.

Upstate manufacturing employment peaked in the 1950s and the region began a long economic decline which has continued to the present day. Major manufacturers have downsized, moved operations offshore, or left the region altogether. An outmigration of people, including recent university graduates, has exacerbated economic stagnation. A 2004 Brookings study of the upstate economy found that in the 1990s, upstate's population growth of 1.1% for the decade was lower than that of any state except West Virginia and North Dakota. Nearly 30% of new residents arriving in upstate New York in the 1990s were prisoners (the construction and operation of prisons for America's growing prison population was seen as a promising source of employment in the 1980s; although mostly the expected gains did not materialize). Personal income grew at half of the national rate in the 1990s, and over half of this meager growth reflected increases in government transfer payments from sources, such as Social Security, Medicare, Medicaid, and the earned income tax credit. Successive democratic and republican governors have acknowledged, and grappled with, the upstate economic malaise.

Historically, the government of the state of New York has driven economic growth through large scale public investments, such as the Erie Canal, the New York State Thruway, the major infrastructure projects undertaken in New York City during the Robert Moses era, the establishment of the Olympics infrastructure at Lake Placid, and the creation of one of the foremost university systems in the world. The Tech Valley developmental effort is the most recent manifestation of this tradition, involving a sustained series of public investments on a scale and over a time frame rarely seen in other states.

Governor Mario Cuomo launched a number of initiatives in the 1980s to revive the upstate economy through investments in university-based innovation. His graduate research initiative paid higher salaries to attract leading faculty to the SUNY system, and in 1993 Cuomo designated SUNY Albany as a Center for Advanced Technology. One of the young faculty members drawn to upstate New York thanks to Cuomo's efforts was Alain Kaloyeros, who has played a central role in the creation of Tech Valley. In the mid1990s, then governor George Pataki assembled a group of industry and academic leaders to devise a strategy for reversing the economic decline of upstate New York. Encouraged and advised by the multinational IBM, the group hammered out a program for combined research, education, and commercial efforts based on centers of excellence affiliated with universities.

Nanotechnology

Pataki's working group identified as an important theme for the innovation-based development effort as nanotechnology—the manipulation of matter on the atomic and molecular scale—because of its potential application across many sectors, including electronics, fluidics, sensors, biomedicine, and photonics. Over the following decade, a multifaceted effort was mounted with the bipartisan support of state political leaders (Pataki, senate majority leader Joseph L. Bruno, and assembly speaker Sheldon Silver) to promote nanotechnology-based economic growth in upstate New York. The initial nanotechnology focus was on the semiconductor industry, a sector in which IBM had long been active in research efforts to progressively reduce the size—while simultaneously increasing the capability—of electronic devices.

Government/Industry/University Collaboration

The primary institutional mechanism utilized to create Tech Valley has been the public private partnership, featuring collaboration between the state government, universities, and private companies. These partnerships are one of the most common modes of economic development globally and may take many forms. An interesting feature of the New York approach is that, in the Tech Valley effort, most of the state funding was invested in university-based research infrastructure, not in companies. This approach was supported by IBM and other companies, which made substantial additional financial contributions to the universities. This approach meant that state contributions were investments on a university campus and that would remain in-state even if corporate partners were to abandon the effort. Reflecting the growing recognition of the region's success, in 2013 US Secretary of Commerce Penny Pritzker said that public–private research collaborations at SUNY Albany were "absolutely" a model for the rest of the country to emulate (Williams, 2013).

In seeking to create an innovation-based cluster in the upstate region, the state benefited from an established base of technology-intensive companies which understood the state's economic challenges. In the 1990s, IBM bluntly warned state leaders that absent changes in state government policies, it would have little choice but to relocate to another region. The state government responded promptly and effectively. At the same time, in cooperation with the state university, IBM took a proactive approach helping to lead the development of key initiatives. These included:

- choice of nanotechnology as theme for economic development efforts;
- development of SUNY Albany as a world-class nanotechnology center;
- creation of a new institution, the CNSE with a USD 100 million commitment by IBM and USD 50 million from the state;
- establishment (in collaboration with the state) of a 675-employee R&D center for semiconductor packaging, to be owned and operated by CNSE;
- formation of International Venture for Nanolithography (INVENT); and
- research collaboration with AMD/GlobalFoundries and transfer of assets to GF.[1]

More recently, in an effort to capture new federal Manufacturing USA funding, GE, IBM, GlobalFoundries, and other companies launched the New York Power Electronics Manufacturing Consortium in collaboration with the state government and CNSE. This effort was not successful, but did result in a new commitment to a high-tech development policy by the state government.

SUNY Albany

The centerpiece of New York's effort to create Tech Valley was a series of major investments which, over time, transformed SUNY Albany from a teacher's college with no engineering program into the foremost academic center for nanotechnology science and engineering in the world. A remarkable civic entrepreneur, Alain Kaloyeros, spearheaded this effort. He developed close relations with multiple governors and key members of the State Assembly, emphasizing the need for close collaborations between university research and the private sector. In 1988, the state supported the establishment of an advanced semiconductor research program at SUNY Albany and in 2001 the School of Nanosciences and Nanoengineering was established at the University. In 2001, investments of USD 50 million by the state and a remarkable USD 100 million contribution by IBM enabled the creation at the university of a current-generation 200 /300 mm clean room for semiconductor process R&D and prototype, and pilot manufacturing. No industrial centers in the United States had a clean room facility of this scale and with such cutting-edge equipment. Continued investments by the state and IBM in SUNY Albany helped that institution to attract top faculty and graduate students in the nanotechnology field. In 2004, Kaloyeros presided over the establishment of the CNSE. During the following decade, CNSE trained a nanotechnology work force, eventually yielding some 800 graduate and undergraduate students per year.[2]

As noted, most of the state's investments in nanotechnology were directed toward research infrastructure rather than to individual companies. The result was the creation of "neutral" common research space [referred to by some as an "industrial commons": see for example, Pisano and Shih (2009)] richly endowed with state-of-the-art equipment and expertise which could be used by many different semiconductor manufacturers, and materials and equipment suppliers to prove and refine production tools, materials, and processes. The existence of CNSE and its facilities, together with state incentives and outreach by Governor Pataki, Kaloyeros, and others, were key factors in the decision by SEMATECH, the US semiconductor consortium, to establish a research center at SUNY Albany (2002) and eventually to relocate entirely to Albany from its original site in Austin, Texas (2007).[3]

As a result of the superb research facilities at CNSE, other major players in the semiconductor industry subsequently made investments in the Albany region, including ASML, Vistec Lithography, Tokyo Electron, Applied Materials, Infineon, Micron Technology, and AMD/GlobalFoundries.

Large Public Investments

The state of New York has invested over USD 2 billion in research infrastructure at SUNY Albany and elsewhere in the Capital Region. This state investment has leveraged a far higher level of investment in the region by high-tech companies attracted by the nanotechnology research center—according to one estimate, about USD 14 billion of private investment in research infrastructure. The catalytic impact of these investments was substantial, providing additional impetus to the CNSE's reputation and activities. The active participation of high-tech companies is a key feature of the CNSE's success, but it would not have been possible without the corresponding investments by the state.

INITIAL IMPACTS

Attracting New Talent

Highly-educated people associated with semiconductor companies have moved into the region, at least partially mitigating the region's longstanding "brain drain." Albany now ranks eighth in the United States in percentage of population with a graduate degree. A 2013 Brookings study noted the Capital Region ranked 18th out of all metropolitan areas in the United States in terms of patents issued to a million residents (Grondahl, 2013). A 2014 study by the Business Journals ranked the Albany-Schenectady-Troy metropolitan area the 11th "smartest market" among the nation's 102 largest metropolitan areas (Rogers, 2014).

The Move to Semiconductor Manufacturing

While New York's principal initial technology-oriented economic development investments were in university-based research infrastructure, state planners expected that such investment would eventually lead to the establishment of a major high-tech manufacturing presence and the creation of thousands of high-skill, high wage jobs within the region. To realize this vision, from 1998 state and local economic development professionals mounted an extraordinary effort to attract inward investment by semiconductor manufacturers and their associated suppliers. To a remarkable degree, this effort was locally driven with decisive help at critical phases from private, state, and (modest) federal support. In addition to the investments in research infrastructure at SUNY Albany, this involved:

- development of deep expertise on semiconductor manufacturing by the development team, including the retention of expert consultants;
- extensive outreach through participation in semiconductor industry trade shows, conferences, and other similar events;
- visits by regional delegations to individual semiconductor manufacturers to better understand their requirements, the opportunity represented in attracting a major fab,[4] and the nature of the global competition;
- preparation of an extremely sophisticated and detailed proposal for chip fabs to be located at what was arguably the best site in New York; and
- preparation at the state level of substantial incentives packages which were fully competitive with other global semiconductor manufacturing regions (e.g., Dresden, Singapore, and Israel). This integration of regional initiatives and state investment policy is a key feature of the Albany/Malta cluster development.

Role of Development Organizations

New York has over 600 economic development organizations, including public, private, and partly state-controlled entities operating at the state, regional, local, and individual site level (Table 7.1). The state's ultimately successful effort to secure additional semiconductor manufacturing—AMD, and later GlobalFoundries—essentially reflected the collaborative efforts of four such organizations:

In addition, a publicly regulated private utility serving upstate New York, National Grid (owned by the UK group of that name), was an active player in promoting technology-based economic growth in the upstate region. As the

TABLE 7.1 Economic Development Organizations in New York State

Organization	Scope
ESD	Statewide
CEG	11-County Capital Region
SEDC	Saratoga County
LFTCEDC	LFTC

CEG, Center for Economic Growth; ESD, Empire State Development Corporation; LFTC, Luther Forest Technology Campus; LFTCEDC, Luther Forest Technology Campus Economic Development Corporation; SEDC, Saratoga Economic Development Corporation.
Source: Wessner, C.W., Howell, T. (forthcoming). *Tech Valley: New York's Nanotechnology Initiative.*

provider of electricity for the region, National Grid's economic interests were linked to the economic development of the region. The prospect of a semiconductor fabrication facility was especially attractive given the very high volumes of high quality, ultra-reliable electricity required for the production of semiconductors.[5] National Grid took an enlightened approach, providing funding to support promotional efforts, consultants permitting reviews as well as support for a myriad of other steps needed to develop the site, such as engineering, aerial mapping, and environmental and vibration studies. Moreover, National Grid's public advocacy of the benefits of the proposed investment played a powerful role.

The effort to create a chip fab site and to secure a semiconductor manufacturing tenant was led by the local development organization, the Saratoga Economic Development Commission (SEDC), and its affiliate, Luther Forest Technology Campus Economic Development Corporation (LFTCEDC). The Empire State Development Corporation (ESD) and the Center for Economic (CEG) growth played key supporting roles, intervening frequently and at important intervals with financial support for the local groups' efforts. ESD and CEG funds paid for environmental and engineering studies, purchases of land, marketing efforts directed at semiconductor manufacturers, preparation of permit applications, and retention of consultants. ESD was the principal provider of state incentives for semiconductor companies interested in locating to New York.

Shovel-Ready Sites

State, regional, and local economic development teams undertook a major effort to create "shovel-ready" sites for semiconductor manufacturing operations, including:

- *Identification of sites* with the best geological and locational characteristics for semiconductor manufacturing.

- *Educational outreach* to affected communities, including sponsorship of visits by local leaders to other US communities where chip fabs were located.
- *"Prepermitting"* the sites, securing zoning approvals from local town boards for generic semiconductor manufacturing operations (at the 300 nm level).
- *Infrastructure development* was undertaken to ensure that the necessary infrastructure to support a chip fab would be in place in a timely fashion. This is a critical variable for a multibillion dollar investment and required coordinated efforts, including engineering studies, wetlands reviews, and some initial construction.

As a direct result of these efforts, in 2006, AMD, one of the world's leading semiconductor manufacturers, announced that it would build a chip fab at the LFTC in the towns of Malta and Stillwater, New York State, to be operational by 2012. Key factors in its decision were as follows:

- The site itself was one of the best in the world in terms of its reliable power, abundant water, geological features, as well as its geographical proximity to CNSE.[6]
- A site in the US was a hedge against global risks, for example, SARS epidemics, earthquakes, and distance with respect to sites located outside the US.
- The state's proposal was highly professional and accurately depicted the new fab's cost structure.
- The state offered a substantial, internationally competitive incentives package. This was a critical factor in attracting the AMD/GlobalFoundries investment.
- State political leaders offered strong and sustained support, with both ad hoc funding for studies to further site development as well as the political will to offer a major incentives package.

The Incentives Package

The incentives package was key to the successful effort to attract a major fab to Tech Valley (Table 7.2). Neither the strong educational infrastructure at RPI and the CNSE, nor the exceptional natural site would have proved remotely sufficient to attract a semiconductor facility without an internationally competitive incentives package. As AMD CEO Hector Ruiz said, the incentive package was "the key" in the company's choice of the New York site. Then New York Governor George Pataki commented that *"philosophically we'd prefer not to have to offer incentives, but without the package, AMD would have gone elsewhere."* The package itself was substantial. It successfully outbid competitors in Dresden, Germany, and Singapore, but it was not different in character from the competing bids, notwithstanding the pretense of limits on state aid to industry. In addition to the advantages of the site itself, its position in the US market, and its proximity to the world's leading center for nanotech research, the New York

TABLE 7.2 New York State's Successful Incentives Package to AMD

Item	Amount (USD million)
State grant for buildings and equipment	500
State grant for R&D	150
Empire Zone tax credits/incentives	250 est.
Infrastructure (includes some federal funds)	300 est.
Total	1200

AMD Commitment:
- To create 1205 jobs by 2014
- Maintain 1205 jobs for 7 years (already surpassed by GlobalFoundries—3000 jobs)

Source: From Lyne, J., 2006. "New York's Big Subsidies Bolster Upstate's Winning Bid for AMD's $3.2—Billion 300–MM Fab," Site Selection. Available from: http://siteselection.com/ssinsider/bbdeal/bd060710.htm.

proposal was simply more generous financially than the very substantial bid offered by Dresden. (although then Senate Majority Leader Bruno said that New York offered a package that outbid Dresden's by about USD 100 million).

As a result of subsequent financial difficulties, AMD eventually spun off its manufacturing operations to GlobalFoundries, an entity owned by the sovereign wealth fund of Abu Dhabi, which proceeded to build the fab and commence operations in late 2011.GlobalFoundries committed to some 1200 jobs over 7 years as a part of the incentive package. As noted, by 2015 GlobalFoundries directly employed about 3,500 workers at its Malta site in New York State. Equally important, in 2015, GlobalFoundries was able to absorb IBM's semiconductor manufacturing operations, which involved a further 1780 at the East Fishkill facility.

The value of these jobs is significant for the region, both in terms of the salaries themselves and the multiplier effects of this type of high-end manufacturing employment. As one local official remarked, *"They are the highest-paying jobs outside of the finance industry,"* adding that they are wealth-creating and impossible to overstate in terms of the value to the local economy (Rulison, 2008). As of 2016, GlobalFoundries alone disperses some USD 350 million per year in salaries to its multibased employees. This does not include the thousands of construction workers or the former IBM semiconductor manufacturing employees that are now a part of GlobalFoundries. While not a part of the GlobalFoundries incentive package, it is important to note that in 2015 an estimated 4000 workers were employed at the CNSE's Albany Nanotech Complex. These complimentary investments by the state are a key feature underpinning the success of the Albany Nano cluster.

Manufacturing Infrastructure

Building the infrastructure needed to support a semiconductor fab in Luther Forest, where it is located, required the collaboration of a number of state, regional, and local development authorities, the Board of Supervisors of Saratoga County, a number of Town Boards, the Saratoga Water Authority, two electrical utilities, a Saratoga County environmental advocacy organization, numerous private entities and individuals, and state political leaders. The process was not smooth or free of acrimony. Some landowners objected to, and resisted construction of pipelines, power lines, and roads crossing their property. But at the end of the process, when the GlobalFoundries fab was ready to start operations at the end of 2011, the infrastructure needed to support it was in place. Observers of the process credit the fact that most of the key players sought the same basic outcome, that is, economic growth in the region through semiconductor manufacturing regionally and the high-tech jobs associated with it. An added factor underlying the infrastructure success was the skill and efficiency of local engineering and construction firms (including the Austrian firm M&W Zander), which generally completed projects on time and within budget once the necessary approvals were secured. This cooperation was essential to attract and prepare for an investment on the scale of the GlobalFoundries facility.

Local Impact

The arrival of GlobalFoundries in the Saratoga County towns of Malta and Stillwater in New York State has had several positive economic effects. The company's presence has attracted elements of the semiconductor global supply chain, inducing at least 200 other companies to expand their operations in the Albany area. Construction of the fab resulted in thousands of construction-related jobs—many of which have been sustained through ongoing construction over the last 4 years. Currently, GlobalFoundries employs over 3000 staff directly, and its local supply chain firms permanently employ some 500 on-site. As noted, GlobalFoundries greatly exceeded what was required (Table 7.2).

A plant on this scale also necessarily involves major expenditures in the region on services, with significant impact on residential construction and hospitality services (e.g., hotels and restaurants). For every direct employee, an estimated additional five jobs have been created in the region. This is a significant multiplier, however it reflects the particularly positive impact of high-tech manufacturing employment. The Semiconductor Industry Association (SIA) affirms that the *"employment multiplier for the U.S. semiconductor industry is relatively high compared to multipliers in other industries. This means that the US semiconductor industry has an outsized positive effect on job creation in other sectors compared to many other industries"* (Yinug, 2015). Travis Bullard, a GlobalFoundries spokesperson, would use higher multipliers than the SIA. Bullard estimated in 2012 that for every job inside the fab, *"there are four to five support jobs outside, such as workers who take care of the clean-room clothing."* In addition to such supply chain-related jobs: *"are maybe an additional five to six indirect jobs, such as openings in new restaurants. Many of those workers need new apartments, grocery stores, and day-care centers"* (Scherer, 2012).

This view is also supported by academic analysis conducted by Moretti (2013). As he notes, *"My research, based on an analysis of 11 million American workers in 320 metropolitan areas, shows that for each new high tech job in a metropolitan area, five additional local jobs are created outside of high tech in the long run. In essence, in Silicon Valley, high-tech jobs are the* cause *of local prosperity, and the doctors, lawyers, roofers and yoga teachers are the* effect"(p. 60, original emphasis).

Moretti offers several explanations for the extremely high multiplier effects exerted by innovative tradable industries like the semiconductor industry. Average wages are far higher than the regional averages, resulting in more disposable income to spend locally. High tech companies require many local business services, including information technology support, graphic design, business consultants, and specialized legal and security services. Finally, high-tech manufacturers support particularly dense clusters of supply chain firms which themselves tend to pay higher average salaries and demand specialized services (ibid., p. 62).

Substantial investments were required to construct the top-quality infrastructure necessary to support the fab (abundant water, quality power, and new transportation infrastructure). These investments now benefit local residents, but equally importantly, provide a foundation for additional manufacturing investment. Property taxes in towns near the GlobalFoundries facility have fallen, displaced by the scale of GlobalFoundries' contribution to the local tax base. GlobalFoundries also contributes to the quality of life in the region. In addition to the major resources, it has committed to the local school systems. It has also developed partnerships to enhance training for high tech jobs with the Hudson Valley Community College (see later). The firm has also directly and indirectly contributed to the improvement of recreational infrastructure, including trails and athletic fields.

Jobs Created

Perhaps the most salient measure of success is the jobs created by the investment generated by the efforts to develop the site and the incentives package offered by the state. If one applies the industry multiplier to GlobalFoundries' employment, the total of 3538 on-site jobs would yield 17,300 indirect jobs. Application of the same multiplier at GlobalFoundries' East Fishkill site produces another 10,196 jobs.[7] Similarly, the European Semiconductor Industry Association uses a multiplier virtually identical to that employed by the SIA, calculating that the 200,000 direct jobs attributable to the industry in Europe in 2011 supported 1,000,000 indirect jobs. By any measure, this represents substantial employment generation.

Workforce Initiatives and Education

New York State's educational system at all levels has played an important role in attracting high-tech investment from outside the state. The state's school system compares favorably to those of most other states, which has proven an important draw for companies and individuals to relocate to the state. In the Capital Region, SUNY Albany, RPI, and SUNY Polytechnic (as CNSE is known after spinning off from SUNY Albany) have produced a stream of graduates with sophisticated engineering and scientific skills. In cooperation with industry, community colleges like Hudson Valley Community College have implemented curricula providing training and retraining in semiconductor manufacturing. Reflecting this effort, 50% GlobalFoundries' new hires of technicians (comprising two-thirds of its total work force) are drawn from within the region—a major additional benefit.

Encouraging Start-Ups

The Tech Valley story to date is essentially one which has seen established firms from outside the region moving operations to the Albany area. The number of start-ups originating at SUNY Polytechnic has been promising but, while growing, remains relatively limited. A number of local observers comment that venture capital is available *"if you have a good idea."* Based on the evidence so far, either the statement is not entirely accurate or there has been a dearth of good ideas for commercializing research results. Indeed, this statement reflects a common misperception that *"good ideas will inevitably be funded,"* a view normally not shared by entrepreneurs or venture capitalists. Nobel Prize-winning research suggests that information asymmetries result in much more problematic investment decisions.[8]

Moreover, in contrast to Silicon Valley, social acceptance of business failure is limited in the region, which chills risk-taking. In addition, some local leaders believe that there are not enough individuals in the region with the skills needed to start and run a small business. The availability of start-up capital and, importantly, follow-on funding, is limited despite the proximity of the New York City capital markets. There may also be an absence of serial entrepreneurs and the demonstration effect they offer. Whatever the cause, the start-up culture that has contributed so substantially to the success of Silicon Valley and Boston has not fully taken root in upstate New York, but it is also true that the Albany region as a whole has not made a sustained effort to increase support for start-ups, nor does it make a sustained effort to benefit from federally-financed innovation programs, such as the Small Business Innovation Research program.

Diversifying the Nanotech Economy

To date, the story of Tech Valley has centered on the creation of a vibrant semiconductor research and manufacturing cluster in the Albany region. However, state leaders have always envisioned that public investments in nanotechnology research infrastructure would result in the emergence and growth of sectors beyond the field of microelectronics and in areas of upstate New York beyond Albany. CNSE has facilitated this diversification by developing a curriculum which embraces a wide range of nanomaterials fields, including biological materials, metals, polymers, chemicals, cybersecurity, and medicine. Reflecting these efforts and initiatives by the National Cancer Institute, CNSE now offers a PhD program in Nanomedicine. Recently, major nanotech initiatives have been launched in upstate New York outside the field of microelectronics and outside the Capital Region.

- At the request of the governor, CNSE is supporting the establishment of a nanotechnology research center in Buffalo, which would be oriented toward the life sciences.
- New York and the DoE are investing in the Photovoltaic Manufacturing Consortium, which will apply nanoscience in photovoltaics manufacturing in the Rochester area.
- The state of New York announced plans in 2013 to create the Nano Utica initiative in collaboration with CNSE; in 2015, GE and an Austrian sensor manufacturer announced plans to establish a manufacturing plant at the new Nano Utica site. These are encouraging additional high-tech investments for the region which will strengthen the cluster while also bringing reputational benefits.

National Interests at Stake in Tech Valley

Tech Valley was created by the state of New York for regional economic development motives, but the initiative has implications for US high-tech manufacturing as well as major implications for national security. The establishment of a major cutting-edge semiconductor manufacturing presence in upstate New York, together with the associated research and supply chain infrastructure, mitigates a longstanding trend toward offshore movement of US semiconductor manufacturing and research capability, particularly to East Asia. Until GlobalFoundries, no state-of-the-art semiconductor foundry existed in the United States, with the result that an increasingly "fab-less" US semiconductor design industry was progressively more dependent on offshore manufacturers to remain in business. Semiconductor foundries manufacture integrated circuits and transistors on behalf of other companies. The high labor and massive capital equipment costs required for the production of semiconductors creates a niche for these companies. They are upstream on the value chain from the "fab-less" (referring to the fabrication plant) chip-design semiconductor companies that create schematics for chips but outsource the manufacturing to semiconductor foundries. The dramatic increase in cost of semiconductor fabrication facilities has meant that most new semiconductor companies have opted for the fab-less model, relying on foundries for the production of their chip designs (ThinkEquity Industry Research, 2008).

The offshoring of semiconductor manufacturing has meant a loss of domestic high-skill, high-income jobs to other regions, exacerbated by the outmigration of supply chain firms. Even a partial reversal of this trend is significant, both in terms of retention of manufacturing capability, related applied research, the maintenance of high-value supply chains, and national security.

As most US defense systems are built around semiconductors, the offshore movement of semiconductor production deeply concerns defense planners. With the semiconductor industry's center of gravity shifting to facilities in Asia that churn out hundreds of millions of chips for consumer-electronics devices, the Pentagon has much less influence on an industry it helped fund and develop in the 1960s and 1970s. While military users accounted for as much as one-quarter of global chip demand in the early 1980s, this has now fallen to less than 0.1% by the turn of this decade according to the Trusted Access Program Office, which coordinates buying for the Pentagon and intelligence agencies (Cameron, 2016).

On the one hand, the globalization of supply offers reliable, very low-cost, "off-the-shelf" commercial components, enhancing the ability to maintain up-to-date capabilities and make military budgets go further. On the other hand, reliance on manufacturing sources located on the other side of the world, near or even inside a potential adversary (China), poses intrinsic risks. The geology of East Asia in itself poses serious risks. The vulnerability of those manufacturing sources to earthquakes has been demonstrated by recent seismic events in Taiwan (1999) and Japan (2011), which involve serious disruptions to supply. Cybersecurity raises another level of concern, with US planners wary of the potential for tampering with devices that are made in Asia and incorporated into US defense systems. In addition, forms of advanced manufacturing, including semiconductor fabrication, confront cyber threats, which include theft of data and intellectual property, theft of know-how associated with manufacturing processes, attacks on operations, and various forms of malicious hacking. Plants where chips are assembled have long been viewed by the Pentagon as a vulnerable part of the military supply chain. The biggest concerns are over technology theft and insertion of rogue elements that could be remotely triggered to access equipment or implement so-called "kill switches" that could render equipment useless (Cameron, 2016).

The advent of GlobalFoundries establishes a secure source of advanced semiconductor manufacturing within the United States that is not subject to earthquake risk and far less vulnerable to cyberattack and industrial espionage. The GlobalFoundries fab, located in Albany, New York, is well outside the Pacific "Rim of Fire" earthquake zone and is constructed on a 120-foot thick cushion of glacial sand which greatly reduces the risks associated with seismic shocks. While no industrial site is completely impervious to cyber threats, GlobalFoundries' location at a secure inland site within the United States makes the tasks of cyber protection significantly easier. Given these advantages for national security, it is remarkable that the infrastructure necessary for the

facility was developed largely without federal support, as was the very substantial investment incentive package needed to attract this multibillion dollar
investment.

Emerging Challenges

Despite this remarkable success, a closer examination of the actual circumstances in upstate New York suggests that continuing the state's go-it-alone
approach may have potentially significant limitations including:

- *Ongoing talent loss*: the recent influx of technology-intensive manufacturing and jobs, while welcome and impressive, has not reversed broader longstanding trends of relatively high unemployment and outmigration of talent
  even in the immediate Capital Region itself.
- *Limited support*: economically-distressed areas in Albany, Troy, and other
  communities in the Capital Region are largely isolated from the "Tech Valley" phenomenon, often reflecting prosaic problems, such as the inadequacy
  or absence of transportation links.
- *Funding talent:* local universities and community colleges confront financial pressures which threaten their ability to support necessary development
  of the work force.
- *Slow emergence of a start-up culture*: the Capital Region is not fostering
  innovation-based start-ups on a scale seen in other innovative regions;
- *Sectoral concentration*: "Tech Valley" is highly concentrated in one volatile
  sector, semiconductors, and has not yet seen the parallel emergence on a
  major scale of industries, such as biomedicine and software.
- *Diversification (or dispersion)*: state leaders face understandable pressure
  for geographical diversification of economic development resources, which
  may offer substantial returns and be politically necessary. The question is
  whether this will distract from efforts to sustain the continued development
  of the Tech Valley nanotech cluster.

Arguably, federal programs exist which could assist Tech Valley to broaden
its impact in economically distressed areas, make better use of local human
resources, and diversify into nationally significant areas, such as defense cybersecurity, alternative energy, sustainability, and health care. One contemporary
example is the DoD's 2015 decision to contribute USD 110 million in grant
money to support the establishment of a USD 600 million Manufacturing USA
institute focusing on photonics innovation in the Rochester area.

Sustaining Momentum

The creation of Tech Valley represents a singular achievement by the state of New
York and the individuals and institutions that were at the center of this effort. However, the experience of numerous US regions illustrates how emerging innovation

clusters are vulnerable to shifts in global competitive patterns, erratic government policies, and the vagaries of the business cycle. Toledo, Ohio for example, developed a promising photovoltaics cluster led by the University of Toledo, but the future of this initiative has been cast into doubt in the wake of the collapse of global photovoltaics markets in 2012. Similarly, Tech Valley confronts multiple challenges in sustaining the momentum it has achieved in the past 15 years.

Leadership Challenges

The original players behind the creation of Tech Valley have largely passed from the scene. At the political level, Governor Pataki and legislative leaders Bruno and Silver no longer occupy positions of leadership. At the operational level, the generation of economic development professionals who spearheaded outreach to the semiconductor community has largely moved on. Similarly, Professor Kaloyeros stepped down in September 2016. Until then, he was a key player in the regional policy and a driver of the development of the new Buffalo life sciences nanocenter. And IBM, which played a leading role in the Tech Valley effort with its own investments and advice to state leaders, has exited semiconductor manufacturing, raising questions about its contributions going forward. The town of Malta, where GlobalFoundries' fab is located, has become increasingly ambivalent in its stance toward further expansion of manufacturing in the Luther Forest Technology Campus. GlobalFoundries itself is questioning whether the state and the region remain willing and able to supply the infrastructure improvements it requires for further growth. Public officials tend to see the initial investment as a success, and some see no reason to continue to give incentives to established companies. The challenge is that investments in new infrastructure and other support are beyond the capabilities of even established companies. Moreover, competitors around the world are very willing to provide substantial incentives to attract these types of investments with their powerful regional and national impacts.

Systemic Issues

In addition to inevitable transitions in leadership, the effort to establish Tech Valley—while broadly successful—has underscored certain regional characteristics that will challenge even the most effective leadership team. Upstate New York is characterized by a multiplicity of governmental jurisdictions and fragmentation of authority among various bodies working on economic development. Town boards and county boards of supervisors, who must be responsive to the concerns of their citizens, are unlikely to support economic development initiatives that do not have local majority support. That reality was demonstrated in 1999 when the town of North Greenbush rejected a proposed chip fab, a potentially transformative investment. Even where such support is present, an organized minority can use various approval processes required by law to delay regulatory approvals and/or extract costly concessions. Such challenges were overcome in the effort to bring a chip fab to Luther Forest. However, when confronting such issues in the future, high-tech manufacturers capable of locating anywhere in the world may indeed choose to go elsewhere.

Workforce Limitations

Despite an excellent system of universities and numerous work force and K-12 initiatives, the availability of a local manpower base to support high-tech businesses remains constrained. Not enough curricula exist to facilitate the transition from an academic milieu to a high-tech company. University graduates continue to leave the region, with Millennials drawn to urban centers like New York City.

Continued Commitment

As noted earlier, a major area of uncertainty is the state's continued commitment to developmental incentives to attract companies to Tech Valley. Financial incentives play a major role in high-tech companies' locational decisions. With the exception of GlobalFoundries, the Luther Forest Technology Campus has not attracted semiconductor or other high technology manufacturers, a fact which may reflect the end of LFTC's status as an Empire Zone eligible for tax benefits. In addition, the Town of Malta recently adopted a "no incentives" stance toward LFTC, a policy changed in January 2016, but one nonetheless reflects the impact of local politics on the region's economic development efforts. Moreover, Governor Andrew Cuomo is reportedly directing state resources to upstate regions apart from the Capital Region which suffer from weaker economies—a move which can be justified on grounds of equity and relative need, but which clouds the future of Tech Valley itself.

These caveats notwithstanding, the New York nanoinitiative has been a major success. The original purpose of Tech Valley was to provide the basis for a broad regional economic turnaround based on new high-skill, high-income manufacturing jobs. Many thousands of such jobs have been created since 2000, both directly by high-tech design and manufacturing firms and indirectly as a result of the development of supply chains, as well as many driven by the local presence of those firms and the demand they create for goods and services in housing, food, banking, and related services. Certain areas, such as Saratoga County, are faring very well in the new technology-based environment.

CONCLUSIONS; CORE LESSONS FROM THE NEW YORK EXPERIENCE

- *Vision*: the state and regional governments cooperated closely on a shared vision. One that combined existing assets into a more productive whole.
- The importance of *entrepreneurial leadership*: Albany has benefited from multiple leaders who shared a vision of what the region could become. The

leaders emerged first in the university with strong support from industry partners, and then in local and regional development organizations. These efforts in turn benefited from a strong state commitment. The federal government played a supportive but essentially minor role.

- *Long-term commitment*: the effort to develop the nanocluster was sustained over a decade, with steady, incremental investments in educational institutions, and investment packages for supply chain development.
- *New institutions*: the creation of CNSE, and close operations with IBM and its supplier network, generated outstanding facilities for researchers in nanotechnologies, new semiconductor designs and tests, and a platform for the benchmarking of semiconductor fabrication equipment; the facilities, equipment, and membership makes this facility the leading global center for nanoresearch and its applications.
- *Leverage*: the development of global quality research facilities through the college of nanoscale science and engineering, the presence of a modern fab, and the support of regional educational institutions, such as RPI providing well-trained engineers enabled the region to leverage these assets to attract a major semiconductor fabrication facility.
- *Significant and sustained support*: the state government, under the leadership of Governor Pataki, allocated significant resources in terms of grants, tax abatements, and crucially, support for new educational institutions. The assistance to CNSE, which provided major benefits both to CNSE and industry, was made available in the form of university facilities and equipment. This provided a neutral and permanent location, which made it easier to justify public investments on this scale, particularly in the American context.
- *Acceleration of scale*: the arrival of GlobalFoundries accelerated regional development and generated major direct/indirect job creation throughout much of the region. A substantial USD 1.2 billion investment package was key in winning the international competition for bringing what is now one of the most modern foundries in the world to the New York Capital Region. This investment package offered major strategic advantages, providing a geologically stable and geopolitically secure site for some of the world's most advanced manufacturing. Importantly, the foundry also now benefits from the substantial talent, patent portfolio, and research capabilities of the IBM acquisition.

LIMITATIONS AND CAVEATS

While the Tech Valley complex represents an undeniable success for state and regional investment policies, major challenges remain. Some of these challenges include the volatile nature of the semiconductor industry itself, which can involve major swings in demand, and therefore the long-term viability of the investment. The semiconductor space also remains vulnerable to the efforts of mercantilist policies elsewhere, which have the potential of seriously disrupting the balance of supply and demand. For example, China has launched a major effort to vertically integrate its semiconductor industry and has set aside substantial funds to do so. Previous efforts by the Chinese government to enhance its semiconductor capabilities have not been fully successful. But firms benefiting from substantial state support, captive markets, and operating without market discipline can be very disruptive (The Economist, 2016). Talent retention remains an ongoing issue. Graduates of leading universities, such as SUNY-Poly and RPI, continue to exit the region. The "millennial generation" places a high-value on living in urban centers, this region cannot offer on the scale of San Francisco, Boston, or New York. One of the most important challenges, as noted, will be whether the state has the focus, and political and financial wherewithal to continue to invest in the existing nanotech cluster as a means of sustaining its growing global reputation and attracting further supply chain development. It is possible, but by no means certain, that other sources of financial support will appear, for example, through federal programs, as the recognition of the importance of this cluster for security becomes more apparent, although this potential investment remains subject to the vagaries of US national politics. Lastly, a fundamental weakness in the region's development efforts is the extreme fragmentation of the political units that are necessarily involved in the processes of permitting, infrastructure, development, and education. This fragmentation is potentially compounded by the traditional discomfort at the federal and state policy levels with the provision of financial support for "successful companies and regions."

From an international perspective, perhaps one of the key lessons of this review of the experiences of the nanotechnology cluster in Albany, New York State would be that investments in R&D and research facilities alone (particularly research facilities focused on basic research) will not in themselves ensure dynamic, and regional economic development. Such investments do, of course, generate employment in their own right, but the dynamic efforts are greatly enhanced by close cooperation with industry and its needs, rather than a focus primarily on basic research and publications. Accordingly, one of the key lessons is the creation of the "industrial commons": in other words, state-of-the-art applied research facilities necessarily involve close cooperation with industry, and ideally include industry contributions in finance and equipment. Indeed, one could argue that New York has succeeded in creating its own Fraunhofer type nanosystem. In fact, the Fraunhofer system has served as a model for the Obama Administration's NNMI. Undeniably, the construction of the state-of-the-art facilities only makes sense if there is genuine industry interest and presence. In this regard, the presence and contributions of IBM as a corporate regional anchor were crucial to the success of the CNSE, which in turn played a major role in generating an environment attractive to semiconductor manufacturers and suppliers.

Another key lesson of international relevance might be the importance of cooperation and coordination, both in developing the vision of the region's future and in providing the educational and infrastructural foundation for high-tech investments. This latter point is of course a major feature of the "Smart Specialization" strategy adopted by the European Commission. If implemented flexibly and creatively, this Smart Specialization approach offers the potential over time for renewed innovation-based growth in Europe and the rest of the world.

ACKNOWLEDGMENTS

This analysis is drawn from an ongoing study of the development of the Tech Valley region now underway at Georgetown University. I would like to thank my assistant, Kevin Carter, formally of Georgetown University, for his contributions to the preparation of this analysis.

ENDNOTES

1. In 2009, AMD's manufacturing facilities were acquired by GlobalFoundries, itself owned by the Advanced Technology Investment Company, which is wholly owned by Mubadala, an investment company of Abu Dhabi.
2. State University of New York (SUNY) Poly is increasingly known for its innovative experiential curriculum. As the school leadership describes its program, "SUNY Poly is committed to building a bright future for New York State by graduating highly skilled students who understand that creating knowledge is the key to innovation and that innovation is the key to success. The innovation-driven educational model in New York State is designed to enable SUNY Poly to provide its students with a world-class learning experience, and the skills and knowledge necessary to emerge as leaders in the 21st century global economy." May 7, 2016. Available from: http://www.sunycnse.com/Newsroom/NewsReleases/Details/16-0507/SUNY_Poly_Graduates_Largest_Class_to_Date_at_42nd_Annual_Commencement.aspx
3. The SEMATECH consortium was established in 1987 to coordinate the research efforts of US Semiconductor companies as part of a multipronged effort to restore US competitiveness in this leading high-tech industry. The consortium was successful and has been widely imitated by policy makers around the world (Wessner, 2003).
4. A fab is a common term for a semiconductor fabrication plant.
5. Initial estimates of energy use suggested that the fab would need about 40 megawatts of electricity, that is, the average use of 20,000–30,000 homes. Reliable power supply was critical because a chip fab cannot normally be without power for an average of more than 100 milliseconds without the manufacturer suffering significant financial loss.
6. A key selling point for the Luther Forest site was its geographic proximity to the College of Nanoscale Science and Engineering (CNSE) research infrastructure at SUNY Albany. John Frank, Senior Vice President of M&W Zander, the engineering company specializing in building semiconductor fabs, observed that CNSE was "a critical enabler in the eyes of a chip manufacturer. To be this close to a center of excellence in nanotech research, development, and manufacturing can be a major factor in the success of a new plant."
7. The European Semiconductor Industry Association uses a multiplier virtually identical to that employed by SIA, calculating that the 200,000 direct jobs attributable to the industry in Europe in 2011 supported 1,000,000 indirect jobs.
8. George Akerlof, Michael Spence, and Joseph Stiglitz received the Nobel Prize in 2001 *"for their analyses of markets with asymmetric information."*

REFERENCES

Cameron, D.,2016, "Pentagon Hires Foreign Chips Supplier." The Wall Street Journal. Available from: http://www.wsj.com/articles/pentagon-takes-foreign-chips-partner-1465159332

Grondahl, P.,2013. "Region thrives amid high-tech revolution," The Times Union, Albany. Available from: http://www.timesunion.com/local/article/Region-thrives-amid-high-tech-revolution-4364916.php

Moretti, E., 2013. The New Geography of Jobs. Mariner Books, Boston and New York.

Pisano, G.P., Shih, W.S., 2009. "Restoring American Competitiveness," Harvard Business Review, July–August issue. Available from: https://hbr.org/2009/07/restoring-american-competitiveness

Rogers, M., 2014. "We're Smarter Than Buffalo and Rochester and Syracuse and …". Albany Business Review. Available from: http://www.bizjournals.com/albany/print-edition/2014/03/14/were-smarter-than-buffalo-and-rochester-and.html

Rulison, L. (2008), 'A Future Filled with Promise', The *Times Union (Albany, NY)*, April 20. Available from: http://bit.ly/2dPE1YF

Scherer, R., 2012. "Can American manufacturing really be cornerstone of economic revival?," The Christian Science Monitor. Available from: http://www.csmonitor.com/USA/Politics/2012/0208/Can-American-manufacturing-really-be-cornerstone-of-economic-revival

The Economist, 2016. "The march of the zombies," The Economist. Available from: http://www.economist.com/news/business/21693573-chinas-excess-industrial-capacity-harms-its-economy-and-riles-its-trading-partners-march

ThinkEquity Industry Research, 2008. "Semiconductor Foundries."

Wessner, C.W. (Ed.), 2003. Securing the Future: Regional and National Programs to Support the Semiconductor Industry. National Research Council of the National Academies, Washington DC, Available from: https://www.nap.edu/read/10677/chapter/1.

Williams, S., 2013. "Cabinet official praises nanocollege," The Daily Gazette. Available from: http://www.dailygazette.com/news/2013/jul/30/cabinet-official-praises-nanocollege/?print

Yinug, F., 2015. U.S. Semiconductor Industry Employment, Semiconductor Industry Association (SIA). Available from: http://bit.ly/2dK5dee

Chapter 8

New Structural Economics and Industrial Policies for Catching-Up Economies

Justin Yifu Lin

Center for New Structural Economics, National School of Development, Peking University, Beijing, China

Chapter Outline

Academic Highlights

- The nature of economic development is a process of continuous structural change with technological innovation and industrial upgrading raising labor productivity, and with improvements in hard and soft infrastructure reducing transaction costs.
- New structural economics, which applies the neoclassical approach to study the determinants of economic structure and its evolution, postulates that the industrial structure in an economy is endogenous to its endowment structure.
- New structural economics argues that the key for developmental success is to have an enabling state using industrial policy to facilitate firms' entry to latent comparative-advantage industries in a competitive market by overcoming the first-mover's externality issue and coordinating the required improvements in hard and soft infrastructure so as to turn the latent comparative-advantage industries to the nation's competitive advantages.

Advances in the Theory and Practice of Smart Specialization. http://dx.doi.org/10.1016/B978-0-12-804137-6.00008-5
183

Policy Highlights

- For a middle-income country in the catching-up process, its industrial policies may be classified into five different categories based on the industry's distance to the global technological frontier, and the state may play a facilitating role accordingly:
  - Industrial policy for catching up higher-income countries' industries.
  - Industrial policy for maintaining a leading-edge industry's technology leadership globally.
  - Industrial policy for leapfrogging high-income countries in short innovation-cycle industries.
  - Industrial policy for helping firms exit from comparative advantage-losing industries.
  - Industrial policy for developing comparative advantage defying, national defense-related industries.

Rapid, sustained economic growth is a modern phenomenon, emerging only in the 18th century. Before then, the average annual growth of per capita Gross Domestic Product (GDP) in Western Europe was just 0.05%. At that rate, it would take an economy 1400 years to double its per capita GDP (Maddison, 2006). From the 18th century to the mid-19th century, the annual growth of per capita GDP in Western European countries accelerated to 1%, enabling it to double in just 70 years. From the mid-19th century to the present, the per capita GDP growth rate accelerated to 2% a year, shrinking the doubling time to 35 years. The impetus for accelerating growth was the Industrial Revolution of the mid-18th century: continuous technological innovations and industrial upgrading made possible the acceleration of labor productivity and income growth that boosted per capita GDP.[1]

In other words, modern economic growth is a process of continuous technological innovation, which raises labor productivity in the existing industries, and industrial upgrading, which moves an economy from low value-added industries to higher value-added ones, thereby raising labor productivity as well. However, taking advantage of the potential of technologies and new industries requires well-functioning hard infrastructure to get products into large domestic and foreign markets. As the scale of trade increases, market exchanges are at arm's length, thus requiring contracts and contract-enforcing legal systems. Moreover, as the scale and risk of investment increase with the upgrading of technology and industries, the financial structure has to adapt too. Improvements in hard and soft infrastructure reduce transaction costs for investment and trade (Harrison and Rodríguez-Clare, 2010; Kuznets, 1966; Lin and Nugent, 1995). While modern economic growth appears to be a process of rising labor productivity, it is actually a process of continuous structural change in technologies, industries, and hard and soft infrastructure.

A developed country's high-income and labor productivity indicate that its technology and industry are on the global frontier. As such, it requires the indigenous invention of new technology and industry to achieve technological innovation and industrial upgrading. Inventions of new technology and industry are costly and risky. A developing country's technological innovation and industrial upgrading occur mostly behind the global technological and industrial frontier. Most of its innovation and upgrading can rely on the adoption of technology and industry that are new to the country but mature elsewhere in the world, and thus have a lower cost and risk compared with an advanced country. In other words, a developing country enjoys the latecomer advantage in technological innovation and industrial upgrading. Potentially, a developing country can grow faster than an advanced country and catch up with it.

After World War II (WWII), most countries in the developing world shattered the shackles of colonialism or semicolonialism, starting their independent pursuit of modern economic growth. Till 2008, only two of them moved up from low to middle income and finally to high income, and only 13 of such countries moved up from middle to high income (Agenor et al., 2012). This means that, among around 200 developing economies, most have remained trapped in a low- or middle-income status since WWII, despite the latecomer advantage. As Keynes said, "it is ideas, not vested interests, which are dangerous for good or evil." These countries' poor development performance reflected the failures of developmental ideas. In this chapter, I review the ideas embodied in two previous waves of development thinking, introduce new structural economics as the third wave, and propose a practical guide for formatting industrial policies in developing countries to accelerate technological innovation and industrial upgrading.

WHY WE NEED TO RETHINK DEVELOPMENT ECONOMICS

Economic theories help us understand the underlying causalities of observed economic phenomena. More than logic exercises, theories have practical relevance: economic agents—governments, firms, households, and individuals—use them to guide their actions so as to achieve the desired results. If existing theories fail to help us understand the underlying causalities of the observed phenomena or if decisions based on these theories fail to achieve their intended goals, we have to rethink them. Development economics is in need of rethinking.

Development economics is a young field in modern economics. It emerged after the WWII to guide the reconstruction of war-ravaged countries and the nation building of newly independent former colonies.

The first wave of development thinking was structuralism. It posited that, if a developing country wanted to catch-up with developed countries in income, it needs to have the same labor productivity as developed countries. In turn, this requires developing countries to build up modern capital- and technology-intensive industries similar to those in developed countries. Yet those industries never emerged in developing countries. Why not? Economists blamed market failures arising from structural rigidities for the failure of such industries to develop spontaneously (Arndt, 1985). Structuralism recommended that governments adopt import-substitution strategies to overcome market failures through mobilizing and allocating resources to directly build those industries (Prebisch, 1950; Rosenstein-Rodan, 1943).

Capitalist, as well as socialist countries pursued, after WWII, the strategies advocated by structuralism (Chenery, 1961). However, countries that adopted import-substitution strategies typically experienced a pattern of rapid growth driven by large-scale investments, followed by economic crises and long periods of stagnation (Krueger and Tuncer, 1982; Lal, 1994; Pack and Saggi, 2006).

The failure of structuralism as a catching-up guide for developing countries led to the emergence in the 1980s of the second wave of thinking, neoliberalism. At that time, government intervention was pervasive in developing countries, leading to rent seeking, bribery, and embezzlement, as well as to multiple economic distortions and inefficient resource allocation. To improve economic performance and close the gap with developed countries, developing countries were advised to build a well-functioning market economy by implementing the measures referred to collectively as the "Washington Consensus": privatization, marketization, and liberalization (Williamson, 1990). Governments were advised not to pick winners to support technological innovations and industrial upgrading.

Again, the logic seemed sound. Yet countries that applied this shock therapy often experienced economic collapse, stagnation, and frequent crises, and the gap between developing and developed countries widened further (Cardoso and Helwege, 1995). Growth rates were lower and economic crises more frequent under Washington Consensus policies in the 1980s and 1990s than under the structuralist policies of the 1960s and 1970s. Some economists referred to this period as the "lost decades" for developing countries (Easterly, 2001; Easterly et al., 1997).

During this time, some economies in Asia were pursuing an entirely different development approach. From the 1950 to 70s, Japan and the four Asian tigers—Korea, Taiwan, Singapore, and Hong Kong—grew rapidly by adopting an export-oriented development strategy, developing initially labor-intensive, small-scale industries, and gradually climbing the industrial ladder to larger, more capital-intensive industries with proactive government support (Amsden, 1989; Chang, 2003; Wade, 1990).

In the 1980 and 90s, under the sway of the Washington Consensus, economists branded planned economies as less efficient than market economies and called for transforming them into market economies through shock therapy: removing all economic distortions by ending government interventions and by leaping in a single bound from a planned to a market economy. However, China adopted a dual-track transition, continuing to protect and subsidize nonviable state-owned firms in the old prioritized capital-intensive industries, while liberalizing the market entry for the previously repressed labor-intensive industries. Many economists predicted such an approach would lead to rampant rent seeking and deteriorate resource allocation. In reality, however, economies that experienced stability and rapid growth, such as Cambodia, China, and Vietnam, all followed the dual-track transition approach.

Policies based on structuralism and neoliberalism failed to achieve their goals. The structuralism and neoliberalism also did not explain the rare economic development and transition successes that occured. A third wave of development thinking is in order.

WHAT IS NEW STRUCTURAL ECONOMICS?

New structural economics as a third wave of development thinking uses a neoclassical approach to study the determinants of economic structure and its evolution in a country's economic development, which is the nature of modern economic growth (Lin, 2011).[2]

What is the core hypothesis of new structural economics? In brief, a country's economic structure at any given time is endogenous to its factor endowments—the amounts of capital, labor, and natural resources at that time. Countries at different development stages vary in their relative abundance of factor endowments. In developing countries, capital is generally relatively scarce, while labor and often natural resources are comparatively abundant. In developed countries, capital is relatively abundant, while labor is comparatively scarce. Although an economy's factor endowments are given at any particular period, they can change over time. New structural economics posits an economy's factor endowments as the starting point for development analysis because they determine an economy's total budget and relative factor prices at that time, which are two of the most important parameters in economic analysis.

Relative factor prices determine a country's comparative advantage. For example, countries with both relatively abundant labor and scarce capital would have a comparative advantage in labor-intensive industries because production costs will be lower than in countries with relatively scarce and more expensive labor. A prerequisite to achieving competitive advantage for a country is developing its industries according to its comparative advantages determined by factor endowments (Porter, 1990).

In developed countries, income and labor productivity are high because the countries' relative capital abundance means that their industries and technologies are capital-intensive. If a developing country wants to catch up to the income and industrial structure of developed countries, it first needs to increase the relative abundance of capital in its factor endowment structure to the level in advanced countries. The ultimate goal of economic development is to raise a country's income, the intermediate goal is to develop capital-intensive industries, and the immediate goal should be to accumulate capital quickly, so that the country's comparative advantages change to more capital-intensive industries. In other words, boosting a country's income requires industrial upgrading, which in turn requires change in country's endowment structure (Ju et al., 2015).

How can a country accumulate capital quickly? Capital comes from saving economic surpluses. If a country's industries are all consistent with its comparative advantages, as determined by its endowment structure, the country will be competitive in both domestic and international markets and generate the largest possible surplus. If all investments are made in industries that are consistent with the comparative advantages determined by a country's endowment structure, the returns to investment will be maximized and the propensity to save will be at its highest. With the largest possible surplus and the highest incentives to save, capital will be accumulated in the fastest way possible. The changes in endowment structure and comparative advantages pave the way for change in industrial structure and the accompanying hard and soft industrial infrastructure.

Yet comparative advantage is an economic concept. How is it translated into the choices of technologies and industries made by entrepreneurs? Entrepreneurs care about profits. They will invest in industries in which a country has a comparative advantage if relative factor prices reflect the relative scarcities of factors in the country's endowments (Lin, 2009; Lin and Chang, 2009). If capital is relatively scarce, the price of capital will be relatively high; if labor is relatively scarce, the price of labor (wages) will be relatively high. If the price system reflects the relative factor scarcity, profit-maximizing entrepreneurs will use a relatively inexpensive factor to substitute for a relatively expensive factor in their choice of production technologies, investing in industries that require more of a relatively inexpensive factor and less of a relatively expensive factor. A price system with these characteristics can arise only in a competitive market. Therefore, a well-functioning market is essential for the success of economic development.

Economic development is a process of structural change with continuous technological innovations, industrial upgrading, and improvement in infrastructure and institutions. When the factor endowment structure changes, it requires first movers to enter new industries that are consistent with changing comparative advantages. The risks for first movers are high. If they fail, they will bear all the losses, and if they succeed, then other firms will follow them into the industry. The resulting competition will eliminate any monopoly profit (Aghion, 2009; Romer, 1990). There is an asymmetry between the losses of failures and the gains of successes for the first movers (Hausmann and Rodrik, 2003).

No matter whether the first movers succeed or fail, they provide society with useful information. The government should encourage first movers and compensate them for the information externality they generate. Otherwise, there will be little incentive for the firms to be first movers in technological innovation and industrial upgrading (Harrison and Rodríguez-Clare, 2010; Lin, 2009; Lin and Monga, 2011; Rodrik, 2004). In addition, the success or failure of the first movers also depends on whether improved hard and soft infrastructures match the needs of the new industries. Improving infrastructure and institutions is beyond the capacities of individual firms. The government needs to either coordinate firms' efforts to improve infrastructure and institutions or to provide those improvements itself. Therefore, a facilitating state is also essential for economic development to happen dynamically.

New structural economics helps to understand why structuralism failed. The import-substitution strategy advocated by structuralism advised governments to give priority to capital- and technology-intensive industries in capital-scarce developing countries, thus defying developing countries' comparative-advantages. Firms in those industries were not viable in open and competitive markets. Without government protection and subsidies, entrepreneurs would not voluntarily invest in those industries. After their establishment, the nonviable firms had to rely on the government's subsidies and protection to survive as well.

New structural economics also helps to understand why neoliberalism failed. In developing countries, market distortions were endogenous to the government's need to protect and subsidize nonviable firms that had been promoted by the government's previous import-substitution strategies. Eliminating protections and subsidies would doom nonviable firms, resulting in large-scale unemployment, and social and political unrest. To avoid those consequences and to continue to prop up nonviable capital-intensive industries that were still considered the cornerstone of modernization, governments had no choice but to continue its protection and subsidies. Even if the firms were privatized, soft budget constraint problems would continue. The subsidies to the nonviable firms could even increase due to the private owners having greater incentives to lobby for subsidies and protection (Lin and Li, 2008). The new protections and subsidies were usually less efficient than the old ones, especially in the transition economies of the former Soviet Union and Eastern Europe (World Bank, 2002). In addition, neoliberalism threw the baby out with the bath water, vehemently opposing any role for governments in facilitating structural change. Chile was a typical example. A model student of Washington Consensus reform, Chile diligently implemented the Washington Consensus reforms in the 1980s and then removed all government protections and subsidies. Chile ranks high among developing countries on the World Bank's Doing Business Index, based on indicators of the ease of doing business and investment. However, Chile has not seen dynamic structural change for more than 30 years, and as a result unemployment is high, income gaps have widened, and Chile remains mired in "the middle-income trap."

New structural economics also justifies the use of gradual, dual track approach to reform an economy with distortions caused by import-substitution strategies. Dual-track reform, which the conventional economic thought labeled the wrong approach to transition, maintains stability by providing transitory protections to nonviable firms in the old priority sectors and achieves dynamic growth by removing restrictions to entry and facilitating the development of previously repressed industries that are consistent with the country's comparative advantages. The dynamic growth of the sectors consistent with comparative advantages helps the economy to rapidly accumulate capital and change the factor endowment structure.

That makes some formerly nonviable firms in capital-intensive industries viable. Once firms in the new sectors are viable, the transitory protection and subsidies can be eliminated, bringing the transition to a market economy to a smooth end (Lau et al., 2000; Lin, 2009, 2012, 2013; Naughton, 1995; Subramanian and Roy, 2003).

NEW STRUCTURAL ECONOMICS AND SMART INDUSTRIAL POLICY FOR DEVELOPING COUNTRIES

Economic theories are intended not only to help people understand but also to change the world. How can the government in a developing country apply new structural economics to achieve dynamic structural change and catch up with high-income countries? To leverage the government's limited resources for the largest possible impact on structural change and economic growth, the government needs to know which new industries are consistent with the country's latent comparative advantages. In other words, the government should know in which industries it has low factor costs of production based on the country's endowment structure but lacks global competitiveness due to high transaction costs. Moreover, the government should know which infrastructures and institutions require improvements to reduce transaction costs so as to enable those new industries to thrive.

In other words, new structural economics suggests that government should identify industries of latent comparative advantages and then provide incentives for the first movers to overcome coordinating failures in improving infrastructure and institutions to turn them into the nation's competitive advantages. Theoretically, industrial policy should be a useful instrument for the government to achieve its facilitating role. In practice, industrial policies have largely failed in developing countries, tainting their reputation in mainstream economics. But if the government does not facilitate the development of industries in line with the country's comparative advantage, old industries may die due to loss of comparative advantages, while new industries are unlikely to emerge spontaneously due to the lack of first movers and appropriate hard and soft infrastructure. One result would be deindustrialization. Without new industries, countries cannot achieve robust economic growth, solve the job-generation challenge, and escape the low-income or middle-income trap.

To reject all industrial policy because of past failures is to miss the opportunity to understand why most industrial policies failed and to improve them in the future. They failed because in many cases the government in a developing country, with the best intentions and unaware of the endogeneity of industrial structure, tried too ambitiously to support advanced industries before the economy had the right endowment structure to make these industries into the country's comparative advantages. The firms in targeted industries were not viable in open and competitive markets, so governments had to protect and subsidize them, granting them monopoly rights, providing low-price capital, raw material and land, or giving preferential taxes. Such distortive interventions created economic rents that stimulated rent seeking, embezzlement, and corruption (Krueger, 1974; Krugman, 1993).

A desirable industrial policy should aim instead to facilitate the growth of industries, which are the country's latent comparative advantage, enabling them to become the country's competitive advantage in the market quickly. The latent comparative advantage refers to an industry with low factor costs of production relative to the rest of the world. This is determined by the economy's endowment structure and too high transaction costs (due to poor hard and soft infrastructure) to be competitive in domestic and international markets. Firms will be viable and the sectors competitive once the government helps the firms reduce transaction costs by overcoming coordination and externality issues to improve hard and soft infrastructure.

In addition to facilitating the growth of industries with latent comparative advantage, an industrial policy may also help firms exit from industries in which the country loses comparative advantages, or relocate to other countries with lower income and wages.

The industries in a middle-income country may be classified into five different types, depending on their distance to the global technology frontier: (1) catching-up industries, which have lower technology and value-added than similar industries in higher-income countries; (2) leading-edge industries, which are global technology frontier industries; (3) comparative advantage losing industries, which the country is about to exit due to changes in endowment structure and comparative advantages; (4) "corner-overtaking" industries, which have short innovation cycles, allowing a middle-income country to compete directly with high-income countries; and (5) strategic industries, which go against the country's comparative advantages but are developed due to the need for national security. I will discuss how the government may play a facilitating role in each of the five types of industrial policy aforementioned.

Type I: Catching-Up Industries

How can governments identify industries with latent comparative advantages in the process of catching up with industries in higher income countries? History offers many lessons of what to do and what to avoid.

Since the 16th and 17th centuries, successful economies have shared a common feature: industrial policies in these countries aimed to help firms enter the industries that had flourished in dynamically growing and slightly more developed countries. They were able to exploit the latecomer's advantage. For example, the Netherlands was the most developed country in the world in the 16th and 17th centuries, with a highly developed wool textile industry. Britain's wool textile industry was immature by comparison. The British government implemented policies to encourage the imports of machinery and skilled workers from the Netherlands. Those policies worked. At the time, per capita income in Great Britain was 70% of the Dutch level. That meant that their endowments and comparative advantages were quite similar.

Following the Industrial Revolution, Great Britain became the most advanced economy in the world. In the late 19th century, France, Germany, and the United States used similar policies to catch up with Great Britain. Their per capita incomes at that time were already about 60%–75% of Britain's (Gerschenkron, 1962). In the 1950s and 1960s, Japan imitated industries in the United States at a time when its per capita income exceeded 40% of that of the United States. Later, the four Asian tigers (Korea, Taiwan, Singapore, and Hong Kong) succeeded by imitating Japan's industries. Their per capita incomes were about 30%–40% of Japan's at the time (Akamatsu, 1962; Chang, 2003; Ito, 1980; Kim, 1988).

Other countries also targeted and tried to imitate industries in the United States after the WWII but failed. One reason was that their income levels were less than 20% of that of the United States. For example, in the 1950s China targeted and tried to imitate US industries even though its per capita income was just 5% of the United States level. With the government's efforts to build up advanced industries, China was able to test atomic and hydrogen bombs in the 1960s and launch satellites in the 1970s. These achievements came at a very high price to the economy. In 1979, when China began its transition to a market economy, its per capita income was less than one-third of the average of sub-Saharan African countries.

Drawing on the experience of successful economies and the theory of comparative advantage, I propose a new growth identification and facilitation framework for the catching-up type of industrial policy. This framework has two tracks and six steps (Lin and Monga, 2011).

Step 1. Identifying tradable goods industries. When the government of a developing country seeks to facilitate industrial upgrading in nonresource manufacturing, it should identify the tradable goods industries in countries that have been growing dynamically for the previous 20–30 years and whose per capita income is about 100%–200% higher than its own. Although experience suggests that 100% has been a successful reference point, a larger leap could be justified because technology and industrial upgrading happen much faster today.

The tradable goods and services produced in the target countries have a good chance of being those in which the pursuing country has a latent comparative advantage. If a country has grown rapidly in the last 20–30 years, the industries in its tradable sectors must be consistent with its comparative advantage. Yet, because of rapid capital accumulation and wage increases, the industries that were consistent with the comparative advantages of the targeted country's previous factor endowment structure will soon lose their comparative advantage. The sunset industries that are about to lose their comparative advantage in the targeted country will become the sunrise industries because of latent comparative advantage in the catching-up country, which has a similar endowment structure and a somewhat lower per capita GDP.

Step 2. Identifying obstacles. Among the industries identified in step 1, the government may give priority to those which some domestic firms have already entered spontaneously, and identify the obstacles impeding these firms from up-grading the quality of their products and the barriers limiting entry by other private firms. The usual barriers are related to high transaction costs. Is the primary impediment deficient infrastructure, poor logistics, inadequate financial support, or a limited pool of skilled workers? Obstacles can be identified using value-chain analysis or the growth diagnostic framework suggested by Hausmann et al. (2008). The government can then take steps to ease those binding constraints, using randomized controlled experiments to test the effectiveness of these measures before scaling up policies at the national level (Duflo, 2004).

Step 3. Encouraging firms in other, more advanced economies to relocate to the country trying to catch-up. Some of the industries identified in Step 1 may be new to the country. The government could adopt measures to encourage firms in the targeted higher income countries to relocate to its country so as to take advantage of lower wages. The government could also establish incubation programs to catalyze the entry of domestic private firms into these industries.

Step 4. Paying attention to successful businesses in new industries. Technology changes fast, which means that there are industries today that did not exist 20 years ago. Some domestic entrepreneurs may discover new profitable opportunities that were not identified in step 1. Consider information services in India in the 1980s. In the beginning, Indian firms outsourcing to US companies used satellite communication, which was extremely expensive. The Indian government built fiber-optic systems that greatly reduced communication costs, helping Indian information service companies gain a competitive advantage over other companies in the world. When new technology brings new opportunities and domestic private firms have already discovered them, the governments should pay close attention to their success and provide support to scale up those industries. Each country may also have some unique endowments. If entrepreneurs in the country discover opportunities to use such endowments profitably, the government may also provide support to scale up those opportunities to become competitive industries.

Step 5. Using special economic zones to attract domestic and foreign companies. In developing countries with poor infrastructure and an unfriendly business environment, budget and capacity constraints prevent governments from making necessary improvements to benefit every industry in all locations of the country within a reasonable timeframe. Instead, the government can use industrial parks, export processing zones, or special economic zones to attract private domestic and foreign firms to invest in the targeted industries. Improvements in infrastructure and the business environment within these special areas can reduce transaction costs and facilitate the development of industries with latent comparative advantage. The special economic areas also have the advantage of encouraging industrial clustering, which can lower logistical costs.

Step 6. Compensating pioneering firms for the externalities they generate. The government may provide limited incentives to pioneering domestic or foreign firms that invest in industries identified in steps 1 and 4 to compensate them for the public knowledge created by their investments. The incentives should be limited in time and budget allocations because the targeted industries should have a latent comparative advantage that enable them to become competitive in domestic and foreign markets once transaction costs fall. The incentives may be in the form of a corporate income tax holiday for a limited number of years, priority access to credit (in countries with financial repression), or priority access to foreign reserves for importing key equipment (in countries with capital controls). To minimize the risk of rent seeking and political capture, the incentives should not be in the form of monopoly rent, high tariffs, or other distortions. The government may reward the firms that discovered successful new industries by themselves (see step 4 aforementioned) with a prize or other forms of special recognition for their contributions to economic development.

This kind of compensation for externalities differs from the protections and subsidies of the old import-substitution strategy that aimed to help nonviable firms in priority industries stay in business. Under this new framework, the firms encouraged have low factor costs of production and are viable in the market, so their profitability can be ensured by improving their management once soft and hard infrastructure are enhanced and transaction costs lowered.

Type II: Leading Edge Industries

When a country reaches the middle-income stage, some of its industries may enter into areas which high-income countries have exited due to limited value-added (from these high-income countries' viewpoint). In such cases, the former country becomes the highest income country in the industry worldwide and it possesses leading edge technology. One example is household appliances, such as color TVs, refrigerators, microwave ovens, and other electronic white goods, in China. For the country to maintain leadership and competitiveness in these industries, it is necessary that the firms in these industries engage in indigenous R&D for new technologies and products.

Two different kinds of activities are involved in indigenous R&D: the development of new products and new technologies, and delivering the breakthroughs in the basic science needed for the new technologies and products. A firm can be rewarded by a patent if its efforts to develop a new product or technology are successful. Therefore, the development of new products and technology should be the firm's responsibility. However, research in basic science requires large capital inputs and is very risky, while its outputs are typically in the form of academic papers, which are public goods. Individual firms may be reluctant to do basic research.

In advanced countries, such as the United States, most of the industries are leading-edge industries worldwide. The basic research related to those industries is mainly carried out by either universities or research institutions, funded by the National Science Foundation, the National Institutes of Health, the Defense Department, and other government sources (Mazzucato, 2013). Similarly, basic research in other advanced economies, such as Japan and some European countries is also carried out by government-funded institutions. All these facts suggest that, in order to maintain global competitiveness and leadership in its leading-edge industries, a middle-income country should adopt a similar approach to support the basic research required to catalyze the innovation of new technologies and products. The government should also strengthen the protection of intellectual property rights.

To be more specific, governments of middle-income countries can promote the development of new products and technologies by using fiscal allocations to set up research funds to support research institutions in related fields or to encourage cooperation between research institutions and firms in the industries. The governments can also financially support firms in the industry to set up joint research platforms, which can be used to tackle common technical bottlenecks. Firms may develop new products or technology separately, based on the breakthrough in the common technology. Lastly, the government can use procurement to help firms rapidly scale up production so as to reduce unit costs and increase international competitiveness.

To expand the market globally, it is essential for firms in the relevant industries to establish worldwide networks for sales, processing of products, and after-sale services. The government may help firms in this type of industries go abroad by providing personnel training, legal service, and consular protection.

Type III: Comparative Advantage—Losing Industries

For labor-intensive industries, wage is one of the most important components of the cost of production. In a rapidly growing developing country, such as China, wages will rise very quickly. Labor-intensive industries will turn from the country's comparative advantages to its sunset industries. In the face of such change, some of the firms in the labor-intensive export processing industries may upgrade to the two ends of a "smile curve" where the added-value is higher, such as branding, R&D, quality control, marketing, sales, etc. However, for most firms the way out is to relocate their production to countries with lower wages, as the textile, garments, and electronic firms in Japan did in the 1960s and firms in similar industries in the four Asian Tigers did in the 1980s. Relocating allows the firms to put their tacit knowledge in technology, management, and marketing to continual use and it also changes these firms' production from the country's GDP to the country's gross national product (GNP). Moreover, the overseas success of these firms can speed up the industrial upgrading in their home country by releasing resources for new industries and generating demand for intermediate parts or machineries used in the labor-intensive industries, which are in general more capital/technology intensive and of higher added value.

Most of the labor-intensive export processing firms are clustered. The government may use two types of policies to help these firms. The first one is to provide training on design, R&D, and marketing, which can help some firms move up to the two ends of a "smile curve." The second policy is to facilitate processing firms go abroad. Specific measures include offering information on host countries and training personnel needed for overseas operations, or establishing export-processing zones together with the host governments so as to provide adequate infrastructure and business environments for the firms. Examples of export processing zones include Singapore's Industrial Park in Suzhou, China.

Type IV: "Corner-Overtaking" Industries

The coming of the information age creates opportunities for a developing country to compete directly with developed countries in certain industries, such as software and mobile devices, where innovations rely mainly on human capital and where the innovation cycle is relatively short (Lee, 2013). The innovation of a new medicine may take decades and will require billions of dollars, whereas the design of a piece of software or a mobile phone may take only a few months and be accomplished by a small team of engineers. Since the required capital input to support the innovation is relatively small, the disadvantage of a relatively capital-scarce developing country in the innovation of such types of products is, compared to a relatively capital-abundant developed country, not insurmountable. Such industries provide a developing country with the opportunity to overtake developed countries on a corner. The government in a developing country can facilitate the development of such industries by investing in the education of related human capital, setting up incubators, reinforcing the protection of property rights, encouraging venture capital, providing preferential taxes, facilitating start-ups run by creative talents at home and abroad, and using government procurement to support the production of new products.

Type V: Strategic Industries

Every country needs national defense. National defense industries are usually characterized by high capital-intensity, long R&D cycles, and large-scale economies. In general, such industries are not compatible with a country's comparative advantages, and especially so in the case of developing countries. However, some of those industries may be essential for national defense and the country needs to own them domestically. Firms in such industries will not be viable in an open, competitive market. Subsidies and protections from government are indispensable. The structuralist perspective discussed in Section, "Why We Need to Rethink Development Economics" of this chapter proposed the use of distortions in factor prices and of market monopolies as means of subsidies/protection for comparative advantage-defying advanced industries. A better approach is to subsidize these firms directly by R&D grants or indirectly through procurement of products. This is similar to the practices in the United States and other advanced countries. In a developing country, the government's fiscal capacity to subsidize strategic industries is limited. Therefore, the choice of strategic industries should be very selective and their number should remain small. In effect, only those industries essential for national defense and having a large externality to civil industries should be chosen.

CONCLUSIONS

This chapter reviewed the evolution of development economics since its formation in the wake of WWII and proposed new structural economics, as an alternative approach. Every developing country has the potential to grow dynamically and avoid the middle-income trap. However, that can only happen if the government plays an appropriate facilitating role in a market economy by supporting the development of industries connected to the country's latent comparative advantages.

Achieving such a result will require a change in mindset. In the first two waves of development thinking, economists used high-income countries as the reference. They examined what those countries had (capital-intensive industries) and could do well (well-functioning market) and recommended that developing countries follow suit. New structural economics turns this model upside down. It recommends that developing countries look at what they have at the present time (their endowments) at and what they can do well based on what they have (their comparative advantages). Governments should compensate for the externalities generated by the first movers to the industries in which the country has latent comparative advantages, and coordinate or provide improvements in hard/soft infrastructure to reduce transaction costs so that the industries in question become the nation's competitive advantages and, thus, profitable. Competitiveness will create the foundation for sustained growth, income generation, poverty reduction, and fast upgrading of endowment/industrial structure leading to catch-up with high-income countries. I hope that the industrial policies for the five types of industries discussed in this chapter will help governments in catching-up European countries to tap their growth potentials and achieve development success.

ACKNOWLEDGMENT

I would like to thank Slavo Radosevic for helpful comments and suggestions in the preparation of this chapter.

ENDNOTES

1. The Industrial Revolution was still in its infancy when Adam Smith was writing *An Inquiry into the Nature and Causes of the Wealth of Nations*. Consequently, Smith paid little attention to technology innovation and industrial upgrading; rather, he focused on trade and specialization within given technologies and industries.
2. By convention, the name for such studies should be "structural economics." The "new" is added to distinguish it from structuralism. This practice has precedents in modern economics. For example, Douglass North, who used the neoclassical approach to study institutions in the 1960s, referred to it as "new institutional economics" to distinguish it from the "institutional school," which flourished in the United States in the early 20th century.

REFERENCES

Agenor, P.R., Canuto, O., Jelenic, M., 2012. Avoiding Middle-income Growth Traps. Econ. Premise 98, 1–7.

Aghion, P., 2009. Some Thoughts on Industrial Policy and Growth. Document de Travail 2009–09, Observatoire Français des conjonctures économiques, Sciences Po, Paris. Available from: http://www.ofce.sciences-po.fr/pdf/dtravail/WP2009-09.pdf

Akamatsu, K., 1962. A historical pattern of economic growth in developing countries. J. Dev. Econ. 1 (1), 3–25.

Amsden, A.H., 1989. Asia's Next Giant. Oxford University Press, New York, NY; Oxford.

Arndt, H.W., 1985. The origins of structuralism. World Dev. 13 (2), 151–159.

Cardoso, E., Helwege, A., 1995. Latin America's Economy. MIT Press, Cambridge, MA.

Chang, H.-J., 2003. Kicking Away the Ladder: Development Strategy in Historical Perspective. Anthem Press, London.

Chenery, H.B., 1961. Comparative advantage and development policy. Am. Econ. Rev. 51 (1), 18–51.

Duflo, E., 2004. Scaling Up and Evaluation. In: Bourguignon, F., Pleskovic, B. (Eds.), Annual World Bank Conference on Development Economics 2004. World Bank, Washington, DC.

Easterly, W., 2001. The Elusive Quest for Growth: Economists' Adventures and Misadventures in the Tropics. MIT Press, Cambridge, MA.

Easterly, W., Loayza, N., Montiel, P.J., 1997. Has Latin America's Post-Reform Growth Been Disappointing? World Bank Policy Research Paper 1708. World Bank, Washington, DC.

Gerschenkron, A., 1962. Economic Backwardness in Historical Perspective: A Book of Essays. Belknap Press of Harvard University Press, Cambridge, MA.

Harrison, A., Rodríguez-Clare, A., 2010. Trade, foreign investment, and industrial policy for developing countries. Rodrik, D. (Ed.), Handbook of Economic Growth, vol. 5, North-Holland, Amsterdam.

Hausmann, R., Rodrik, D., 2003. Economic development as self-discovery. J. Dev. Econ. 72 (2), 603–633.

Hausmann, R., Rodrik, D., Velasco, A., 2008. Growth diagnostics. In: Serra, N., Stiglitz, J. (Eds.), The Washington Consensus Reconsidered: Towards a New Global Governance. Oxford University Press, Oxford, UK.

Ito, T., 1980. Disequilibrium Growth Theory. J. Econ. Theory 23 (3), 380–409.

Ju, J., Lin, J.Y., Wang, Y., 2015. Endowment Structures, Industrial Dynamics, and Economic Growth. J. Monet. Econ. 76, 244–263.

Kim, Y.H., 1988. Higashi Ajia Kogyoka to Sekai Shihonshugi (Industrialisation of East Asia and the World Capitalism). Toyo Keizai Shimpo-sha, Tokyo.

Krueger, A., 1974. The political economy of rent-seeking society. Am. Econ. Rev. 64 (3), 291–303.

Krueger, A., Tuncer, B., 1982. An empirical test of the infant industry argument. Am. Econ. Rev. 72 (5), 1142–1152.

Krugman, P., 1993. Protection in developing countries. In: Dornbusch, R. (Ed.), Policymaking in the Open Economy: Concepts and Case Studies in Economic Performance. Oxford University Press, New York.

Kuznets, S., 1966. Modern Economic Growth: Rate, Structure and Spread. Yale University Press, New Haven, CT.

Lal, D., 1994. Against Dirigisme: The Case for Unshackling Economic Markets. International Center for Economic Growth, ICS Press, San Francisco.

Lau, L., Qian, J.Y., Roland, G., 2000. Reform without Losers: an interpretation of China's dual-track approach to transition. J. Polit. Econ. 108 (1), 120–143.

Lee, K., 2013. Schumpeterian Analysis of Economic Catch-up: Knowledge, Path Creation, and the Middle-income Trap. Cambridge University Press, Cambridge, UK.

Lin, J.Y., 2009. Economic Development and Transition: Thought, Strategy, and Viability. Cambridge University Press, Cambridge, UK.

Lin, J.Y., 2011. New structural economics: a framework for rethinking economic development. World Bank Res. Obs. 26 (2), 193–221.

Lin, J.Y., 2012. Demystifying the Chinese Economy. Cambridge University Press, Cambridge, UK.

Lin, J.Y., 2013. Against the Consensus: Reflections on the Great Recession. Cambridge University Press, Cambridge, UK.

Lin, J.Y., Chang, H., 2009. DPR debate: should industrial policy in developing countries conform to comparative advantage or defy it? Dev. Policy Rev. 27 (5), 483–502.

Lin, J.Y., Li, Z.Y., 2008. Policy burden, privatisation and soft budget constraint. J. Comp. Econ. 36, 90–102.

Lin, J.Y., Monga, C., 2011. DPR debate: growth identification and facilitation: the role of the state in the dynamics of structural change. Dev. Policy Rev. 29 (3), 259–310.

Lin, J.Y., Nugent, J., 1995. Institutions and economic development. Srinivasan, T.N., Behrman, J. (Eds.), Handbook of Development Economics, vol. 3, North Holland, Amsterdam.

Maddison, A., 2006. The World Economy. OECD, Paris.

Mazzucato, M., 2013. The Entrepreneurial State: Debunking Public vs. Private Sector Myths. Anthem Press, New York.

Naughton, B., 1995. Growing Out of Plan: Chinese Economic Reform 1978-1993. Cambridge University Press, Cambridge, UK.

Pack, H., Saggi, K., 2006. Is there a case for industrial policy? A critical survey. World Bank Res. Obs. 21 (2), 267–297.

Porter, M.E., 1990. The Competitive Advantage of Nations. Free Press, New York.

Prebisch, R., 1950. The Economic Development of Latin America and its Principal Problems, New York: United Nations. Reprinted in Economic Bulletin for Latin America 7 (1) (February 1962), pp. 1–22.

Rodrik, D., 2004. Industrial Policy for the Twenty-First Century. Harvard University, Cambridge, MA.

Romer, P.M., 1990. Endogenous technological change. J. Polit. Econ. 98 (5), S71–S102.

Rosenstein-Rodan, P., 1943. Problems of industrialization of eastern and southeastern Europe. Econ. J. 111, 202–211.

Subramanian, A., Roy, D., 2003. Who can explain the Mauritian Miracle: Mede, Romer, Sachs, or Rodrik? In: Rodrik, D. (Ed.), In Search of Prosperity: Analytic Narratives on Economic Growth. Princeton University Press, Princeton, NJ.

Wade, R., 1990. Governing the Market. Princeton University Press, Princeton, NJ.

Williamson, J., 1990. What Washington means by policy reform. In: Williamson, J. (Ed.), Latin American Adjustment: How Much Has Happened?. Institute for International Economics, Washington, DC.

World Bank., 2002. Transition, the First Ten Years: Analysis and Lessons for Eastern Europe and Former Soviet Union. Washington, DC.

Chapter 9

Smart Specialization With Short-Cycle Technologies and Implementation Strategies to Avoid Target and Design Failures

Keun Lee

Seoul National University, Seoul, South Korea

Chapter Outline

Academic Highlights

- Neither neoclassical nor neo-Schumpeterian thinking on growth and development offers sound theoretical ideas regarding the specialization or comparative advantage for middle-income countries that suffer from the middle-income trap.
- The latter group of countries has to seek a sector where they may be able to survive by competing effectively with the incumbents and expect improved growth prospects.

Advances in the Theory and Practice of Smart Specialization. http://dx.doi.org/10.1016/B978-0-12-804137-6.00009-7

- Qualified middle-income countries have comparative advantages in techno-logical sectors with a short-cycle time because in such sectors dominance by the incumbent is often disrupted, and new technologies tend to emerge more frequently and offer high growth prospects.
- The criterion of cycle time of technologies is better than those criteria based on product spaces and is complementary to the idea of latent comparative advantage of Lin (2012a) and Chapter 8.

Policy Highlights

- A key idea for the implementation of this policy of specialization is for indus-trial policy to involve private firms and avoid targeting and design failures from the beginning.
- Policy makers can organize a public–private joint taskforce, conduct a survey, and consult with existing private firms and entrepreneurs by asking about the types of business items or technological areas in which they see near-future potential, as well as about the opportunities, risks, and bottle-necks in entering or starting these future areas.
- The business areas to be identified are those areas where private sectors see strong market potential, but are new or short-cycle technology based and facing technological, financial, and other environmental (regulations) uncer-tainties.
- Policy intervention should promote these identified areas by mobilizing pub-lic and private resources and competences, thereby correcting market and coordination failures.

INTRODUCTION

Despite a large, steady volume of literature on economic growth, the de-terminants of such growth remain an important question in economics (North, 2005). Therefore, initiating and sustaining economic growth in de-veloping or peripheral countries have become very difficult. Neoclassical growth theories do not shed sufficient light on this topic because they do not explicitly consider the theoretical possibility and reality that the mechanisms of economic growth significantly differ between developed and developing countries or across stages of development, and that, therefore, a different specialization/strategy must be adopted by countries at various stages of de-velopment. Moreover, neoclassical growth theory assumes that as long as the capital is in place, the technologies and practices being used in developed economies can be easily transferred to and mastered by developing coun-tries. However, this strong assumption has limited applicability in the context of developing countries (Nelson and Pack, 1999). Development economists that adopt the Schumpeterian tradition emphasize the importance and pro-cesses of learning and capability building in local contexts; they identify the difficulty of learning and technology transfer as key factors hindering latecomers from catching up (Bell, 1984; Bell and Figueiredo, 2012; Bell and Pavitt, 1993; Katz, 1984).

The importance of capability building in developing countries is uncontested. However, "where (which sectors) to utilize" such capability remains unknown. Given that latecomer firms are not only "resource/capability poor," but also "late entrants" (Mathews, 2002a), they have to determine the points of entry in the established international division of labor for their survival; they are late entrants in the sense that when they begin their manufacturing activities, the value chain of production is already well established in their chosen market segment and is already occupied by firms from advanced countries (Ernst and Guerrieri, 1998; Sturgeon and Gereffi, 2009). Therefore, latecomer firms have no choice but to inherit some, often low-end, segments left by firms from advanced economies or to start from original equipment manufacturing (OEM) or subcontracting (Amsden, 1989; Hobday, 1995).

Developing countries, especially low-income ones, have comparative advantages in low-end, often labor-intensive, segments or sectors in which they have to specialize. However, specialization alone will not help these countries catch up or move beyond the middle-income stage. Although OEM and subcontracting may serve as channels for exporting and earning foreign exchanges, they have limited applications as long-term strategies. Specifically, a successful OEM can lead to increased wage rates, and new, cheaper labor sites in "next tier down" countries will emerge to replace the position of a country in the global value chain. Consequently, these countries will fall into the "middle-income trap," unless they upgrade themselves into a higher-end segment with higher capabilities.

The middle-income trap results from the positioning of middle-income countries (MICs) between low-wage manufacturers and high-wage innovators; given their very high wage rates and low technological capability, these countries cannot compete with low-wage exporters and advanced countries (World Bank 2010, 2012; Yusuf and Nabeshima, 2009). To free themselves from this trap, these countries must build their innovation capabilities and find a new niche or segment in which they can upgrade their specialization (Lee, 2013a,b). This study is focused on the latter option.

"Where and how to specialize" is an important challenge for MICs. However, the solution to this problem lacks theoretical guidance. This challenge contrasts the situation of low-income countries, for which conventional endowment-based specialization (i.e., labor- or resource-intensive sectors) is offered as a solution. After these countries reach the middle-income stage, they do not have any theoretical guidance as to what capital-intensive sector they must enter.

This study is motivated by the fact that neither the neoclassical nor Schumpeterian perspectives on growth and development offer a sound basis for the specialization or comparative advantage of MICs stuck in the middle-income trap. Latecomer firms and economies need both capability building and "smart specialization." Although such a requirement holds true for both low- and middle-income developing countries, the latter face great difficulty in developing their specialization because they are located close to the frontier (high-income countries) and face more competition or entry barriers in the higher-end segments of the international division of labor. Therefore, these countries must look for a sector in which they may obtain better growth prospects or survive by competing effectively with the incumbents.

This study proposes a new economic specialization criterion and an implementation strategy for MICs. Specifically, it proposes the cycle time of technologies as a criterion that is better than the criteria based on product spaces, as suggested by Hausmann et al. (2007) and Hidalgo et al. (2007), and complements the latent comparative advantage idea of Lin (2012a,b). Cycle time of technologies refers to how fast technologies change or become obsolete over time (Jaffe and Trajtenberg, 2002). Based on the country panel growth regression results obtained by Lee (2013a) using cycle time variables, this study argues that qualified MICs have relative advantages in specializing in technological sectors with a short-cycle time because short-cycle technologies imply that the dominance of the incumbents is often disrupted and new technologies tend to emerge and offer higher growth prospects. Aside from indicating low entry barriers and high profitability, a minimal reliance on existing technologies is associated with few collisions with the technologies of advanced countries, less royalty payments, and first- or fast-mover advantages (Lee, 2013a). We also propose concrete action plans for implementing this idea of specialization.

The idea of MICs specializing in short-cycle sectors is consistent with the notions that the mechanisms of economic growth differ across various levels of income, especially in the case of low- and high-income countries, and that a narrow transition path bridges these two country groups. Specialization into short-cycle sectors is a transition strategy that can help MICs go beyond their middle-income levels and reach high-income status.

The section, "Criteria for Specialization" discusses and evaluates the extant economic specialization criteria for developing countries, particularly MICs, as well as the requirements for these criteria to become viable. Late entrants search for a sector in which they may enter, expect better growth prospects, and survive by competing effectively with the incumbents. In this case, the criterion is "entry/survival possibility with some growth prospects." The section "Specializing in Short-Cycle Technology–Based Sectors" introduces the cycle time concept and argues that MICs must specialize in sectors with short-cycle technologies, which can help them upgrade their growth mechanisms. The section, "Implementing the Ideas: Avoiding Failures in Targeting Versus Designing" discusses how MICs can avoid both targeting and designing failures by combining the short-cycle idea with the entrepreneurial discovery (ED) proposed in the "smart specialization" framework (Foray, 2015). The section, "Summary and Concluding Remarks" concludes the chapter.

CRITERIA FOR SPECIALIZATION

Traditional, Endowment-Based Comparative Advantages

Proposed by Ricardo, the comparative advantage framework considers the natural and physical resources of a nation, including its labor force, as the basic criteria for specialization. Given that many developing countries initially face labor abundance, as revealed by Lewis (1954), they are advised to specialize in labor-intensive sectors. Consistent with Hecksher–Ohlin trade theory or its variations (Kahn, 1951; Sen, 1957), capital–labor ratio is a key variable in such a criterion. Despite some criticisms, this allocation criterion is useful and workable because the shift of the industrial structure from agricultural sectors to labor-intensive manufacturing sectors characterizes the typical process of development and structural transformation (Kuznets, 1966).

However, this investment strategy does not offer any answers as to what countries must do when the increasingly scarce and expensive labor drives them to enter capital-intensive sectors. An exemplar country is South Korea, which started out as a labor-surplus economy in the 1950s and later experienced an economic boom after entering the labor-intensive manufacturing sector. In the early 1970s, South Korea reached the Lewis turning point of scarce labor, during which the rapid growth of light industries increased the wage rates, thereby driving the country to enter capital-intensive sectors (i.e., automobile, steel, shipbuilding, and chemicals) in the mid-1970s. Given the large number of capital-intensive sectors, nations need to be guided as to which sector they must enter. However, the endowment-based theory of comparative advantages neither distinguishes one capital-intensive sector from another, nor suggests a criterion for choosing among these sectors.

Dynamic or Latent Comparative Advantages

As one of the first to investigate the limitations of static comparative advantage, Viner (1958) applied dynamic modifications on comparative advantage, which was further developed by Lin (2012a,b) into latent comparative advantages. Lin argued that endowment is not necessarily given or exogenous, but can change endogenously as the country grows or accumulates more capital. Therefore, developing countries must match their present endowment structure to that of forerunning countries (countries with a GDP per capita that is twice higher), and then target the mature or leftover industries from these countries. Lin (2012a,b) also suggested that the government should prescribe comparative advantage–following industrial policies based on the changing endowment structure of their countries.

This theory of late advantage is a step forward, in that it suggests a criterion to help choose from among the potentially many capital-intensive sectors; namely, to choose a sector that is new to a country, but old to the bench mark the countries ahead of it. In this way, apart from avoiding direct competition, latecomer countries also inherit the declining or advantage-losing sectors from the forerunning countries. Although this strategy can help in their catching up with the forerunning or incumbent economies, latecomer countries always remain behind these economies. Some aspects of the actual experience of South Korea are consistent with this suggestion; however, the country not only inherited old sectors (i.e., steel and automobile), but also leapfrogged into emerging sectors (i.e., telecommunication equipment) and directly competed with the forerunning economies to catch up (Lee, 2013a). This story makes more sense for those countries that are shifting from labor- to capital-intensive sectors (i.e., South Korea in the 1970s), especially to those sectors with a high degree of technologies (i.e., equipment and facilities) that cannot be easily entered by those countries that do not have the necessary facilities (Jung and Lee, 2010). Therefore, although this strategy may prove useful for lower-level MICs, the same cannot be said for those upper-level MICs attempting to upgrade their industrial structure to match that of emerging or close-to-frontier sectors. We still need additional theoretical criteria for the sectoral specialization of MICs.

Product Spaces and Diversification

Hausmann et al. (2007) developed the product space concept to determine the sophistication of the trade structure of a country. They divided the specialization pattern of a country into core versus peripheries based on the sophistication of its products. They proposed that a country can achieve gradual sophistication (and diversification) in its trade structure by moving into neighboring spaces or capturing low-hanging fruits. Therefore, the export structure of a country must be diversified into highly sophisticated products to achieve sustained export performance and economic growth. However, such an idea has some limitations from the point of view of developing countries.

Hausmann et al. (2007) and Hidalgo et al. (2007) considered the proximity among product spaces as an important variable in determining the feasibility of diversification. However, their criterion does not disclose much information about the "directions" of diversification because of the numerous neighboring spaces. In other words, they focus on the "distance" rather than on the "directions" of diversification. The distance-based argument of diversification fails to ask in which sectors the latecomer economies must diversify first.

The empirics of Hausmann et al. (2007) and Hidalgo et al. (2007) are based on trade data, which do not contain any information on the value added of traded products or about how products are made. Therefore, the technological (or value-added) content cannot be assessed based on such data (Sturgeon and Gereffi, 2012). Although a developing country exports high-tech goods, as reflected in its trade data, the most valuable value-added components of these goods are often produced in a third-world country.[1] Hausmann et al. (2007) and Hidalgo et al. (2007) also used income level as the weighting factor to calculate the degree of sophistication; in other words, those countries that produce the goods currently exported by high-income countries are considered highly sophisticated. This method makes such a measure tautological; in other words, a country can become rich by producing goods currently made by wealthier countries.

However, this strategy does not consider the ability of a country to compete in the international market. Specifically, the strategy informs latecomer countries that they must try to produce those products being made by the incumbents, but do not inform them about how to compete with these incumbents in the same or similar sectors. Instead of avoiding direct collision with the incumbent countries, latecomer countries must find a niche for them to survive and compete effectively in the market.

In sum, Hausmann et al. (2007) and Hidalgo et al. (2007) did not propose an effective way for MICs to reach the core structure, but merely argued that "countries can reach the core only by traversing 'empirically infrequent' (meaning long) distances," which is a very difficult task to achieve. However, Hausmann et al. (2007) and Hidalgo et al. (2007) do not discuss how these countries can traverse the long distance to reach the core space. This observation may help us understand why poor countries have trouble developing more competitive exports and fail to match the income levels of rich countries.

Criteria for Technological Specialization

Leaving trade-based specialization, we now consider technology-based specialization, for instance, specialization into sectors with high technological opportunity or high originality.

First, the idea of specializing in a sector with high technological opportunity sounds appealing because of the better growth prospects. Technological opportunity can be measured by the growth rate of patents in a sector/field. This variable has been used in the literature as an indicator of "good" technological specialization, but a robust relationship between technological opportunity and economic growth is yet to be found. For instance, Meliciani (2002) failed to confirm any significant relationship between technological specialization and economic growth. Lee (2013a, Chapter 4) also found no significant relationship between technological opportunity and technological catch-up in the cases of South Korea and Taiwan. Although these economies are considered the most successful catching-up economies, their shares in US patent classes have not significantly increased in high-opportunity sectors. From the perspective of a latecomer, a specialization in high-opportunity sectors is desirable, but involves increased risk because such sectors are crowded with established companies. In other words, high-opportunity sectors involve increased levels of competition, which may also serve as a high entry barrier for latecomers with weak technological capabilities.

Second, specializing in sectors with highly original technologies may be considered. Originality is often considered similar to creativity. According to

Jaffe and Trajtenberg (2002), a technology with high originality is defined as that based on knowledge from diverse fields, and highly original patents are defined as those citing the patents from a wide variety of areas. In other words, a country that has more patents relying on knowledge from various fields is regarded as a country with a highly original patent portfolio. Advanced countries show a much higher degree of originality than developing countries (Lee, 2013a, Chapter 3). However, the country panel econometric analysis in Lee (2013a, Chapter 3) failed to establish a causal or correlational relationship among economic growth and high originality. Interestingly, Latin American countries have a higher degree of originality than do South Korea and Taiwan, but failed in sustained economic growth compared to the latter, which did not demonstrate a rapid growth of patents in high-originality sectors (Lee, 2013a). Consistent with the results at the country or sector level, the regressions using South Korean and American firm data failed to establish a robust relationship between financial performance and the number of patents of firms in high-originality sectors (Lee, 2013a, Chapter 5).

Given the aforementioned limitations, we must identify other variables that can be used as criteria for technological specialization. Therefore, we propose the cycle time of technologies as a criterion, and then discuss what makes it a viable criterion.

Requirements of Viable Criteria

The previous discussion gives latecomer firms and economies, particularly those at the middle stage of development, some ideas on what to look for in a viable specialization criterion. Given their weak capabilities, latecomers need to establish their niche in the international division of labor and participate in a sector where they can achieve better growth prospects and survive by competing effectively with the incumbents. In this case, "entry/survival possibility with some growth prospects" presents a viable criterion.

Static or latent comparative advantages suggest that countries must enter a highly competitive market by inheriting those sectors left behind by forerunning economies because of their weak growth prospects. The sophistication of a country's trade structure along the product space is also oriented toward the same idea, but does not provide directions among many neighboring spaces. By contrast, technological opportunity or originality is biased toward growth prospects without considering the possibilities of entry and survival.

SPECIALIZING IN SHORT-CYCLE TECHNOLOGY–BASED SECTORS

We propose the cycle time of technologies as a new criterion for technological specialization (Lee, 2013a). The cycle time of technologies measures how fast technologies change or become obsolete over time (Jaffe and Trajtenberg, 2002;

Lee, 2013a; Park and Lee, 2006). Lee (2013a) argued that qualified latecomers can achieve great advantages by targeting and specializing in technological sectors with a short-cycle time because short-cycle technologies indicate that the dominance of the incumbents is often disrupted and that the continuous emergence of new technologies can generate new opportunities. A minimal reliance on existing technologies represents both low entry and profitability, which are associated with few collisions with the technologies of advanced countries, less royalty payments, first- or fast-mover advantages, or product differentiation (Lee, 2013a). In other words, a sector that is based on technologies with a short-cycle time satisfies the two requirements of a viable criterion, namely, entry possibility and growth prospects. This is because a short-cycle technology–based sector has minimal reliance on existing technologies and can leverage the great opportunities resulting from the emergence of new technologies. For example, information technologies have a shorter cycle than pharmaceuticals in the sense that new innovations in information technology tend to rely less on existing or stock knowledge.[2]

The advantage of specializing in short-cycle technologies is consistent with the leapfrogging concept, in which the emerging generations of technologies allow catching-up countries to have a head or same start because both incumbents and latecomers start from the same starting line, and incumbents often stick with their existing technologies from which they derive their supremacy.[3] Leapfrogging is similar to the "long jumps" (Hidalgo et al., 2007) that economies must perform to shift themselves to those product spaces located far away from their current position and thus achieve subsequent structural transformation.

When combined with the latent comparative advantage concept and the growth identification and facilitation framework of Lin (2012b), the idea of technological specialization along the cycle time of technologies may provide a comprehensive policy framework for the economic growth of developing countries. Lin (2012b) advised latecomers to observe forerunning countries, and then target the mature industries in those countries as their latent comparative advantages. After inheriting the mature sectors from their forerunning countries in the first step, developing countries can then enter sectors with a shorter-cycle technology or leapfrog into new or emerging sectors. In other words, a sustainable catching-up growth not only requires entering mature industries (which are still new to the latecomers), but also leapfrogging into emerging industries that are new to both advanced and developing countries.

The technological development of South Korea over the last 3 decades (Lee, 2013a) reflects the increasing specialization of South Korean industries into short-cycle technologies during its catch-up period. South Korea began to specialize in labor-intensive (low value–added, long-cycle technology) industries, such as the apparel or shoe industry, in the 1960s. The economy then moved to the shorter- or medium-cycle sectors of low-end consumer electronics and automobile assembly in the 1970s and 1980s; to the shorter-cycle sectors of telecommunication equipment (telephone switches) in the late 1980s; and to memory chips, cell phones, and digital televisions in the 1990s. South Korean industries kept moving to shorter-cycle technologies to achieve technological diversification.

Fig. 9.1 shows the actual trends in the cycle time of technologies as calculated from the US patents jointly held by South Korea and Taiwan and those held by China. The numbers on the vertical axis represent the average cycle time of patents held by these economies. Jaffe and Trajtenberg (2002) defined average cycle time as the time difference between the application or grant year of the *citing* patent and that of the *cited* patents. For example, a value of 8 on the vertical axis indicates that the average cycle time of patents is 8 years (i.e., the patents held by South Korea and Taiwan tend to cite 8-year-old patents on average), and that the related technologies are considered outdated or useless after 8 years. Since the mid-1980s, South Korea and Taiwan have traveled toward technologies with increasingly short-cycle times. Therefore, the average cycle time of those patents held by Korea and Taiwan was shortened to 6–7 years by the late 1990s. This duration is 2–3 years shorter than the average cycle time of patents held by European G5 countries, whose patents have cycle times ranging from 9 to 10 years since the late 1980s because of their strong performance in high value–added, long-cycle sectors, such as pharmaceuticals and machine tools. Consequently, the patent portfolios of South Korea and Taiwan are completely different from those of advanced countries (Lee, 2013a). We consider the mid-1980s as an important turning point because that was when South Korea and Taiwan faced the middle-income trap, but were able to escape the trap after this period. Both countries reached the middle-income level during this period, and the GDP per capita of South Korea reached 25% of that of the

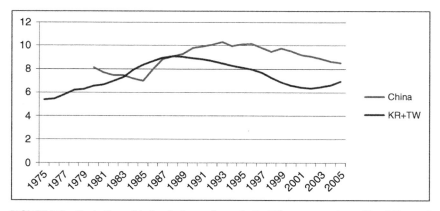

FIGURE 9.1 Cycle time of technologies as shown in the US patents registered by China and South Korea (SK)/Taiwan (TW). The *y*-axis measures the average cycle time of technologies, which in turn is measured by the mean backward citation lags (Jaffe and Trajtenberg 2002). The figures for the earlier years, such as the 1970s, must not be taken seriously because of the very small number (around 20) of US patents registered by these countries during those years. Values have been calculated by the author following the method of Lee (2013a).

United States. Since then, South Korea and Taiwan have continued to increase their R&D expenditures, and their R&D/GDP ratio eventually surpassed the 1% level. Along with this upgrading of technological capabilities, these countries have journeyed toward short-cycle technology–based sectors, such as various information technology products.

After achieving technological catch-up, the specialization of these countries must reach maturity. Fig. 9.1 shows that when South Korea and Taiwan reached their maturity in the 2000s, their technologies turned in the opposite direction toward long cycles, such as biological- or science-based technologies. Lee (2013a) considered such strategy a "detour" because the latecomer countries do not directly and immediately replicate the path and industries of advanced economies that specialize in long-cycle technologies. Instead, those countries that successfully catch up moved first toward a sector with short-cycle technologies and then, after reaching some maturity, turned toward the long-cycle based technologies. In other words, in contrast to Hausmann et al. (2007), who suggested that a developing country should become similar to a rich country, we propose that the transition strategy of a developing country must involve entering sectors that are based on short-cycle technologies instead of those that are dominated by rich countries, such as long-cycle technologies. However, as countries reach the point of technological maturity and a somewhat high level of capabilities (as South Korea did in the early 2000s), they are now driven to adopt long-cycle technologies, such as biomedical or pharmaceutical industries, which is what Samsung has been trying to achieve recently.

Therefore, the prospects of a country beyond the middle-income stage depend on whether the country is experiencing a "technological turning point" to enter short-cycle technologies along the curve of the cycle time of technologies. Based on Lee (2013a), Fig. 9.1 shows that China passed such a turning point in the mid-to-late 1990s, approximately 10–15 years after South Korea. The top 30 technologies in the US patents of China (Table 8.4 in Lee, 2013a) are similar to those of South Korea and Taiwan from 1980 to 1995. China holds more patents for semiconductors, information storage, telecommunications, electrical lighting, electrical heating, X-rays, and computer hardware and software. The weighted average cycle time of Chinese technologies from 2000 to 2005 was 8.07 years, which was closer to the South Korean/Taiwanese average of 7.69 years from 1980 to 1995, than to the Brazilian/Argentinean average of 9.26 years in the same period (Lee, 2013a).

Overall, in contrast to the comparative advantages in trade (trade-based specialization) determined initially by endowment conditions, we suggest that the dynamic comparative advantages in technology (technological specialization) are determined not by natural resource endowments, but by R&D and design capabilities accumulated over time. This technology-based specialization complements trade-based specialization along the latent comparative advantages or the new structural economics of Lin (2012a,b). The latter focuses on low- or lower-level MICs (e.g., China in the early 1980s) that are choosing between the right latent and the wrong comparative advantage sectors, whereas technology-based specialization focuses on upper-level MICs (e.g., China today) that are choosing between short- (and low-originality) and long-cycle (and high-originality) technologies. In a sense, short-cycle technologies provide latecomers with a niche, and ensure a higher rate of profitability, as revealed in the firm-level analysis of Lee (2013a, Chapter 5). By contrast, directly replicating the activities of forerunning economies and focusing on highly original and long-cycle technologies may lead to a continuous reliance on foreign advanced countries, thereby decreasing the chances of consolidating indigenous knowledge bases. Latin American economies may serve as examples of such specialization with very long average–cycle times (longer than 10 years) in their US patent portfolio.

Increasing the specialization in short-cycle technologies results in technological diversification. As shown in their cycle time curves, South Korea and Taiwan have gradually shortened their cycle times since the mid-1980s. However, this gradual shortening does not indicate that these economies have specialized in a few sectors; rather, they continued to enter progressively newer sectors with shorter-cycle times, essentially a process of industrial diversification into new or unrelated fields at times of paradigm shifts or lower entry barriers.

Fig. 9.2 shows the number of technological fields in which countries have registered patents from out of the 417 three-digit fields in the US patent classification system. High-income countries have registered patents in about 40% of the 417 classes in the US patent system. South Korea and Taiwan demonstrated an impressive catching-up performance compared to other MICs: they began from the same starting point and eventually surpassed the average level of

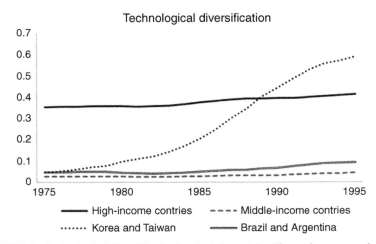

FIGURE 9.2 **Technological diversification in selected countries.** The y-axis represents the number of fields with registered patents divided by the total number of classes: 417. *(Taken from Figure 9.1 of Lee K., 2013. Schumpeterian analysis of economic catch-up: knowledge, path-creation, and the middle-income trap. Cambridge University Press, London; drawn by the author based on the NBER patent data.)*

high-income countries by the early 1990s. This achievement is very important because many scholars, such as Hausmann et al. (2007), consider the diversification of export structure as a necessary condition for sustained export performance and economic growth, as well as an important challenge faced by developing countries.

Given that diversification and specialization in short-cycle sectors occur simultaneously, one cannot determine which of the two is "driving" the other. However, we consider the cycle times of technologies as a policy guide variable that indicates the direction in which an economy must diversify. Developing countries must diversify themselves by moving into short-cycle, technology-based sectors. Our criterion is dynamic because we do not suggest that catching-up economies must target a specific or fixed list of short-cycle technologies. These economies must keep moving into shorter-cycle technologies to achieve technological diversification. Therefore, the chances of catching-up can be determined by whether a country experiences a turning point where it switches from long to short cycles along the curve of the cycle time of technologies.

Both Korea and Taiwan exhibit dual diversification, which is both intersectoral and intrasectoral. Intersectoral diversification involves entering new industries with high added value, whereas intrasectoral diversification involves entering high value–added segments within the same industry. Examples of intrasectoral upgrading or diversification are the Korean and Taiwanese semiconductor firms that move up the value chain. Numerous examples of successive entries into higher value–added industries also exist, such as those of Tatung in Taiwan and the Samsung Group in Korea.[4]

The old sectors in this dual diversification and upgrading do not simply give up, but are instead upgraded into high value–added segments within the same industry. These new, high value–added segments are based on short-cycle technologies. This process is also a type of diversification, that is, intrasector diversification into the high-value areas. Cycle times are gradually shortened when an economy engages in both intra- and intersector diversification. A middle-income economy that fails to realize this dual diversification may become a victim of the so-called adding-up problem and middle-income trap. An economy's early success with initial comparative-advantage industries, which are often based on low wage–based labor industries, tends to elevate its own wage rates. Thus, the economy has to move upward to engage in high value–added activities that afford high wage rates. Moreover, new and cheap labor sites in next-tier countries constantly emerge to take their positions in the global value chains, which is the situation of the adding-up problem.[5] Therefore, an economy should find new industries or activities that are beyond the capabilities of these next-tier countries because old industries often mature and degrade into low value–added activities. Otherwise, the economy is doomed to remain in low-wage activities or industries, with minimal chances of long-term success.

Lee and Kim's (2009) study is one of the few studies on the issue of different growth mechanisms in developing and developed countries. Their country panel analysis shows that economic growth in developing countries is positively related to basic human capital (i.e., primary and secondary enrollments) and political institutions, whereas in the upper middle– and high-income countries economic growth is positively associated with innovation (i.e., R&D expenditure or patents) and tertiary education. These findings are consistent with the perception that economic growth in developing countries is not innovation driven but low value–added activity driven, which can be realized by labor with primary or secondary education.

A thorny issue is the process of transition from the one growth mechanism to the other growth mechanism found in developed economies. The prevailing answer is capability building or increasing expenditure for R&D, with a view to increasing the R&D-to-GDP ratio or the number of patents filed. The answer can also lie in terms of building a national innovation system that enables innovation. Building a national innovation system is challenging. However, it may only be half of the story. The issue of specialization also has to be considered during the transition period. Sound transition requires both capability building and smart specialization into a niche where latecomers can find their own room (position) for survival in the international division of labor. Thus, the results of the country panel growth equation in Lee (2013a, Chapter 3) show that for the four Asian economies, economic growth (measured as growth in per capita income) has a negative and significant correlation with the cycle time of technologies. This unlocks the secret for a successful transition. Fast-growing Asian economies, such as Korea and Taiwan, managed to catch up with high-income countries by specializing in short-cycle sectors over time or since the mid-1980s. Short-cycle sectors are their niches, as shown by the high growth record of these economies, but also by the fact that having more patents in short-cycle technologies was significantly related to the higher profit rate of the Korean firms, as shown by the firm-level analysis in Lee (2013a, Chapter 5). In contrast, a wrong transition strategy would be to specialize in long-cycle sectors, which can be regarded as an attempt to directly replicate the knowledge base of high-income countries by specializing in high-quality and very original technologies. Several advanced Latin American countries, such as Brazil and Argentina, have tried this path because they boast of an advanced level of academic research in science. However, the present analysis indicates that specialization in highly original technology is not significantly related to economic growth. Therefore, countries on this trajectory must continue to rely on the patents held by advanced economies. Countries on the high road failed to catch up in the 1980s and 1990s.

Short cycles provide opportunities to catch up with those that command a certain degree of technological capability. However, frequent changes in technologies may serve as an additional barrier against catching up because these changes interfere with learning and lead to the truncation of the learning process. Thus, going along the path of short-cycle technologies may not always be smooth and easy. Selecting the road of short-cycle technologies requires a certain threshold level of technological capability in firm- and national-level institutions and policies. Such a level of capabilities would only be available to some upper middle–income countries. Inheriting mature industries from countries with high-income levels may help build such capabilities; thus, in this sense, this idea complements Lin's idea of latent comparative advantage. However, refusing to take risks means the middle-income trap continues, while taking risks does not guarantee success. The transitional path is an insufficient but necessary condition for eventual upgrading.

IMPLEMENTING THE IDEAS: AVOIDING FAILURES IN TARGETING VERSUS DESIGNING

Avoiding Targeting Failure

This section deals with the implementation of specialization in short-cycle technology–based sectors. Given that this idea is based on the past experience of South Korea and Taiwan, an intriguing question is whether the policy makers in these countries had the criterion of short-cycle time in mind as they conducted their industrial policy. The answer to this question is "No," but they always asked themselves, "What's next?" They looked keenly at which industries and businesses were likely to emerge in the immediate future and thought carefully about how to enter the emerging ones. New or emerging industries or businesses are often those with short-cycle technologies because they rely less on existing technologies.

This way of dealing with the idea of short-cycle technologies is consistent with the view that the essence of the idea is not about a fixed list of short- or long-cycle technologies, but that the latecomer economies should keep moving into the sectors with a "shorter"-cycle time than those they currently specialize in. The issue of "how much shorter than now" depends upon the existing level of capabilities of the concerned firms or sectors and upon the emergence of exogenous window of opportunities, such as the arrival of new technologies, new demand, or new promotions by the government. When the existing level and experience of the concerned firms are not high, a safe choice is not to make a "long jump" in less-related fields, but a "small jump" within the existing sector or into more-related fields. However, a long jump or leapfrogging is possible when the firms have a relatively high level of capabilities and absorptive capacity to take advantage of new innovations.

The criterion for technological specialization is less about the cycle length itself, and more about the technological sectors that rely less on existing technologies and offer great opportunities with newly emerging technologies. IT service may also be a promising sector because it depends on short-cycle technologies and may promote leapfrogging into service by bypassing manufacturing. The advantages of IT services, such as low entry barriers, have already been taken advantage of by India in promoting IT services, an example of how

India managed to leapfrog over IT manufacturing (Lee, 2013a, Chapter 8 on India). There are also successful cases of public–private collaboration in Latin America, such as the software company, ARTech Consultores in Uruguay (Sabel et al., 2012, Chapter 10) and the software sector in Belarus.[6]

Avoiding the Design Failure

Another issue is the identification of the sector or business items corresponding to shorter-cycle technologies than the current businesses. A method that is consistent with the idea of ED suggested by the smart specialization framework (Foray, 2015) can be adopted. Policy makers should organize a public–private joint taskforce, which includes representatives from the private sector, and administer a survey to existing private firms and entrepreneurs on the nature of business items or technological areas where they see near-future potential, opportunities, risks, and bottlenecks when entering or starting out in these future areas. The business areas to be identified by surveys are those areas where the private sectors see certain market potential and short-cycle times, but with some technological, financial, and other related environmental (regulation) uncertainties. Private firms may know better where the next markets are, but cannot be sure whether they will be able to develop the necessary and right technologies and whether they will be able to raise the funds for such R&D and initial marketing. In other words, new business/technology areas with more certain market potential but uncertain technological, financial, and regulatory uncertainty will be targetable areas. Policy intervention promotes these identified areas by mobilizing public and private resources and competencies that correct market and coordination failures.

An example is the Korean electronics industry in the early 1990s. The TV industry was a fast-growing market globally and new technologies, such as high-definition (HD) TVs, emerged. HD TV technologies had two alternatives: the analog HD technologies pioneered by Japanese firms and the digital technology–based HD TVs by Western firms. Thus, the Korean latecomer firms knew with certainty that the market was there, but they faced three choices: keep making the old (non-HD) analog TV, follow the Japanese firms to license analog HD TV technologies, or leapfrog into digital TV technologies. Lee et al. (2005) explained that the public–private R&D consortium chose the third option to develop their own digital TV technologies. Japanese firms were locked in for a while with their own analog HD TVs. Thus, Korean firms became the leader in digital TV, which was the turning point for the Korean firms (i.e., Samsung), and surpassed Japanese firms (i.e., Sony) in the display industry.

This case in Korea can be contrasted with a case in South Africa, where they developed their own electric cars called "Joule." Swart (2015) explained that the South African government provided the initial funding and established Optimal Energy in 2005. Optimal Energy is a start-up business with the objective of "establishing and leading the Electric Vehicle industry in South Africa and expanding globally." The company initially succeeded and had four roadworthy prototypes by December 2010. The Joule electric vehicle was a "born electric" five-seater passenger car that sported a totally new vehicle design, which incorporated a locally developed battery, motor, and software technologies. However, the company closed in June 2012 despite the technical success and an impressive network of partners and suppliers. The government, who was the major shareholder, decided to stop the funding required to start large-scale production of the electric cars because of uncertainties in marketing success.

The failure of "Joule cars" was caused by the lack of involvement of private companies to take the role in volume production and sales. Thus, existing foreign multinational companies and local auto companies did not want this new "disruptive innovator," a state-owned company, to grow as another rival that sells cars. The government should have formed a public–private consortium with the plan that volume production would be carried out by private actors after the consortium developed the prototype. Thus, this South African case can be considered one of "design failure" rather than a "targeting failure."[7]

The reason that the process should involve private firms in terms of design is twofold: they know where market demand is, and they eventually run the show. However, public sector agents have improved capabilities to deal with technological and financial uncertainty. The situation could have been favorable if the South African project had involved private firms throughout. Caution against government activism often does not distinguish whether the sources of failure are due to targeting or design. The sources are often mixed together. While one might expect more cases of targeting failure, this is not always the case. Uncertainty diminishes if targeting is seen in terms of identifying the potential or existing markets, as long as the private sector with knowledge about the markets is involved. If not on the frontier, the targets may be obvious because there often exists a clear benchmark case, and then one might attempt to identify niches between existing firms and projects. Numerous public initiatives fail because of design or capability failure, where the latter means low execution capabilities.

A Scheme for the Two Types of Upgrading Diversification

A concrete action plan for utilizing the idea of "capability upgrading and smart specialization for activities with shorter-cycle time of technologies" is briefly discussed in this section. The plan is divided into a small jump and a long jump. The former is about intrasector (functional) upgrading and smart specialization, and the latter is about intersector upgrading and smart specialization.

Numerous examples of intrasector (in the same sectors) upgrading are found in East Asia. Semiconductor firms in South Korea and Taiwan started from integrated circuit (IC) packaging or testing (i.e., low value–added activities), and moved to IC fabrication and IC design (i.e., highest valued added) (Lee and Mathews, 2012). This upgrading is similar to the functional upgrading along the three stages of OEM–ODM–OBM, which represent a move from low to high end or from low value– to high value–added activities. Often, this upgrading may be equivalent to a move from long-to short-cycle activities within a sector, to the extent that low value–added activities in the same sector (i.e., packaging in the semiconductors) have relatively longer cycles than do higher value–added activities (i.e., designing).

In any case, targeting or specialization is easy because the obvious targets are the functional activities at the next tier– or high tier–value segments. For instance, packaging firms may, or should, target fabrication and design. Failure to realize such upgrading is the source of the middle-income trap. Only Korean and Taiwanese firms in the semiconductor sector made such upgrading compared with Malaysia, which is still struggling. Uncertainty is not primarily about whether the next target activities are promising markets or not, it is more about whether firms can implement the activities physically and financially (i.e., technological and funding uncertainty). The latter type of uncertainty should be handled by public interventions or public–private joint consortia, as in examples from Taiwan or South Korea. Interference in this type of upgrading discussed in Lee et al. (2015a) is often caused by the incumbent firms (brand owners) who do not want the former (OEM) suppliers to rise as new rivals (as own-brand owners). The latecomer firms should be prepared for possible counterattacks by incumbent firms in the same sector, such as dumping and intellectual property rights (IPR) law suits.

Possible counterattacks by the incumbents or IPR disputes with the incumbents may justify the strategy of leapfrogging by creating one's own technological path rather than following the path of the forerunners. For example, South Korean firms that considered upgrading into HD TV chose to leapfrog into digital TV rather than follow the Japanese leadership with analog HD TV. That was a deliberate choice by the Korean consortium. Digital TV is a product that corresponds to shorter-cycle technologies than the analog-based HD TV. The former relies on more recent technologies. Thus, the idea of a shorter cycle may also apply to intrasector upgrading or diversification. The original idea of the short-cycle technologies is a concept at the level of sector or fields. In other words, a product relies on recent technologies for policy purposes. Park and Lee (2015) proved that latecomer firms tend to utilize more recent technologies than the incumbent using patent-and firm-level regressions (Park and Lee, 2015).

The second type of upgrading is intersector upgrading or diversification, which involves the issue of sector-level specialization. An early example is Nokia, which entered the telecommunication equipment industry from being a company for pulp and wood products. This is a clear example of a long jump, which is different from a small jump into neighboring product spaces. This is also an example of entry into short-cycle technologies. Additional examples can be found in East Asia (Lee and Mathews, 2012), for example, Taiwanese firms made a long jump into notebook computers in the 1980s from small calculators (Lee, 2005; Mathews, 2002b). Furthermore, the Samsung group in South Korea is well known to have made successive entries into new industries for over 60 years: apparels and textiles in the 1960s, black and white TVs in the 1970s, semiconductors in the 1980s, and telecommunication equipment in the 1990s. Such intersector entries and diversification are needed because the existing activities often become mature or turn into small profit margins with eventual decline. Therefore, firms and regions always have to move to new future growing market areas and activities.

Private firms know best where the future markets are, but are often unsure about technological feasibility, funding uncertainty, and marketing (competition) uncertainty. Thus, the scheme is to first initiate a process of ED to identify the future growth areas by listening to the private firms and forming a public–private consortium to overcome technological and financial uncertainty. In the case of Taiwan's entry into notebooks, market demand was emerging in notebooks, but entry into notebooks was a big jump for the small firms that only made calculators. Thus, the job was done by a public research institute, which developed the architecture for the notebooks and transferred it to the private firms (Mathews, 2002b). This was an important momentum for the upgraded and sustained growth of the electronics firms in Taiwan.

A more difficult part would be how to win in the actual market, which is a different issue from whether market demand exists or not. In other words, the problem arises for the latecomer firms even if there is enough market demand because of rival incumbents or established firms. Thus, latecomer firms must choose short-cycle items with low entry barriers. Assistance from the public sector may be needed to help market competition or guarantee initial markets. The role of the government in the typical examples in East Asia was not just in the collaborative development of new products, but also in marketing and market competition in various forms of industrial policy, such as exclusive standards, public procurements, and tariffs (Lee, 2005, 2013b). In the case of Nokia, a decisive help was the European Union's decision to allow GSM to be the single and exclusive standard against the Motorola phone, which was based on the analog standard.

Space for Industrial Policy under the WTO Regime

The WTO regime has reduced the space of industrial policy for catching-up countries. However, some room is still available, as discussed in Lee et al. (2015b).

First, latecomer economies are advised not to take the WTO restriction on industrial policies as an excuse for not trying such policies. Members can deviate from WTO discipline, provided that no other member initiates legal action (and makes the case) against that measure, a situation that is likely to happen only when industrial policies become significantly successful.

Second, R&D subsidies have not been restricted or classified as green-light subsidies. Subsidies on exports are prohibited. However, those on production for domestic markets are "green-light subsidies," in other words they have not been prohibited, unless they are deemed as specific and causing adverse effects on other member countries (UNIDO/UNCTAD, 2011). Moreover, the WTO clause on Subsidies and Countervailing Measures (SCM) does not prevent governments from subsidizing activities, particularly through regional, technological, and environmental policies, provided that governments have sufficient ingenuity to present such subsidies as WTO compatible (UNCTAD, 2006). Developing countries may attempt to take advantage of the fact that many rules in the WTO SCM have loopholes or room for flexible interpretation, such as the "yellow"-light classification for certain types of subsidies. The lengthy process and enforcement are sometimes dubious, even if a country is brought into the WTO process.

Third, the global south may be able to use some "nonspecific" subsidies because these subsidies are not prohibited by the WTO. In other words, subsidiaries are regarded as not specific when they are not limited to "certain enterprises or industries," but are available on the basis of "objective criteria or conditions."

SUMMARY AND CONCLUDING REMARKS

The mechanisms and context of economic growth differ markedly in developed and developing countries. Thus, a different specialization/strategy is needed at varying stages of development. Neither neoclassical nor neo-Schumpeterian thinking on growth and development offers sound theoretical ideas regarding the specialization or comparative advantage for MICs that suffer from the middle-income trap. Latecomer firms and economies are "resource poor, late entrants," and thus need both "capability building" and "smart specialization." This is true for both low- and middle-income developing countries. However, the latter group faces a difficult choice in terms of specialization because it is close to the frontier (higher-income countries) and thus faces increased competition or entry barriers in high-end segments of the international division of labor. MICs have to seek a sector where they may be able to survive by competing effectively with the incumbents and where they expect improved growth prospects.

This study proposed the concept of cycle time of technologies as a policy-relevant criterion that can help MICs make this choice about specialization. The criterion and an effective transition path to an upgraded mechanism of growth suggest that the cycle time of technologies is better than criteria based on product spaces and is complementary to the idea of latent comparative advantage of Lin (2012a). Qualified MICs have comparative advantages in technological sectors with short-cycle time because short-cycle technologies imply that dominance by the incumbent is often disrupted, and new technologies tend to offer high growth prospects.

The chapter also discussed strategies for implementing this policy of specialization. The key idea is for industrial policy to involve private firms and avoid targeting and design failures from the beginning. Concrete schemes are different. The schemes depend upon diversification and whether the goal is intrasector upgrading or intersector upgrading. However, the main idea is as follows.

First, policy makers can organize a public–private joint taskforce, administer a survey, and consult with existing private firms and entrepreneurs by asking about the types of business items or technological areas where they see near-future potential and about the opportunities, risks, and bottlenecks in entering or starting these future areas. The business areas to be identified by surveys are those areas where the private sector sees strong market potential, but which are new or short-cycle technology based, and where the private sector is facing technological, financial, and other environmental (regulations) uncertainties. The process will require more than the typical technology foresight analysis, which is usually strong in identifying technological opportunities, but often weak in assessing market opportunities. Then, policy interventions should promote these identified areas by mobilizing public and private resources and competences, thereby correcting market and coordination failures. This idea is discussed with numerous examples, such as the digital TV consortium in Korea, contrasted with the example of a design failure in launching electric cars in South Africa.

ACKNOWLEDGMENTS

This paper benefits from the workshop on Smart Specialization held in November 2015 in Bucharest, Romania. The author thanks the participants of the workshop, especially Slavo Radosevic, Lena Tsipouri, Niko Maroulis, and Imogen Wade, for their comments and feedback, as well as the financial support provided by the National Research Foundation of Korea (Grant no. NRF-2010-330-B00093).

ENDNOTES

1. For example, only $4 out of the $299 retail price of an Apple iPod goes to China (Linden et al. 2007).
2. For this reason, not all emerging technologies are considered short cycle because even new products in pharmaceuticals tend to rely heavily on existing or stock knowledge depending on the nature of such innovations (i.e., disruptive or competence enhancing). Therefore, information technology is more prone to disruptive innovations than long-cycle sectors.
3. Replacing analog technologies with digital ones provides a window of opportunity for some latecomers, especially South Korea. The digitalization of products and production processes entails fewer disadvantages for latecomers because the functions and quality of these products are determined by electronic chips rather than by the skills of engineers, who are more critical in analog products.
4. See Mathews (2005) for the semiconductor case. See Khan (2002) for Tatung's story.
5. The adding-up problem may provoke a protectionist response in the form of tariffs, quotas, or other barriers in markets, including those of advanced countries (Spence 2011).
6. Belarus has already exported USD 800 million worth of software services through several emerging brands in IT services. This point was made by Slavo Radosevic. For example, see https://www.epam.com
7. Slavo Radosevic observes that the European discussion on smart specialization is more about targeting domains, but less about smart designing. The whole entrepreneurial discovery (ED) is confined to bringing all stakeholders around targeting, not about designing the next stage.

REFERENCES

Amsden, A., 1989. Asia's Next Giant: South Korea and Late Industrialization. Oxford University Press, New York, NY.

Bell, M., 1984. Learning and the accumulation of industrial technological capacity in developing countries. In: Fransman, M., King, K. (Eds.), Technological Capability in the Third World. Macmillan, London, p. 404.

Bell, R.M., Figueiredo, P.N., 2012. Building innovative capabilities in latecomer emerging market firms: some key issues. In: Amann, E., Cantwell, J. (Eds.), Innovative Firms in Emerging Market Countries. Oxford University Press, Oxford.

Bell, R.M., Pavitt, K., 1993. Technological accumulation and industrial growth: contrasts between developed and developing countries. Ind. Corp. Change 2 (1), 157–210.

Ernst, D., Guerrieri, P., 1998. International production networks and changing trade patterns in East Asia: the case of the electronics industry. Oxford Dev. Stud. 26 (2), 191–212.

Foray, D., 2015. Smart Specialization. Routledge, London.

Hausmann, R., Jason, H., Dani, R., 2007. What you export matters. J. Econ. Growth 12 (1), 1–25.

Hidalgo, C.A., Bailey, K., Barabási, A.-L., Hausmann, R., 2007. The product space conditions the development of nations. Science 317 (5837), 482–487.

Hobday, M., 1995. Innovation in East Asia: The Challenge to Japan. Edward Elgar Publishing, London.

Jaffe, A.B., Trajtenberg, M., 2002. Patents, Citations, and Innovations: A Window on the Knowledge Economy. MIT Press, Cambridge.

Jung, M., Lee, K., 2010. Sectoral systems of innovation and productivity catch-up: determinants of TFP gap between the Korean firms and the Japanese firms. Ind. Corp. Change 19 (4), 1037–1069.

Kahn, A.E., 1951. Investment criteria in development programs. Qtly. J. Econ. 65 (1), 38–61.

Katz, J.M., 1984. Domestic technological innovations and dynamic comparative advantage: further reflections on a comparative case-study program. J. Dev. Econ. 16 (1), 13–37.

Khan, H.A., 2002. Innovation and growth: a Schumpeterian model of innovation applied to Taiwan. Oxford Dev. Stud. 30 (3), 289–306.

Kuznets, S., 1966. Modern Economic Growth: Rate, Structure and Spread. Yale University Press, New Haven.

Lee, K., 2005. Making a technological catch-up: barriers and opportunities. Asian J. Technol. Innov. 13 (2), 97–131.

Lee, K., 2013a. Schumpeterian analysis of economic catch-up: knowledge, path-creation, and the middle-income trap. Cambridge University Press, London.

Lee, K., 2013b. Capability failure and industrial policy to move beyond the middle-income trap: from trade-based to technology-based specialization. In: Lin, J., Stiglitz, J. (Eds.), Industrial Policy. Revolution I. Palgrave, New York.

Lee, K., Kim, B.-Y., 2009. Both institutions and policies matter but differently for different income groups of countries: determinants of long-run economic growth revisited. World Dev. 37 (3), 533–549.

Lee, K., Mathews, J., 2012. Firms in Korea and Taiwan. In: John Cantwell, Ed Amann (Eds.), The Innovative firms in the Emerging Market Economies. Oxford University Press, Oxford.

Lee, K., Lim, C., Song, W., 2005. Emerging digital technology as a window of opportunity and technological leapfrogging. Int. J. Technol. Mgmt. 29 (1–2), 40–63.

Lee, K., Jooyoung, K., Song, J., 2015a. An exploratory study on the transition from OEM to OBM: case studies of SMEs in Korea. Ind. Innov. 22 (5), 423–442.

Lee, K., Shin, W., Shin, H., 2015b. How large or small is the policy space? WTO regime and industrial policy. In: Jose, A., José, O. (Eds.), Global Governance and Rules for the Post-2015 Era (UN Series on Development). Bloomsbury, London.

Lewis, W.A., 1954. Economic development with unlimited supplies of labour. The Manchester School 22, 139–191.

Lin, J.Y., 2012a. New Structural Economics: A Framework for Rethinking Development and Policy. World Bank Publications, Washington DC.

Lin, J.Y., 2012b. The Quest for Prosperity: How Developing Economies can Take off. Princeton University Press, Princeton.

Linden, G., Kraemer K.L., Dedrick J., 2007. Who captures value in a global innovation system? The case of Apple's iPod. PCIC Working Paper. Personal Computing Industry Center, University of California, Irvine.

Mathews, J.A., 2002a. Competitive Advantages of the latecomer firm: a resource-based account of industrial catch-up strategies. Asia Pac. J. Mgmt. 19 (4), 467–488.

Mathews, J.A., 2002b. The origins and dynamics of Taiwan's R&D consortia. Res. Pol. 31 (4), 633–651.

Mathews, J.A., 2005. Strategy and the crystal cycle. Calif. Mgmt. Rev. 47 (2), 6–31.

Meliciani, V., 2002. The impact of technological specialisation on national performance in a balance-of-payments-constrained growth model. Struct. Change Econ. Dyn. 13 (1), 101–118.

Nelson, R.R., Pack, H., 1999. The Asian miracle and modern growth theory. Econ. J. 109 (457), 416–436.

North, D., 2005. Understanding the Process of Economic Change. Princeton University Press, Princeton.

Park, K.H., Lee, K., 2006. Linking the technological regime to the technological catch-up: analyzing Korea and Taiwan using the US patent data. Ind. Corp. Change 15 (4), 715–753.

Park, J., Lee, K., 2015. Do latecomer firms rely on "recent" and "scientific" knowledge more than incumbent firms do? Asian J. Technol. Innov. 23 (Suppl. 1), 129–145.

Sabel, Charles, E., Fernandez-Arias, R., Hausmann, A., Rodriguez-Clare, E., Stein (Eds.), 2012. Export Pioneers in Latin America. IDB, Washington DC.

Sen, A.K., 1957. Some notes on the choice of capital-intensity in development planning. Qtly. J. Econ. 71 (4), 561–584.

Spence, M., 2011. The Next Convergence: The Future of Economic Growth in a Multispeed World. FSG Books, New York, NY.

Sturgeon, T.J., Gereffi, G., 2009. Measuring success in the global economy: international trade, industrial upgrading and business function outsourcing in global value chains. Transnat. Corp. 18 (2), 1–36.

Sturgeon, T.J., Gereffi, G., 2012. Measuring success in the global economy: international trade, industrial upgrading, and business function outsourcing in global value chains. In: Lall, S., Pietrobelli, C., Rasiah, R. (Eds.), Evidence-Based Development Economics. University of Malaya Press, Kuala Lumpur.

Swart, G., 2015. Innovation lessons learned from the JOULE EV development. In: Pretorius L., Thopil, G.A., (Eds.), Proceedings of the Twenty-Fourth Annual IAMOT Conference. 8–11 June 2015, Cape Town, Africa.

UNCTAD, 2006. Trade and Development Report. United Nations, Geneva.

UNIDO/UNCTAD, 2011. Economic Development in Africa Report 2011. United Nations, Geneva.

Viner, J., 1958. Stability and progress: the poorer countries' problem. In: Hague, D.C. (Ed.), Stability and Progress in the World Economy: The First Congress of the International Economic Association. Macmillan, London.

World Bank, 2010. exploring the middle-income-trap. World Bank East Asia Pacific Economic Update, vol. 2. The World Bank, Washington, DC.

World Bank, 2012. China 2030 Building a Modern, Harmonious, and Creative High-Income Society. The World Bank, Washington, DC.

Yusuf, S., Nabeshima, K., 2009. Can Malaysia escape the middle-income trap? A strategy for Penang. Policy Research Working Paper, no. WPS 4971. World Bank, Washington, DC.

Chapter 10

Lessons for a Policy Maker From Real-Life Self-Discovery in Economies With Weak Institutions

Ksenia Gonchar*, Yevgeny Kuznetsov**, Imogen Wade†,‡
*Institute for Industrial and Market Studies of the National Research University Higher School of Economics, Moscow, Russia; **Migration Policy Institute and The World Bank, Washington, DC, United States; †University College London (UCL), London, United Kingdom; ‡Institute for Statistical Studies and Economics of Knowledge of the National Research University Higher School of Economics, Moscow, Russia

Chapter Outline

Academic Highlights

- The chapter provides historical evidence of innovation-led structural changes at the subnational level in high-middle-income economies, particularly emphasizing economies with a significant knowledge base and weak institutions.
- Proposes a three stage-model (based on previous work by Teubal and Kuznetsov, 2012) to conceptualize self-discovery, each posing different problems:
  - *micro level*: first mover problem (proof of concept for a new domain);

Advances in the Theory and Practice of Smart Specialization. http://dx.doi.org/10.1016/B978-0-12-804137-6.00010-3
225

- *regional level*: collective action (regional cluster coordination) problem; and
- *global level*: critical mass problem (how to acquire a bundle of highly specialized and interrelated institutions).
- Illustrates the model with empirical examples of self-discovery, entrepreneurship, and experimentation from Argentina, Russia, and Israel—examples of real-life smart specialization processes.
- Three-stage model stems from the logics of incremental institutional development which does not mandate any institutional preconditions.
- Regional development is usually a byproduct of national or global success of private first movers that can initiate exclaves but may fail to become developed regional clusters.

Policy Highlights

- The key implication of the three-stage model is that even in institutionally weak economies there are always some regions, firms, sectors, or institutions that are working well; the key policy challenge is to discover them and assist them to enlarge their activities.
- The heterogeneity argument implies that the policy agenda for advanced and less developed regions has to be designed and implemented differently.
- For advanced regions (stages 2 and 3 of the model), the single focus is on strengthening existing and building new collective action institutions;
- For less developed localities (stage 1), the issue is searching for dynamic institutional segments in the public and private sector which are exceptions from the general rule of ineffective and dysfunctional institutions.
- Solving the problems of collective action (regional cluster coordination) and critical mass (when the region should acquire specialized competences to become competitive and globally known) are decisive for success in RIS3 processes.

INTRODUCTION

Middle-income nonfrontier economies outside the EU have limited experience with innovation policies with regional development effects, particularly when they are focused on activities generating emergence of new domains on the basis of existing activities. Examples of regional economies in catching-up countries with weak institutions successfully making innovation-based structural changes are very rare. Yet, learning lessons from these exceptional cases may be instructive for the design and implementation of the current RIS3 policy, and should improve our understanding of the link between innovation process, policies, and institutions. This chapter intends to start bridging the gap between the normative perspective on smart specialization—as it emerges in the 6-step EU guide (European Commission, 2012), and actual processes of self-discovery. The normative perspective—the EU guide—is based on the endowment view of development: it assumes that the main institutional endowments are already in place, and prescribes to create whatever endowments are missing. Shedding light on actual experience of self-discoveries (the objective of the chapter) will help to develop a workable and operationally useful policy model of the smart specialization process—one that can facilitate the creation of investment projects in addition to a multiplicity of funding applications, plans, studies, and vision documents.

In this chapter, we draw upon the concept developed in (Foray, 2014), which distinguishes between RIS3 as process and RIS3 as policy. According to this distinction, the RIS3 process may not necessarily be planned and governed by the policy; instead, it may be initiated by private actors, and survive in path dependent and institutionally weak environments. The interaction of innovations through entrepreneurial discovery and location in this respect is guided by the notion of absorptive or learning capacity (Cohen and Levinthal, 1989), which is understood by the authors as the firm's ability to identify, assimilate, and exploit knowledge from the environment that will permit it to do something quite different from what it is already doing. This concept is particularly instrumental in combination with the literatures on agglomeration economies (Audretsch, 1998), technology diffusion (Keller, 2004), and economic growth (Aghion and Jaravel, 2015; Hausmann and Rodrik, 2003). These literatures establish that knowledge spillovers can theoretically drive cross-regional convergence, although the outcome depends on various conditions, starting from the size of the technological gap, the combination of advantages and disadvantages of backwardness (Gerschenkron's catch-up), to the efficacy of various institutions or policies that encourage innovations in catching up economies. Aghion and Jaravel (2015) provide examples of institutional reforms and policies which are conductive to frontier innovation, but may be less efficient in driving imitation in nonfrontier locations, and show complementarity between absorptive capacity and external knowledge. Muscio et al. (2015) provide empirical evidence that the potential of smart specialization strategies in European transition economies is seriously constrained by weak governance and inadequacies of absorption capacities.

Finally, we are interested in the literature on the interaction of weak institutions and growth with the notion that weak national institutions in some subnational locations may be offset by relatively more efficient regional institutions in other parts of the country or by improvements in regional dynamic economic capabilities. For example, Acemoglu and Robinson (2008) build on the formal and informal institutional differences between regions and explain income disparity within a country by local institutional variation. Rodrik (2008) and Acemoglu et al. (2006) point to the possibility of counterbalancing inefficient institutions, showing that when formal institutions are weak, the business environment can still be conductive to growth in the presence of informal (or more precisely, poorly understood) substitutes to weak institutions or improvements in dynamic incentives, which compensate for the efficiency losses from institutional weaknesses. Empirically, these theories have been tested on Russian FDI location data by Bessonova and Gonchar (2015): they show that subnational institutional and economic heterogeneity explain why FDI inflow into Russia grew in the 2000s despite a generally weak institutional environment.

The principles for identifying cases for our analysis are borrowed from Sabel et al. (2012). We are interested in the emergence of new activity, which experiences strong growth to become a national frontier, export or global chain participant and possibly provide a good fit with the comparative advantage of the given location. Our analysis tries to answer the following research questions. What are the most binding obstacles to the self-discovery process first movers initiate and how do they manage to overcome them successfully? How do these obstacles depend on local specialization and local institutions? What role do government interventions play in supporting or preventing the self-discovery process in the new domains? How do the successful first movers affect local economies? To answer these questions, we document problems and solutions within four cases in two countries with comparable income distribution, path dependence, and institutional problems: Russia and Argentina. We also document a case from an advanced economy (Israel) that has been able to overcome the problems of critical mass, the final stage in the sequential model we develop here.

The chapter is structured as follows: Section "Entrepreneurial Discovery in Two Contrasting Policy Perspectives" elucidates our conceptual framework and casts high-middle-income, resource-based economies with weak institutional environments as peculiar labs for the self-discovery. Section "Empirical llustration of the Three-Staged Policy Model," central in the chapter, outlines a three-stage model on the basis of a policy perspective of incremental institutional development which does not mandate any institutional preconditions. A largely empirical Section "Resolving the Collective Action Problem: the Need for Complementarity of Diverse Public Support Policies" wells on the need for a complementarity of diverse support policies. The final Section "Conclusions" concludes and derives relevant lessons for a policy maker engaged in the design and implementation of innovation-led growth policies.

ENTREPRENEURIAL DISCOVERY IN TWO CONTRASTING POLICY PERSPECTIVES

There is a consensus among economists that higher industrial productivity, often instigated by innovation, triggers economic growth. There is renewed debate, however, on the role of the government in helping countries or regions to facilitate innovation leading to higher productivity. In explaining economic success, both economic science and economic practice focus on good institutions. Over the last 25 years, the endowment view has been challenged from a variety of perspectives, both neo-Schumpeterian and neo-classical. The most compelling challenge is associated with names Dani Rodrik, Ricardo Hausmann, and Charles Sabel (Hausmann and Rodrik, 2003; Sabel et al., 2012). This view shifts policy makers' attention away from general endowments towards the binding constraints to growth.

An entrepreneur (coined a "first mover" in the business literature) is a central institution of development who discovers both opportunities for growth and ways, and means to ameliorate binding constraints. A key notion of the self-discovery process from this policy perspective is positive variations in performance. Positive variations emerge on a microlevel—an entrepreneur creating her firm. Then these positive variations may (but do not necessarily) reach the mezzo-level—the level of regional agglomerations and cross-national value chains, and may eventually spread to the national level (economic transformation). In other words, the key problem is how positive variations diffuse, propagate and coalesce, not why positive variation emerges: the notion of entrepreneurship already assumes that entrepreneurs are tenacious enough to be able to grow through asphalt. The key policy question is how micro and cluster-level growth spurts (positive variations in performance) can be translated into sustained growth performance.

Following this focus on positive variations of performance, the central hypothesis of this chapter is that agents with new capabilities develop together. By such agents, we mean a new private sector (which learns to innovate by connecting to the world economy) and a new public sector (capable of providing complementary public inputs for private-sector research). In other words, self-discovery can be conceptualized as proceeding in three stages, consequently posing the following three problems:

1. *micro level*: first mover problem (proof of concept for a new domain)—which is the first investment project to test the new domain? How to identify collaborators for this project? In what follows, the first mover problem is illustrated by the cases of IPG-Photonics of Russia and INVAP of Argentina (Section "Microlevel; First Mover Problem—IPG-Photonics and INVAP").
2. *regional level*: collective action (regional cluster coordination) problem—how to supply complementary and usually specialized public inputs to transform first mover investment into a portfolio of diverse projects supplying public and club goods? In what follows, the collective action problem is illustrated by an account of two regional wine clusters in Argentina.
3. *global level*: critical mass problem—how to acquire a bundle of highly specialized and interrelated institutions to become globally known and competitive? Section "Global-Level; High-Tech Cluster of Israel" elucidates the third stage in the evolution of positive variation in performance by making a reference to venture capital in Israel, which managed to reach global prominence.

This is, of course, not the first attempt to develop a policy model in stages. In a series of elegant papers, Teubal and collaborators (Teubal et al., various years) introduced a three-phase model of the emergence of a global innovation cluster in Israel. There is a poignant irony, however, that even paragons of the Schumpeterian and evolutionary economics (a category to which the authors of the model undoubtedly belong) follow the preconditions perspective. The first stage of the Teubal's model mandates background conditions—in terms of both institutional and human capital, and R&D endowments. Until those conditions are met, one cannot move to stage 2—experimentation in business sector and venture financing.

Our point is that from the perspective of a policy maker, the background-conditions model in general, and its rendering in Teubal's three-stage model in particular, is not practical. How is one to know whether the background conditions are met? Probably only by hindsight and thus that model cannot guide policy action. What are the appropriate actions of a policy maker when the background conditions are not met? Should one just wait? Answering those questions would lead us to a phased bootstrapping model, which dispenses with the notion of preconditions altogether.

To test the validity of our approach, we take an extreme-case approach looking at two high middle-income economies with notoriously weak institutions (pervasive corruption, rent seeking public sector) yet surprising incidences and diversities of self-discovery episodes.

EMPIRICAL ILLUSTRATION OF THE THREE-STAGED POLICY MODEL

Microlevel: First Mover Problem—IPG-Photonics and INVAP

The first case is about a company of Russian origin, which is currently positioned as a world leader in the design and manufacturing of high power fiber lasers and amplifiers. This is a remarkable success story, which started as a purely entrepreneurial innovation-led initiative with few links to government policy. These links, however, strengthened when the company moved to the world technology frontier, although the established political connections had little to do with mainstream industrial policy in support of national champions.

Several lessons may be learnt from this story. First, "business as usual" is rarely an option in places characterized by weak institutions, resource scarcity, and high degree of uncertainty. The success is often an exception, generated by a highly entrepreneurial first mover. Yet, however successful and promising, first movers with a killing novel product do not generate regional clusters, which require much more than just colocation of innovators. Moreover, regional demand is too weak to support the new infant industry, and regional development is often only a by-product of global success rather than the initial goal and result of the project.

IPG-Photonics as a company in its current format was incorporated in 1998. It pioneered the commercial development and manufacturing of optical fiber lasers for use in manufacturing, automotive, heavy industry, aerospace, and electronics sectors. IPG was not the first to design fiber lasers, which were developed four decades ago. Yet, it contributed to the technology with significant innovations, which increased output power levels and decreased costs by developing improved optical components and advancements in semiconductor diode technology. The company is currently headquartered in the United States, with the largest R&D and manufacturing facilities located in (Oxford)

Massachusetts, (Burbach) Germany, and (Fryazino) Russia. The largest customers are located in China, Russia, and the United States. The company is fully vertically integrated in order to maintain a technological lead over competitors, keep trade secrets, and ensure the supply of critical components. Total sales amounted to USD 769.9 million in 2014, and the total number of employees exceeded 3000 as of December 2014. Annual R&D expenditures accounted for USD 53 million in 2014. This R&D effort is mostly concentrated on the development of new applications for the core technology.

The history of the company is mostly associated with the name of its founder, Dr. Valentin Gapontsev (born in 1940). He served as a senior scientist of laser physics in the Institute of Radio Engineering and Electronics in Moscow under the Soviet Academy of Sciences prior to market reforms in Russia. Dr. Gapontsev has been the Chief Executive Officer and Chairman of the Board of IPG since the very start of the company, and he controls the majority stake.

The initial entrepreneurial idea of Dr. Gapontsev was to commercialize conventional laser technologies on the basis of one production shop leased from NPO Polus in the town of Fryazino. This first venture failed as a commercial undertaking and its only value added for the future global company was in increasing international connectedness and in establishing contacts to possible consumers on the world market. Ital Tel was among these contacts, which commissioned the first R&D contract for fiber lasers to the small team of three Russian research entrepreneurs. One of the technologies developed within this contract proved promising, and the team kept the intellectual property for this technology despite financial difficulties and pressures to sell exclusive rights for the newly developed product. The next large R&D contract was commissioned by the German company Dornier. This contract was conditioned by the relocation of design and manufacturing to Germany. Thus, the first incorporation took place in the form of a FDI subsidiary in Germany in 1994, when Dr. Gapontsev purchased the bankrupt manufacturing plant near Frankfurt from Deutsche Bank. Currently, this is one of the largest manufacturing facilities of the IPG Photonics corporation, which employs 800 people. The same strategy was used when the company expanded to the US market, acquired manufacturing facilities, and incorporated as IPG Photonics in 1998.

IPG is innovating extensively in various directions, pursuing the clear strategy of innovation-led growth. It is due to IPG's new products and new applications of older technologies that the firm's annual growth rate reached 27% between 2010 and 2014. It continues to displace the carbon dioxide gas lasers in metal cutting with fiber lasers. The newest technology for laser sintering in 3D printing brought about a 100% growth of sales in 2014, and plans to expand the new products and technologies to health care and biomedicine. The answer to low-cost competition from China was to design a new lower-priced pulsed laser specifically to compete with low-end providers.

Given the purpose of this chapter, it is interesting to study how IPG interacts with its home-country local economy after global success was achieved. Does the regional economy benefit from the global innovation star firm with roots in the town of Fryazino? Is the scale and network of IPG in Russia and in the world sufficient to start and develop a regional cluster?

The small town of Fryazino, the home for the future IPG, is located in the northern part of Moscow region. It has a population of almost 60,000 people. The city has historically hosted research organizations and high-tech manufacturing, starting with the community of German migrant scientists and engineers, who were displaced from the Soviet zone of occupation at the end of WWII and launched TV and communication technologies in the former Soviet Union. Similar to many regions surrounding the city of Moscow, Fryazino underwent several waves of structural changes and saw the decline of defense-related R&D and manufacturing, and further commercial growth during the 2000s. According to the city mayor, the town suffers from outmigration of skilled personnel to the country's capital, an ageing population, and various other socioeconomic challenges. However, Fryazino is considered economically quite well-developed relative to many towns in Russia, and the local administration is pragmatic and responds positively to initiatives from local firms to expand and develop as high-tech innovators.

Together with other selected science-intensive locations in Russia, in the 1990s Fryazino was awarded the status of a "town of scientific excellence" (*naukograd*). However, not a single project application from Fryazino-based research firms and institutions received funding from the state program of support to scientific towns. The problem was the requirement to target innovations to local demand. Needless to say, novel laser technologies and applications had no chance to meet local, regional, or even national demand. The market for the infant industry had still to emerge. Thus, the region's contribution to the future success at the initial stage of the venture was to provide a relatively friendly environment with good quality human capital and minimal red tape.

Today's contribution of IPG to the local economy is twofold. First, it built a high-quality R&D and manufacturing facility at the premises of its subsidiary Science and technology society "Institute of radio engineering and electronics—Polus" (IRE-Polus) in Fryazino, which is currently the largest affiliate among IPG factories, with 860 jobs as of 2014. Since 2012, this has been the largest firm in Fryazino by volume of sales. The Russian subsidiary provides components, tests equipment, and sells finished fiber devices to customers in Russia and neighboring countries, components to US and German manufacturing facilities, as well as finished pulsed lasers to an IPG subsidiary in China. The chances for future expansion are high, although in the vertically integrated corporation this would mean a second production shop belonging to IPG rather than outsourcing to other local producers and start-ups. However competitive and sophisticated the local firms, they do not have many chances to become integrated into the IPG-led global value chain. As stated in the 2015 annual company report, IPG's strategy in Russia is to expand the existing facility rather than outsource to local producers and R&D centers, and to radically increase the application of laser technologies in various manufacturing sectors inside Russia.

IPG's second contribution to the local economy is its initiative to network with the local science-intensive firms and pragmatic town administration and apply jointly for the status of a federally funded special economic zone, "Istok," which will further be complemented with an innovation cluster "Fryazino." Moreover, IPG and Istok, the so-called "anchor residents" of the proposed new economic zone, have long been competing with each other for the right to launch their own version of an innovation cluster.

Istok and IPG currently intend not only to merge their administrative power, but to develop synergies between VHF electronics (the specialization of Istok) and fiber lasers, and to increase the applications of both technologies in various incumbent and new industries on the Russian market. Small firms—residents of the new cluster—serve as possible integrators of new technology applications. IPG took responsibility for the new investments and new jobs, while the cluster provides tax advantages, access to land and technical facilities, a customs terminal, and access to the best graduates in the city of Moscow and the Moscow region.

The question whether IPG has sufficient scale and market power to advance local cluster development does not have a simple answer. On the one hand, we may safely assume that IPG's global reputation and achievements were decisive in the successful outcomes of the long lobbying process which culminated in the visit of Russia's Prime Minister to IRE-Polus in Fryazino and in the further approval of the cluster initiative. On the other hand, the lessons from the failure to establish an innovation cluster centered only around IPG suggest that the cause may lie with the problems in forming a critical mass of participating actors. The first-mover success proved insufficient to generate a local cluster even within the borders of a small town. Teaming up with the second largest firm locally, the support of Rosnano, as well as the establishment of small firms backing linkages to potential customers of the new applications of fiber lasers in telecommunication, biomedicine and other sectors seem to provide capabilities to jointly bypass the institutional weaknesses of the Russian innovation system.

IPG Photonics seems to have a first-mover twin in Argentina with a similarly unexpected global success in a technologically complex field with very high entry barriers. INVAP[1] is a public agency located in Bariloche, Argentina (1700 km southwest of Buenos Aires). It was the first mover in the production of satellites and nuclear reactors, and is now a global, hi-tech R&D enterprise also active in the aerospace, industry, and medical systems fields. Created in 1976, it is state-owned (by the province of Rio Negro), yet operates as an unlisted private company. INVAP focuses on designing and constructing complex technological systems, and has operated for more than 30 years on the domestic market and for more than 20 internationally. It is focused on the development of state-of-the-art technology in different industrial, scientific, and applied research fields, thus creating "technological packages" with high added value. It now has global contracts for design, development, fabrication, and operational work. It is the sole company in Latin America that has worked with NASA (the US National Aeronautics and Space Administration) for complete space projects. As of 2012, INVAP had annual sales totaling USD 200 million, USD 500 million in sales orders backlog, and 970 employees. The firm had subsidiaries in Brazil and US, with branches in Australia, Egypt, and Venezuela. At the time of writing, INVAP directly employs 1330 people (around 80% of whom are highly qualified technicians and professionals) and has a surface area of over 10,000 square meters comprising laboratories, workshops and office space.

Interestingly, now INVAP designs and assembles a broad and wide-ranging portfolio of technologically complex products (Seijo and Cantero, 2012), such as nuclear reactors from experimentation. In addition to nuclear reactors, this portfolio includes artificial satellites (the main client of which is the national government), radars, aerogenerators (equipment to produce alternative energy from wind), and several more such complex systems (ibid.). This is a clear case of excessive experimentation, as such a broad portfolio is suboptimal. Only nuclear reactors have penetrated the global market, and ironically such a broad product portfolio—a case of accidental smart specialization—is another side of the coin of the global success of nuclear reactors. In most instances, clients for the reactors are national governments—of countries which do not have their own nuclear machine-building capabilities. It is well-known that bidding for such complex public contracts involves significant, upfront fixed costs and is highly uncertain. There are many bidders: both established and well-known (such as France, US, and Russia), and emerging (such as Argentina). Dealing with such uncertainty was one motivation for the innovation cluster with INVAP in its center to engage in spontaneous smart specialization by drawing on its high absorptive capacity to venture into products that stem from its core competencies of complex technological design but are nevertheless sufficiently remote in the product space.

Mezzo-Level: Collective Action Problem in Argentinian Wine Clusters

In this section we address the collective action problem, which arises when various parties need to come together to form credible commitments.

Two Wine Clusters in Argentina

In Argentina, two wine-producing regions' differing responses to a national economic crisis in the late 1980s—generally and in the wine industry specifically—resulted in divergent outcomes in their wine industries, illustrating the importance of collective institutions. Argentina is a country with generally weak social capital and institutions, and for a long time had a backward wine industry, until the last decade of the 20th century.

The case we describe briefly here is effectively a natural experiment and is based on the extensive research published in McDermott (2007). Argentina did not export any wine until the 1990s, after which Argentinian wine subsequently did very well, accounting for approximately 3% of the over USD 14 billion global wine market by 2004. The Mendoza province alone accounted for 90% of Argentina's wine exports (average for 2000–2003), compared to just 6% of the total coming from San Juan (McDermott, 2007, p. 111). Moreover, Mendoza shifted to higher value added wine production by the end of the 1990s. In 2002, 65% of Mendoza's harvest came from so-called high- and medium-quality grapes compared to only 26% of San Juan's grape harvest in that year.

What explains these divergent vinicultural outcomes? San Juan and Mendoza are neighboring provinces in the west of Argentina, with San Juan being the more northerly. San Juan has a population of just under 740,000 as of 2015 while Mendoza had almost 1.9 million people in 2010. Both regions have very similar institutional environments, geographies, and natural endowments. Hence, socioeconomic endowments are of little importance in determining why Mendoza firms, and its wine industry overall, were able to upgrade so successfully over a decade, while firms in San Juan were not.

Instead, the explanation hinges on the different political approaches to reform taken by the provincial governments in Mendoza and San Juan. The Mendoza province implemented a "participatory restructuring" approach that enabled novel and inclusive public–private institutions to be formed for industrial upgrading, while San Juan's political leadership pursued a "depoliticization" approach favoring arm's-length incentives but worsening social fragmentation. Thus, we may hypothesize that the construction of collective action institutions—firm associations, public agencies, design bureaus, certification, quality, standards, etc.,—as well as meaningful cooperation between them, affects outcomes in any given industry.

Mendoza

First, let us turn to Argentina's Mendoza province. This province implemented a "participatory restructuring" approach to reforming its provincial wine industry. A participatory restructuring approach refers to the organization of policy-making power, i.e., getting a greater number of diverse public agencies and sectoral associations involved in the policy-making process from the beginning. One political explanation for why Mendoza took such an approach to reform in 1987 is that the newly elected governor (Bordon of the Peronist Party) did not control the provincial legislature. Thus, Bordon was willing from the start of his term of office to work with everyone so as to increase support for his party among a variety of stakeholder groups. These groups included industry associations, such as the Association of Wine Cooperatives, relevant firms, wine business associations representing firms in the different areas within the province, as well as public agencies, such as the Rural Development Institute and the National Agricultural Technology Institute (or INTA, the acronym by its Spanish name). Slowly, the provincial government won the trust of these agencies and associations. All parties involved shared the risks and benefits of the reform process. As a result, the government and associations learned how to combine resources and cogovern new public–private institutions that introduce upgrading programs (greater and varied policy experimentation). These networks became embedded to form a dense network of organizations.

In term of policy, Mendoza's state-owned winery "Giol" was restructured into a federation of cooperatives (Fecovita) to effectively become a public–private partnership (PPP). Fecovita introduced various credit programs, technical and legal advice, special leasing rates, etc., to encourage the creation of cooperatives. The region signed up to—and actually implemented (in contrast to San Juan)—a 1993–1994 accord with neighboring San Juan as a response to a very cold winter, which caused great changes in grape prices and big losses for firms. This accord created new institutions to stabilize grape prices and share new policies. In total, Mendoza implemented more than 75 programs and policies targeting the wine industry in the 1990s—certainly evidence that the region had an elaborate policy portfolio for wine industry. This is testimony to the regional leadership's willingness to be experimental in policy making.

San Juan

San Juan took a contrasting approach to reform, namely a "depoliticization" approach, from that taken by Mendoza's government. This method was top-down and nonparticipatory in governance, and involved rapidly introducing new economic incentives at arms-length (e.g., investment incentives to encourage restructuring of the agricultural sectors, particularly wine and grapes). The restructuring led to some upgrading in San Juan's wine sector (i.e., a shift from lower to higher value economic activities via using local innovative capabilities to make continuous improvements in processes, products, and functions). However, it was mostly big companies—from outside the province—who gained from the upgrading. They were primarily interested in getting results in the short-term and importing new technologies, rather than in experimenting and building up their capabilities in vineyard management and transformation. Hence, the upgrading was not broad-based and did not help to establish novel capacities for collective innovation. The San Juan government reflected—in a review of its agricultural policies in the 1990s written by the provincial Ministry of Economy—that it had not introduced any policy innovations or institutional resources in that period, except for a handful of federal programs that were excessively bureaucratic and did not match local demand from firms (McDermott, 2007, pp. 116–118).

Another result of San Juan's wine policy-making approach was more conflicts between stakeholder groups and the provincial government. New aggregating structures that could coordinate different actors were blocked from being formed. Finally, San Juan had almost no horizontal ties between associations and government bodies: the wine producer associations were essentially lobbying bodies operating to influence provincial government policy for grape and wine prices on an ad hoc basis. Consequently, both associations and the San Juan government grew to distrust each other. Collaboration and cooperation between the firm associations and public agencies were virtually absent in San Juan; at best, the province had isolated first mover firms.

In terms of policy relevant for the wine industry in San Juan, the region has implemented a federal-level tax incentives program for smaller and poorer provinces since 1983. The earlier mentioned 1993–94 accord with the Mendoza province was never implemented in San Juan. Three attempts between 1989 and 1999 to set up a provincial export agency all failed because of a lack of substantial public–private cooperation between the government and the sectoral associations (e.g., inability to agree on priorities and sharing costs, not allowing associations to take part).

One can also see several similarities in the evolution of the successful nano-technology regional cluster ("Tech Valley") in Albany, New York, US (Chapter 7) and the way Argentina's Mendoza province successfully transformed and upgraded its wine industry. First, both regions had effective, consensus-building political leadership (universities, private sector, and political authorities). This can be considered key to successful regional transformation over a 10–20 year period. Second, "Tech Valley" in Albany, New York and Mendoza province had substantial and sustained state (i.e., regional or provincial) leadership. Third, the federal government played only minor roles in both cases (the US and Argentina are both decentralized countries). The role of the federal government in Tech Valley has been valuable particularly on regulatory issues, yet limited when it comes to scope and impact (e.g., DARPA designated SUNY Albany as one of four national "focus centers" for semiconductor research, as well as the role of the US Department of Transportation). Mendoza participated in several relevant federal programs/initiatives, e.g., Cambio Rural (CR), launched by INTA in the early 1990s.

Fourth, both regions (Tech Valley and Mendoza) introduced and developed (PPPs), which turned out to be key institutional mechanisms. In Tech Valley's case, the PPP involved collaborations between the New York state government, universities, and private companies. In Mendoza, the PPPs consisted of collaborations between provincial government and industry associations.

One difference, however, between the US Tech Valley and Argentina's Mendoza province concerned the leadership role. The Albany cluster in New York state was initiated by a civic entrepreneur called Alain Kaloyeros, who involved industry and then applied for state funding (i.e., market-driven, then state support came in later). Mendoza's wine industry transformation was initiated and spearheaded by its provincial governor, who saw the need for a participatory governance approach to restructure the region's wine industry and was willing—from the very beginning of his term of office—to work with everyone because his party did not control the provincial legislature (i.e., more politics-driven). Both the market-driven and politics-driven approaches have their trade-offs; which one is chosen depends on the specific political and economic context.

Global-Level: High-Tech Cluster of Israel

There are only a few globally competitive clusters in high middle-income economies, none of them in Argentina and Russia. These have been well examined in the literature (see Teubal and collaborators, various years for Israel; and Breznitz, 2007 for Taiwan, both high middle-income economies in the 1970s when the formation of the clusters started).

The critical mass problem stems from the increasing returns when forming the necessary specialized institutions. For high-tech clusters, private support structures [such as early stage venture capital (VC) and specialized business development services] for technology entrepreneurship *respond to* rather than *create* commercial opportunities in clusters of innovative start-ups. If those existing commercial opportunities—actual projects—are small in number and size, we will not see specialized business development services and funding mechanisms (such as early-stage venture capital) that are needed to develop the technological and marketing capabilities of firms. However, without these highly specialized business development services and funding mechanisms, globally successful clusters will not develop. This is a classic chicken-and-egg problem. One manifestation of this problem is a pervasive deal flow problem: early-stage VCs are confronted with many ideas to fund but have little or no actual projects to fund. They have to create rather than just fund projects. The same applies to other funding structures, such as Rosnano, which we will discuss in detail in Section "Resolving the Collective Action Problem; the Need for Complementarity of Diverse Public Support Policies". In more technical economic parlance, generating private and public institutions for business innovation is subject to strategic complementarity. That, in turn, results in two equilibria: low-level equilibrium, wherein the process halts at stage 2 or even stage 1, at which our examples from Russia and Argentina are stuck; and high-level equilibrium, the stage 3 at which the critical mass problem is resolved. Examples of the latter include Ireland, Taiwan, and Israel (Breznitz, 2007).

Therefore, synergy and coevolution of public and private support structures for technoentrepreneurship are crucial. As we just hinted, this coevolution tends to proceed in three stages. In the first stage, which generates a diversity of support institutions and programs, they are predominantly public, as in our Argentinean cases. In the second stage, intense private–public institutional experimentation occurs: commercial and private actors develop a portfolio of institutions to address the critical mass problem. In the third stage, critical mass is achieved and a full-fledged private venture capital industry with seed and early-stage segments emerges. The well-known work of Avnimelech and Teubal (2006) (Avnimelech et al., 2010, see also Breznitz, 2007) trace the development of the Israeli VC industry through three phases: the creation of background conditions (1949 to the early 1970s), preemergence (early 1970s–92), and emergence (1993–2000). Box 10.1 recasts Teubal's classic three phases, developed from the background conditions perspective, as the three stages proposed in this chapter.

BOX 10.1 Three-Stage Model in the Emergence of Israeli Innovation Cluster

First mover stage; diversity of start-up (SU) companies (1949-early 1970s)
Horizontal Grants to Business Sector R&D → *Creation of R&D performing companies, of R&D/Innovation capabilities; and Creation of civilian High-tech industry and first start-up companies*

Collective learning stage: venture capital (VC) experiments (mid-1970s–1992)
- Business Experiments and Informal VC activity → New Model of SU ("born global" with links to global capital/product markets)
- Sharp increase in Business sector R&D grants. Incubator and Magnet program (supporting cooperative, generic R&D). First VC support program (Inbal) → Business Sector R&D expansion → Increased rate of SU formation → increased Demand for VC services → Learning from Inbal's failure and from Business Experiments → Identification of System Failure (absence of significant VC) & Selection of Limited Partnership form of VC Organization
- A critical mass of about 300 SUs reached by 1992, some of them of high quality (a few having IPOs NASDAQ). Once VC funding was made available, it could trigger a market-driven, virtuous VC-SU coevolutionary process.
Background factors: Liberalization of Trade, Capital Markets, Foreign Exchange market, etc. Favorable global context: liberalization of global communications markets; new possibilities of immigration from the former Soviet Union, beginnings of the Software Industry, etc.

Critical mass stage: accelerated growth of R&D and high-ech (1993–2000)
Targeted Support of VC (Yozma Program); continuation of all Innovation Policy programs, R&D Grants peaked in 2000 → Emergence of a VC industry and EHTC → Accelerated growth of SU segment and High-Tech; large numbers of IPOs and M&A, etc.

Source: *Adapted from Teubal, M., Kuznetsov, Y., 2012. Sequencing Public Interventions to Support Techno-entrepreneurship, in Promoting Inclusive Growth: Challenges and Policies, L. de Mello and M. A. Dutz, eds., Paris: OECD.*

The following section examines how the collective action problem of stage 2 is addressed at the regional level in Russia.

RESOLVING THE COLLECTIVE ACTION PROBLEM; THE NEED FOR COMPLEMENTARITY OF DIVERSE PUBLIC SUPPORT POLICIES

Raising productivity and innovativeness in institutionally and economically weak regions is a fundamental challenge for geographically diversified countries like Russia. However, in recent years much went wrong on the path to convergence, with the gap between wealthy regions and the rest having increased over time in spite of significant regional subsidies and high growth rates of laggard regions during the 2000s, when the country experienced significant economic growth (Zubarevich, 2009). Yet, the economic structure of subsidized, fast-growing weak territories became too dependent on federal support, and their new specialization focused on providing government services with little or no link to their core endowments, comparative advantages, or institutions. Thus, the political machine failed to revive the forces which stimulate the desired trajectory of local growth.

This failure has led to a debate about the optimal design for structural and innovation policies, in which two polar views compete. The choice is to be made between financing of the frontier regions ("territories of growth"), while providing the weak areas with some basic social infrastructure and the opportunity to capitalize on innovations made by somebody else. The second option is to keep struggling for innovation-led growth in all locations, strong and weak, or, as postulated in the recent government document about innovation strategy, to *"eliminate the "white spots" on the innovation map in Russia"* (Government of the Russian Federation, 2015). From the perspective of regional development, it is therefore important to learn *how realistic it is to rely on smart specialization in places which lack sufficient local resources, competences, and networks*, especially when the previous experience of government interventions in promoting economic growth via innovation has been questioned. In this section, we hypothesize that the complementarity of policies and colocation of projects funded from various sources might be a condition for more efficient regional economic policy designs.

An argument in favor of *a selective rather than inclusive approach* derives from the obvious observation that science and innovation activities cluster in space. Clusters are more capable than other locations to endogenously generate and diffuse knowledge, benefiting from specialization, diversity, and favorable combinations of knowledge supply and demand (Saxenian, 1996; Audretsch and Feldman, 1996). Clusters are more competitive than less dense and isolated places in attracting government R&D subsidies, especially in the form of matched grants (Broekel et al., 2015). Moreover, the impact of proinnovation policies on economic performance is higher in more developed territories, especially if they are more open to globalization. Laggard regions, in turn, are less competitive in receiving government support for innovation, so they are also much less responsive to innovation incentives. If so, the question may be how to increase the initially low response of weak regions to proinnovation policies.

To answer this question, we address the allocation of granted R&D subsidies, using data about projects funded by the Russian Ministry of Education and Science in the framework of matched grants schemes. The successful applicants needed to fit the design of subsidy programs, which generally aim to stimulate innovation based on excellence in research, and are conditioned by certain requirements for skills and competences of participants and cofunding from commercial partners. Participation in federal programs is not restricted to specific regions and in theory is meant to be as inclusive as possible. As a result, the design of the programs translates into specific organizational structures, which are more likely to receive grants (large universities, research institutes, and firms). The spatial structure of projects proves the dominance of developed urban agglomerations as host locations. Thus, Russian R&D subsidies tend, as elsewhere, to cluster in space.

The data show the details of this clustering: Moscow and St. Petersburg hosted almost 64% of all projects funded between 2005 and 2015, while the 15 top locations (from 65 participating regions) concentrate 89% of projects. Moreover, the top regions which host a R&D subsidy program often also receive other kinds of federal support programs, such as innovation clusters, Rosnano centers, and SME development grants. How can we interpret this concentration within the convergence targets of the overall regional policy? Table 10.1 shows the distribution of R&D and innovation subsidies, federal transfers from all sources and Gross regional product (GRP) per capita across Russian regions, comparing the ranks of regions in all three indicators (the top position equals 1, the lowest—65).

Table 10.1 indicates that allocation of R&D grants and general subsidies do not show clear codevelopment patterns. Some exceptions are positioned on the top of the table, which show that the 10–15 top spenders of R&D subsidies are simultaneously positioned as important beneficiaries from federal transfers and report relatively high GRP per capita levels. Among them are regions, which are usually ranked high on innovation and economic performance: Moscow city and St. Petersburg, Tatarstan, Novosibirsk region, Tomsk, Kaluga, and Moscow regions. These are territories which were also selected to host innovation clusters. Simple regression analysis of these data shows that the R&D grants are positively and significantly (at a 3% significance level) associated with GRP per capita and have no link to the total general subsidies.

To sum up, we found little complementarity in overall and proinnovation government policies in Russia, which may be regarded as a matter of reduced efficiency, duplication, and waste of scarce resources. R&D subsidies, associated with the high income level of the region, most probably increase the development gap across regions, while overall government subsidies seem to complement the proinnovation support only in the wealthier regions. When firms located in laggard regions get incentivized by government R&D grants, these grants—even when firms make the most of available resources—are incapable of stimulating innovation clusters and the region itself can hardly reap any benefits from the technological advances of the selected local firms. Many programs do not fulfil their aims in regional economic development as their budgets are too small compared to the size and level of complexity in regional economic structure. They cannot do much to tackle population ageing, outmigration, or political tensions, which are often associated with backwardness. When weak subnational institutions in laggard regions prevent overall federal subsidies from being effective, the laggard regions linger too long, and the government support for innovation would most probably be wasted as an instrument to support economic growth.

TABLE 10.1 The Ranks of Subnational Regions in Russia as Recipients of R&D and General Subsidies (2005–2011)

	R&D subsidies	Federal transfers	GRP per capita
Moscow (city)	1	13	4
Saint-Petersburg	2	11	7
Novosibirsk oblast	3	24	32
Moscow oblast	4	6	14
Tatarstan	5	3	12
Nizhny Novgorod oblast	6	20	30
Tomsk oblast	7	48	11
Kaluga oblast	8	55	35
Sverdlovsk oblast	9	17	16
Ulyanovsk oblast	10	37	49
Mordovia Republic	11	32	54
Yaroslavl oblast	12	50	31
Primorie	13	10	23
Rostov oblast	14	7	42
Belgorod oblast	15	29	17
Chelyabinsk oblast	16	19	27
Krasnodar krai	17	5	33
Khanty-Mansijsk autonomous okrug	18	65	1
Voronezh oblast	19	21	44
Irkutsk oblast	20	15	22
Vladimir oblast	21	43	46
Samara oblast	22	31	19
Krasnoyarsk krai	23	8	8
Omsk oblast	24	27	26
Smolensk oblast	25	62	45
Marij El	26	58	59
Tver oblast	27	46	38
Karachayevo-Cherkessia	28	56	63
Komi Republic	29	61	6
Kabardino-Balkaria	30	41	64
Perm krai	31	33	15
Bashkortostan	32	12	29
Bryansk oblast	33	34	58
Tambov oblast	34	36	50
Penza oblast	35	28	56
Altai krai	36	9	55

TABLE 10.1 The Ranks of Subnational Regions in Russia as Recipients of R&D and General Subsidies (2005–2011) (*cont.*)

	R&D subsidies	Federal transfers	GRP per capita
Murmansk oblast	37	45	9
Kursk oblast	38	54	37
Saratov oblast	39	22	47
Leningrad oblast	40	53	13
Kaliningrad oblast	41	35	24
North Ossetia-Alania	42	42	60
Volgograd oblast	43	26	36
Karelia	44	60	25
Kemerovo oblast	45	18	21
Daghestan	46	2	62
Ivanovo oblast	47	44	61
Pskov oblast	48	57	52
Ryazan oblast	49	52	40
Tula oblast	50	49	39
Arkhangelsk oblast	51	23	10
Stavropol krai	52	14	57
Udmurtia	53	47	34
Republic of Sakha (Yakutia)	54	4	5
Orenburg oblast	55	39	18
Tyumen oblast	56	25	2
Astrakhan oblast	57	51	41
Buryatia	58	16	43
Novgorod oblast	59	64	28
Oryol oblast	60	59	48
Chuvashia	61	38	51
Lipetsk oblast	62	63	20
Kirov oblast	63	30	53
Chechen Republic	64	1	65
Sakhalin oblast	65	40	3

Note: The R&D project funding is the indicator of the rank of the region as a recipient of R&D subsidies from the Ministry of Education and Science. The indicator of general subsidies to the regions was constructed from the regional consolidated budgets by adding up all the income line items that come from the federal budget (subventions, general subsidies, subsidies, and equalization grants). The value of this indicator is the rank of the region in the total sum of transfers received between 2005 and 2011. GRP per capita is the rank of the region in the average annual GRP per capita between 2005 and 2011.
Source: From Ministry of Education and Science of the Russian Federation for R&D project funding. For general subsidies, we used the database on economic and political indicators for the Russian regions in 1998–2014, created by the International Center for the Study of Institutions and Development of the National Research University-Higher School of Economics.

Shifting now from national support programs to specific policies and innovation support agencies, let us examine the case of Rosnano. Rosnano has the status of a joint-stock company, which helps it work with investors and partners. It is currently the largest technological investor in Russia. The initial aim was to commercialize research in nanotechnologies, which it achieves by investing in high-tech projects on a cofinancing basis and supporting the creation of infrastructure for nanotechnology. It seems that regional development is also only an unintended by-product of Rosnano projects. The second regional effect of Rosnano is stimulating local entrepreneurship. These development incentives are highly concentrated in space and colocate with innovation clusters and R&D projects funded by the Ministry of Science. While it may be too early to evaluate the success of Rosnano cofunding or infrastructure creation, we can see some actual impacts regionally. These include introducing nanotechnology-related new specializations in regions of scientific excellence (while encouraging a diversity of specializations), assisting strong regions to apply for other kinds of federal funding, and stimulating local entrepreneurial initiatives.

There are three main regional effects of Rosnano projects. First, the initiative to establish *technology transfer centers* in 12 regions (in total, there are 85 regions in Russia, including the Republic of Crimea and the federal city of Sevastopol since 2014). This network of nanotechnology centers was created between 2010 and 2013.

Data indicate that all but two of the active 11 centers are in regions with existing centers of scientific excellence—though not necessarily in nanotechnology. The exceptions are two regional technology transfer centers in Ulyanovsk and the Republic of Mordovia specialized in traditional manufacturing, hardly related to high technology.

Most regional nanotechnology centers are created based on existing patterns of regional specialization, and in partnership between several different stakeholders. The latter include universities, research institutes (usually affiliated to the Russian Academy of Sciences), and commercial firms specializing in technologies related to nanotechnologies (for example, ICT, electronics). While the new specialization(s) of nanotechnology (nanomaterials, nanoelectronics, etc.) was imposed from earlier on the centers, as a condition of Rosnano cofunding, regions' existing specializations were also built upon. We see quite a lot of diversity in specializations across the 11 regional centers (for example, biotechnology, new energy, electron-beam technologies, (nano)electronics, and aviation). In other words, the nanotechnology specialization was linked to areas of existing strengths. This aligns with the intentions of RIS3-type policies in the EU, which were never intended to reduce variety in regions, although this was sometimes how policy makers interpreted such policies (Kroll, 2015). On the other hand, the high-tech bias of all these Rosnano-funded nanotechnology centers goes against the academic advice for RIS3 policies to focus on adapting general purpose technologies in various domains of the economy, whether high-, low-, or medium-tech (Kroll, 2015).

Second, another regional effect is that all 11 regions with a Rosnano nanotechnology center also have a federal cluster, another policy initiative. These clusters were formed either concurrently with, or a few years after, the nanotechnology centers. Several regions have more than one cluster, with St Petersburg and the surrounding region faring particularly well (10 clusters in St Petersburg and Leningrad oblast). The nanotechnology center in Novosibirsk has different specializations (nanomodified metals, nanostructured coatings, chemical vapour deposition coatings, etc.) from the ICT and biopharmaceutical technologies-focused federal cluster in the same city. Hence, different development policies can coexist regionally and can help to build up a sufficient number of diverse R&D and innovative projects.

Third, we see some evidence of local entrepreneurial initiatives stimulated by Rosnano funding. The small company "Toytemic Inventions" makes robot toys for children, a rapidly emerging and globally competitive field. It won a 3 million RUB (approx. USD 100,000 as of 2012) innovation prize in a 2012 competition run by Skolkovo innovation center in Moscow city.

Our analysis clearly shows that, from the perspective of regional policy, there is a sound economic basis for smart specialization in more developed regions, where innovation clusters, beneficiaries of R&D grants and federal transfers, and better subnational institutions colocate. Despite the weaknesses of the Russian innovation system and of institutions, top regions which engaged in various proinnovation subsidy schemes may achieve certain synergies and increase the efficacy of public support. In lagging regions, the development gap can hardly be closed through proinnovation policies. This does not mean that there is no scope for innovation policy in the lagging regions, but rather only that such policy needs to include institution building efforts to ensure adequate public–private and public-to-public coordination.

CONCLUSIONS

The contribution of this chapter is twofold.

First, it provides an exposition of the three stage-model illustrating it with empirical examples from Argentina, Russia, and Israel (Section "Empirical Illustration of the Three-Staged Policy Model"). The key implication of the three-stage model is that even in institutionally weak economies there are always some regions, firms, sectors, or institutions that are working well. Furthermore, the self-discovery process in this institutional context, central in the RIS3 concept, is mostly about carving out a new space within the national or subnational economy capable of growth and development. The second finding is that solving two types of problems is decisive on the road to success. The first problem is that of collective action, which is about regional cluster coordination. The second is the critical mass problem, when the region should acquire specialized competences to become competitive and globally known. A policy conclusion of the three-stage model is that dynamic regional development is often an unintended by-product of global or national success, rather than an end in itself. However, global or national success may be of limited scope: in our accounts, successful first movers do not necessarily generate local clusters. For instance, the Russian firm IPG-Photonics is an example of a so-called "born global" firm—a firm that acquired an international presence within 2 years of existence, becoming a global leader without relying on its local region or generating a critical mass of local linkages. In Bariloche (Argentina), an innovation cluster exists, yet its effects on generating employment are very weak. Hence, individual technology and business successes are not necessarily economic regional success stories.

Second, focusing specifically on the collective action problem of stage 2, we provided an argument that more focus should be given to policy implementation and complementarity of policies in regions with differing institutional and income levels (Section "Resolving the Collective Action Problem: the Need for Complementarity of Diverse Public Support Policies"). Wealthy and more developed subnational regions are well suited for the logic and instruments of RIS3, and they benefit from a complementarity of policies supported by various funding sources.

Third, the heterogeneity argument developed in the chapter implies that the policy agenda for advanced and less developed regions has to be designed and implemented quite differently. For advanced regions (stages 2 and 3 of the model), the single focus is on strengthening existing and building new collective action institutions with a diversity of funding sources. For less developed localities (stage 1), the issue is searching for dynamic institutional segments in the public and private sector which are exceptions from the general rule of ineffective and dysfunctional institutions (for instance, the National Atomic Commission and INVAP were such exceptions in the early days of the development of the Bariloche cluster). So, the policy agenda for the less developed regions is twofold: on the one hand, policy makers should accelerate the emergence and growth of "first mover" organizations and disseminate their experience—turn them into role models for others to follow. Matching grant schemes are well suited for this purpose. On the other hand, policy makers should facilitate collective action among those dynamic exceptions, so that they may coalesce and diversify. One policy instrument for that objective is competitive funding of private-public project consortia.

ACKNOWLEDGMENT

The work of Ksenia Gonchar on this chapter was supported by the Basic Research Program at the National Research University Higher School of Economics. Yevgeny Kuznetsov would like to thank Bob Hodgson (Zernike, UK) and Miguel Lengyel (Centro Interdisciplinario de Estudios en Ciencia, Tecnología e Innovación, Buenos Aires, Argentina) for useful feedback and discussions of the concepts of the chapter. Imogen Wade would like to acknowledge support for work on this chapter within the framework of the Basic Research Program at the National Research University Higher School of Economics and supported within the framework of a subsidy by the Russian Academic Excellence Project "5-100".

ENDNOTE

1. Sources: INVAP official website (http://www.invap.com.ar/en); PowerPoint presentation by INVAP General Manager and CEO Héctor Otheguy, October 31, 2012, Open Innovations Forum, Moscow (http://sk.ru/foundation/events/october2012/forinnovations/p/urban_session.aspx).

REFERENCES

Acemoglu, D., Robinson, J.A., 2008. Persistence of Power, Elites, and Institutions. Am. Econ. Rev. 98 (1), 267–293.

Acemoglu, D., Aghion, P., Zilibotti, F., 2006. Distance to Frontier, Selection, and Economic Growth. J. European Econ. Ass. 4, 37–74.

Aghion, P., Jaravel, X., 2015. Knowledge Spillovers, innovation and growth. Econ. J. 125, 533–557.

Audretsch, D.B., 1998. Agglomeration and the location of innovative activities'. Oxford Rev. Econ. Policy 14 (2), 18–92.

Audretsch, D.B., Feldman, M.P., 1996. R&D spillovers and the geography of innovation and production. Am. Econ. Rev. 86 (4), 253–273.

Avnimelech, G., Teubal, M., 2006. The emergence of Israel's venture capital industry: how policy can influence cluster dynamics. In: Braunerhjelm, P., Feldman, M. (Eds.), Cluster Genesis: Technology-Based Industrial Development. Oxford University Press, Oxford.

Avnimelech, G., Rosiello, A., Teubal, M., 2010. Evolutionary Interpretation of Venture Capital Policy in Israel, Germany, UK and Scotland. Sci. Public Policy 37 (2), 101–112.

Bessonova, E., Gonchar, K., 2015. Bypassing weak institutions in a large late-comer economy. J. Institutional Econ. 11 (4), 847–874.

Breznitz, D., 2007. Innovation and the State: Political Choice and Strategies for Growth in Israel, Taiwan, and Ireland. Yale University Press, New Haven and London.

Broekel, T., Fornahl, D., Morrison, A., 2015. Another cluster premium: Innovation subsidies and R&D collaboration networks. Res. Policy 44, 1431–1444.

Cohen, W.M., Levinthal, D.A., 1989. Innovation and learning: two faces of R&D'. Econ. J. 99 (397), 569–596.

European Commission, 2012. Guide to Research and Innovation Strategies for Smart Specialisations (RIS 3). Available from: http://s3platform.jrc.ec.europa.eu/s3pguide.

Foray, D., 2014. From smart specialisation to smart specialisation policy'. Euro. J. Innovat. Manag. 17 (4), 492–507.

Government of the Russian Federation, 2015. National report on innovation in Russia 2015 a draft document, Ministry for Economic Development, Open Government, Russian Venture Company, Moscow (Natsionalnyi doklad ob innovaciiah v Rossii 2015. Proekt. Ministerstvo ekonomicheskogo razvitiya, Otkrytoe pravitelstvo, RVK, 2015). Available from: http://xn----7sbbhhb-3acaml2aagi4k.xn--p1ai.

Hausmann, R., Rodrik, D., 2003. Economic development as self-discovery. J. Dev. Econ. 72, 603–633.

Keller, W., 2004. International technology diffusion. J. Econ. Lit. 17 (1), 752–782.

Kroll, H., 2015. Weaknesses and Opportunities of RIS3-type Policies: Seven Theses, Fraunhofer Institute for Systems and Innovation Research ISI, September. Available from: http://www.isi.fraunhofer.de/isi-wAssets/docs/p/de/publikationen/Thesenpapier_RIS3.pdf.

McDermott, G., 2007. The politics of institutional renovation and economic upgrading: recombining the vines that bind in Argentina. Politics Soc. 35 (1), 103–143.

Muscio, A., Reid, A., Rivera Leon, L., 2015. An empirical test of the regional innovation paradox: can smart specialisation overcome the paradox in Central and Eastern Europe? J. Econ. Policy Ref. 18 (2), 153–171.

Rodrik, D., 2008. Second-Best Institutions. Am. Econ. Rev. 98 (2), 100–104.

Sabel, C., Fernandez-Arias, E., Rodriguez-Clare, A., Stein, E. (Eds.), 2012. Export Pioneers in Latin America. Inter-American Development Bank, David Rockefeller Center for Latin American Studies, Cambridge, MA.

Saxenian, A.-L., 1996. Regional Advantage: Culture and Competition in Silicon Valley and Route 128. Harvard University Press, Cambridge, MA.

Seijo, G.L., Cantero, J.H., 2012. ¿Cómo hacer un satélite espacial a partir de un reactor nuclear? Elogio de las tecnologías de investigación en INVAP [transl. "How to make an artificial satellite out of a nuclear reactor. In praise of research technology management at INVAP"]. REDES: Revista de estudios sociales de la ciencia y la tecnología 18 (35), 13–44, Available from: http://www.iesct.unq.edu.ar/index.php/en/publications/redes-journal/past-issues/item/182-redes-35.

Teubal, M., Kuznetsov, Y., 2012. Sequencing Public Interventions to Support Techno-entrepreneurship. In: de Mello, L., Dutz, M.A. (Eds.), Promoting Inclusive Growth: Challenges and Policies. OECD, Paris.

Zubarevich, N., 2009. Regional development and regional policy in Russia during ten years of economic growth, Zhurnal Novoy Economicheskoy Assotsiatsii 1–2, 160–174 (in Russian).

FURTHER READING

Kuznetsov, Y. (Ed.), 2013. How Can Talent Abroad Induce Development at Home? Towards a Pragmatic Diaspora Agenda. Migration Policy Institute, Washington, DC.

Chapter 11

Transnationalizing Smart Specialization Strategy

Louis Brennan*, Ruslan Rakhmatullin**
*Trinity College, Dublin, Ireland; **European Commission,
Joint Research Centre (DG JRC), Seville, Spain

Chapter Outline

Academic Highlights

- An analysis of Global Value Chains (GVCs) in the context of RIS3 is provided.
- A novel methodology that regions can employ to engage with GVCs and that is built around a three-tier approach is developed.
- The challenges of engaging with GVCs are explored.

Policy Highlights

- Regional institutions can play an important role as conduits/boundary spanners in forging engagement between local actors and GVCs.
- In relation to the critical issue of data deficits, the EU should facilitate a dialog to identify where the paucity in data hinders the full exploitation of GVCs and what data deficits need to be addressed.
- Private/public dialog can be crucial but how such dialog works in the context of mixed actors (local, national, and multinationals) is important to consider.

Advances in the Theory and Practice of Smart Specialization. http://dx.doi.org/10.1016/B978-0-12-804137-6.00011-5
249

INTRODUCTION

This chapter[1] examines smart specialization in the context of global value chains (GVCs). Technology upgrading is highly dependent on whether countries and regions use global value chains and international R&D networks as linkages, levers, and mechanisms of learning (Mathews, 2002). The key challenge for RIS3, which is still very much unexplored, is how can the local production stage of GVCs become a building block of regional innovation strategy? There are policy views suggesting that GVCs are key to technology upgrading. Linking is key; countries or regions should link up only when they are able to benefit, that is, they need first to build endogenous technological capability and only then link up.

In the past, a dominant feature of earlier regional and national research strategies was an excessive inward orientation or domestic-led modernization. However, starting with RIS3, there is a requirement to provide evidence that each RIS3 strategy is sufficiently outward-looking. While outward-looking can mean an inward-oriented RIS3, which has taken into account the global context, within the EU context it also means taking account of what other regions are doing and where complementarities arise, engaging with those other regions. On the other hand, there are limits of exclusively GVC-led upgrading. This chapter explores how to transationalize RIS3 and offers insight into the key elements that need to be incorporated into a policy toolbox to help policy makers achieve such an objective.

With respect to that, the chapter argues that institutional capacity for RIS3 is critical. RIS3 presumes different types of public–private coordination, both in design and implementation, more than can be found in many member states (MS) (Karo and Kattel, 2015). The attainment of institutional preconditions for RIS3 is one of the major challenges. The factors involved in addressing this challenge are considered in the context of GVCs and the transnationalization of RIS3.

The smart specialization principle, which was initially defined by the "Knowledge for Growth" Expert Group in 2008, requires EU regions and member MS to build on their own strengths and to manage a priority-setting process in the context of national and regional research and innovation strategies. Research and innovation strategies for smart specialization (RIS3) have been placed at the core of the new European cohesion policy as an important driver for the achievement of the Europe 2020 strategy objectives from a regional perspective.

Smart specialization, as a rationale for research and innovation policies, aims to promote collaboration between the regional and national authorities in charge of taking decisions on the design and implementation of the innovation policies and the relevant stakeholders involved in such a process (i.e., firms, entrepreneurs, universities, research centers, civil society). An assessment of existing national/regional assets implies looking "inside" the country/region; however, this might be insufficient for a smart specialization strategy. An important aspect of the RIS3 approach is that each country/region has to make its strategic decisions by taking into account their position relative to other regions of Europe. Whereas, having done so, a region may decide to operate on an autonomous basis, ignoring other regions, the RIS3 approach encourages the quest for learning and synergies from other regions.

The RIS3 approach requires looking beyond the national/regional administrative boundaries. In other words, a country/region should be able to identify its competitive advantages through systematic comparisons with other countries/regions, mapping their national and the international context in search of examples to learn from, or to differentiate from, and performing effective benchmarking and leading to interregional or global value chain (GVC) cooperation. Yet effective benchmarking takes account of not only priorities, but also of the modes of delivery of those priorities. With respect to this, the principles of linkage, leverage, and learning (Mathews, 2002) can usefully be brought to bear in terms of securing cooperation with other regions and GVCs. Thus, the development of links by the country/region with GVCs and their leveraging to foster the growth of local firms and to provide learning for them can be a significant means of increasing their competitiveness.

A country/region should be able to identify relevant linkages and flows of goods, services, and knowledge revealing possible patterns of integration with partner regions. However, this is not a trivial exercise, with paucity of extant data and data deficits being a major impediment. The issue of data is critical and will be returned to later in this chapter. The availability of data is important in the case of both developed and less developed countries/ regions, which would often need to source know-how and technology from elsewhere and are hence in need of data that can guide that process.

The significance and role of GVCs merit consideration, and so do the ways of engaging with them. The position of businesses within global value chains is a crucial element to be considered. This is particularly important as the RIS3 concept warns against "blind" duplication of investments in other European regions. Any such duplication of efforts could lead to excessive fragmentation, loss of synergy potential, and ultimately could hamper the reaching of the critical mass required for success. This can be avoided by engaging in benchmarking. On the contrary, interregional collaboration should be pursued whenever similarities or complementarities with other regions are detected. In the context of a radically transformed global competitive landscape where competition is increasingly based between the triad of the North and South America, East Asia including China, and the European Union, duplication of investments in the European regions may undermine still further Europe's global competitiveness, particularly in the absence of critical mass and intra-European cooperation. Potentially beneficial opportunities may lie in reshoring/near-shoring of extant GVC activities, whether afforded by the competitive realities underpinning GVCs or by the embrace of new technologies and the development of the requisite human capital capabilities and skills to ensure effective implementation of those technologies. Engaging with the leading GVC multinational enterprise (MNE) is an essential element if such opportunities are to be realized.

This chapter offers an approach to the transnationalization of smart specialization strategy. With regard to that, the aforementioned considerations lead this chapter to focus on the development of a methodological approach to analyzing a country's (region's) position in GVCs in terms of activities, resources, assets, and relationships. It also proposes an approach to the process of building linkages between regions and GVCs. It is argued that analyzing a country's (region's) position in GVCs can reveal where along the value chain the industry is positioned and the extent of that positioning. Thus, the analysis can point to opportunities for maintaining/extending/deepening the country's positioning on the GVC. Furthermore, by applying a similar analysis to other locations, a place can ascertain who else occupies significant parts of the industry value chain, how strong their positions are, and whether those clusters of GVC activities in these other competing regions/countries are similar or complementary to their own activities. Taking account of the previously identified linkages, this can indicate whether there might be opportunities to capitalize on complementarities in other locations and the development of interregional/trans-European linkages. This can be a very significant exercise, as leading GVC MNEs often have cognitive gaps insofar as the potential contribution of the local actors in the region are concerned. An absence of and/or scant local knowledge of the extant industrial commons in terms of its constituents and their capabilities can be a source of these cognitive gaps. If such gaps on the part of MNEs are to be overcome, it may require local regions to engage with GVC players.

Transnationalizing smart specialization is important for several reasons. These include the benefits that can flow to countries (regions) from engaging and cooperating with other regions that are complementary in nature and that have capabilities in place that the region lacks. It is also important given the critical role that GVCs play in economic activity. GVCs can be a source of knowledge, know-how, expertise, and learning. They can provide access to opportunities for the region offering an entry point into international markets via the GVCs themselves or via networking that can emerge from engagement with GVCs.

However, there are knowledge gaps insofar as the current positioning of the region with GVCs is concerned. There are also knowledge gaps relating to the process that is required to insinuate actors within the region into GVCs. This chapter addresses those knowledge gaps by:

1. providing a methodological approach to analyzing a country's (region's) position in GVCs; and
2. proposing an approach to the process of building linkages between regions and GVCs.

GLOBAL VALUE CHAINS

The value chain describes the full range of activities that firms engage in to bring a product from its conception to its end use and beyond. This includes design, production, marketing, distribution, and support to the final consumer.

The activities that comprise a value chain can be contained within a single firm or divided among different firms. Value chain activities can produce goods or services, and can be contained within a single geographical location or spread over wider areas.

GVCs can be divided among multiple firms and dispersed across wide swaths of geographic space, hence the term.[2] In some instances, activities of the value chain may be embedded in established clusters that specialize in that particular activity. Cluster analysis reveals the extent to which a cluster forms part of a global value chain and can provide important insights on GVC participation. On the contrary, GVCs can lead to fragmentation of national and regional spaces.

GVCs represent the enactment of globalization, which at its heart is about flows: flows of materials, goods, information, knowledge, finance, and people. GVCs are the basis of such flows. The ongoing construction, deconstruction, and reconstruction of such chains provides the infrastructure through which globalization is enabled. At the same time, it can be argued that GVCs rely on infrastructure represented by national and regional clusters or ecosystems with which they interact. The design, configuration, and coordination of such chains to achieve maximum business performance are central to the role of MNEs. The integration of technologies into such chains to create symbiotic business systems that yield maximum performance is the key to competitive advantage in today's globalized world.

GVCs make it possible to bring together all the raw materials and components that combine to make a product or service; to deliver it into use through distribution systems; to support users on a 24-h basis; and to recover and integrate residue that may subsequently be incorporated into earlier stages of the chain. These chains span the world, so that even mundane items now commonly involve the coordination of flows of goods, information, finance, and people across several continents while navigating customs crossings, security screenings, and identity verification. A global value chain may involve US designers, Indian software writers, Asian manufacturers, and European system integrators and support provision.

GVCs are *organizational systems* that operate across multiple nations and are integrated. Their global integration is complex and their technology base, or "engine," is information and communication technologies (ICT). Thus, consistent with the role of ICT and related key enabling technologies (KETs) as a means of upgrading activities in some sectors in countries/regions, KETs can also play an important role in GVC participation. GVCs drive firm-level competitive advantage through integrating global and local competitive and comparative advantages (firm-specific and location-specific advantages).

In the context of today's competitive realities, where competition is less interfirm and more inter-GVC, developing and maintaining the competitiveness of the GVC is critical. Thus, GVCs must build and defend longer-term competitive advantage through complex and hard-to-imitate firm-level assets or capabilities. GVCs evolve through stages of development, or may be "born global." Thus, for example, if we consider the value chain for the JCB 3CX backhoe loader, it evolved from having virtually all of its inputs locally sourced in the 1970s to the point where about two thirds of its inputs were globally sourced by 2010. By contrast, some firms, such as those operating in the internet space may operate within a value chain that is global from the birth of the firm. GVCs incorporate "traditional" or "conventional" activities and functions, but also involve "whole system" activities from sourcing to customer support, and embody materials, information, financial, and people flows and assets.

GVCs are complex. The complexity that can be inherent in GVCs raises operational and orchestration challenges for the lead firm. For example, these challenges were particularly acute for Boeing with its Dreamliner aircraft.

The value chain takes an *end-to-end* perspective in terms of activities, resources, assets, capabilities, relationships, and financial and operating data. This facilitates thinking holistically across the chain and identifying opportunities in terms of new ideas and innovations that could emerge from a questioning of what is, what is not, and what could be.

As firms have sought to maximize returns, they have embraced various strategies directed toward value capture, including slicing the value chain, outsourcing, off-shoring (either in-house or contracted out), repositioning on the chain, and/or collaborating with other parties on the industry value chain. Thus, leading firms determine *value chain configurations*, that is, the way in which the activities of the value chain are spatially arranged within the constraints of product physical and knowledge characteristics.

They take account of a multiplicity of factors that can include cost factors, such as wage rates, productivity and inflation, the quality of business environments including the extent of political and economic risk, regulatory and tax considerations, technology, cluster effects involving related value-creation activities, logistics considerations including value-to-weight ratio and just-in-time practices, degree of digitization, economies of scale, and customer needs (that influence the requirement for, and location of buyer-related support activities) (Daniels et al., 2013). Other considerations that may obtain, particularly in the case of high-end manufacturing, can include adequate infrastructure, talent availability, IP protection, energy costs, and domestic supply networks.

GVC analysis concentrates on how different tasks, activities, and types of operations positioned in the value-chain are distributed across locations (Suder et al., 2014). Higher volumes of intermediate products, such as parts, components, and intermediate services are being produced in stages or processes across different countries and then exported to other countries for further production. As highlighted by UNCTAD (2013), a country's exports can be divided into domestically produced value added and imported (foreign) value added that is incorporated into exported goods and services. Furthermore, exports can either go to a foreign market for final consumption or as intermediate inputs to be exported again to third countries (or back to the original country).

The analysis of GVCs takes into account both foreign value added in exports (the upstream perspective) and exported value added incorporated in third-country exports (the downstream perspective). Today, almost 60% of trade in goods is in intermediates and the average import content of exports is around 40% (Lamy, 2013). Given the increasing complexity and sophistication in GVCs, it has been difficult to identify who produces what kind of value for whom and by what kind of activity in the chain (Suder et al., 2014).

Growing GVCs means that a country's exports can increasingly rely on significant intermediate imports (i.e., value added by industries in upstream countries where value chain stages are based that preceded those of the country in question). A country's imported intermediates from another can contain intermediates from third countries and sometimes from the first country itself. When these quantities are completely calculated so that the origin of all primary factor inputs in exports is identified, we have factor-content trade,[3] which is referred to as value added trade. Thus, we can have a measure of how much value is generated in the region by considering the difference between gross exports and imported intermediaries.

Three Measures of GVCs

The GVC participation index indicates the extent to which a country is involved as part of a multistage trade process involving a vertically fragmented production process, both as a user of foreign inputs for its own exports (measured as the value of imported inputs in the overall exports of a country, backward participation), and as a supplier of intermediate goods or services used in other countries' exports (measured as the percentage of exported goods and services used as inputs to produce other countries' exports, forward participation). The higher the foreign value-added embodied in gross exports and the higher the value of inputs exported to third countries and used in their exports, the higher the participation of a given country in the value chain. The overall participation indices together with the backward and forward participation indices for the EU28 MS for 2011 are displayed in Fig. 11.1.

The annual percent change in GVC participation from 1995 to 2011 is also displayed in Fig. 11.1. The data presented in Fig. 11.1 is sourced from the OECD-WTO TiVA database.[4]

The index of distance to final demand addresses the question of where countries are located in the value chain. It measures how many stages of production are left before the goods or services produced by an industry in a given country reach final consumers.

The GVC length: The participation index does not provide information about the length of the value chain, that is, the number of stages of production involved. The index of the number of production stages indicates how long the global value chains are. It also highlights the domestic and international part of the value. This dimension may also be useful in providing an indication of the

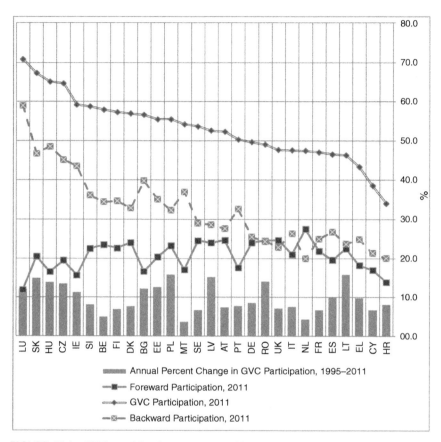

FIGURE 11.1 GVC participation data for EU28. *(Trade in value-added and global value chains: statistical profiles, WTO. Available from: https://www.wto.org/english/res_e/statis_e/ miwi_e/countryprofiles_e.htm)*

scope for countries upgrading within GVCs, assuming that one can argue that longer (more fragmented) value chains provide more opportunities since they offer a greater number of participation possibilities, that is, greater opportunities for targeting via joining the chain

ENGAGING WITH GVCs—WHAT ARE THE POSSIBILITIES?

In their analysis of the participation of developing countries in GVCs, Kowalski et al. (2015) argue that, although GVCs are often considered a defining feature of the current wave of globalization, little is known about: what drives GVC participation, what are the benefits associated with growing participation, and how countries engage and benefit from GVCs. Nonetheless, they conclude that the evidence indicates there are important benefits due to wider involvement in terms of enhanced productivity, sophistication, and diversification of exports, while structural factors, such as geography, size of the market, and level of development are found to be key determinants of GVC participation. They also conclude that trade and investment policy reforms, as well as improvements of logistics and customs, intellectual property protection, infrastructure, and institutions can, however, also play an active role in promoting further engagement.

The emergence of GVCs suggests major paradigm changes (Cattaneo et al., 2013). These include a change of relevant strategic framework, from countries to firms and GVCs. Since a country cannot develop a competitive offer of goods or services in isolation, imports are a means for firms to access the most efficient inputs and free resources to focus on core competences. In addition, trade and FDI, both inward and outward, should be treated in an integrated framework.

A second paradigm change relates to a change of relevant economic framework, from industries to tasks and business functions. With regard to this, the objective is not to develop domestic industries that would capture all the segments of production or the whole value chain. Rather, it is to identify the country's best position in the GVC and the most competitive supply of tasks or business functions and acknowledging that an efficient manufacturing sector requires efficient and competitive services (e.g., financial intermediation, R&D, logistics, and marketing), as well as a skilled workforce and continuous innovation in products, processes, and business models. Thus, it has been concluded that countries do not need to develop vertically integrated industries to participate in global trade but rather to develop capacities in specific segments (stages of production, tasks, or business functions) of the value chain. With respect to this, Baldwin's TOSP (tasks, occupations, stages, and product) framework (Baldwin, 2012) provides a useful means of identifying the possibilities for GVC positioning (Baldwin, 2011). By pointing to tasks that are involved in the different stages of the GVC and assessing the capacity of the region to meet those task requirements or to develop those task capabilities, a region can determine the extent to which it is feasible to seek to position itself in particular stages of the GVC under consideration. There has been some suggestion that Baldwin (2011) positions policy prescriptions derived from the local systems of innovation/smart specialization literature and the GVC literature as being diametrically opposed. We, however, would view the RIS3 approach and the GVC approach as having high potential for complementarity and in fact can at times be mutually reinforcing. This can arise given the overlapping focus on capacities and the development and/or expansion of regional capacities.

A further paradigm change relates to a change in the relevant economic assets from endowments and stocks to flows (Cattaneo et al., 2013). GVCs have become the main channel of transfers, such as capital, knowledge, technology standards, and value-added services.

Trade and participation in GVCs are just intermediary objectives (Cattaneo et al., 2013). Instead, the key consideration is how much value is captured by the country in terms of jobs, income, technology diffusion, sustainable development, etc. The ability of a country to participate in global trade and benefit from the transfers that will generate growth and development is now partially linked to its ability to join GVCs. *Thus, competitiveness is not measured in terms of a country's capacity to develop an integrated industry, but its capacity to identify its best position in GVCs.* A country's competitiveness can be assessed at three levels relating to its capacity to join GVCs, remaining part of GVCs, and move up the value chain within GVCs. A further issue is a country's capacity to disrupt GVCs, which requires a somewhat different set of considerations. Radosevic and Ciampi Stancova (2015) highlight that, from a RIS3 perspective, there are three important aspects to consider in relation to GVCs. These are, first, related to the choice of GVC that is suited to regional RDI and manufacturing and services capacities. Second, how firms can be assisted to "climb the ladder" or move from process, to product, to functional, or value chain upgrading. The third and final aspect that they highlight relates to the discovery of "new ladders" or new production and market uses for existing capabilities, not originally envisaged by either the foreign or local partners.

Finally, in considering the potential to benefit from participation in GVCs, trade in integrated regions, such as the European Union are more attractive to GVC-led firms for several practical reasons, due to greater ease and lower costs of flows. Leading firms in GVCs carry brands and sell branded products and systems in final markets to individual consumers, other businesses, or government agencies. These firms initiate, or *lead*, the GVC's activities by placing orders with suppliers, giving them market power over suppliers (Sturgeon and Kawakami, 2010). With respect to this, the European Union could develop a number of competitive industries through forming regional value chains as already demonstrated in the case of Airbus in aeronautics.

In addition, it has been observed that a number of value chains tend to be regional, such as the bulk of the automotive industry (Sturgeon et al., 2009). However, it has been argued that the objective is not necessarily to develop an integrated industry, but to capture an important part of the chain's value-added by providing a regional bundle of tasks or services at pinch points of the GVC where opportunities can arise (Cattaneo et al., 2013).

WHAT IS REQUIRED FROM A RIS3 PERSPECTIVE?

We now consider what is needed in terms of exploring GVCs within the context of RIS3. This is a multistage undertaking that involves a process, which can be effected within the context of the region and which also provides an in-depth understanding of GVCs.

The first stage encompasses a number of general principles to be followed. These entail the following:

1. *Engaging* with the industry and its stakeholders on a continuous basis.
2. *Anticipating* the likely evolution of the industry globally.

3. *Assessing* the challenges and opportunities that are likely to ensue from future industry trajectories.
4. *Responding* to those challenges and opportunities in a proactive manner. This process of engaging, anticipating, assessing, and responding (*EAAR*) should be followed on an ongoing basis and must involve the active participation of all stakeholders.

The ongoing success of Ireland in the changing pharmaceutical industry is an instructive example of RIS3 in action from which specific lessons can also be derived:

1. The provision of a compatible and supportive environment via a relevant infrastructure that encompasses a robust regulatory framework, research and technology, and education.
2. The upgrading and sustaining of a national innovation system.
3. The development of the requisite human capital pool.
4. The supporting and nurturing of collaboration among all stakeholders.
5. The engagement in upgrading of existing activities in the industry.
6. The anticipating and targeting of areas of growth within the industry.

A further stage, which is directed at gaining detailed insight into GVCs, requires the following five steps of analysis referred to as the M3DA process (Brennan and Rakhmatullin, 2015):

1. *Mapping*, as in plotting out their various stages across geographies and firms.
2. *Digging* into each stage in terms of activities, resources, assets, capabilities, relationships, and financial and operating data.
3. *Determining* the chain orchestration in terms of actors, linkages, and flows.
4. *Decomposing* the activities at each stage into occupations and associated tasks.
5. *Ascertaining* the participation possibilities by considering not only the status quo from 1 to 4 points mentioned in this list, but by also anticipating likely future chain trajectories.

The outputs from the application of the M3DA process to a GVC provide a multilevel perspective on the GVC that includes its spatial positioning, its attributes, operations, and functional breakdowns. At the same time, the analysis can reveal where along the value chain the industry is positioned and the extent of that positioning. Thus, the analysis points to opportunities for maintaining/extending/deepening the country's/region's positioning on the GVC. Furthermore, by applying a similar analysis to other locations, a place can ascertain who else occupies significant parts of the industry value chain, how strong their positions are, and whether those clusters of GVC activities in these other competing regions/countries are similar or complementary to their own activities. Taking account of the previously identified linkages, this can indicate whether there might be opportunities to capitalize on complementarities in other locations and the development of interregional/trans-European linkages. To explore such opportunities requires engaging in the digging (D) stage of the MD3A process. This implies a focus on the extant clusters of the industry GVC.

Since the data required at the digging stage may be unavailable or indeed difficult to access, there is a need to identify conduits/boundary spanners who are connected to the industry and have a deep knowledge of the industry cluster and its characteristics. These conduits/boundary spanners are likely to be found within the national and regional development agencies and/or enterprise development agencies. For each location, one such individual might be assigned a RIS3 responsibility within the context of the industry GVC. Platforms—real and virtual—would need to be developed to facilitate engagement among such conduits/boundary spanners so that opportunities for intraregional industry GVC linkages can be precisely identified and pursued and matchmaking takes place.

In relation to some methodological perspectives, we have already observed that the macroanalysis involved in the mapping stage of our M3DA process offers only preliminary insights into the industry within a GVC context. However, this represents only the first stage of the M3DA process. The subsequent stages of digging, determining, decomposing (3D), and ascertaining (A) call for microlevel analyses. These are particularly important if regional authorities are to play a role in cocreating and developing European industrial value chains based on smart specialization priorities.

This calls for interregional knowledge building, mapping the match-making potential around GVCs between regional smart specialization priorities, identifying some pilot examples of interregional value chains, key stakeholders, available equipment and facilities, and relevant actors/skills in smart specialization areas. Furthermore, it entails applying the methodology described earlier to identify examples of matching of national and regional cluster organizations in identified value chains of smart specialization areas.

A SYSTEMATIC APPROACH TO TRANSNATIONALIZING A SMART SPECIALIZATION STRATEGY

In considering a systematic approach, the crucial importance of data needs to be emphasized yet again. GVCs are complex and, to capture that complexity with a view to appreciating the opportunities that they may offer, the region requires better data. Thus far, the indicators for measuring GVCs are very aggregate in nature and can be viewed more as refined trade measures rather than value chain measures. To effectively interrogate GVCs requires "system level" analyses and measures. While some regions may have such data available to them, these are likely to be the exception rather than the rule. With respect to that, the EU should facilitate a dialog across the regions of the EU to promote learning but also to identify where the paucity in data hinders the full exploitation of GVCs and what data deficits need to be addressed. Resolving those deficits may

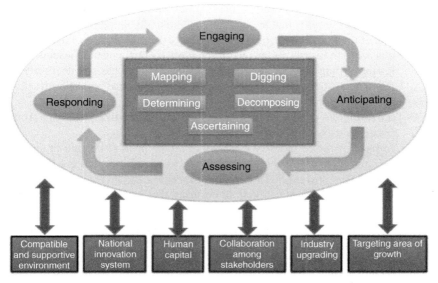

FIGURE 11.2   An approach to upgrading a country's/region's position in a specific RIS3 area (industry driven).

require not only Eurostat, but also the other pertinent international institutions, such as the OECD and the WTO.

For regions to profitably engage with GVCs, we propose a three-tier approach to upgrade country's/region's position in a specific RIS3 area (industry-driven) (Fig. 11.2).

This involves the following three steps:

1. A high-level policy/strategy level encompassing the four EAAR principles applied to individual RIS3 niches. Thus, in line with the EAAR principles, this requires:
   a. *Engaging* with the industry and its stakeholders on a continuous basis
      Rather than viewing engagement as an one-off or intermittent process, it is necessary for the region and its institutions to engage continuously with the industry and its stakeholders. This includes, along with leading MNEs, the entire panoply of actors that are already involved in the industry or have the potential to be involved. Thus, in the case of the biopharma sector, these would include academia and research institutes, SMEs and start-ups, health care organizations, such as hospitals, sources of capital that specialize in the sector, such as VCs, and industry, professional, and trade organizations.
   b. *Anticipating* the likely evolution of the industry globally
      Industries today are in a state of constant flux whether from the impact of disruptive technologies, of new business models, or of new discoveries. The only certainty is change in the nature, structures, and trajectories of

industries. It is therefore of crucial importance that regions benefit from scooping exercises that are directed toward anticipating the likely evolution of their target industries globally. Here the global aspect must be emphasized. Industries today tend to be globally connected. Consequently, having insights into the target industry on a global basis is necessary if the region is to be able to anticipate the challenges and opportunities that are likely to arise in the future.

   c. *Assessing* the challenges and opportunities that are likely to ensue from future industry trajectories
   In light of future industry evolution, regions need to engage in an ongoing assessment of the challenges and opportunities that are likely to ensue. This process has a twofold purpose. In the first instance, identifying the challenges can help in ensuring that a region acts to maintain its current positioning in the industry GVC. In the second instance, an assessment of the opportunities can shed light on the possibilities for extending and upgrading of the region's position in the GVC.

   d. *Responding* to those challenges and opportunities in a proactive manner
   Responding proactively to the challenges and opportunities identified in the previous step is critical if the region is to address the challenges identified and to capitalize on the opportunities identified. This might involve addressing changes to the regulatory environment, developing and implementing initiatives aimed at forming and/or upgrading of pools of human capital, and forging specific relationships between the leading MNEs and the industry stakeholders.

2. A focus on cluster-related activities
   GVCs are frequently related to clusters. By virtue of their constituents and their dynamics, clusters can offer a useful unit of analysis in which to consider engagement with GVCs. With respect to this, the RIS3 guidelines provide the basis for initiatives aimed at supporting clusters and their potential engagement with GVCs. The authors of the European Commission's RIS3 Guide argue that in many regions clusters can provide an adequate platform to facilitate the interactions between various regional innovation stakeholders, which should lead to better results in terms of regional industrial competitiveness and growth. It is further suggested that during the design stage, regional/national RIS3 authorities should involve key representatives of cluster organizations in the RIS3 entrepreneurial discovery process (EDP), as clusters are often very aware of the existing regional (industrial) strengths and weaknesses. This would allow them to contribute to identifying the right RIS3 priorities. In regions with better-performing clusters, such organizations can help the authorities in charge of RIS3 to mobilize both the necessary resources and key actors. During the RIS3 implementation stage, clusters can also facilitate interregional, as well as cross-sectoral cooperation.
   The European Commission suggests that the support of clusters in the RIS3 context may imply important political decisions regarding the development

and the use of cluster initiatives. It is argued that regional/national authorities can consider launching such new initiatives, should these be seen as important in the implementation of RIS3 and if they can be supported in the future. Many cluster initiatives can often result in more fragmentation and less synergies. The development of new linkages between any existing clusters could make them stronger and more capable to adapt to changing markets.

Here, the importance of connecting local SMEs with foreign MNEs is well established. Sauvant (2015) has highlighted that the single most important mechanism to transfer the tangible and intangible assets and capabilities of foreign affiliates to domestic firms is through the mechanism of linkages, such as domestic firms becoming suppliers to foreign affiliates and ideally part of their GVCs. He emphasizes that governments can institute linkage programs to upgrade potential domestic entities.

Inserting SMEs into GVCs can be the means by which they engage in exporting. SMEs can gain important advantages from engaging with lead GVC MNEs, gaining a new market for their outputs and gaining the credibility and kudos that can further advance their development and their penetration of GVCs. Of course, local institutions have a key role to play in acting as facilitators and even enablers of such engagement.

Kaczmarski (2015) highlights Singapore as an example of a region that has successfully created the links for local SMEs to forge relationships with lead MNEs. He reports that, as long ago as 1986, Singapore established its Local Industry Upgrading Program (LIUP), an entity charged with supporting knowledge transfer from MNCs to SMEs, initially in the electronics sector. The LIUP strengthened MNC-SME links by improving SMEs' operational efficiency, introducing and transferring processes from large international companies to smaller local firms, and by helping to establish a joint product. The success of the LIUP can be observed in the degree of participation by both SMEs and MNEs. Kaczmarski (2015) reports that, by the turn of the millennium, 670 SMEs and 30 MNCs were engaged, representing other sectors beyond electronics.

3. Project-level activities: supporting emerging value chains

Once a specific subarea (such as *3D Printing*) is identified within a specific RIS3 niche (e.g., *advanced manufacturing systems—additive manufacturing*), regional policy makers could provide further assistance by following the M3DA process:

a. *Mapping*, as in plotting out their various stages across geographical locations and firms:

– *From a regional perspective, this could include a definition of a regional innovation ecosystem and the mapping of regional stakeholders. When mapping regional knowledge generators, the regional authorities might consider sharing this information through a webpage similar to the one built by the Romanian authorities (http://www.erris.gov.ro/).*

- *If a cluster organization exists in this subarea, the task will be somewhat easier; if it does not, then regional capabilities represented by MNEs present in the region should be identified.*
- *Transregional/transnational cooperation: at this point, the regional authorities might need to initiate some external contacts with other regions/MS that have either indicated similar RIS3 priorities or have strong capabilities (as indicated by figures from the Orbis database).*[5]
- *Regional authorities would perhaps need to understand the needs of their regional stakeholders before reaching out to their international partners. Here, a combination of investment promotions agency (IPA)/regional enterprise type of institutions could be used to capture the perspectives of the pertinent actors:*
  - **(i)** *These regional institutions could then be employed to build:*
    - **A.** *A wide network of boundary spanning individuals/organizations.*
    - **B.** *Specific projects (joint calls) could be initiated at this point.*
- **b.** *Digging* into each stage in terms of activities, resources, assets, capabilities, relationships, and financial and operating data:
  - *Ideally, this could be done via a database of possible resources/services/etc. available in this specific subarea (such as 3D Printing) in each region (country).*
- **c.** *Determining* the chain orchestration in terms of actors, linkages, and flows.
- **d.** *Decomposing* the activities at each stage into occupations and associated tasks.
- **e.** *Ascertaining* the participation possibilities by considering not only the status quo from the digging stages through the decomposition stage aforementioned, but by also anticipating likely future chain trajectories.

At the same time, there are some specific action points that were earlier derived from our analysis of the success of the Irish biopharma sector (Brennan and Rakhmatullin, 2015).

1. Provision of a compatible and supportive environment via a relevant infrastructure that encompasses a robust regulatory framework, research and technology, and education:
   One of the key lessons from our study of the Irish biopharma sector is the importance of providing a compatible and supportive environment via a relevant infrastructure that encompasses a robust regulatory framework, research and technology, and education. Being proactive in this respect can give the region an advantage insofar as securing/maintaining and extending its position in the industry GVC.
2. Upgrading and sustaining of a national innovation system:
   Having in place a vibrant regional/national innovation system provides a means for industry stakeholders, especially start-ups and SMEs, to develop and acquire the capabilities to develop linkages into the GVC.

3. Development of the requisite human capital pool:
Likewise, having in place the requisite human capital pool is vital to joining/ maintaining/ extending and upgrading in the GVC. The more the requisite capital pool is anticipated and steps put in place to develop the requisite labor and knowledge capabilities, the better positioned the region is in relation to the GVC.

4. Supporting and nurturing of collaboration among all stakeholders:
In the world where the centrality of collaboration to success is well established, the supporting and nurturing of collaboration among all stakeholders is key to ensuring a region is well positioned to meet challenges and take advantages of the opportunities arising. However, some evidence on the changing role of the MNC subsidiary raises some concern about the degree to which MNE subsidiaries located in a region can engage in such collaboration. Reilly and Sharkey Scott (2013) argue that many subsidiaries now adopt a more narrowly defined, specialized implementer role, while also experiencing greater levels of monitoring and control from the parent company. Since MNEs now have considerably greater ability to frequently monitor subsidiary activities, this encourages tighter control (Scott and Gibbons, 2011) and may limit the subsidiary's autonomy and scope for embedding into the local region. The subsidiary's ability to act in a locally responsive manner can be reduced since its freedom to act without first obtaining headquarters' permission is reduced, while increased monitoring by headquarters will lower the level of slack or unused available resources in the subsidiary system that previously might have been directed toward engagement with the local ecosystem. This combination of decreased autonomy and decreased slack means that both the subsidiary's decision-making ability and its resources to execute them are decreased (Scott and Gibbons, 2011). Diminished subsidiary autonomy might also be impacted by the structural organization of the multinational corporation. Multinationals now have the option to allocate strands of activities from across the value chain to subsidiaries. Scott and Gibbons (2011) argue that this breakdown of subsidiary activities into combinations of possibly randomly assigned value chain activities, closely monitored and with little autonomy, substantially reduces the subsidiary's ability to adopt a strategic perspective. This again can reduce its ability to productively engage with the local region.

5. Engagement in upgrading of existing activities in the industry:
In an evolving, dynamic, and fast-paced changing industry context, it is not possible for the region to stand still in its positioning on the industry GVC. Standing still guarantees the erosion of the region's position on the GVC and its likely exit. Thus, engagement in extension/upgrading of existing activities needs to be pursued. Otherwise, a vicious circle of decline is likely to ensue. The region therefore needs to invest in the upgrading of scientific infrastructure and human capital.

6. Anticipating and targeting of growth areas within the industry:
As well as defending its position in the GVC, the region can benefit from anticipating and targeting areas of growth within the industry. Doing so can help embed the region more firmly in the GVC and drive a virtuous circle, with the region's role becoming more critical within the GVC. This further assists in embedding the region even more in the GVC, which in turn makes the region's contribution to the GVC more significant.
The aforementioned approach is not dissimilar to that proposed elsewhere around production transformation and development in the context of GVCs. Primi (2015) derives five pillars of successful transformation regardless of the variety in institutional setting and objectives: anticipation, adaptation, maximization of learning potential, capacity to operate in networks, and embeddedness. These are derived from the five features of success for transformation and upgrading: namely, being forward-looking, being flexible, dealing with networks, activating learning and self-discovery, and creating resilient linkages. Both this approach and the one described earlier share explicitly the principle of anticipation. Arguably, much of the focus of regions can be overly tilted to the past and present, with insufficient attention paid to anticipating change and proactively putting in place policies that address the challenges and opportunities that emerge from such an anticipatory process. There is therefore a need to balance the trade-off between evidence-based policy with policies that are capable of embracing change and addressing the future. Likewise, there is a similarity with our approach, particularly with the pillars of adaptation capacity, interconnectedness propensity, learning and upgrading potential, and embeddedness potential.

CONCLUSIONS

This chapter has focused on transnationalizing RIS3. To this end, we presented a three-tier approach to upgrading a country's/region's position in a specific RIS3 area (industry driven).
The proposed methodological approach allows you to analyze a country's position in GVCs (in terms of activities, resources, assets, and relationships). By revealing where along the value chain the country's industry is positioned and the extent of that positioning, the analysis can point to opportunities for maintaining/extending/deepening the country's positioning on the GVC. In addition, by applying a similar analysis to other regions and countries, a region can explore who else occupies significant parts of the value chain, and how strong their positions are. This would allow regions and countries to discover whether clusters of GVC activities in these other regions/countries are complementary to their own activities in related smart specialization niches. Taking account of the previously identified linkages, this can indicate whether there might be opportunities to capitalize on complementarities in other locations and the development of interregional/trans-European linkages.

While the chapter has considered many important factors, there remain others that need to be addressed. Among those still to be grappled with are the learning dimension and how activating learning dynamics can benefit from linkages with GVCs. Can other factors beyond top-down strategies play a role here?

It also needs to be emphasized that it is important for a region to have a clear vision linked to RIS3 as the foundation for engaging in the process of seeking to benefit from, and indeed to potentially shape, GVCs.

The challenge of the functional regional dimension remains. Production systems can extend beyond formal regions defined by government or other bodies into the areas surrounding it. Interacting with production systems can entail a greater need for planning at a functional rather than administrative level.

Finally, in terms of policy recommendations, private/public dialog can be crucial. Consideration needs to be given to how such dialog works in the context of mixed actors (local, national, and multinationals). What are the factors that are not too *ad hoc* and matter in engaging in a positive dialog? What does this mean at the level of policies? What are some of the institutional implications?

ENDNOTES

1. The early sections of this chapter draw extensively from the earlier work by the authors (Brennan and Rakhmatullin, 2015).
2. www.globalvaluechains.org
3. The amounts of primary factors used in the production of a good or service that are traded.
4. Available from: http://www.oecd.org/industry/ind/measuringtradeinvalue-addedanoecd-wto-jointinitiative.htm
5. ORBIS International Corporate Database provided by Bureau van Dijk (BvD). Available from: http://www.bvdinfo.com/en-us/our-products/company-information/international-products/orbis

REFERENCES

Baldwin, R., 2011. Trade and industrialisation after globalisation's 2nd unbundling: how building and joining a supply chain are different and why it matters. NBER Working Paper, 17716.

Baldwin, R., 2012. Global supply chains: why they emerged, why they matter, and where they are going. Working Paper FGI-2012-1, Fung Global Institute.

Brennan, L., Rakhmatullin, R., 2015. Global value chains and smart specialisation strategy, thematic work on the understanding of global value chains and their analysis within the context of smart specialisation, EUR 27649 EN, doi 10.2791/44840.

Cattaneo, O., Gereffi, G., Miroudot, S., Taglioni, D., 2013. Joining, upgrading and being competitive in global value chains: a strategic framework. Policy Research Working Paper no. WPS 6406, The World Bank.

Daniels, J.D., Radebaugh, L.H., Sulivan, D.P., 2013. International Business: Environments and Operations. Pearson Education, Upper Saddle River, NJ.

Kaczmarski, M. 2015. Are IPAs the missing link in the SME supply chain? Available from: www.fdiintelligence.com

Karo, E., Kattel, R., 2015. Economic development and evolving state capacities in Central and Eastern Europe: can "smart specialization" make a difference? J. Econ. Policy Reform 18, 172–187.

Kowalski, P., et al. 2015. Participation of Developing Countries in Global Value Chains: Implications for Trade and Trade-Related Policies, OECD Trade Policy Papers, No. 179, OECD Publishing, Paris. Available from: http://dx.doi.org/10.1787/5js33lfw0xxn-en

Lamy P., 2013. Emerging Economies: "Shapers and Makers" in Changing Landscape. WTO News: Speech by DG Pascal Lamy at Bigli University, Istanbul.

Mathews, J.A., 2002. Competitive advantage of the latecomer firm: a resource-based account of industrial catch-up strategies. Asia Pac. J. Manage. 19 (4), 467–488.

Primi, A., 2015. Production Transformation Policy Reviews (PTPRs): A Policy Assessment and Guidance Tool to Improve the Effectiveness of Production Transformation Strategies. OECD Development Centre.

Radosevic, S., Ciampi Stancova, K., 2015. Internationalising smart specialisation: assessment and issues in the case of EU new member states. J. Knowl. Econ. 2015, 1–31.

Reilly and Sharkey Scott. 2013. Subsidiary innovation: a phenomenon under threat? Available from: http://arrow.dit.ie/buschmanart/19

Sauvant, K.P., 2015. Attracting foreign direct investment and benefiting from it: challenges for the least developed countries. Transnatl. Corp. Rev. 7, 125–137.

Scott, Gibbons, 2011. Emerging threats for MNC subsidiaries and the cycle of decline. J. Bus. Strategy 32 (1), 34–41.

Sturgeon, T., Kawakami, M., 2010. Global value chains in the electronics industry: was the crisis a window of opportunity for developing countries? Policy Research Working Paper 5417, The World Bank.

Sturgeon, T., Memedovic, O., Van Biesebroek, J., Gereffi, G., 2009. Globalization of the automotive industry: main features and trends. Int. J. Technol. Learn., Innov. Dev. 2, 7–24.

Suder, G., Liesch, P.W., Inomata, S., Mihailova, I., Meng, B., 2014. The evolving geography of production hubs and regional value chains across East Asia: trade in value-added. J. World Bus. 50, 404–416.

UNCTAD. 2013. Global Value Chains and Development. Available from: http://unctad.org/en/publicationslibrary/diae2013d1_en.pdf

Chapter 12

Can Smart Specialization and Entrepreneurial Discovery be Organized by the Government? Lessons from Central and Eastern Europe

Erkki Karo, Rainer Kattel, Aleksandrs Cepilovs
Tallinn University of Technology, Tallinn, Estonia

Chapter Outline

Academic Highlights

- RIS3 and entrepreneurial discovery (ED) can be analyzed as elements of the broader experimental governance trends in the European Union.
- Organization of RIS3 and ED processes matters for the eventual outcomes:
  - RIS3 processes led by ministries or regional agencies for research and development are more likely to lead to academic bias and "science push"–based approaches.
  - Ministries and agencies responsible for economic development and innovation may be better equipped for engaging business actors and entrepreneurs in policy processes.

Advances in the Theory and Practice of Smart Specialization. http://dx.doi.org/10.1016/B978-0-12-804137-6.00013-9
269

- The maturity, or level of development, of national, regional, and sectoral innovation systems in terms of actor capabilities and networks determines the depth and quality of RIS3 and ED processes.

Policy Highlights

- RIS3 and ED remain vague and emerging concepts for most Central and Eastern Europe policy makers: there is a need for better articulation and operationalization of the RIS3 conceptual and especially policy making–related underpinnings to aid national and especially regional policy makers.
- In Central and Eastern Europe economies, RIS3 and ED seem to occur through two phases: fast specialization based on consciously broad and vague specializations, followed by actual and ongoing implementation of RIS3.
- The second stage of implementing RIS3 could be the phase where ED at the level of "granularity" could happen.
- The implementation requires significant policy experimentation (design of novel and flexible policy interventions), which is highly challenging and unlikely without the European Union's conscious support by explicitly allowing and encouraging flexible approach to European Structural and Investments Funds rules and regulations.

INTRODUCTION

One of the key "innovations" of the smart specialization initiative is the adoption of the concept of *entrepreneurial discovery* (ED) as part of the smart specialization strategies (RIS3) and regional policy (Foray et al., 2009; RIS3 Guide, 2012). As Foray (2014, p. 11) succinctly summarizes: "A smart specialisation strategy emphasises the formation of capabilities and the design of institutions to support entrepreneurial discovery and the early growth of most promising activities that have been discovered." Further, according to Coffano and Foray (2014) "specialization" in RIS3 does not mean deduction of specializations from historical data on development paths, but implies a more experimental approach to searching and developing *new* specializations by leveraging the regionally specific concentration of knowledge and competencies. In this context, "strategy" "involves putting in place a process whereby such dynamics can be facilitated through targeted interventions undertaken by the government in order to support in a preferential way the most promising new activities in terms of discovery, experimentation, potential spillovers, and structural changes" (ibid., p. 35). In other words, the emphasis of RIS3 should not be on defining and agreeing upon "smarter" specializations per se, but on developing systems and capabilities for continuous ED based on close interactions and agile coordination between and within states, academia, and businesses.

Yet, as with any policy concept, RIS3 and ED have also lived their own lives (Foray et al., 2011). RIS3 was initially proposed as a *policy* concept and the *economics* of smart specialization are still debated (McCann and Ortega-Argiles, 2015) (Chapter 1). The European Union adopted RIS3 as an *ex-ante* policy conditionality with an open-ended vision and broad guidelines regarding the content of the strategy, and how ED should be supported and implemented (RIS3 Guide, 2012). It was hoped that this EU-guided and -monitored "nudge" would be enough to steer EU regions away from the tendency of overextended policy convergence in priorities and instruments (Izsak et al., 2014) and toward more contextually relevant and customized policies and interventions. However, implementation of this concept with desired outcomes seems to be quite challenging. A recent study of RIS3 priorities chosen by different regions (Sörvik and Kleibrink, 2015) found that while only a few regions have selected similar combinations of priorities, there is still an overall convergence around groups of domains closely linked to the EU strategic priorities (Iacobucci, 2014).

In this chapter, we leave the debates on the economics of smart specialization aside and focus on RIS3 as a policy concept that has to be implemented by member states and their regions. We treat RIS3 as one of the many industrial and innovation policy concepts within the multilevel governance of economic policies in the European Union that proposes one novel focus—ED—to complement already existing processes of policy making (such as consensus building, policy coordination, instrument and policy mix design, and organization of implementation). We analyze how policy makers have understood ED as part of RIS3, integrated it into policy-making processes, and organized it administratively in the weaker-performing member states and regions from Central and Eastern Europe (CEE). As the European Union rejected most first-draft documents for RIS3 by the CEE countries discussed here, it must have some sort of understanding what RIS3 and ED should be. Still, CEE member states have been engaged in trial-and-error processes to determine what these concepts mean in their specific contexts.

In the next section, we frame our analysis by focusing on some of the key elements potentially affecting the evolution of RIS3 and ED as policy concepts—structural and ideational differences between polities, in styles of policy coordination and stakeholder participation—and discuss how RIS3 and ED fit into the different policy-making contexts in the European Union. Thereafter we look at the experiences of CEE economies in organizing and implementing RIS3 and ED. We show that during the first attempts to draft RIS3, the process was treated as a traditional bureaucracy-led policy planning exercise where historical data–based and foresight-like analytical exercises were combined and further legitimized through country-specific stakeholder inclusion and policy coordination practices. A common CEE feature seems to be the difficulty of engaging private actors into such detailed policy-making exercises. Further, as RIS3 has been designed as part of the national-level policy processes, there has been a common tendency to define specializations relatively broadly and vaguely, mainly for political reasons. While tendencies for broad/vague specializations have been also noted in more-developed Scandinavian regions, in these cases such choices may be justified by economic structure (Chapter 4). Finally, there has been limited focus on internalizing ED as one of the central elements of policy-making and implementation processes. As a result, we argue that the ideal-typical ED has not yet happened as part of RIS3, or has been postponed to the policy implementation phase, where it will be further influenced by the prevalent styles of policy implementation and governance.

ENTREPRENEURIAL DISCOVERY AND THE DIVERSITY OF POLICY CONTEXTS IN THE EUROPEAN UNION

One of the key RIS3 policy–related debates focuses on how RIS3 and ED fit into the generic models and traditions of policy making. Some are critical, arguing that the bottom-up logic of ED makes it incompatible with the top-down policy–making traditions, and therefore it is unlikely to have a significant impact on policies (Boschma, 2014; Iacobucci, 2014). Others are more positive, arguing that ED and supportive institution building is in fact necessary, as a learning, information, and feedback source, to change existing policy-making styles and their outcomes (Coffano and Foray, 2014; Foray, 2014).

This RIS3 debate mirrors similar debates on the new industrial policy (Chapter 1). Hausmann et al. (2008) differentiate between two complementary analytical lenses on industrial policy. *Industrial policy "in the small"* focuses on searching for and supporting productivity enhancements in existing economic activities through experimental and ED-like policy actions that are codesigned and codelivered by public and private actors. *Industrial policy "in the large"* focuses on betting strategically on future domains, sectors, and activities that may sustain national economic growth and development in the long term. This lens requires strategic and future-oriented policy capabilities at the system level (such as analytical skills and long-term vision, patient planning, and financing). This simplified dichotomy emphasizes how different policy focuses may require different time horizons, styles of policy making, stakeholder participation, policy coordination approaches, and also diverse policy mixes and organizations to implement them (Karo and Kattel, 2016).

We can think of RIS3 and ED as a strategic attempt by the European Union to strengthen the focus and capabilities of policy experimentation and "experimental governance" (as an alternative to principal–agent–based models, such as New Public Management) under conditions of "strategic uncertainty" (Sabel and Zeitlin, 2008, 2010). Yet how this experimental approach is accepted and adopted by different polities depends on their broader governance context. Thus, differences in the *development levels* of "mature" versus "emerging" innovation systems (Chaminade et al., 2011), in the *styles of politicoeconomic coordination* (Amable, 2003; Schmidt, 2002), and in *politicoadministrative structures* and *styles of policy making* (Kuhlmann and Wollmann, 2014; Pollitt and Bouckaert, 2011) have to be considered to understand the feasibility of and potential barriers to the adoption of experimental policy making and governance approaches.

Next to the variety in economic and innovation capabilities, as measured for example by innovation scoreboards, recent studies of RIS3 argue theoretically (Karo and Kattel, 2015; McCann and Ortega-Argiles, 2015) and show empirically (Charron et al., 2014; Kroll, 2015) that the European Union is characterized by significant differences in RIS3-related policy, administrative capabilities, and traditions, and in prevalent modes of policy coordination and stakeholder participation. In terms of institutional preconditions, RIS3 and ED may be more suitable for consensual (or corporatist) and decentralized polities with explicit regional governance architectures and policies, established routines of close government–academia–business interactions, and coordination with sufficient policy space for policy experimentation and agility. Thus, RIS3 and ED may be more easily adoptable, though with limited added value to the actual innovation performance, in the core Continental European countries and regions (Kroll, 2015) (Chapter 5) and in Scandinavia (Chapter 4). In other types of polities, similar institutional complementarities and preconditions may be lacking or be less effective, and the adoption of RIS3 and ED may be more difficult.

In countries following market-based (and neoliberal) policies and governance approaches—where the role of the state is limited to securing broad framework conditions through horizontal policy interventions—the styles of public–private interactions and policy coordination may also be more formal, hierarchical, and distanced (principal–agent style). To unpack differences in policy-making styles, Schmidt (2008) proposed a distinction between *simple* and *compound* polities. Simple polities (e.g., unitary states with strong executive powers) tend to rely more on formalistic policy coordination and stakeholder participation patterns (see Arnstein, 1969 on different types of participation practices) to legitimize policies and ideas developed by the executive. Compound polities (e.g., unitary or federal states with strong access and veto powers for nongovernmental and regional actors) tend to rely on more substantive coordination and participatory patterns, not only for legitimization, but also for policy deliberation and selection purposes. This distinction could also be used to analyze specific policy domains where national governance styles fuse with sectoral approaches.

The CEE economies are a rather special case in the European Union. The region has experienced more recent institutional transformations (from democratization and marketization to Europeanization) than the more-stable systems of Western Europe. Thus, there is also a higher likelihood of institutional immaturity and possibly less-stable links between institutional setups and economic performance (Bohle and Greskovits, 2012; Karo et al., 2017; Reinert and Kattel, 2014). We can treat the Baltic States as closest to the simple polity ideal type and Slovenia to the compound model (Karo and Looga, 2014), while Visegrad systems show intermediate models (Bohle and Greskovits, 2012). At the same time, the processes of Europeanization are pressuring these economies to converge toward the neoliberal model (Hermann, 2007; Stanojevic, 2014; Streeck, 2014).

In terms of innovation, CEE economies are some of the weakest innovation performers in the European Union. Only Slovenia and, in some years, Estonia have been considered as "innovation followers" or "strong" innovators, while most other countries and regions (except for some capital regions such as Prague) are considered "moderate" or "modest" innovators. Their innovation policies have been driven largely by the "European Paradox" narrative, focusing on policies supporting networking and commercialization, while overlooking domestic demand conditions and actor capabilities (Izsak et al., 2014; Karo, 2010). This policy focus has arguably (Myant and Drahokoupil, 2012) kept industrial structures and global integration patterns similar since the 1990s. The Visegrad countries and Slovenia can be described as *dependent market economies* where integration is based on exporting relatively complex manufactured goods increasingly produced by foreign-owned multinational corporations (MNCs) with limited linkages with the broader innovation systems (Dulleck et al., 2005). The Baltic States can be described as *peripheral market economies* integrating via less-stable manufactured goods exports and characterized by more financialization and economic instabilities (Reinert and Kattel, 2014). Furthermore, these policies have been financed by growing dependence on European Structural and Investments Funds (ESIF) (Veugelers, 2014; Table 12.1), with its specific ex-ante conditionalities and resulting pressures for policy and governance convergence. This has been illustrated by similar models of strategic planning (most countries adopt innovation strategies compatible with the EU fiscal framework), emulation of EU-wide policy goals and targets (Lisbon Agenda goals, common technological priorities), establishment of principal–agent–style policy design and implementation systems through "agencification" and ex-ante determined and generic performance indicators, and by common emphasis on procedural and administrative accountability and "absorption capacity" (Karo and Kattel, 2010, 2015; Suurna and Kattel, 2010). As in most CEE economies the networks and institutions the inclusion of private actors in new EU-initiated policy domains have been relatively fragile (Karo and Kattel, 2015; Tulmets, 2010), these policy focuses and governance conditionalities seem to be destabilizing existing coordination and public–private interaction patterns in more corporatist and coordinated economies as well (Karo and Looga, 2014; Karo et al., 2017; Reinert and Kattel, 2014; Stanojevic, 2014).

In sum, we can conjecture that the CEE economies, despite the within-group variations, tend to have more legalistic-, hierarchical-, centralized-, and bureaucracy-led styles of policy making, and more weakly established and formalistic types of government–academia–business interaction and public–private coordination (Bouckaert et al., 2008; Randma-Liiv, 2008). Such systems—also found in Southern Europe (Kuhlmann and Wollmann, 2014) (Chapter 6)—require *ex-ante* formalization of policy processes and their outcomes (performance indicators and targets), which is contrary to the essence of policy experimentation (Sabel and Zeitlin, 2008, 2010). Still, RIS3 as an *ex-ante* conditionality is likely to create some "windows of opportunities" for changes in policy-making practices. This

TABLE 12.1 Basic Characteristics of the Cases

	Estonia	Latvia	Lithuania	Slovenia	Poland	Czech Republic
Polity dimensions	Neoliberal, simple polity (unitary, executive government driven)	Neoliberal, simple (unitary, executive government driven)	Neoliberal, simple (unitary, executive government driven)	Neocorporatist, compound (unitary, consensus based), but changing	Embedded neoliberal, somewhat compound and decentralized (fading legacy of stakeholder power)	Embedded neoliberal, somewhat compound and decentralized (fading legacy of stakeholder power)
Innovation capacities (IUS, 2015)	Moderate innovator	Modest innovator	Moderate innovator	Innovation follower	Moderate innovator	Moderate innovator
Economic integration patterns (Myant and Drahokoupil, 2012)	Financialized, exporter of low value–added products (MNC subcontractor)	Financialized, exporter of low value–added products (MNC subcontractor)	Financialized, exporter of low value–added products (MNC subcontractor)	Exporter of relatively complex manufacturing goods (MNCs and domestic firms, gradually financializing)	Most mixed economy in CEE (largest agricultural sector), less financialized	Exporter of relatively complex manufacturing goods (MNCs), less financialized
Quality of governance: EU ranking; regional variations (Charron et al., 2014)	16 No regional variation measured (single NUTS2)	21 No regional variation measured (single NUTS2)	23 No regional variation measured (single NUTS2)	17 No regional variation measured (single NUTS2 until recently)	24 Low variation across regions	18 Moderate regional variations (includes best CEE regions)
GERD 2013 (Eurostat[a])						
% Of GDP	1.74%	0.6%	0.95%	2.6%	0.87%	1.91%
% Financed by government	47.2%	23.9%	34.5%	26.9%	47.2%	34.7%

(Continued)

TABLE 12.1 Basic Characteristics of the Cases (cont.)

	Estonia	Latvia	Lithuania	Slovenia	Poland	Czech Republic
% Of funds from "abroad"	10.3%	51.6%	37.1%	8.9%	13.1%	27.2%
ESIF allocations to R&D as a % of GBOARD (2007–13[b])	79%	211%	96%	59%	107%	56%
Share of research and innovation funds in 2014–20 ESIF[c]	11.15% (first priority) R&I, ICT, SMEs themes together 36%	6.81% (sixth priority) R&I, ICT, SMEs: 20.3%	7% (sixth priority) R&I, ICT, SMEs: 21%	10% (third priority) R&I, ICT, SMEs: 27.3%	8% (fourth priority) R&I, ICT, SMEs: 21.2%	7.8% (third priority) R&I, ICT, SMEs: 15.6%

CEE, Central and Eastern Europe; GBAORD, government budget appropriations or outlays for research and development; GDP, gross domestic product; GERD, gross domestic expenditure on R&D; ESIF, European Structural and Investments Funds; ICT, information and communications technology; MNC, multinational corporations; NUTS2, Nomenclature of Territorial Units for Statistics 2; R&I, research and innovation; SME, small- and medium-sized enterprises.

[a]Available from Eurostat database: http://ec.europa.eu/eurostat

[b]Calculations by Veugelers (2014).

[c]Calculated by authors as a % of total planned funding for 2004–20 based on the latest from the ESIF database (February 2016). Available from: https://cohesiondata.ec.europa.eu

may be the first important outcome of RIS3, even if the ideal outcomes in terms of "smarter" specializations may not be achieved in the short and medium terms.

ORGANIZING ENTREPRENEURIAL DISCOVERY IN CEE

In this section, we analyze—based on existing RIS3 strategies, official documents, secondary literature, and interviews with policy makers and other experts[1]—how CEE countries and regions have organized ED as part of RIS3 and whether the expectations outlined earlier in this chapter hold. We first look at three countries closer to the simple polity spectrum (i.e., Estonia, Latvia, and Lithuania). Thereafter, we look at three Central European countries closer to the coordinated/compound polity spectrum (i.e., Slovenia, Poland, and Czech Republic). In the latter cases, we could expect a relatively more substantive policy coordination, stakeholder participation, and regional focuses in RIS3, but these countries also have significant legacies of centralized innovation policy making. Table 12.1 summarizes the basic characteristics of the cases, while Table 12.2 gives an overview of RIS3 priority domains.

TABLE 12.2 RIS3 Priority Domains

Country	RI3 priority domains in Eye@RIS3 database (February 2016)
Estonia	• *Use of ICT in industry*: data analysis and information management, embedded systems and robotics, and production automation and industry 4.0 • *Biotechnologies in medicine and healthcare (red)*: prognostics and diagnostics, treatment therapies using biotechnology, laboratory products and services, biobanking, and early phase medicine development and production • *E-health*: remote management and remote diagnostics, decision support for clinicians and patients, and person-centered health information management • *Materials technologies*: nanotechnologies in new materials, surface coating technologies, and oil shale in the chemical industry • *Knowledge-based construction*: digitalization of construction processes, automation of construction processes, renewable energetics in construction, and development of timber utilization technologies • *Biotechnologies in food production and other areas (green and white)*: food that supports health, and systems technologies
Latvia	• Smart energy • Advanced ICT • Knowledge-intensive bioeconomy (in national documents includes all traditional industries) • Biomedicine, medical technologies, and biomedicine • Smart materials, technology and engineering (in national documents includes also machinery and heavy engineering)

(Continued)

TABLE 12.2 RIS3 Priority Domains (*cont.*)

Country	RI3 priority domains in Eye@RIS3 database (February 2016)
Lithuania	• Energy and sustainable environment • Health technologies and biotechnologies • Agricultural innovations and food technologies • New production processes materials and technologies • Transport, logistics, and ICT • Inclusive and creative society
Slovenia (priorities summarized by the Authors)	• Networks for transition to circular economy (bio mass, materials, energy etc) • Sustainable food production (value chain) • Mobility (energy, materials, technologies) • Sustainable tourism and creative cultural and heritage based societies • Smart use of resources • Smart cities and communities • Smart buildings and homes • Industry 4.0 (smart factories) • Health/ medicine
Poland (grouped by the Authors)	• *Innovative technologies and industrial processes* (*horizontal approach*): smart networks and geoinformation technologies, smart creative technologies, optoelectronic systems and materials, automation and robotics processes, electronic conducting polymers, sensors (including biosensors) and smart sensor networks, multifunctional materials and composites with advanced properties, including nanoprocesses and nanoproducts • *Natural resources and waste management*: modern technology sourcing, processing and use of natural resources and the production of substitutes, minimizing waste (including unfit for processing and use of materials and energy waste: recycling and other recovery methods), innovative technologies, processing water recovery, and reducing its consumption • *Healthy society*: production of medicinal products, medical diagnosis and treatment of lifestyle diseases, personalized medicine, medical engineering technologies, including biotechnologies • *Sustainable energy*: smart and energy efficient construction; high efficiency; low-emission and integrated circuits manufacturing; storage, transmission, and distribution of energy; environmentally friendly transport solutions • *Bioeconomy and environment*: healthy food (high quality and performance of production), biotechnological processes and products specialty chemicals and environmental engineering, innovative technologies, processes and products of the agrifood and forestry wood
Czech Republic	• Transport means (automotive and aerospace, including connected ecosystem of supplying and supporting industries) • Engineering industries and electrotechnics • ICT, automatization, and electronics • Healthcare and medical technology and devices

Source: Available from: http://s3platform.jrc.ec.europa.eu/eye-ris3

Organizing ED in the Baltic States

In terms of the structure of polities, the Baltic States are executive-led unitary states treated in the European Union as single Nomenclature of Territorial Units for Statistics 2 (NUTS2) regions. Local and regional entities have traditionally had a very limited role in economic and innovation policies. All countries have strong legacies of "no policy" industrial policy, and governments have mostly focused on improving the framework conditions and rectifying market failures with limited targeting/specializations in policies. Access to the European Union brought both the rhetoric and funds (ESIF) to build horizontal innovation policies with a strong high-tech orientation. Politicians have largely been inactive in innovation policy debates and priority setting. Styles of stakeholder participation and policy coordination have been rather formal (stakeholders lack real institutional pathways). The key exception has been the relatively well-organized academic sector, affecting R&D and innovation policies in all countries. (Karo, 2011) As a result, dual R&D and innovation systems seem to have emerged: government-financed and basic research–oriented academic R&D systems versus less-active business sectors with limited demand for academic R&D. Thus, one can expect that introducing RIS3 and a more experimental, ED-type policy approach in such contexts would require both policy and institutional innovations in the form of more targeted (regional) policy approaches and new forms of state–market interaction patterns, such as experimental spaces for ED-like activities (Hausmann et al., 2008).

Yet, in all the Baltic States, RIS3 is actually implemented at the national level, while political debate and interest in it have been moderate. Looking at policy-making styles, all Baltic States appear relatively conventional, as they have relied on quantitative analyses of specializations, foresight-type exercises, management consultants and foreign experts to highlighting global trends, and formal consultations with stakeholders. ED has been interpreted as a process of public–private coordination and stakeholder discussion with limited awareness of the need to focus on supporting experimentation, search, and discovery.

Furthermore, different policy logics seem to have come into conflict. On the one hand, local policy makers have argued that the smallness of the countries justifies, on efficiency grounds, nationally coordinated policies and planning. On the other hand, the same actors argue that at the national planning level, it is often not feasible to focus on very specific domains because interests from the wide spectrum of specializations found across the nation need to be considered. This argument goes hand in hand with the general unwillingness to follow policies seemingly similar to "picking winners" in more neoliberal polities. Further, as all governments have been investing significant sums of ESIF into R&D and innovation (Table 12.1), this has created significant stakeholder pressures and expectations (especially from academia) to keep funding already established entities. Thus, while there may be economic arguments for specialization even in small-state contexts, the political and administrative constraints make the actual policy-making situation more complicated.

Overall, in designing of RIS3 and ED, all countries seem to have been influenced by their specific legacies. First, given the legacy of high-tech innovation policies, RIS3 and ED are formally coordinated by the ministries for education and research in all of the three Baltic States, which have stronger links and networks with academia than with businesses. Consequently, in all cases business sector participation in the initial drafting phase of RIS3 has been relatively sporadic, academic interest has been dominant, and the consciously vague priorities tend to have a strong high-tech focus and logic (Table 12.2). Second, given the strong time pressures on ESIF planning (a key source of investments in R&D and innovation), there has been no time to build new participatory and coordination practices and experimental policy spaces. Thus, while a broad set of actors from business and academia were formally informed and consulted about potential priority areas, these activities could be classified as formal/symbolic ways of participation (Arnstein, 1969).

In *Estonia*, the Ministry of Education and Research initiated early exercises (engaging academics and the Ministry of Economic Affairs) to quantitatively derive specializations using the traditional NACE statistics–based industry analysis that provided rather broad insights for RIS3. The later stages of more qualitative analysis and policy formulation and coordination were contracted out to the Estonian Development Fund, a foresight and venture capital agency under the Parliament. Given its prior focus on start-up support and recent personnel changes substituting experienced civil servants with people from the private sector, the agency has been better at interacting with the start-up community than with traditional industry, and has found it also difficult to coordinate RIS3 with a broader group of policy stakeholders. In parallel to RIS3, the Ministry of Economic Affairs, in active interactions with sectoral industry associations, started to draft the first-ever green paper for industrial policy in Estonia, but these two processes were never consciously coordinated. This led to a strong criticism of the RIS3 by traditional industries regarding the high-tech– and academia-driven operationalization of research and innovation needs in RIS3.

Overall, policy makers have found it difficult to explain the whole process of RIS3 and selected specializations to both domestic counterparts and the European Union. In the Eye@RIS Database, Estonia lists six domains (Table 12.2), but domestically these are discussed through three broad domains [horizontal application of information and communications technology (ICT), healthcare technologies, and more efficient use of natural resources]. There has been no in-depth policy discussion on either the focus on "horizontal application of ICT" (i.e., developing ICT capabilities in and for traditional sectors), or on what is actually meant by "more efficient use of natural resources." Further, the original RIS3 strategy covered five policy measures and approximately 140 million EUR of ESIF activities; however, in late 2014, the European Union requested the RIS3 to cover almost all EU cofinanced activities in R&D, innovation and entrepreneurship (as well as resource use–related aspects of environmental policy). This increased the RIS3 coverage by 17 policy measures and

660 million EUR, but no significant adjustments were made in policy measures and strategies. Rather, it is expected that RIS3 priorities will be taken into account during project selection and implementation. In practice, most current policy instruments (such as technology development centers, centers of excellence, and R&D programs) have been taken over from the previous ESIF periods. Effectively, as Estonia's funding priorities were ICT, biotechnology, and material sciences also in the 2000s, the broadly similar priorities continue to be applied under somewhat different headings, albeit within a similar administrative structure and processes (competitive open calls).

In *Latvia*, the initial analysis for RIS3 was written up in very short time by a civil servant normally responsible for macroeconomic analysis. The actual process (drafting and stakeholder engagement) was contracted out to a management consultant with a 3-month deadline. This resulted in a relatively limited participation of business representatives, as most participants came from high and medium–high technology companies focusing on electronics, ICT, chemical, and pharmaceutical industries. Despite the fact that policy makers often emphasized the need to concentrate limited resources to achieve stronger impact, the ED process resulted in five broad priority areas (Table 12.2) that essentially include all sectors of Latvian economy. Most of the policy makers interviewed argued that instead of specialization, smart diversification is needed in Latvia, as the economy is already relatively specialized, especially in exports structure (though, the latter is not fully corroborated by comparative international statistics).

To date, the R&D and innovation policy mix proposed for the 2014–20 period has been almost entirely transferred from the 2007–13 period, with somewhat more pronounced emphasis on science–industry R&D collaboration. Therefore, the ED process is supposed to continue throughout the implementation of the Operational Programs (OPs). Previous experience, lack of political commitment to RIS3, as well as lack of resources and competences of the organizations involved suggest that a significant change of policy mix is rather unlikely without a conscious focus on developing relevant policy and administrative capabilities.

In *Lithuania*, the government had already tried to build some sectoral focuses into its policies through "integrated science, studies, and business centers," or "valleys" in the 2007–13 strategic period. According to local experts, this approach did not follow ED-like processes, but rather tried to replicate global trends. For RIS3, it created strong stakeholder pressures, as recipients of government funds expected continuity. In the end, Lithuania had to conduct two rounds of specialization analyses. First, six broad domains were defined through business–academia panel discussions, but these were criticized for being too vague. Second, this step was followed by a more-detailed foresight exercise (including relevant ministries next to business and academia) to define more-detailed focuses based on future trends and existing capabilities. The Lithuanian RIS3 also uses the EU "societal challenges" approach to better align national processes with EU priorities (Paliokaite et al., 2015). This may have led to more a systemic agreement on RIS3 than in other Baltic States and to better policy coordination (Paliokaite et al., 2016), but the specializations seem to be on a much higher level of "granularity" than expected in academic and policy discussions (Foray, 2014).

In principle, the idea of RIS3 is not challenged by business and academic actors in the Baltic States. It is in fact—at least rhetorically—praised. However, for these actors the process of executive-led ED and selection of specializations seems counterintuitive because of the weak traditions of government-led prioritization and low expectations regarding bureaucratic capabilities. Arguably, the ideal-typical ED envisioned by EU policy makers and expert communities has not yet happened, and RIS3 seems to be going through two phases. First, "fast" specialization or conscious selection of broad priorities was carried out to satisfy the *ex-ante* conditionalities of ESIF. In this stage, ED was understood as consultations with entrepreneurs and academics based on existing formalistic traditions. Second, this is followed by more routine work to develop specific policy measures, and evaluation and monitoring principles that try to satisfy both the expectations of RIS3 and other policy interests. Thus, the second step of RIS3—policy implementation—is the stage where real ED processes could start and more "granular" specializations emerge. Still, the Europeanization of R&D and innovation policies has established a rather specific style of policy making in these countries, with a predominant focus on "rational' strategic planning in 7-year policy cycles, cost efficiency, and detailed procedural and administrative regulations and accountability. Thus, implementation of RIS3 still seems to happen through multiyear policy measures where potential recipients (firms and academics) are either competing among themselves, or are asked to self-organize ED and propose new ideas and avenues that government will cofinance.

Organizing ED in Central Europe

The Central European countries seem to represent a more mixed group of polities. Formal regional decentralization (except in Slovakia and Slovenia) and a history of relatively established sectoral interests' representation in policy making [e.g., labor and specific traditional industries (Bohle and Greskovits, 2012] have been counteracted by centralized styles of R&D and innovation policy making. Yet, we can also see some recent trends toward the decentralization of economic policies in some countries. For the 2014–20 financial framework, Slovenia was transformed from a single region into two NUTS2 regions, but the RIS3 is still coordinated nationally. In Poland, the 2014–20 period is expected to bring substantial increase in ESIF allocated for research and innovation and a more active role for the 16 NUTS2 regions (EC, 2014). In Czech Republic, a more conscious division of labor seems to be emerging through RIS3 whereby formal top-down and analytical planning is carried out nationally, supported by more systemic regional-level RIS3 initiatives. Yet, in all cases these regional policies and initiatives are emerging only gradually. Three main challenges stand out.

First, as in the Baltic States, organizing RIS3 and ED nationally creates two-stage processes: definition of either vague or extensive lists of specializations, while expecting the detailed specializations and ED to emerge during later phases of policy implementation. Second, again as in the Baltic States, academic interests seem to be better organized and able to steer RIS3 discussions at the national level. Third, a policy challenge peculiar to compound polities is that while the countries have had their own specific styles of stakeholder participation and policy coordination, which are somewhat more substantive than in the Baltic States, they must combine these styles with the European Union's evolving expectations about RIS3 and ED. Thus, despite more extensive ED-like processes, the European Union has still been unhappy with the outcomes and procedural approaches. In the following discussion, we focus on this last challenge.

While *Slovenia* is rather similar to the Baltic States in size and unitary state structure, in terms of stakeholder participation and policy coordination mechanisms, it seems much closer to the compound ideal type. Different interest groups have always had an important role in and access to policy making. Further, the innovation system seems more balanced, with much more active R&D performance by firms than in the Baltic States. Yet access to the European Union and Eurozone, together with the impact of the financial crisis (austerity measures and dealing with the financial sector's problems), has brought significant political instabilities, increasing conflicts and pressures to shift toward a simple polity-type model (Karo and Looga, 2014; Karo et al., 2017).

Consequently, RIS3 has suffered from political instabilities and inconsistencies as well. The national negotiations were significantly delayed, reorganized, and RIS3 was accepted by the European Union only in late 2015. Still, the central government has managed to organize more visible and widespread consultation rounds as compared to those in the Baltic States. For example, organizations, such as the Chamber of Commerce and Industry, were involved in the RIS3 process from the beginning, proactively providing inputs and arguably organizing their own ED-type activities. As one of the focuses of RIS3 debates has been on how to integrate into and move up in the global value chains, the development of RIS3 seems to have had less academic and high-tech bias than in the Baltic States.

Paradoxically, one of the early European Union's criticisms was that ministries were insufficiently involved in the initial RIS3 processes. Thus, the Government Office for Development and European Cohesion Policy—the main government-level office for ESIF planning and implementation—took over the leading role. Later versions of RIS3 strategies have been broader and more vague in their priorities than the earlier versions (but still much more detailed than in the Baltic States). The greater political importance of the Government

Office led to higher-level political debates, but also criticism of extremely close ties between the industry and government. Furthermore, the early plans regarding policy instruments (strategic partnerships and a special fund/facility for pilot projects to test policy ideas) seem more flexible and allow more space for extending ED than the more hierarchical– and procedural accountability–driven focuses in the Baltic States. At the same time, the delays in the strategy-making process mean that the actual policy implementation pathways remained unclear even in late 2015.

In *Poland*, the conflicts between the national traditions of policy making and EU expectations seem to be even starker. Policy makers and local experts argued that, between 2007–13, the European Union discouraged Poland from developing sectoral approaches and convinced it to keep focusing on horizontal policy approaches. Thus, the introduction of RIS3 was a somewhat surprising policy shift. In addition, a local expert noted that ED as a concept remained confusing for most actors, and the rhetoric of RIS3 sounds to some policy makers like a return to socialist economic specialization policies (blamed for the erosion of Poland's nascent computer industry). Furthermore, for around 8 years before RIS3 became a conditionality, Poland had been running a similar process as part of foresight activities initiated by different ministries (Mieszkowski and Kardas, 2015; Nazarko et al., 2013; Okon-Horodynska, 2007). In addition, specialization and concentration of resources was also attempted within the public research sector. However, these were nationwide efforts of prioritization led by academic interests, and led to long lists of specializations with broad coverage.

Thus, when RIS3 and ED were introduced as a formal requirement for ESIF, Poland had already identified certain areas of sectoral and technological specialization and developed respective policy mixes. The results of these foresight activities were used as input for developing RIS3, but this was initially not accepted by the European Union, which expected RIS3 to be developed according to its broad guidelines. At least initially, this negative stance of the European Union created some resistance both from the authorities and from businesses, as another properly conducted round of ED-like activities was considered too burdensome. Ultimately, the European Union and the Polish authorities agreed that the output of foresight projects could still be used when devising RIS3, albeit with some revisions and additions.

Thus, while the prior specialization efforts seemed legitimate within Poland, for the broader legitimation of RIS3, Poland opted to contract in advisory and monitoring work from the World Bank. External expertise was deemed necessary, as the ministry in charge of RIS3 was not confident of its ability to engage all relevant stakeholders in ED. While the prior ESIF-related funding had been designed and implemented by the Ministry of Regional Development, RIS3 was perceived as a sectoral economic policy to be led by the Ministry of Economy, which lacked experience in EU and ESIF policies. Overall, the RIS3 has not yet changed much in terms of policy making nationally, as many seemingly similar activities had previously been planned and implemented. Yet, through the process, some ideas for experimental policy making have emerged, such as the Polish Agency for Enterprise Development's plans to establish an innovation policy lab.

RIS3 seems to have more impact on regions, which have suddenly found themselves responsible for innovation policy and tasked with initiating local RIS3 and ED processes. Given the history of centralized management of R&D and innovation policy, many regions have not developed similar strategies based on active stakeholder participation and coordination previously. As a result, regions with prior experiences in cluster policies seem to have found it easier to initiate RIS3 and ED processes. At the same time, the evolving understanding of RIS3 and ED among EU officials and related conflicting feedback complicated these processes for even these "first-mover" regions. For example, The South-Eastern Podkarpackie region is considered to be one of the success stories for regional-level RIS3 in Poland. This region has developed a historical specialization in aviation industry over 5 decades, with many attributes of a functioning cluster (Nijkamp and Kourtit, 2014). Nevertheless, a domestic expert argued that even in such a context the participation of industry representatives in developing RIS3 was challenging. Another perceived success story in terms of developing and implementing RIS3 is Pomorskie, a region with an above-average economic performance and a relatively high proportion of business R&D. Pomorskie has developed its own approach to ED, focusing on economic activities with a high level of export orientation and value added, and based on jobs requiring high-level skills. In the Warsaw capital region, a major RIS3 challenge has been the diversity of economic activities. This has turned RIS3 into a highly contested and partly "politicized" process and priority areas have been defined relatively broadly to include a wider range of interest groups.

In the *Czech Republic,* most innovation policy has been developed and implemented centrally. There is general recognition that both local- and national-level policy actors have limited experience in dealing with large amounts of R&D funding, while the support system for innovation is perceived to be overly complicated. As in many other cases, the European Commission (EC) rejected the first National Innovation Strategy on the grounds that it was only developed at the level of the central government and was not based on RIS3 principles, including ED. Thus, a new strategy was developed within a very tight schedule (1 year) along with development of the OPs for the 2014–20 period.

Initially, the Ministry of Education, Youth, and Sports (MEYS) was given the responsibility to develop national RIS3 supplemented by regional annexes. MEYS opted to outsource most RIS3 activities to consultants from preparing guidelines for regional RIS3 processes, capacity building, and training of actors to coordination and supervision of all processes. During this process, one of the most important challenges was to ensure business participation, especially of MNCs. This was a challenge both nationally and regionally, as even in one of the most proactive regions (South Moravia), representatives of MNCs largely neglected the process of defining regional specializations. Another important challenge was the lack of full comprehension by MEYS and the Government Office for Science, Research, and Innovation (section within the Office of the Government led by the Deputy Prime Minister of Science, Research, and Innovation) regarding the actual meaning of RIS3 and ED and how these should be organized. When the revised RIS3 was submitted to the EC, the responsibility for further implementation and development of RIS3 was transferred from the MEYS to the Government Office to reduce the workload of MEYS and to find a more legitimate and capable actor. While it is premature to judge whether the transfer of responsibility had any significant effect on the outcomes in terms of specializations and policy instruments, our interviewees suggested that the Government Office may have been more successful in engaging a wider array of stakeholders, especially from business. In addition, the Government Office may be more effective in coordinating regional initiatives and processes, especially given the varying innovation capabilities and policy needs of different regions.

Still, the early lessons of policy implementation mirror the experiences across the CEE overall. Given the pressures to open the ESIF as soon as possible, some of the funding has been distributed on the basis of policy instruments devised disregarding RIS3 and ED. Most of the policy instruments proposed so far are horizontal, and this has attracted some criticism from the EC. One of our interviewees suggested that to satisfy the EC's requirements for more vertical policy instruments aimed at specific areas of specialization, new policy instruments will be gradually phased in after the midterm evaluation in 2018.

Next to the national policies, some local regions have tried to build regional strategies since the early 2000s to prepare for MNCs' inevitable decisions to move their production facilities to cheaper locations. The regions of Prague, South Moravia, and Moravia–Silesia are much more developed compared to other regions and have experience with regional innovation policies. For example, South Moravia has built one of the most-established networks and institutions (e.g., the South Moravian Innovation Centre) that could be used to organize ED before RIS3 was introduced. Yet, policy makers from even such proactive regions recognized that they lack sufficient technological and innovation policy–related knowledge to be able to translate this into indigenous policy actions. Thus, copying instruments from other countries seems to still prevail (Charles et al., 2012). Prague seems to have similar conceptual challenges with RIS3 as Warsaw and countries, where RIS3 is carried out at the national level. As a capital region, it is dominated by service industries, while also being home to several national universities, as well as the majority of R&D organizations that aim to serve the needs of all regions (thus, most research organizations collaborate with firms from outside the Prague region).

In summary, while both Slovenia and the Visegrad countries look more like compound polities with participation and coordination styles more conducive to ED-like processes, the unequal regional economic and institutional capabilities and centralized nature of policy making seem to make both the central and regional actors less equipped for such tasks. Central governments and capital regions with the most diverse economies encountered "politicization" of specialization similar to the Baltic States. For regions, the main challenge is to build basic instruments and processes for engaging with business and academic actors. Further, the pressures to open up ESIF to increase funding for innovation and investments, while still consolidating national finances, have forced all regions to rush policy implementation, even though the substantive questions of RIS3 and ED have not been fully resolved. Nevertheless, based on their current plans for implementing RIS3 activities, it seems that the concepts of policy experimentation and ED are slightly better comprehended than in the Baltic States.

CONCLUSIONS

To understand the evolution of RIS3 and ED in CEE and the European Union in general, one should not underestimate the implications of the evolving understanding of RIS3 and ED in both academic and EU-level policy discussions (Foray, 2014; Foray et al., 2011; RIS3 Guide, 2012). Although we have conceptualized RIS3 and ED as elements of the experimental governance approach, we enjoy the benefits of hindsight. For most policy makers in CEE, these concepts have been confusing and difficult to operationalize and implement. In other words, despite the differences in both polity and economic structures and legacies, all CEE cases encountered similar challenges with RIS3 and ED.

First, the institutional preconditions for such experimental governance—from styles of policy coordination and stakeholder participation to basic technology, innovation policy capabilities, and policy experimentation skills—seem to be lacking generally (in the Baltic States), or differ from the EU expectations (in the Central European countries). Moreover, emergent concepts, such as RIS3 and ED, compete with other policy drivers and interests that are conceptually more understandable and politically better institutionalized, that is, fiscal consolidation, procedural transparency, and accountability, demonstrating policy impact in increasingly shorter time frames, opening the new period of ESIF as fast as possible, and maintaining funding flows for instruments and institutions created previously. Thus, further development and conceptualization of RIS3 and ED seem to be very much needed.

Second, RIS3 and ED seem to happen through two phases in CEE. All countries have now completed the first phase of "fast" specialization to formally satisfy EU conditionality and ease domestic pressures for opening ESIF funding for R&D and innovation. ED was interpreted in this phase as a process of formal consultation and coordination with stakeholders to legitimize some specializations. Carrying these processes out nationally and relying on existing policy-making styles have led to relatively broad and vague specializations, which seem to best satisfy those interested in the *status quo*. In the Baltic States, we seem to witness a more symbolic/formal legitimization of an executive-led approach to RIS3. In Central Europe, more substantive approaches with longer traditions seem visible, but these still differ from the (seemingly evolving) EU expectations. In all cases, academic interests seem to have been better organized, while business participation has usually been weaker and uneven. The inclusion of the business sector has been challenging for at least two reasons: (1) having ministries of education and research in charge of RIS3, and (2) businesses' weak interest in engaging in long-term strategic deliberations (as MNC subsidiaries follow the strategies of their headquarters; financialization reduces strategic time frames).

The second phase of RIS3 consists of the design and implementation of policy interventions by national and regional organizations. In this stage, more focused ED could happen through experimental codesign and coimplementation of novel ideas and policy approaches. Indeed, in some countries and regions, policy makers seem to be discussing the introduction of more experimental policy instruments and approaches through institutional innovations, such as innovation policy labs (Poland) and special funds for experimentation (Slovenia). In general, though, these seem to be rather isolated efforts. The predominant routines of hierarchical policy making, the emphasis on procedural accountability and cost efficiency in the governance, and management of ESIF finances seem to carry policy makers in a different direction. Most countries and regions still seem to feel pressure from the European Union (or simply prefer, given their own understanding of ESIF rules) to distribute ESIF through conventional policy instruments based on clearly defined ex-ante rules and regulations, as opposed to initiating flexible and experimental approaches where both risks and failures, but also substantive learning and discovery, may be more likely. In other words, in most cases the process of drafting RIS3 and ED has not yet led to a significant overhaul of how policy instruments and interventions are designed and structured.

The main reason for these developments seems to be the legacy effect of prior ESIF governance rules and approaches. These have created specific routines in CEE bureaucracies, which have been reinforced by the recent responses to fiscal austerity (increasing the reliance on ESIF for funding R&D and innovation policies) and the initial challenges with developing RIS3 and ED. In many cases RIS3 governance systems have been already reformed by shifting leadership from one ministry to another, or contracting out core activities to outside consultants. Consequently, early lessons learned from these processes may be lost and policy implementation has to occur while the conceptual ideas of RIS3 and ED remain still vague.

Thus, it seems to be a fair assessment that the open-ended approach toward conceptualizing RIS3 and ED as *ex-ante* conditionalities, while overlooking the institutional varieties across the European Union, might have been a tactical mistake by the European Union that has turned RIS3 into a confusing challenge for many countries and regions. To support the emergence and spread of more substantive ED in the RIS3 implementation phase, the European Union needs to consciously support countries and regions trying to design and implement novel approaches as part of RIS3 and ESIF by explicitly allowing and encouraging more flexibility in designing policy instruments and interventions. The latter should be less regulated and determined *ex-ante* in terms of structure, time frames, performance targets, etc. This could be achieved by allowing countries and regions to allocate some amounts of ESIF funding for policy experimentation through, for example, innovation policy labs steered by deliberation councils managed by entrepreneurs (Hausmann et al., 2008) (Chapter 3).

Finally, the comparative lessons emerging from this book raise more fundamental questions about the feasibility and timing of ED-based RIS3 in CEE. One could argue that ED does not work as part of a national-level strategy-making process, as the diversity of interests and policy goals will pressure discussions and negotiations toward broad and vague agreements and incremental changes. Moreover, we have shown that both simple and compound CEE polities seem to find RIS3 and ED more challenging than many more developed regions from Scandinavia and Continental Europe (Chapters 4 and 5). On the one hand, the institutions of innovation policy governance are still only emerging (especially regionally) across CEE, or undergoing significant changes (the gradual neoliberalization of Central Europe). On the other hand, the modest or moderate innovation performance of most CEE economies and regions indicates that institutional thickness, interactions, and the capabilities of innovation system actors (i.e., universities and firms) may be insufficient. In other words, it is not only policy makers who lack experience and skills for ED, but the same may also apply to their academic and industrial counterparts who should contribute to reflexive policy learning and feedback. Besides, this feedback may be highly unequal between different economic sectors, and ED may function better in some fields than in others. As most CEE economies seem to increasingly rely on EU/ESIF funding for R&D and innovation policies, the explicit policy focus of ESIF and RIS3 should not be only on extending RIS3- and ED-type activities, but also on building basic industrial and institutional capabilities for R&D and innovation.

ACKNOWLEDGMENTS

Research for this chapter has been funded by the Estonian Research Council grants IUT19-13, ETF9404, and the JSPS KAKENHI Grant Number 15F15760.

ENDNOTE

1. We carried out 16 interviews with policy makers and experts. In the case of Estonia, we also rely on our participant observations, which we undertook as part of the Research and Innovation Policy Monitoring Programme. In the case of Lithuania, we refer to similar RIS3 analysis by Paliokaite et al. (2015, 2016), corroborated by an additional interview with a policy maker (from the Research and Higher Education Monitoring and Analysis Centre). In the case of Latvia, we rely on five interviews conducted with policy makers (from the Ministry of Education and Science and Ministry of Economics) and consultants, as well as on the participant

observation of the processes. In the case of Slovenia, we conducted two interviews—one policy maker (from the Government Office) and one international consultant (working both in Latvia and Slovenia)—and discussed our interpretations with other experts contributing to this book. In the case of Czech Republic, we carried out four interviews with policy makers from both central and regional governments (Ministry of Education, Youth and Sports, three regions). In Poland, we interviewed two policy makers (from the Polish Agency for Enterprise Development and one region) and two experts (working on the RIS3 methodology and consulting different actors).

REFERENCES

Amable, B., 2003. The Diversity of Modern Capitalism. Oxford University Press, Oxford.

Arnstein, S.R., 1969. A ladder of citizen participation. J. Am. Inst. Plan. 35 (4), 216–224.

Bohle, D., Greskovits, B., 2012. Capitalist Diversity on Europe's Periphery. Cornell University Press, Ithaca.

Boschma, R., 2014. Constructing regional advantage and smart specialisation: comparison of two European policy concepts. Sci. Region. 13 (1), 51–68.

Bouckaert, G., Nemec, J., Nakrosis, V., Hajnal, G., Tõnnisson, K. (Eds.), 2008. Public Management Reforms in Central and Eastern Europe. NISPACee Press, Bratislava.

Chaminade, C., Lundvall, B.-A., Vang, J., Joseph, K.J., 2011. Designing innovation policies for development: towards a systemic experimentation-based approach. In: Lundvall, B.-A., Joseph, K.J., Chaminade, C., Vang, J. (Eds.), Handbook of Innovation Systems and Developing Countries: Building Domestic Capabilities in a Global Setting. Edward Elgar, Cheltenham, UK, pp. 360–379.

Charles, D., Gross, F., Bachtler, J., 2012. Smart specialisation and cohesion policy—a strategy for all regions? IQ-Net Thematic Paper 30 (2).

Charron, N., Dijkstra, L., Lapuente, V., 2014. Regional governance matters: quality of government within European Union member states. Region. Stud. 48 (1), 68–90.

Coffano, M., Foray, D., 2014. The centrality of entrepreneurial discovery in building and implementing a smart specialisation strategy. Sci. Region. 13 (1), 33–50.

Dulleck, U., Foster, N., Stehrer, R., Woerz, J., 2005. Dimensions of quality upgrading. Econ. Transit. 13 (1), 51–76.

European Commission, 2014., Summary of the Partnership Agreement for Poland 2014-2020. Available from http://ec.europa.eu/contracts_grants/pa/partnership-agreement-poland-summary_en.pdf.

Eye@RIS3 database. Available from: http://s3platform.jrc.ec.europa.eu/eye-ris3.

Foray, D., 2014. Smart Specialisation: Opportunities and Challenges for Regional Innovation Policy. Routledge, Abingdon.

Foray, D., David, P.A., Hall, B., 2009. Smart specialisation—the concept. Knowledge Economists Policy Brief 9, Available from: http://ec.europa.eu/invest-in-research/pdf/download_en/kfg_policy_brief_no9.pdf.

Foray, D., David, P.A., Hall, B., 2011. From academic idea to political instrument, the surprising career of a concept and the difficulties involved in its implementation. MTEI Working Paper.

Hausmann, R., Rodrik, D., Sabel, C., 2008. Reconfiguring industrial policy: a framework with an application to South Africa. Nontechnical Policy Brief. Center for International Development. Harvard University, Cambridge, MA.

Hermann, C., 2007. Neoliberalism in the European Union. Stud. Polit. Econ. 79, 61–89.

Iacobucci, D., 2014. Designing and implementing a smart specialisation strategy at regional level: some open questions. Sci. Region. 13 (1), 107–126.

IUS, 2015. European Innovation Scoreboard. Available from: http://ec.europa.eu/growth/industry/innovation/facts-figures/scoreboards/index_en.htm.

Izsak, K., Markianidou, P., Radosevic, S., 2014. Convergence of national innovation policy mixes in Europe–has it gone too far? An analysis of research and innovation policy measures in the period 2004-12. J. Common Market Stud. 53 (4), 786–802.

Karo, E., 2010. Improving governance of science and innovation policies, or just bad policy emulation? The case of the Estonian R&D system. Admin. Cult. 11 (2), 174–201.

Karo, E., 2011. The evolution of innovation policy governance systems and policy capacities in the Baltic States. J. Baltic Stud. 42 (4), 511–536.

Karo, E., Kattel, R., 2010. The copying paradox: why converging policies but diverging capacities for development in Eastern European innovation systems? Int. J. Inst. Econ. 2 (2), 167–206.

Karo, E., Kattel, R., 2015. Economic development and evolving state capacities in Central and Eastern Europe: can 'smart specialization' make a difference? J. Econ. Pol. Reform 18 (2), 172–187.

Karo, E., Kattel, R., 2016. How to organize for innovation: entrepreneurial state and organizational variety. Working Papers in Technology Governance and Economic Dynamics 66.

Karo, E., Looga, L., 2014. Understanding institutional changes in economic restructuring and innovation policies in Slovenia and Estonia. Journal of International Relations and Development 19 (4), 1–34.

Karo, E., Kattel, R., Raudla, R., 2017. Searching for exits from the Great Recession: coordination of fiscal consolidation and growth enhancing innovation policies in Central and Eastern Europe. Europe-Asia Studies. forthcoming.

Kroll, H., 2015. Efforts to implement smart specialization in practice—leading unlike horses to the water. Eur. Plan. Stud. 23 (10), 2079–2098.

Kuhlmann, S., Wollmann, H., 2014. Administrative Systems and Reforms in Europe. Edward Elgar, Cheltenham.

McCann, P., Ortega-Argiles, R., 2015. Smart specialization, regional growth and applications to European union cohesion policy. Region. Stud. 49 (8), 1291–1302.

Mieszkowski, K., Kardas, M., 2015. Facilitating an entrepreneurial discovery process for smart specialisation. The case of Poland. J. Knowledge Econ. 6, 357–384.

Myant, M., Drahokoupil, J., 2012. International integration, varieties of capitalism and resilience to crisis in transition economies. Europe-Asia Studies 64 (1), 1–33.

Nazarko, J., Glinska, U., Kononiuk, A., Nazarko, L., 2013. Sectoral foresight in Poland: thematic and methodological analysis. Int. J. Foresight Innov. Pol. 9, 19–38.

Nijkamp, P., Kourtit, K., 2014. Aviation clusters: new opportunities for smart regional policies. Paper presented at the Fifth Central European Conference in Regional Science. Available from: http://www3.ekf.tuke.sk/cers/files/zbornik2014/PDF/Nijkamp,%20Kourtit.pdf.

Okon-Horodynska, E., 2007. Foresight—identification of science and technology priorities of economic development (the case of Poland). In: Piech, K. (Ed.), Knowledge and Innovation Processes in Central and Eastern European Economies. Institut Wiedzy i Innowacji, Warsaw, pp. 164–168.

Paliokaite, A., Martinaitis, Ž., Reimeris, R., 2015. Foresight methods for smart specialisation strategy development in Lithuania. Technol. Forecast. Social Change 101, 185–199.

Paliokaite, A., Martinaitis, Ž., Sarpong, D., 2016. Implementing smart specialization roadmaps in Lithuania: Lost in translation? Technol. Forecast. Social Change 110, 143–152.

Pollitt, C., Bouckaert, G., 2011. Public Management Reform: A Comparative Analysis-New Public Management, Governance and the Neo-Weberian State. Oxford University Press, Oxford.

Randma-Liiv, T., 2008. New Public Management versus the Neo-Weberian State in Central and Eastern Europe. NISPAcee J. Pub. Admin. Pol. 1 (2), 49–71.

Reinert, E.S., Kattel, R., 2014. Failed and asymmetrical integration: Eastern Europe and the Non-financial origins of the European crisis. In: Sommers, J., Woolfson, C. (Eds.), The Contradictions of Austerity: The Socio-Economic Costs of the Neoliberal Baltic Model. Routledge, London.

RIS3 Guide, 2012. Guide to Research and Innovation Strategies for Smart Specialisations (RIS3). European Commission, Brussels.

Sabel, C.F., Zeitlin, J., 2008. Learning from difference: the new architecture of experimentalist governance in the EU. Eur. Law J. 14 (3), 271–327.

Sabel, C.F., Zeitlin, J. (Eds.), 2010. Experimentalist Governance in the European Union: Towards a New Architecture. Oxford University Press, Oxford.

Schmidt, V.A., 2002. The Futures of European Capitalism. Oxford University Press, Oxford.

Schmidt, V.A., 2008. Discursive institutionalism: the explanatory power of ideas and discourse. Annu. Rev. Pol. Sci. 11, 303–326.

Sörvik, J., Kleibrink, A., 2015. Mapping innovation priorities and specialisation patterns in Europe. S3 Working Paper Series, no. 8/2015.

Stanojevic, M., 2014. Conditions for a neoliberal turn: the cases of Hungary and Slovenia. Eur. J. Ind. Relat. 20 (2), 97–112.

Streeck, W., 2014. Buying Time: The Delayed Crisis of Democratic Capitalism. Verso Books, London.

Suurna, M., Kattel, R., 2010. Europeanization of innovation policy in Central and Eastern Europe. Sci. Pub. Pol. 37 (9), 646–664.

Tulmets, E., 2010. Experimentalist governance in EU external relations: enlargement and the European neighborhood policy. In: Sabel, C.F., Zeitlin, J. (Eds.), Experimentalist Governance in the European Union: Towards a New Architecture. Oxford University Press, Oxford, pp. 297–324.

Veugelers, R., 2014. Undercutting the future? European research spending in times of fiscal consolidation. Bruegel Policy Contribution, no. 2014/06.

Chapter 13

From Strategy to Implementation: The Real Challenge for Smart Specialization Policy

Alasdair Reid*, Nikos Maroulis**

*European Future Innovation System Centre, Louvain-la-Neuve, Belgium;
**Technopolis Group, Brussels, Belgium

Academic Highlights

- This chapter combines a series of concepts from the public policy literature with the smart specialization theory. We use a typology of policy instruments to examine the policy mix used to implement S3.
- The chapter extends the literature on smart specialization. It considers S3 over the policy cycle and examines how entrepreneurial discovery processes can be prolonged into implementation by experimental instruments or novel forms of delivery arrangements (platforms).

Policy Highlights

- The chapter is one of the first attempts to examine cases of the implementation of S3 policies via the European Structural and Investment Funds (ESIF) programming processes.
- We find evidence of novel multiactor/multilevel delivery arrangements in Finland and Scotland: open innovation platforms. While there is potential for

Advances in the Theory and Practice of Smart Specialization. http://dx.doi.org/10.1016/B978-0-12-804137-6.00012-7

replicating such models in Greece and Poland, the current ESIF management arrangements remain dominated by a traditional public agency/management authority model that leaves little room for more experimental and strategic initiatives.

INTRODUCTION

This chapter examines the extent to which smart specialization strategies for research and innovation (S3) (R&I) are translated into a set of instruments (a policy mix) to foster the desired "transformative economic change." Based on Foray et al. (2009), the European Commission's Regional Policy Directorate-General adopted the S3 concept as a strategic planning tool for the European Structural and Investment Funds (ESIF) for 2014–20.[1] An S3 is an *ex-ante* conditionality for ESIF funding for R&I. Across the EU28, the ESIF funding planned for R&I is over EUR40 billion, although the share of total ESIF funding for R&I varies from 4.5% in Romania to 34% in the Netherlands.

An S3 sets priorities for competitive advantage by matching R&I strengths to business needs to address coherently emerging opportunities and market developments, while avoiding duplication and fragmentation of efforts (European Union, 2013a). Critically, an S3 should define the policy mix used to stimulate private R&I investment by taking account of "entrepreneurial knowledge" on technological and market opportunities.

A key to this outcome is that an S3 is designed via what Foray and Goenaga (2013) term as the entrepreneurial discovery process (EDP). Entrepreneurs are defined broadly to include all actors (such as innovative firms, research leaders in higher education, suppliers, users, etc.) that can contribute to jointly discovering the R&I domains in which a region is likely to excel given its existing capabilities and productive assets. As Foray (2014) underlines, the EDP helps develop vertical policy interventions, in addition to horizontal measures, that enable a region to diversify by developing and consolidating new specialties or activities that facilitate the transformation, revival, and renewal of productive structures, and also generate spillovers toward the rest of the economy. Ideally, the EDP should extend beyond the strategy phase with entrepreneurial actors involved in the design and delivery and then updating of the S3. The European Commission has recommended involving entrepreneurs in the design of instruments and of the innovation support system (such as financial support to R&I projects, cooperation platforms, support services, infrastructure, etc.)

Significant experience has been accumulated since the 1990s in developing and implementing regional innovation strategies in European regions (Landabso, 2014). While many regions, with diverse innovation capabilities and profiles, have designed good strategies based on public–private partnerships, the implementation of the strategies through the Structural Fund has proved harder (CSIL, 2016; Technopolis Group, 2006). Indeed, Muscio et al. (2015) found that the regional innovation paradox (the greater need of lagging regions to invest in innovation alongside their relatively lower capacity to absorb funding compared to more-advanced regions) meant that Structural Fund support for R&I has not improved the capacity of Central and Eastern European countries to close the gap with the more-advanced Western European regions.

During 2014–20, the challenge for ESIF-managing authorities is to administer increased R&I funding using novel instruments (such as multisector, crosscutting technologies, multiactor, etc.). Foray and Rainoldi (2013) note that S3 will not succeed "if the policy making capability at regional level does not reach high levels of competence and commitment. This is not a surprise: smart specialization is part of the family of the so-called 'new industrial policy' that aims at designing and deploying sophisticated instruments to make compatible vertical choices for concentrating resources and market dynamics."

In short, smart specialization strategies do not conclude with priority setting. Rather, the EDP should be extended throughout the policy cycle. This chapter draws on concepts from the public policy literature to compare four national cases of implementing smart specialization strategies.

A FRAMEWORK FOR ASSESSING S3: THE POLICY CYCLE, INSTRUMENTS, DIMENSIONS, AND INTERACTIONS

A policy cycle (Fig. 13.1) begins from a "political" decision to reach an objective (or goal). This decision is developed into a strategy that in turn sets agreed targets (or priorities). A policy strategy sets out what a government wants to change: its agenda, and the ways in which public agencies will act to help it achieve this agenda (Stewart, 2004). A strategy is developed into a portfolio of specific policy initiatives that can take various forms: regulatory frameworks, grant funding, indirect (tax) subsidies, equity stakes, the creation of "agencies" or public–private partnerships, etc. Learning from evaluations and feedback from users and stakeholders is used to update the strategy (Fig. 13.1).

For Howlett (2009) successful policy design requires that: (1) policy aims, objectives, and targets be coherent; (2) implementation preferences, policy instruments, and policy tools should also be consistent; and (3) policy aims and implementation preferences, policy objectives, policy instruments, policy targets, and policy tools should also be congruent and convergent.

Once strategic objectives are agreed upon, the next step is to select the set of instruments that a government or public–private partnership should deploy to reach the agreed objective. Hood and Margetts' (2007) NATO typology defines four types of instruments[2] each with a limiting factor in terms of effectiveness:

- **Nodality:** the property of being in the middle of a social network; it provides the government with a strategic position it can use to influence stakeholders and society. The limiting factor is credibility.

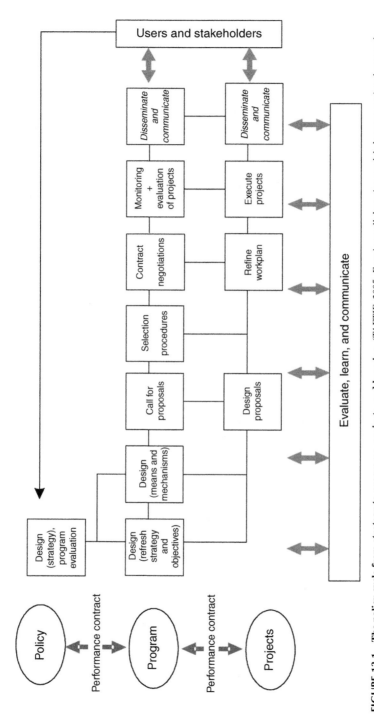

FIGURE 13.1 The policy cycle from strategy to programs, projects, and learning. *(TAFTIE, 2005. Framing collaboration models between national research and technological development programmes. Available from: http://www.taftie.org/content/report-task-force-programme-management-era-era-august-2005)*

- **Authority:** the possession of legal or official power gives the government the ability to determine how other actors in society should act, in a legal or standard setting sense. The limiting factor is a mix of reputation and enforcement capacity.
- **Treasure:** a stock of money or anything that provides value to the policy target. The limiting factor is available funds.
- **Organization:** the stock of people with skills, which gives the government the ability to act directly. The limiting factor is capacity both in terms of the number of people and their technical skills.

Instruments can be used to gather information or influence actors:

- **Detectors:** the instruments used for taking in information (e.g., to inform policy-making choices or to regulate actors).
- **Effectors:** the tools used to try to make an impact on the economy or society.

A second useful distinction (Howlett, 2005) is between:

- **Substantive** policy instruments that directly intervene in social or economic life, and
- **Procedural** (or soft) instruments that seek to affect the participation of selected actors in the policy process itself.

The concepts provide a framework (Table 13.1) to classify policy measures by type of instrument, by their substantive or procedural nature, and by whether they are being used as detectors (D) or effectors (E).

TABLE 13.1 Categorizing Policy Instruments: An Illustrative Framework

	Nodality	Authority	Treasure	Organization
Substantive	Advisory and information services to businesses (E) Online services/portals (D/E)	Laws/regulations (E) Legal (tax, etc.) reporting obligations (D)	Subsidies/grants to companies, research units, training institutes (E)	Government departments or agencies (E) Public–private partnerships (E) Task forces (D/E)
Procedural	Data/statistical collection and analysis (D) Studies and surveys (D) Open data (D/E)	Stakeholder conferences (D/E) Voluntary/self-regulation (E)	Subsidies and grants to support interest group activities or mobilization (D/E)	Interest group creation (D/E) Public consultations conferences (D)

D, Detector; E, effector.
Source: Adapted from Hood, C., and Margetts, H.Z., 2007. The Tools of Government in the Digital Age, second ed. Palgrave, London; Howlett, M., 2011. Designing Public Policies: Principles and Instruments. Routledge, New York, NY; calculations by authors.

While theoretically instruments can be used interchangeably, in practice, specific instruments may be effective in addressing different objectives or target groups. When considering the choice of possible S3 instruments, four main criteria can be used:

- Visibility in budgeting and policy review activities,
- Intrusiveness or degree of coercion required for effectiveness,
- Cost (absolute cost, but also relative effectiveness), and
- Automaticity or use of existing structures versus creation of new structures.

The criteria serve to calibrate instruments to targets, thus enabling a choice of instruments that target most precisely the factors and actors concerned (Fig. 13.2). As an example, a government agency may choose to boost business R&D expenditure through: information campaigns encouraging companies to invest in innovation, legislation (standards or regulations leveraging investment), and financial measures (such as grants, R&D tax breaks, etc.), or by supporting new private or public–private risk-taking investors (such as business angels, etc.). Each choice has a different likelihood of achieving the desired aim: an information campaign may be low cost, but is unlikely to have a significant impact. Similarly, tax relief may have a lower administrative cost and be more "automatic" than grant funding, but it does not target "underinnovating" businesses.

In practice, governments design a policy mix of instruments that provides the best chance of meeting the stated objective in the context of national or regional innovation systems (Izsák et al., 2015; Reid, 2011). Nauwelaers et al. (2014) argued that S3 policy mixes need to evolve from silo- to outcome-driven

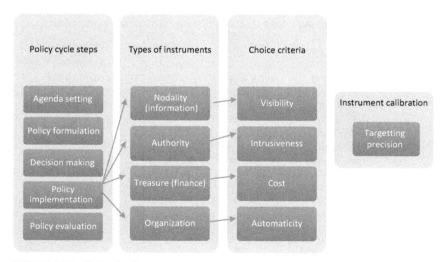

FIGURE 13.2 Policy implementation: instrument choice criteria and calibration. *(Adapted from Howlett, M., 2011. Designing Public Policies: Principles and Instruments. Routledge, New York, NY.)*

approaches, implying that "the design of policy mixes should start from policy objectives (desired outcomes) rather than from a realignment of the instruments seen from a policy managers' perspective." Hence, an S3 policy mix should:

- imply more than incremental improvements in existing portfolios,
- incorporate both vertical and horizontal instruments,
- span domains and vary per specialization area, and
- avoid one problem: one-policy instrument approaches.

S3 implementation procedures should foster innovation platforms that create a framework (legal, organizational, resources, facilities, digital, funding, etc.), enabling many actors to be involved, and provide comprehensive support to the entire innovation cycle, including financial, technological, productive, and market capabilities (Komninos et al., 2014). Moreover, the Commission stressed that ESIF funding should be combined with other private and public national or European funds to deliver S3 objectives.

Other dimensions and interactions in the S3 process can complicate the choice and design of priorities and instruments. In large or federal countries, the regional S3 needs to take account of national S3 priorities (whether developed earlier or in parallel). During both the design and implementation phases, an innovation agency needs to align interventions with those of other organizations supporting economic development (e.g., skills agencies). From an open innovation perspective, there is a rationale to ensure that regional firms can access complementary expertise and technologies through global value chains (Brennan and Rakhmatullin, 2015). The Vanguard Initiative's work on interregional value chains and thematic S3 platforms in energy or agrifood is an example of efforts that are required to generate interregional synergies on S3 priorities.

Our assumption is that these various dimensions, interactions, and tensions between instruments (in line with Flanagan et al., 2011) introduce a layer of complexity to policy design and delivery that may complicate the effective implementation of smart specialization.

ASSESSING S3 IMPLEMENTATION IN FOUR COUNTRIES: ARE POLICY INSTRUMENTS COHERENT WITH S3 RHETORIC?

In the aforementioned conceptual framework, S3 is part of a policy cycle that requires the translation of selected priorities into instruments calibrated (and adjusted over time) to the needs of entrepreneurial actors. In this section, we review the S3 policy cycle process in four countries with diverse innovation systems and levels of performance, governance quality, and degrees of dependence on ESIF (Table 13.2). For each case, we consider three main questions:

- Has the EDP extended beyond the strategy phase into implementation?
- How are S3s translated into ESIF Operational Programs (OPs)?
- Do the ESIF OPs incorporate novel or systemic S3 instruments?

TABLE 13.2 Case Selection

Cases	Economic and innovation performance	Policy approach to smart specialization	EPD
Finland	High income/close to technology frontier ESIF provides marginal share of RDI funding	National strategy targets four business ecosystems S3 at regional level as part of growth pact with national government	Regional partnerships mobilizing Active international positioning (e.g., Vanguard Initiative)
Scotland	High income, weak business innovation ESIF declining source of R&I funding	National strategy focused on six key growth sectors and entrepreneurial culture, strong emphasis on low-carbon economy	Driven by enterprise agencies and industry leadership groups Efforts to identify higher value–added niche
Poland	Catching-up country with strong economic growth, but weak business innovation ESIF important source of funds for RDI	National strategy aims to "rebalance" by increasing business R&D and science–industry linkages	National S3 priorities are "science based" Regions used variety of EDP approaches to design RIS3
Greece	Innovation and economy laggard ESIF critical funding source for R&I system	Emphasis is placed on key sectors for national economy and improving their export potential	National S3 priorities are to a large extent "science based" Regional priorities are more business based, agrofood, etc.

EPD, Entrepreneurial discovery process; ESIF, European Structural and Investment Funds; RDI, research, development, and innovation; R&I, research and innovation.

Before examining the S3 implementation process, we sketch the recent trends in the economic and innovation systems of the four countries. Of the four, only Poland emerged "untouched" after the financial crisis, enjoying an increase in gross domestic product (GDP) per capita since 2008 (Fig. 13.3). Due to a weakly diversified economic structure and export profile, the Finnish economy suffered from both structural decline (e.g., information technology sector post-Nokia and the paper industry) and external shocks (in its largest export market, Russia). Scotland's significant financial sector was hit and the economy fell back after 2009 and had not returned to 2008 standards by 2014. Greek GDP per capita dropped from near EU28 average in 2008 to 72% of the EU average in 2014.

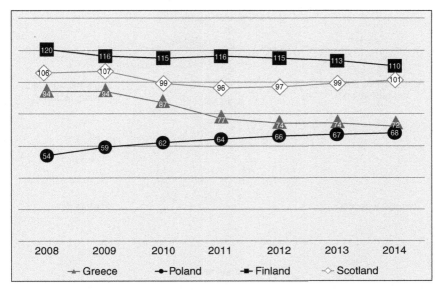

FIGURE 13.3   Gross domestic product (GDP) per capita (in PPS, EU28 = 100). *PPS,* Purchasing power standard. *(Data taken from Eurostat: GDP at current market prices, in PPS (nama_10r_2gdp).)*

The structural crisis in Finland is illustrated by the sharp decline in 2009 in gross value added (GVA) and the further slump in 2012–13. In contrast, Scotland bounced back with higher GVA growth rates since 2011 than the EU28 average. Poland's relative economic health is clear from the positive trend in GVA growth rates. Despite some signs of recovery, structural impediments in the Greek economy weaken the potential for export-led growth (Böwer et al., 2014).

Compared to the three other countries, the employment structure of the Finnish economy is strongly orientated toward high-tech sectors with a notable lead in high-tech knowledge-intensive services (KIS) and a strong position in high–medium tech manufacturing. Scotland lags behind both Finland and Poland in high-tech manufacturing, and does barely better than Poland and Greece in high-tech KIS; however, Scotland has a strong position in financial services.

Greek employment intensity in KI-market services is similar to the intensities of Finland's and Scotland's, but otherwise Greece is structurally weak in high-tech and KI employment. Using arts, entertainment, and recreation employment as a proxy for the creative classes (Florida, 2012) that drive entrepreneurial dynamics, Scotland performs relatively better, followed by Finland. Greece and Poland lag (Fig. 13.4).

Finland remains among the top-ranked countries for R&D expenditure despite falling by 11% between 2011 and 2014 (from EUR7.2 billion to EUR6.4 billion). Gross domestic expenditure on R&D (GERD) as a share of GDP declined from a high of 3.75% in 2009 to 3% in 2015, partly explained by Nokia's

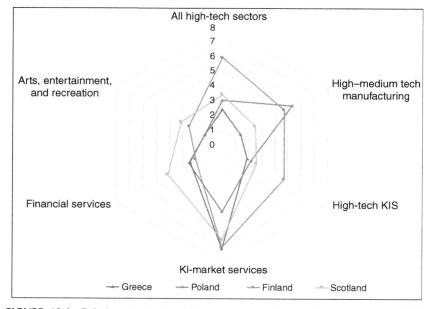

FIGURE 13.4 Relative structures of four economies (% of active employment, 2015). *(Data taken from Eurostat: Employment in technology and knowledge-intensive sectors (KIS) by Nomenclature of Territorial Units for Statistics (NUTS) 2 regions and sex (from 2008 onward, NACE Rev. 2) (htec_emp_reg2).)*

collapse. However, public funding of R&D has also declined. Despite one of the lowest rates in the OECD[3] of government funding (including tax incentives) for business expenditure on R&D (BERD), Finland stands out in terms of the scale of investment by the business sector. This is a specific weak point of Scotland, which, in contrast, has the highest rate (relative to GDP) of R&D investment in the higher-education sector (Fig. 13.5). In per capita terms, Finland invested over EUR1200 per inhabitant in 2013, compared to EUR462 in Scotland, EUR133 in Greece, and only EUR90 in Poland.

The Scottish economy is dominated by medium-tech manufacturing (e.g., food and drink), but is highly specialized in energy. Scotland's internationally excellent university research is not enough to offset the underperforming business sector (low R&D expenditure and weak innovation outcomes).

The business contribution to Poland's GERD exceeds that of higher education. However, in terms of innovation performance, Poland has not achieved the breakthrough required for Polish firms to improve their position in global value chains. The Polish economy remains resource (energy and carbon)-intensive, and has a product specialization biased toward low- or medium–low technology goods, which rely on comparatively cheap employment costs (EC, 2015).

Greece lags the EU average in all R&D and innovation indicators, and its business expenditure at 0.28% of GDP is the lowest in the European Union

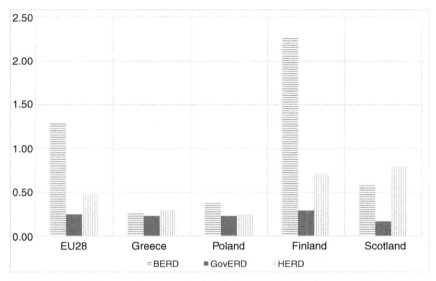

FIGURE 13.5   R&D expenditure as a % of GDP (2013). *BERD*, Business expenditure on R&D; *GovERD*, government expenditure on R&D; *HERD*, higher-education expenditure on R&D. *(Data taken from Eurostat: Total intramural R&D expenditure (GERD) by sectors of performance and NUTS 2 regions (rd_e_gerdreg).)*

(average 1.3%). Public funds accounted for 63% of GERD in 2013,[4] and Maroulis and Mikroglou (2013) estimated that in 2007–13 ESIF and the 7th Research Framework Programme (FP) contributed 17% of GERD and 33% of the Greek research funding.

To sum up, all four countries have structural weaknesses in their economic or innovation system. A common challenge is the economic diversification by developing higher value–added, internationally traded product niches that are complementary to or build on existing capabilities in line with the S3 theory.

From Smart Specialization Strategy to Implementation: Four Cases

In this section, we examine how our four selected countries have designed their S3s through an "EPD," and the resulting policy mix of instruments chosen to implement S3-type policies.

Finnish competitiveness policy has focused on four areas since the mid-2000s: bioeconomy, cleantech, digital (notably games), and health and well-being (BCDH). This reflects an effort to diversify the economy away from traditional core sectors with relatively low value added (such as forestry, basic chemicals, etc.), and to redirect the skilled employees affected by the electronics crisis to help boost other sectors. A key challenge is to internationalize the emerging business ecosystems (composed of smaller technology start-ups) and position them in global value chains (Reid et al., 2016).

The government elected in 2015 maintained the focus on the BCDH priorities, but cut grant support for business R&D (via Tekes, the Finnish Funding Agency for Innovation). It shifted the focus to loan, guarantee, and equity investments in support of start-ups and high-growth firms in the BCDH areas, as well as for restructuring enterprises and internationalization on a horizontal basis. As part of a cost-cutting agenda, the government is pursuing enhanced interagency collaboration through Team Finland,[5] with the colocation of key agencies in one building, signaling a virtual merger. At the national level, the Growth Programmes aim at internationalizing Finnish firms in key sectors and deliver a mix of financial support and services through the multiagency "Team Finland" platform with a budget of EUR51 million for 2015–17 (Halme et al., 2016). Team Finland incorporates the 15 Centres for Economic Development, Transport, and the Environment (ELY Centres), which are responsible for the regional implementation and development tasks of the central government.[6]

Finland's Sustainable Growth and Work (2014) OP covers all the regions. The investment strategy is structured around 10 challenges including "unbalanced economic structure, weakened international competitiveness of business and low number of growth companies" and "expanding the R&I base." Total ESIF funds for Finland for 2014–20 account for roughly 5% of the expected national public investment in the areas supported (EC, 2016a).

The OP stated that the ex-ante conditionality is met by the National Innovation strategy (2011–15), the Innovative Cities Programme (INKA), and the processes for drafting regional RIS3. The first round of INKA was cofunded by the Structural Funds (using 2007–13 money) and aimed to align the objectives of the national innovation strategy and regional R&I strategies. The national ministry selected five main themes, based on areas in which Finnish know-how can be strengthened and used to boost growth, namely, future healthcare, bioeconomy, clean and sustainable industrial technology, intelligent and innovative cities, and cybersecurity. At the regional level, the S3 concept was applied in the development of the strategies for 2014–17, approved by the Regional Assemblies in spring 2014. These strategies clarified the use of ESIF funding regionally, especially in the fields of R&I.

In Finland, the Sustainable Growth and Work OP foresaw that investments would be focused particularly on the development of strong regional sectors, as well as the identification of sectors undergoing change. In 2014, the previous support for regional innovation clusters through the longstanding Centre of Expertise Program (OSKE) was replaced by INKA. Approximately 10% of European Regional Development Fund (ERDF) resources was originally earmarked to INKA, and 12 urban regions were selected, which were created and strengthened to be internationally attractive innovation clusters. The funding awarded by INKA was dedicated to businesses with internationally marketable products tested in real urban environments that solve challenges faced by smart cities.

Although launched as planned in 2014, the Finnish government, elected in 2015, decided to phase out INKA from 2017. A European Investment Bank

SME Instrument initiative was developed to replace it, and EUR40 million from the ESIF and national budget was allocated to leverage commercial lending through a risk-sharing mechanism. The expectation is that the financial instrument will act as a catalyst for private investment and foster job creation within the SME community.[7] However, the new financial instrument is horizontal and no longer aligned with specific priorities.

Nevertheless, the nationally funded Witty (Smart) City initiative (2013–17) supported collaborative projects between business, municipalities, and research bodies to provide companies with opportunities to bring new products and services to the market. In addition, the ESIF OP foresaw that the Integrated Territorial Investments strategy (ITI) would foster open innovation platforms and use open data with a view of sustainable urban development. The Six AIKA (Six Cities) "open and smart services" program was initiated by the largest Finnish cities (i.e., Helsinki, Espoo, Vantaa, Oulu, Tampere, and Turku). The ERDF, the Six Cities, and the Finnish Government made available a funding of nearly EUR80 million to projects in three focus areas:

- open data and interfaces (to support the development of electronic services that span multiple sectors, from online and health services to energy, traffic, logistics, and resource management);
- open participation and "customership" (creating new user-oriented models, by combining the potential of the largest cities on a national level via user- and demand-oriented trials of new public services); and
- open innovation platforms.

Innovation platforms are environments that enable the development of new products, services, and markets, allowing the entire city community to work together to create new services, solutions, and businesses. In other words, innovation platforms are tools that cover the entire life cycle of a service, from idea to testing and from testing to product. These measures are divided into two main activity types. The first focuses on developing innovation platforms, such as tools and operating models. The other is implemented with pilot projects that aim to overcome challenges related to, for example, mobility, local services, well-being, and cultural services (Raunio et al., 2016).

Since 2007, the *Scottish* Government's Economic Strategy (SGES) (updated in 2011 and in 2015)[8] is the overarching framework for all public sector investment in economic and social development, including R&I. The 2015 Strategy kept the emphasis on raising productivity and innovation and on reinforcing internationalization in selected growth sectors (identified in 2011). Importantly, the strategy adds a fourth pillar: inclusive growth (tackling inequality). Economic policy is based on the principle that delivering sustainable growth and addressing long-standing inequalities are reinforcing, and not competing, objectives. Another key change is the adoption of a "One Scotland" approach, whereby strategy implementation is delivered by a partnership of government and public agencies, universities and colleges, the third sector, and the private sector. It is noteworthy that the SGES mentioned European partnerships, such as the Vanguard Initiative, as a means to cooperate on smart specialization and align with European innovation policy.

Prior to 2007, Scotland had standalone science and innovation strategies; however, innovation is now a core element of the economic strategy and universities are one of the six "growth sectors." The economic strategy sets out actions to foster business innovation (including customer-led/supply chain and cooperation between large and small firms), the development of eight industry-led Innovation Centers, workplace innovation, and public sector innovation.

The Scottish OPs adopted the "Growth Sectors" of the Scottish Government's Economy Strategy as the S3 priorities. There was a limited engagement with the S3 concept, partly because of the preexisting strategic focus on the six growth sectors and their associated industry leadership groups, which provide sectoral stakeholder platforms that support an EDP-like process. Moreover, an acknowledged "entrepreneurial deficit" was addressed by a broad-based partnership that developed and agreed to implement the "Scotland CAN DO" action plan (Scottish Government, 2013, 2014). While this is a cross-cutting plan, specific strategic plans have been developed, notably a Manufacturing Future for Scotland action plan in February 2016 (with a strong emphasis on the circular economy), as well as plans for life and chemical sciences, industrial biotechnology, food and drink, as well as other sectors. Moreover, the ESIF OP foresaw that the national enterprise agencies would further refine the focus on specific subsectors and key enabling technologies. The Scottish Enterprise commissioned a cluster-mapping study in 2015 (Izsák et al., 2016).

The Scottish ESIF OPs are designed to maximize the impact of investments, and are structured around specific themes. Large-scale funding allocations (minimum of EUR15 million) known as Strategic Interventions (SI)[9] are administered by lead partners who are responsible for distributing smaller-scale amounts of money to eligible projects. Each SI has a defined aim, for example, to increase the competitiveness of SMEs, or improve the quality of green spaces in Scotland's urban areas. The Business Innovation SI secured an investment of GBP31 million from the ERDF to support businesses to develop new products and services, and collaborate with universities. The Lead Partners are: Scottish Enterprise, Highlands and Islands Enterprise, and the Scottish Funding Council. The overall investment figure is expected to be in the region of GBP78 million till the end of 2018. The SI aims to:

- promote business investment in R&I, develop links and synergy between enterprises, R&D centers, and Scotland's higher-education sector;
- promote investment in the development of products and services, technology transfer, social innovation, ecoinnovation, public service applications, networking, clusters, and open innovation through smart specialization; and
- increase business commercialization and investment in research, technological development, and innovation (RTDI), particularly in sectors identified through smart specialization.

The ESIF OP priority axis foresaw 12 types of actions, including grants for business R&D or technology adoption and innovation vouchers, to help firms engage with academic research. However, as in Finland, there is a shift toward demand-driven and systemic (innovation platform, value chain, etc.) instruments, such as:

- Encouraging business networking, particularly large-to-SME and supply chain development. This includes a Scottish Enterprise open innovation initiative, where smaller firms compete in challenge competitions to solve the innovation needs of larger firms or public sector bodies.
- The Smart Cities SI (led by Glasgow and involving all seven Scottish cities) allocated GBP10 million of ERDF (out of a total budget of GBP40 million) to support the use of innovative technology. This includes opening up access to nonpersonal data to allow the development of new applications and services, and funding of pilots of smart-city technology, which support individual service areas and capture data to allow wider and responsive city management.
- The implementation of the Manufacturing Action Plan is supported by the Resource Efficient Circular Economy SI. A Circular Economy Investment Fund will help manufacturers develop innovative technologies and business models from the proof-of-concept stage through to implementation. A Circular Economy Service will offer support to businesses to redesign their processes and products.

The OP foresaw support related to smart specializations for businesses to engage with EU knowledge and innovation communities (KIC), including use of ESIF Article 70.[10] In practice, Scottish S3 thinking has been driven by the involvement in the Vanguard Initiative pilots on advanced manufacturing (notably on offshore energy-related technologies).

Since accession to the European Union, the *Polish* economy has grown at rates well above the European average, thanks to competitive employment costs and the enhanced access of Polish companies to European industrial and consumer product markets. ESIF has contributed to these developments, by coinvesting in upgrading production capacities and technologies, and in improving infrastructure (such as transport, communications, energy, etc.). However, in the 2017–13 period, most funding was allocated to measures aimed at creating or upgrading academic research infrastructure or for "technology absorption" in the business sector (Klincewicz and Szkuta, 2015).

The national S3 priorities were defined through foresight exercises on scientific and industrial strengths, patent analysis, and a stakeholder consultation. The Ministry of Economic Development led this process that drew up a list of 20 smart specializations.[11] The S3 priorities are not a separate strategy, but are embedded in other strategies and policy documents as guidelines for investment and funding instruments (the Enterprise Development Program, the Research Infrastructure roadmap, and the ESIF OP). However, Miller et al. (2014) argue that there was a lack of leadership of the S3 process due to fragmented responsibilities across national ministries.[12] Moreover, the 16 regions ran their own S3 exercises to define priorities under the regional ESIF OPs. Indeed, there was no attempt to align national and regional S3 priorities before 2015 (Klincewicz and Szkuta, 2015).

However, the S3 concept was not well understood and priorities were defined extensively, incorporating all related technologies and research areas and thus diluting the potential benefits of focused interventions (Klincewicz and Szkuta, 2015). There was also an emphasis on identifying existing key technologies or leading sectors rather than enhancing interaction and exchange and a "self-learning EPD to be carried out throughout 2014–2020" (Miller et al., 2014).

Diverse approaches were used to develop the regional S3 (World Bank, 2015). The Pomorskie (Pomerania) region used an open competition inviting broad-based partnerships to define S3 areas. An international panel evaluated the call and awarded funding from the regional OP to four partnerships: offshore, port and logistics; interactive and information-rich technologies; ecoefficient technology; and medical technologies for lifestyle and aging diseases. However, most regions used a more traditional mix of statistical and consultative methods to analyze regional strengths and potential approaches. This means that most regional S3 were designed using an old-style top-down process, with little involvement from "entrepreneurial stakeholders," especially "nonincumbent" firms (World Bank, 2015).

The Commission approved the national and regional OPs, but asked the Polish authorities to define an on-going EDP, and improve coordination between national and regional S3 priorities. A World Bank project supported five regions to experiment methods, such as crowdsourcing, innovation maps, and smart labs, (World Bank, 2015) to enrich the EDP process.

The national and regional S3 processes are mirrored by a national OP for Smart Growth and 16 regional OPs (ROPs). The OP Smart Growth (OPSG) aspires to build a "more coherent system of support instruments addressing the whole innovation cycle from research to market innovation." The OP is structured in four priorities: support for R&D activity of enterprises (45% of funds), support for the environment and capacity of enterprises for research, development, and innovation (RDI) activity (12%), support for innovation in enterprises (25%), and increase in the research potential (14%). Priority one includes funding for sectoral R&D programs that are developed, partly, in response to S3 priorities. Although grant funding remains the main form of finance, there is a shift to support through financial instruments, so that more private investment can be leveraged. The OPSG accounts for almost 70% of ESIF funding allocated to S3 instruments, and hence most measures will be implemented centrally.

The adoption of the OPSG paved the way for launching a series of new or updated instruments. During the OP negotiation, the Commission expressed concerns that insufficient attention was being paid to the barriers and incentives for business innovation. Klincewicz and Szkuta (2015) argue that most instruments were previously available, but have been streamlined (e.g., proposal evaluation processes better targeting innovativeness and commercial potential). Moreover, the "industry-led" sector R&D programs are more demand driven and are based on a value chain logic rather than on a strict sectoral/industrial classification (Mieszkowski and Kardas, 2015).

Most public funding for business R&D is distributed by the National Centre for Research and Development (NCBR), with instruments covering the "innovation cycle." Preexisting measures include: fast-track open call (decision within 60 days) for business R&D projects, Demonstrator+ targeting pilot installations or proof-of-concept activities, and applied R&D funding by consortia of scientific and business organizations. NCBR manages sectoral programs, such as Innomed (medical technologies), Innolot (aviation), Innochem (chemical engineering), Innotextile (technologically advanced textiles), and InnoSBZ (unmanned aerial vehicles). The agency also oversees strategic national and regional R&D programs consistent with S3 and responding to business needs.

The Polish Agency for Enterprise Development (PARP) manages programs covering intellectual property and technology transfer (including match-making database, innovation vouchers for SMEs to cover R&D services by scientific organizations, and financing IPR protection) and the internationalization of key clusters (selected in a nationwide competition), as well as projects that involve implementing innovations developed or licensed by enterprises that contribute to the launch of new products or services.

Due to the very low use of venture and other equity instruments to support innovative firms (EC, 2016b), the European Fund for Strategic Investments (EFSI) is providing guarantees aimed at high-risk, innovative, or research-oriented companies' needs with the first agreements signed in 2015 between the European Investment Fund (EIF) and Polish banks. Related nonfinancial support includes services to boost the international exposure of innovative companies, such as "Polish technological bridges," and accelerator platforms to help selected high-tech companies expand internationally.

Despite some of the identified weaknesses in the S3 process, in 2016, the new Polish Government adopted an "Action plan for the responsible development of Poland"[13] acknowledging that to "avoid a middle-income trap requires building global specializations of the Polish economy." The action plan places an increased emphasis on inclusive growth and is structured around five main pillars: reindustrialization, development of innovative companies, capital for development, foreign expansion, and social and regional development. The five pillars are underpinned by efforts to create a more efficient state (through e-government and intelligent procurement). The S3 proposes measures to boost R&D innovation in specific sectors and support the deployment of cutting-edge technologies. The Action Plan continues with development programs for priority sectors, such as aviation, armaments, ship building, chemical, food, transport, and IT.

The *Greek* economic policy, since 2010, has been conducted in the context of the EU/IMF economic adjustment agenda. Thus, the proactive economic policies have been solely supported by EU funds. National R&I budgets are used to cover operational costs and salaries of permanent research staff, while funding for research projects, investments, and project-based personnel comes from ESIF and the European Union's Research FP (Tsipouri et al., 2016). The Structural Funds keep the overall R&D system running, while the FP funding has orientated organizations toward EU priorities rather than national specializations. If ESIF R&I funding is focused on S3 priorities, this risks depriving a significant share of the research community of project funding. Hence, there is political pressure against selective funding that applies criteria other than quality.

In terms of past priorities, the Greek competitive advantages (Komninos et al., 2014) are services, such as information and communication technology (ICT) and health, and in industries, such as agriculture and food, biomedical, energy, and chemical. Yet, Greek economic and innovation has largely avoided targeting specific areas, while Structural Funds support for R&I has been nationally managed and has taken no account of regional specificities during 2007–13 (Reid et al., 2012). Despite mentioning S3, the 2016 development law (Hellenic Republic, 2016a) maintains this horizontal approach, although it does provide greater scope for cooperation and cluster actions and for a shift from grants to tax and equity instruments (Hellenic Republic, 2016b).

The General Secretariat for Research and Technology (GSRT) under the Ministry of Education led the design and implementation of the national S3 (GSRT, 2015). In parallel, the regional authorities developed S3 from 2013 without coordinating with the Ministry of Economy (responsible for the design and implementation of the OPs) and the GSRT (national S3). An effort to coordinate started in 2014 with the acknowledgment of the de facto allocation of labor between the GSRT and the regions (Greek Ministry of Development, 2014). The parallel design of the national and 14 regional S3s without early coordination increased complexity and limited potential synergies.

Nationally, the EDP was based on innovation platforms created by the GSRT. The process resulted in a National Strategy for Research, Technological Development, and Innovation (ESETAK) and the identification of eight priority fields. However, the platforms were mainly discussion forums dominated by the research community. Despite the participation of companies, only a few of the platforms (e.g., agrofood) managed to engage businesses actively and set up thematic working groups, which presented specific proposals. However, it is planned that the GSRT platforms, in one form or another, will continue to play a role during the implementation phase.

Due to the mandate of GSRT, the strategy initially focused strictly on R&I without considering synergies with other policy domains, such as entrepreneurship or the national digital strategy. Such synergies were explored only later, during the translation of the S3 into OP objectives and measures. Moreover, the S3 intervention logic was designed in three pillars, without any reference to the specialization areas (investing in the creation and dissemination of new knowledge;

strengthening investment in R&I; and developing innovative attitudes, institutions, and RTDI links with society to address social challenges). These were to be delivered by four forms of intervention: R&I capacity building, support of R&I activities, support of infrastructures, and networking and internationalization.

Regionally, with the encouragement of the European Commission, diverse approaches to EDP were explored, including setting up of Innovation Councils to mobilize the private sector. Although the GSRT proposed a legal status for Regional Research and Innovation Councils (law 4310/2014), a 2016 amendment (law 4386/2016) increased the research community's position at the expense of business and innovation interests. In practice, only a few regions managed to set up a council that was actively involved in S3 planning. During the implementation phase, a new EDP process will be designed for all regional S3s, based on a pilot exercise implemented by the European Commission's Joint Research Centre in Anatoliki Macedonia Thraki (Boden et al., 2016).

The national S3 budget is EUR3.6 billion, of which EUR2.5 billion (69%) is cofinanced by the ESIF and national funds. It is expected that another EUR1.1 billion will be leveraged from the private sector. The OP for Competitiveness, Entrepreneurship, and Innovation (EPANEK) is expected to contribute EUR1.4 billion to this total. However, in practice, only EUR859 million (or 34% of the total planned S3 budget) was "ring fenced" under the R&I thematic objective (TO) for the specialization areas. Under the digital and entrepreneurship TOs, there is no upfront budgetary commitment to support S3 priorities.

From an operational perspective, there are three groups of specific objectives and interventions. The *first group* includes R&I measures, designed by GSRT, and funded under EPANEK, and is expected to address the S3 priorities. However, they are horizontal in character and were designed independently from the S3 priorities. These include a grant scheme for supporting the setting up and development of innovative start-ups (with an indicative budget of EUR540 million), a measure supporting innovative clusters where businesses collaborate with academia (EUR300 million), and a grant scheme to support private RTDI projects (EUR318 million) (Tsipouri et al., 2016).

The *second* group, under the ESIF TOs for digital, entrepreneurship, and human resources, was designed by the Ministry of Economy with limited coordination with the GSRT. It is likely that only a fraction of the funding will be directed to S3 priorities. The *third* group of measures under other OPs (such as agriculture, fisheries, etc.) was designed by other ministries based on their agenda without considering the S3 priorities.

Given the GSRT's mandate, the national S3 initially focused on R&D and innovation without considering the synergies with other policy domains, such as entrepreneurship. Such synergies were explored only later during the translation of the S3 into OP objectives and measures. During the S3 design process, synergies with other policies were identified, such as the need for improving the regulatory framework for public procurement or coordination with sectoral ministries for precommercial procurement. However, no mechanism was specified.

TABLE 13.3 Selected Instruments Relevant to S3 Implementation

	Nodality	Authority	Treasure	Organization
Finland	Open innovation platforms (major cities)	Regulatory issues are key to demand driven policies	Six AIKA "open and smart services" program	Team Finland multiagency delivery
Scotland	"Scotland Can Do" partnership Scottish cities network	Public sector innovation Procurement reform	Open innovation program Innovation centers	"One Scotland" multiagency delivery Strategic intervention partnerships
Poland	National task forces for S3	e-Government administrative improvements Procurement reform	National and regional sectoral/S3 programs	National Innovation Council S3 monitoring system
Greece	GSRT innovation platforms	Reforms to RTDI-related legal framework Procurement reform	Greater emphasis on innovative cluster approaches	Regional Research and Innovation Councils

GSRT, General Secretariat for Research and Technology; RTDI, research, technological development, and innovation.

In the regions, a single public authority was responsible for the design of the entire OP and for combining different policy domains into the S3 to make it a coherent strategy. In contrast to the national OPs, most regions allocated their budget on a priority basis. Most regions (e.g., Attiki, Sterea Ellada, Ionia Nisia, Notio Aigaio, and Ipeiros) structured their strategy around the identified priorities and tailored their interventions to these needs. The regional S3s proposed interesting approaches that brought together activities from various policy domains, and targeted economic activities and technologies along priority value chains. Examples include the metal clusters in Sterea Ellada and Thessaly, the health and well-being cluster in Ipeiros, and the agrofood and tourism priorities in most regions. However, the requirement stipulated by ESIF guidelines to group activities by TOs and by the Fund dismantled the systemic instruments and regrouped the various components into artificial lists of measures serving very broad objectives (Table 13.3).

CONCLUSIONS AND LESSONS FROM S3 IMPLEMENTATION

This chapter has reviewed the experiences of four diverse European countries in adapting existing policy frameworks and governance arrangements to the smart specialization concept. It has also examined the extent to which S3-type strategies have been translated operationally through different types of instruments and operational management setups.

In the two more-advanced countries, smart specialization was not adopted in a systematic way. S3 was an "add-on" to the existing policy systems and was used as a "focusing device" to refine existing competitiveness and innovation priorities. In Finland, S3 was largely ignored at the national level, but adopted more enthusiastically by regions, feeding into a partnership-based planning process structured around lead city regions. In Scotland, S3 has been used as a trigger to "dig deeper" into the emerging opportunities existing in the nationally defined "growth sectors" (without a specific regional differentiation).

In Greece and Poland, the national S3 processes were run in parallel to regional S3 with an initial lack of coordination and with differing approaches. Nationally, the exercises adopted a "technology"-driven approach with "task forces" that included the usual suspects from academia and established firms, rather than mobilizing more entrepreneurial forces. Regionally, the focus tended to be on consolidating perceived business strengths, although efforts to introduce more novel EDP processes were observed regionally in both countries.

In all four countries, there is a relative vagueness with respect to the amount of ESIF funding directly targeted to the defined S3 priorities. Although ESIF funding has been allocated to S3 in all countries, it is unclear to what extent the S3 priorities are effectively translated into operational guidelines that prevent managing authorities defaulting back to a horizontal approach. The translation of "S3 priorities" into the ESIF OPs has been done through implementation guidelines (e.g., S3 priorities imposed as one criterion for project selection). In all cases, significant shares of ESIF funds allocated to S3 are likely to be allocated to standard "horizontal" funding measures for business R&D, industry–academic cooperation, or technology transfer. In Finland, the INKA initiative to support regional S3 processes was shelved as early as 2015, and replaced by a horizontal SME financing scheme.

Summarizing the instruments using the NATO typology, there is a clear distinction between the two more-advanced countries (Finland and Scotland), which have been more active in supporting "nodality." They have done this by encouraging the development of partnerships around, but not necessarily led by, the government, notably giving a leadership role to the major cities (Table 13.4). These measures can be considered as both detector- and effector-type instruments. Similar efforts to structure coalitions of innovative actors exist in Greece and Poland, but these tend to remain part of more formal and "bureaucratic" governance systems (such as task forces, etc.), essentially for detecting needs. Regulatory reform to support the S3 priorities is not given significant attention in any of the four countries, at least formally in the S3 and ESIF programming documents. Nevertheless, all countries have on-going efforts to enhance regulatory and administrative systems, notably the use of innovative public procurement tools.

TABLE 13.4 Policy Actors' Roles in S3 Implementation

Role	Finland	Scotland	Poland	Greece
Policy principal	Ministry of Economic Affairs and Employment	Scottish Government Enterprise agencies	Ministry of Economic Development Regional governments	National ministries (GSRT, Economic Development) Regional Councils
Policy entrepreneurs	Cities and regional partnerships	Industry leadership groups	National S3 task forces Regional partnerships	Innovation platforms Regional Innovation Councils
Policy targets	Innovation platforms Financial institutions	Innovation centers in key priorities Financial institutions	Industry–academic consortia Financial institutions	Universities and research centers Financial institutions
Policy implementation agents	National agencies and regional ELY centres City partnerships	Strategic intervention partnerships City partnerships	Research and enterprise agencies NCBR and PARP	Special management authorities GSRT
Policy beneficiaries	Businesses in selected national or regional priority areas	Businesses in selected national growth sectors	Businesses and public–academic researchers in S3 priorities	Businesses and public–academic researchers in S3 priorities

ELY, Centres for Economic Development, Transport, and the Environment; NCBR, National Centre for Research and Development; PARP, Polish Agency for Enterprise Development.

Both the advanced countries have more experimental demand-driven implementation models, which aim to structure interventions through innovation platforms. These strategic partnerships adopt open innovation methods to tackle societal challenges using innovative technologies and developing new products and public services. The seeds of such approaches exist in Poland (e.g., Pomorskie region) and in Greece (Tsipouri et al., 2016); however, the dependence on ESIF limits the space for deploying more innovative instruments, which increase selectivity, especially in the case of Greece.

Turning to the extent to which ESIF governance arrangements are likely to foster an on-going EDP over the entire policy cycle, Table 13.4 positions key actors in the four countries, applying the roles proposed by Flanagan et al. (2011).

The Finnish and Scottish models (Team Finland and One Scotland) are examples of a shift to multiagency management spanning policy domains and governance levels. The use of strategic partnerships to deliver ESIF interventions (such as bringing together key national agencies with public–private consortia, health sector, city alliances, etc.) illustrates how the four types of NATO instruments can be combined to effectively respond to identified smart specialization–type priorities. Policy experimentation continues poststrategy by involving a wide range of private firms, public agencies, and users in delivery. These types of management models and instruments appear more likely to foster the active experimentation and discovery during implementation that Rodriguez-Pose and Wilkie (2017) underline is a critical feature of a well-functioning EDP.

In contrast, in Poland and Greece, the model remains dominated by a "lead" public agency managing a range of specific measures intended to cover the perceived "innovation cycle." Both Poland and Greece face the challenge of aligning the ESIF funding instruments to the identified S3 opportunities, at both national and regional levels, so that "horizontal" instruments can be better tailored to the needs of entrepreneurial actors in each priority area (EC, 2016b; Tsipouri et al., 2016). The need to extend the EDP process during implementation is acknowledged in both countries, and on-going initiatives are in place. However, the desire to develop more open, demand-driven, and partnership approaches may continue to face obstacles at national level, due to an overprocedural, rigid, and risk averse interpretation of ESIF regulations.

ENDNOTES

1. The European Structural and Investment Funds (ESIF) regulations (European Union, 2013b; Article 9) require Member States to organize their budgets and interventions around 11 Thematic Objectives (TO). The regulations also provide a list of intervention areas (Investment Priorities) that are eligible under each TO. TO1 is dedicated to R&D and innovation, TO2 addresses the digital agenda and information and communication technology (ICT), and TO3 focuses on small- and medium-sized enterprises (SMEs) competitiveness. The regulation sets as an ex-ante conditionality for funding interventions under TO1 and TO2, the existence of R3 at the national or regional level. All funding under TO1 should be directed to S3 interventions (European Union, 2013b; Annex XI). Similarly for TO2, two out of the three investment priorities should be part of a strategic policy for digital growth included in the S3. All other TOs are free from any legal obligation to link to an S3.
2. Bridgman and Davis (2003) suggested that there are four different ways of conceptualizing policy instruments: (1) policy through advocacy: arguing a case, educating, or persuading; (2) policy through money: using spending and taxing powers to shape activity; (3) policy through direct government action: delivering services; and (4) policy through law: legislation, regulation, and authority.
3. http://www.oecd.org/sti/rd-tax-stats.htm
4. Estimation of the authors based on Eurostat data.
5. http://team.finland.fi/en/network
6. http://www.ely-keskus.fi/en/web/ely-en/

7. http://www.rakennerahastot.fi/web/en/home/-/asset_publisher/g9yjWiLx6BQZ/content/finland-implements-sme-initiative-creating-new-opportunities-for-economic-growth-and-jobs/maximized
8. http://www.gov.scot/Topics/Economy/EconomicStrategy
9. http://www.gov.scot/Topics/Business-Industry/support/17404/EuropeanStructuralFunds/StrategicInterventions
10. Article 70(2) provides for up to 15% of European Regional Development Fund (ERDF) support at the level of the priority, and up to 3% of the ESF budget [Article 13(3) ESF] to be allocated to operations located outside the program area.
11. http://www.smart.gov.pl/en
12. Klincewicz and Szkuta (2015) noted that the Ministry of Science and Higher Education published a "Programme for the Development of Higher Education and Science for the years of 2015-2030" in September 2015 that proposes "national research specialisations, as if its authors were not aware of the existence and contents of the national smart specialisation strategy."
13. https://www.mr.gov.pl/media/14909/ResponsibleDevelopmentPlan_pressrelease.pdf

REFERENCES

Boden, M., dos Santos, P., Haegeman, K., Marinelli, E., Valero, S., 2016. Implementing RIS3 in the region of Eastern Macedonia and Thrace: towards a RIS3 tool box. JRC S3 Policy Brief Series No. 20/2016, EUR 27956 EN. Available from: http://dx.doi.org/10.2791/160115

Böwer, U., Michou, V., Ungerer, C., 2014. The puzzle of the missing Greek exports, European economy. Economic Papers 518. Available from: http://dx.doi.org/10.2765/70035

Brennan, L., Rakhmatullin, R., 2015. Global value chains and smart specialisation strategy, thematic work on the understanding of global value chains and their analysis within the context of smart specialisation. Available from: http://dx.doi.org/10.2791/44840

Bridgman, P., Davis, G., 2003. What use is a policy cycle? Plenty, if the aim is clear. Aus. J. Public Admin. 62, 98–102, Available from: http://dx.doi.org/10.1046/j.1467-8500.2003.00342.x.

CSIL, 2016. Support to SMEs—increasing research and innovation in SMEs and SME development. Final Report Work Package 2 Ex post Evaluation of Cohesion Policy Programs 2007-2013. Available from: http://dx.doi.org/10.2776/799378

European Commission, 2015. Commission Staff Working Document. Country Report Poland 2015. COM(2015) 85 final. Available from: http://ec.europa.eu/europe2020/pdf/csr2015/cr2015_poland_en.pdf

European Commission, 2016. Commission Staff Working Document. Country Report Finland 2016. SWD(2016) 94 final. Available from: http://ec.europa.eu/europe2020/pdf/csr2016/cr2016_finland_en.pdf

European Commission, 2016. Commission Staff Working Document. Country Report Poland. SWD(2016) 89 final. Available from: http://ec.europa.eu/europe2020/pdf/csr2016/cr2016_poland_en.pdf

European Union, 2013a. Regulation (EU) 1301/2013 of the European Parliament and of the Council of 17 December 2013. Available from: http://eur-lex.europa.eu/legal-content/EN/TXT/?uri=CELEX:32013R1301

European Union, 2013b. Regulation (EU) 1303/2013 of the European Parliament and of the Council of 17 December 2013. Available from: http://ec.europa.eu/newsroom/dae/document.cfm?doc_id=5247

Flanagan, K., Uyarraa, E., Laranja, M., 2011. Reconceptualising the 'policy mix' for innovation. Res. Pol. 40 (5), 702–713, Available from: http://dx.doi.org/10.1016/j.respol.2011.02.005.

Florida, R., 2012. The Rise of the Creative Class. Basic Books, New York, NY.

Foray, D., 2014. From smart specialisation to smart specialisation policy. Eur. J. Innov. Mgmt. 17 (4), 492–507, Available from: http://dx.doi.org/10.1108/EJIM-09-2014-0096.

Foray, D., Goenaga, X., 2013. The Goals of Smart Specialisation. European Commission, Joint Research Centre Institute for Prospective Technological Studies, Seville, Spain, Available from: http://dx.doi.org/10.2791/20158.

Foray, D., Rainoldi, A., 2013. Smart Specialisation Programmes and Implementation. European Commission, Joint Research Centre Institute for Prospective Technological Studies, Seville, Spain, Available from: http://dx.doi.org/10.2791/19106.

Foray, D., David, P.A., Hall, B., 2009. Smart specialisation—the concept, knowledge economists. Policy Brief no. 9. Knowledge for Growth Expert Group, European Commission. Available from: http://ec.europa.eu/invest-in-research/pdf/download_en/kfg_policy_brief_no9.pdf

Greek Ministry of Development, 2014. 3rd Circular for the Design of the Operational Programmes of the Programming Period 2014-2020. Athens, Greece.

Greek Ministry of Economy, 2014. Operational Programme Competitiveness, Entrepreneurship and Innovation. Athens, Greece.

General Secretariat for Research and Technology, 2015. National Research and Innovation Strategy for Smart Specialisation 2014-2020. Available from: http://www.gsrt.gr/News/Files/New1034/Executive%20Summary-2015-09-17-v04.pdf

Halme, K., Saarnivaara,V-.P., Mitchell, J., 2016. RIO Country Report 2015 Finland. EUR 27861 EN. Available from: http://dx.doi.org/10.2791/528976

Hellenic Republic, 2014. Research, Technological Development and Innovation and Other Provisions 2014 (4310/2014) (in Greek).

Hellenic Republic, 2016. Law 4399 Institutional Framework for Establishing Private Investment Aid Schemes for the Country's Regional and Economic Development.

Hellenic Republic, 2016. The 2016 National Reform Programme.

Hellenic Republic, 2016. Rules for Research and Other Provisions (4386/2016) (in Greek).

Hood, C., Margetts, H.Z., 2007. The Tools of Government in the Digital Age, second ed. Palgrave, London.

Howlett, M., 2005. What is a policy instrument? Policy tools, policy mixes, and policy-implementation styles. In: Eliadis, P., Hill, M., Howlett, M. (Eds.), Designing Government: From Instruments to Governance. McGill Queen University Press, Montreal and Kingston.

Howlett, M., 2009. Governance modes, policy regimes and operational plans: a multi-level nested model of policy instrument choice and policy design. Pol. Sci. 42 (1), 73–89, Available from: http://dx.doi.org/10.1007/s11077-009-9079-1.

Izsák, K., Markianidou, P., Radošević, S., 2015. Convergence of National innovation policy mixes in Europe—has it gone too Far? An analysis of research and innovation policy measures in the period 2004-12. J. Common Market Stud. 53, 786–802, Available from: http://dx.doi.org/10.1111/jcms.12221.

Izsák, K., Markianidou, P., Reid, A., 2016. Scottish Clusters Mapping 2015. Report for Scottish Enterprise. Technical Report.

Klincewicz, K., Szkuta, K., 2015. RIO Country Report 2015 Poland. EUR 27872 EN. Available from: http://dx.doi.org/10.2791/984739

Komninos, N., Musyck, B., Reid, A., 2014. Smart specialisation strategies in south Europe during crisis. Eur. J. Innov. Mgmt. 17 (4), 448–471, Available from: http://dx.doi.org/10.1108/EJIM-11-2013-0118.

Landabso, M., 2014. Guest editorial on and innovation strategies for smart specialisation in Europe: theory and practice of new innovation policy approaches. Eur. J. Innov. Mgmt. 17 (4), 378–389, Available from: http://dx.doi.org/10.1108/EJIM-08-2014-0093.

Maroulis, N., Mikroglou, E., 2013. ERAWATCH Country Report 2011 Greece. JRC Scientific and Policy Reports. Available from: https://rio.jrc.ec.europa.eu/sites/default/files/riowatch_country_report/ERAWATCH%20Country%20Report%20Greece%202011.pdf

Mieszkowski, K., Kardas, M., 2015. Facilitating an entrepreneurial discovery process for smart specialisation. The case of Poland. J. Knowl. Econ. 6 (2), 357–384, Available from: http://dx.doi.org/10.1007/s13132-015-0242-y.

Miller, M., Mroczkowski, T., Healy, A., 2014. Poland's innovation strategy: how smart is 'smart specialization'? Int. J. Transit. Innov. Syst. 3 (3), 225–248.

Muscio, A., Reid, A., Rivera Leon, L., 2015. An empirical test of the regional innovation paradox: can smart specialisation overcome the paradox in Central and Eastern Europe? J. Econ. Pol. Reform 18 (2), 153–171.

Nauwelaers, C., Periañez Forte, I., Midtkandal, I., 2014. RIS3 Implementation and Policy Mixes. S3 Policy Brief Series No. 07/2014. Available from: https://ec.europa.eu/jrc/en/publication/eur-scientific-and-technical-research-reports/ris3-implementation-and-policy-mixes

Raunio, M., Nordling, N., Ketola, T., Saarinen, J., Heinikangas, A., 2016. Open innovation platforms: an approach to city development. Available from: https://avoimetinnovaatioalustat.files.wordpress.com/2016/02/kc3a4sikirja_eng.pdf

Reid, A., 2011. EU innovation policy: one size doesn't fit all! In: Radosevic, S., Kaderabkova, A. (Eds.), Challenges for European Innovation Policy. Edward Elgar, Cheltenham.

Reid, A., Angelis, J., Griniece, E., Halme, K., Regeczi, D., Ravet, J., Salminen, V., 2016. How to improve global competitiveness in Finnish business and industry? Impact study, Tekes, Finland. Available from: http://dx.doi.org/10.13140/RG.2.1.4943.0007

Reid, A., Komninos, N., Sanchez, J., Tsanakas, P., 2012. RIS3 National Assessment: Greece Smart Specialisation as a Means to Foster Economic Renewal. European Commission, Brussels, Available from: http://dx.doi.org/10.13140/RG.2.1.3202.8327.

Rodriguez-Pose, A., Wilkie, C., 2017. Institutions and the entrepreneurial discovery process for smart specialization. In: Kyriakou, D., Palazuelos Martínez, M., Periáñez-Forte, I., Rainoldi, A. (Eds.), Governing Smart Specialisation. Routledge, London.

Scottish Government, 2013. Scotland CAN DO: becoming a World-leading entrepreneurial and innovation nation. Available from: http://www.gov.scot/Resource/0043/00438045.pdf

Scottish Government, 2014. Scotland CAN DO Action Framework. Available from: http://www.gov.scot/Resource/0044/00449131.pdf

Stewart, J., 2004. The meaning of strategy in the public sector. Aus. J. Public Admin. 63 (4), 16–21.

Technopolis Group, 2006. Strategic evaluation on innovation and the knowledge based economy in relation to the Structural and Cohesion Funds, for the programming period 2007-2013. Synthesis Report. Available from: http://ec.europa.eu/regional_policy/sources/docgener/evaluation/pdf/strategic_innov.pdf

Tsipouri, L., Athanassopoulou, S., Gampfer, R., 2016. RIO Country Report 2015 Greece. JRC Science for Policy Report.

World Bank, 2015. Towards an innovative Poland: the entrepreneurial discovery process and business needs analysis. Available from: http://documents.worldbank.org/curated/en/801221468186841613/pdf/106148-REPLACEMENT-v2-English-REPORT-Web.pdf

Chapter 14

Entrepreneurial Discovery as a Foresight for Smart Specialization: Trade-Offs of Inclusive and Evidence-Based Consensus

Radu Gheorghiu*, Liviu Andreescu*, Marian Zulean*, Adrian Curaj**

*Institutul de Prospectiva, University of Bucharest, Bucharest, Romania; **National University of Political Studies and Public Administration (SNSPA), Bucharest, Romania*

Chapter Outline

Academic Highlights

- Given its prescriptive dimension, smart specialization sets a tall normative order for national and regional governments.
- So far, there is limited explicit guidance on how a RIS3-building process should be designed.
- There is also relatively limited past experience, especially in Central and Eastern Europe (CEE) but arguably also in other European regions, in designing and implementing an actual entrepreneurial discovery (ED) process.
- Romania's experience, where policy routines were partly circumvented in the RIS3 elaboration process only to be reintroduced during implementation, is consistent with that of other CEE countries.

Advances in the Theory and Practice of Smart Specialization. http://dx.doi.org/10.1016/B978-0-12-804137-6.00014-0
319

Policy Highlights
- Romania's national RIS3 used a foresight-based, prioritization-centered design.
- The design combined data analytics with widespread consultations focused on consensus-making.
- The large-scale but one-off exercise has so far failed to generate an enduring ED mechanism.
- The "depoliticized" RIS3 process may reflect a tactical choice of the government, which may explain the delayed and, so far, half-hearted implementation.

INTRODUCTION

In its prescriptive function as an enabler of access to European Structural Funds, smart specialization has raised new challenges for national research and innovation (R&I) strategies. Smart specialization urges governments to promote activities that "are new, aim at experimenting and discovering technological and market opportunities and have the potential to provide learning spillovers to others in the economy" (Foray, 2013, p. 58). It also prescribes the "prioritization of knowledge investments" to a limited number of fields which have the potential to enable economic competitiveness on a continental and even global scale. In both these capacities as codiscoverer and priority-setter, a regional or national government should—again following EU policy prescriptions (EC, 2012)—probe the future with visions and scenarios, capture trends, maintain a 'discovery' dialogue with the relevant actors and stakeholders, capitalize on their localized and specialized knowledge, and gain their consent and support for its "smart" decisions.

Under such a tall normative order, the demand for broadly participatory foresight exercises is unsurprisingly on the rise. Nevertheless, although the European Commission (EC) explicitly lists foresight and associated tools as a valuable set of techniques for developing a smart specialization strategy, there is limited explicit guidance on how a foresight exercise should be designed in this specific context, at least in the EC's Guide on R&I strategies for smart specialization (EC, 2012).[1] This may be due to the very absence of substantial previous experiences with RIS3-making, itself perhaps a result of smart specialization's "rash translation from concept to policy" (Kroll, 2015a, p. 2081). Indeed, as national and regional experiences are being analyzed and publicized (e.g., Paliokaitė et al., 2015), they are recorded on the RIS3 platform website maintained by the Commission (EC, 2012).

Fresh out of a national RIS3 exercise, we describe here the design of a national smart specialization strategy and the limited "entrepreneurial discovery (ED) mechanism" deployed in this context. Thus, in the subsequent section we probe briefly into the smart specialization discourse, in particular its assumptions and attendant prescriptions. We then explore several issues in designing a large-scale foresight process for RIS3, which we illustrate with the process of formulating the Romanian National Strategy for Research, Development and Innovation 2014–20 (NS RDI). We focus particularly on the procedural dimension of this process and on the prospects of using data analytics tools to gather and disseminate the evidence base to many stakeholders. Furthermore, we highlight how the foresight process reached an argument-based consensus on the potentially controversial prioritization of a few R&I (sub)fields. In the final sections, we discuss some implications of the exercise.

The ambition of the paper is predominantly descriptive—the presentation of an *actually* deployed RIS3 design. Our main claim is that this design worked, in the limited sense that it was carried out as originally planned (making allowance for the unavoidable, in our view, *ad hoc* decisions occasionally); that its output was delivered as per the client's request; and that it was a straightforward effort to respond to some of the policy prescriptions detailed later (which were explicitly or implicitly part of the terms of reference of the design and its implementation). We do *not* claim that the output was ideal (or close to it) for a smart specialization process by any particular standard other than, perhaps, the narrow procedural one mentioned earlier. Neither do we claim that the client put it to good use. Nevertheless, we argue that the story of Romania's RIS3 is worth knowing about for two reasons. First, because it happened (e.g., it is potential material for an in-depth case study). Second, because it might inspire other consultation-based strategy-making processes in the future.

To these ends, we approach questions of context, constraints, and limitations in the implementation of the project described herein, and briefly discuss its aftermath. We explain design decisions in light of these issues. To reiterate, even if the prose may occasionally suggest otherwise we do not intend the main sections of the chapter to *justify* the design in question, but merely to describe it in outline.

A TEMPLATE FOR SMART SPECIALIZATION?

"Smart specialization" is Europe's household name for a strategic approach to bridging the three "mutually reinforcing priorities" of smart, sustainable, and inclusive growth at the core of the continent's development strategy (EC, 2012, p. 11). The "smart" part specifically aims to strengthen Europe's—and presumably regional and/or national—knowledge and innovation capacity through entrepreneurship, education, and ICT to generate innovative products and services, better jobs, and, ultimately, help tackle the so-called grand societal challenges.

Beyond these continental goals, smart specialization also implies a "place-based" (Rodríguez-Pose et al., 2014) approach to economic development. The presuppositions of this approach are that regions "hold the knowledge about the local innovation systems and have the capacity to mobilize economic actors towards a shared goal" and are "well positioned to develop a thorough understanding" of local assets and challenges (EC, 2012, p. 12). This place-based dimension of smart specialization is relevant for our purposes here. Specifically, we are interested in how foresight techniques can be used in developing a smart-specialization-compliant national strategy for R&I. In the rest of this section, we spell out some of the key assumptions behind the national/regional smart specialization approach and identify several of its prescriptive aspects, which served as guidance for (and implicitly as constraints on) the exercise described in this chapter.

Smart specialization strategies respond to a view of industrial policy where, while market forces and private entrepreneurship remain "in the driving seat," governments are tasked with "a strategic and coordinating role in the productive sphere beyond simply ensuring property rights, contract enforcement, and macroeconomic stability." (Rodrik, 2004, p. 3) Part of this active governmental role consists of maintaining a regular dialogue between government, R&D organizations, and business—the so-called "ED process" to identify business' concerns. Governments should also capitalize on localized entrepreneurial knowledge to facilitate a way out of various market impasses. The result of the discovery process should be governmental prioritization of and support for regional or national "specializations"—economic endeavors which hold substantial promise, are sufficiently particularized (rather than mimetic and fashionable), but remain not yet fully realized due to constraining market factors. The latter may include factors that inhibit risk-taking explorations necessary for innovations, which can enable entry into or upgrading on global value chains. Noting that entrepreneurial knowledge is most often distributed within a regional system, Foray and Goenaga, 2013, p. 4) claim that "the best bet" in prioritization "is entrepreneurial trial and error," whereby "[p]riorities will be identified where and when opportunities are discovered by entrepreneurs."

Smart specialization is thus invested with an important "self-discovery" rationale. Government intervention aims to mitigate the disincentives to private innovators arising from information externalities (such as the low return to private entrepreneurs from pioneering discovery efforts). Consequently, policies by governments assist entrepreneurs as well as policy makers in finding out which new products can be generated at a low enough cost to make a particular field of business profitable (Hausmann and Rodrik, 2002). As a result, smart specialization directs government intervention not only toward getting the policy process right, but also toward choosing outcomes, insofar as it implies an active selection and promotion of "technologies, fields, subsystems, even firms" (Foray, 2013, p. 57).

The earlier mentioned prioritization should be based on a scenario of national or regional economic development enabling the "setting [of] strategic priorities and making use of smart policies to maximize the knowledge-based development potential of any region, strong or weak, high-tech or low-tech" (JRC-IPTS, website). The underlying development scenario, in turn, should rely on analytical evidence and stakeholder support and "should give a clear picture of the evolution of the regional productive structure towards activities that are globally competitive and have a greater potential for value added" (WB, 2013, p. 2). This entails amassing the relevant evidence base for the selection-and-prioritization process, as well as ensuring the participation of relevant stakeholders in both the broad policy dialogue and the more difficult and contentious task of picking out priority R&I fields or niches.

INCLUSIVE EVIDENCE AND ARGUMENT-BASED CONSENSUS: A NATIONAL RIS3 IN ROMANIA

The main concern of this practice-oriented chapter is precisely the process of discovery and selection, as designed in the process of elaborating a national "smart-specialization-compliant" strategy for research, development, and innovation (RDI). This process is, we argue by way of an illustration, particularly amenable to foresight initiatives with an exploratory component. In this section, we present the national RIS3 design deployed in Romania to develop the NS RDI 2014–20. We highlight the use of data analytics tools and large-scale argumentative consultations in the exploration and selection phases.

First, however, some context is in order. Romania first deployed a large-scale foresight exercise in a NS RDI in 2005–06, for the previous programming cycle (2007–13). The result was a substantial change in the funding instruments for RDI, closely following the European Framework Program blueprint. Consequently, this also led to promising short-term growth in scientific productivity, although the premises of this process were soon undermined by the economic crisis and the consequent slashing of the public RDI budget, as well as by cuts in private expenditures for R&D (Gheorghiu, 2015). The foresight exercise that gave birth to this previous strategy (Paunica et al., 2009) proved atypical, at least by local standards, in its ability to draw upon the involvement of an impressive number of stakeholders (reaching overall some 10,000 participants). This set a relatively high bar for the new strategy-building effort.

The making of the new NS RDI, mostly throughout 2013, occurred under different circumstances (not unlike elsewhere in the region): a slow economic recovery, sharp cuts in public R&D expenditures (bringing the national R&D budget to below 2006 levels), and pessimism within the research and development community (Gheorghiu, 2015). There was a time constraint as well, with only around 12 months available until the deadline for the final draft of the Strategy and its main policy instruments (the National Plan for RDI and an RDI-dedicated axis of the Operational Plan for Competitiveness financed from structural funds). Last but hardly least, to enable access to structural funds the Strategy had to be informed by the principles of smart specialization. In other words, it had to prioritize investment in a limited number of R&I directions that had the potential to drive innovation in Romania's competitive economic sectors or those with substantial prospects of future growth.

In Romania, and elsewhere in CEE, innovation policy is formally thought of as primarily the responsibility of the Ministry of Education and Research. Romania also has very limited regionalization.[2] Hence, the Ministry of Education and Research was formally tasked with ensuring the creation of a national RIS3. The ministry outsourced the process to a consortium of around a dozen organizations coordinated by the Executive Agency for the Funding of Higher

Education, Research, Development, and Innovation (UEFISCDI)[3] and backed by the nominal support of more than 100 additional organizations, mostly but not exclusively in the field of R&D. There was little direct involvement of other ministries in the design or coordination of the process described later (beyond occasional meetings with key representatives of these agencies), although members of the central and regional administrative agencies took part in various phases of the consultations.

Regarding the design of the process, as noted previously the EU provides some guidance on how to build a proper RIS3 (EC, 2012), not to mention an overarching continental strategic framework for national/regional strategies in the Europe 2020 strategy and the Innovation Union initiative. However, as far as foresight is concerned, few specifics concerning actual designs are provided. On the other hand, a RIS3 poses special challenges to a participative foresight-based exercise, especially when the latter has a national—rather than a more narrowly regional—scope. Specifically, a RIS3 raises the stakes substantially because of its combination of exploratory and normative dimensions.

While the exploratory component is crucial in preparing the ground for selecting priority fields of smart specialization, the act of setting priorities is exposed to the threat of traditional policy-making routines, rent-seeking, and lock-in (Rodríguez-Pose et al., 2014; Grillitsch, 2015), and is therefore potentially plagued by questions of legitimacy. To alleviate the latter, a broadly participatory design was contemplated and ultimately implemented in Romania. Ideally, all significant RDI actors were to be represented, alongside stakeholders in business, public decision making, and civil society. This, as the literature on participation in foresight emphasizes (van der Helm, 2007), raises its own dilemmas of stakeholder involvement, evidence gathering and presentation, as well as consensus-building among participants. The packaging of evidence was thought to be particularly important, with a focus on enabling participants both to apprehend the RDI system and its parts, and, just as crucially, to recognize themselves in the system.

A key part of the effort was therefore invested in adapting large-scale foresight to the challenges and dilemmas of "discovery'" and prioritization. In a nutshell, the operational goals of the process entailed:

- providing an *inclusive evidence base*, meaning one that supplements the typical "big-picture" approach based on key RDI and economic indicators and that additionally assists actors in tracking their own roles and relative positions on the "systemic map";
- enabling an *argumentative exploration* of prioritization options, that is, allowing participating actors and stakeholders to support their proposals and assessments of priority R&I fields with specific, substantive arguments relative to a set of predefined criteria relevant for RIS3; and
- engineering *consensus* on the selection of priorities *based on shared assumptions* with respect to the RDI system.

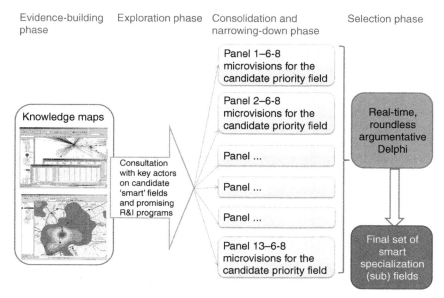

FIGURE 14.1   An outline of the project's main phases.

The resulting foresight consists of four main phases, which we discuss in the following subsections (Fig. 14.1):

1. Development of the evidence base;
2. Exploration of current research interests and strengths in the Romanian RDI landscape;
3. Consolidation of the results of the exploratory exercise; and
4. Selection of RIS3 priorities for the forthcoming programmatic cycle.

The discussion below is concerned chiefly with the design—that is, the procedural dimension—of the strategy-making process. We leave aside numerous questions of substance for reasons of space. For the same reasons, we also fail to touch on a few parallel flows in the strategy elaboration process (such as designing a governance structure and the two key implementation instruments). Finally, it bears repeating that the making of the RIS3 was, formally speaking, the responsibility of the Ministry of Education and Research. This parceling out of responsibilities for RIS3 (and similarly, for meeting other ex-ante conditionalities set by the Commission) is very much in keeping with the traditional policy routines in Romania and indeed, constituted a considerable limitation. It inflated the self-perceived role of research organizations: the NS was seen by the latter, despite efforts to "sell" smart specialization, as primarily the follow-up to the previous strategy. Therefore, the NS arguably did not do enough to discourage traditional R&D actors from positioning themselves as they had in the past. Efforts to engage the business community may have been less successful due to the same perception.

Developing the Evidence Base Through "Knowledge Maps"

As noted earlier, smart specialization strategies are premised, in part, on a process of self-discovery with "a strong learning dimension. The social value of the discovery is that it informs the whole system that a particular domain of R&D and innovation is likely to create new opportunities for the ... economy" (Foray and Goenaga, 2013, p. 6). The policy makers need to amass, distribute, and interpret the analytical evidence to support the prioritization process, and to this end an extensive dialogue with the RDI community and other stakeholders is essential, as usually emphasized in connection with national foresight practice (Gavigan and Scapolo, 1999). Furthermore, it is often argued in research policy circles that in the contemporary, ICT-pervaded, well-networked RDI ecosystems, significant research actors are sufficiently aware of one another to reach out and engage the relevant players if and when needed, provided the right structural incentives are maintained. Under such circumstances, the role of the policy maker would be primarily to ensure, particularly across the different categories of RDI actors (research, business, and investors), channels for communication, incentives for investment, and solutions for "information market" failures (Aghion et al., 2009).

Be that as it may, policy makers in a fragmented RDI ecosystem such as Romania's have to act as facilitators. Policy makers thus should enable the actors to "see themselves" and each other in relation to the broader picture of a large, internally divided system (WB, 2011). The outline, structure, internal demarcations, and local configurations of this system may not always be fully comprehended even by its members. For example, which universities and institutes share similar or neighboring interests or goals, as *actually* revealed in publicly-funded projects, patents, or publications? Which public research organizations (PROs) collaborate closely with each other, and what is the strength of these relationships in comparison to similar links between other PRO clusters in related or different fields? To what extent do the interests, competences, and collaborative links within the RDI community overlap with local or regional business interests, competences, and agglomerations? In other words, self-discovery entails an appreciation by each actor of "where I stand" in complex networks of actors and relationships—something which may be clear to some actors but less so to others. This understanding is important both in the exploratory phase and, subsequently, in reaching a consensus on smart specialization priorities.

In terms of the process examined here, this raised several challenges:

• Overcoming the dearth of reliable and accessible data on research, development, and innovation, so as to amass the evidence supporting the analysis of the current RDI ecosystem and assist in the potentially antagonistic prioritization process.

- Identifying ways of making this information available to a big group of actors and stakeholders participating in a large-scale foresight process.

Given that the priority-selection process could easily end up being construed by participants as a zero-sum game, a *shared* image of the RDI system was deemed vital for participation to work. In light of the well-known limitations of and constraints on stakeholder participation (van de Kerkhof and Wieczorek, 2005; van der Helm, 2007), "packaging" the data in a form that is simultaneously informative, simple to communicate, easy to absorb, and comprehensive can prove a daunting task.

Data analytics tools are now relatively widely available, as are visualization tools. The project adopted a data analytics approach to developing the evidence base. First, it created a repository of data on Romanian research and development as revealed in publicly-funded projects, publications, and patents, plus data on the business environment. This was achievable within the relatively short time frame given the fact that the agency coordinating the project, UE-FISCDI, manages public competitive funding streams for RDI in Romania. Second, it set out to develop intuitive snapshots (social network analysis or SNA-style graphs) of relationships among the various actors. The latter were dubbed "knowledge maps."

Perhaps the most labor-intensive challenge was to collect and compile databases, which had to be cleaned and harmonized. Eventually, these databases covered virtually all the publicly-funded competitive Romanian RDI projects over the last 7–8 years (more than 6000) across the different funding streams; all publications in the main scientific flows (over 100,000 articles in Web of Knowledge and Scopus); all patents awarded over the past decade (7000+); as well as data on more than 500,000 business firms. Although this sounds relatively straightforward (and in countries where such data have been collected systematically for a long time it may well be), the project found that the challenge can be formidable. To provide just one illustration: a single—admittedly large—academic organization was present across the databases under more than 1500 denominations, ranging from the full organizational name to a variety of shortened titles and acronyms, names belonging to its main component entities, abbreviations of small and hard to identify institutes or informal units, and so on. Simply accessing, compiling, and cleaning the data proved extremely time-consuming, especially given the time constraints of the project.

The more innovative part of the evidence-building phase involved creating "knowledge maps" as visual presentations of research networks with the relevant organizational and individual actors. We relied on a SNA package developed for, among others, the intelligence community; on open-source graph manipulation software; as well as on semantic analysis software and a well-known Geographic Information System package for geographical data used in the actual maps. Some examples of visual presentations are provided later.

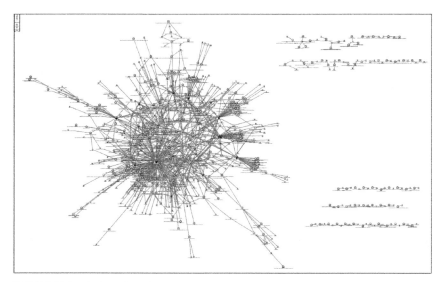

FIGURE 14.2 **A clustering of organizations and projects in the field of "energy."**

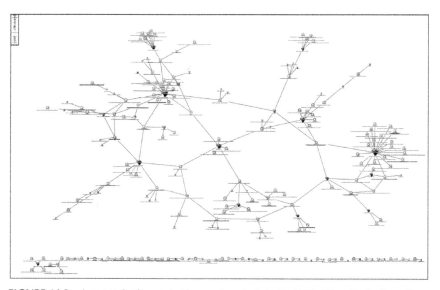

FIGURE 14.3 **A network of organizations and projects in the field of "medical science."**

Pictured in Fig. 14.2 are organizations and their relationships (lines) in terms of participation in a variety of types of projects (in the original graph, green and red dots) in the field of "Energy." Fig. 14.3 provides a similar snapshot for the health sciences. The small, isolated clusters on the right in Fig. 14.2 and at the bottom in Fig. 14.3 are organizations that have only partnered with a few others in carrying out, typically, a small number of projects.

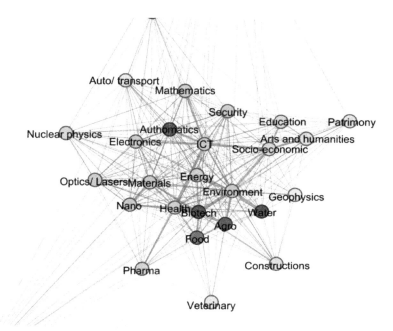

FIGURE 14.4   Linkages among fields resulting from a semantic analysis of a large sample of abstracts of nationally and internationally funded projects. Pictured above are relationships among fields based on their association in competitive projects under the main national competitive funding schemes (the taxonomy was developed in the project).

This type of information was made available to participants in the exploratory, consolidation, and selection phases of the project, but was particularly important in the latter two stages. They were supplemented by more traditional analyses of the current state of affairs consisting of descriptive statistics, aggregate figures, and indicators. Some of these were generated within the project (e.g., an assessment of the outgoing strategy and its outcomes); while others were provided by the public agency for RDI who contracted out the National Strategy project. Examples of the latter kinds of inputs include a JASPERS-ARUP, 2013 analysis of the RDI market in Romania and the World Bank's assessment of Romania's RDI system (WB, 2011). Analyses of current research and publication trends in this country were also provided Fig. 14.4.

The Exploratory Phase

The "knowledge maps" and assorted analyses served as inputs for selecting a long list, followed by a short list, of candidate R&I fields of smart specialization. The next stage was to narrow down the list to a more limited number of smart specialization priorities. Since this gradual selection process involved several stages as well as several types of consultations, from panel work to online Delphi, the knowledge maps served another important function, namely, to identify experts and stakeholders as potential participants. The most active individual actors in the RDI community were tracked down, as were their collaborators. The previous RDI strategy and other broadly participatory foresight exercises in Romania (Paunica et al., 2009; Andreescu et al., 2012) relied for this purpose on stakeholder analysis and snowball sampling (Hill and Jones, 1992; Freeman et al., 2010). The knowledge maps somewhat simplified and expedited this procedure.

The exploratory phase was structured as follows:

- an initial collaborative selection of a larger set of potential smart specialization fields, followed by:
- a narrowing down of the set to a short list of candidate fields; and
- identifying potentially promising R&I programs in the shortlisted fields through a consultation process.

The first selection was carried out by a panel of experts and stakeholders on the basis of knowledge maps and several analyses of the Romanian economy and R&D, consisting among others of predictions concerning sectoral growth performance based on various economic indicators (JASPERS-ARUP, 2013; WB, 2011). This step resulted in an initial set of 29 potential smart specialization sectors, largely based on the list of research specializations within economic sector specializations identified by JASPERS-ARUP (2013, pp. 51–52). This list was subsequently narrowed down by an expert panel to 13 broadly-defined, candidate R&I domains.[4] The key task for this phase of the project was, however, not primarily to identify the potential domains, but to disaggregate them into promising R&I programs (or "subfields") relative to the 2020 time horizon. More specifically, the goal was to identify R&D which shows competitive economic potential and to get the "granularity" right (Foray and Goenaga, 2013). The R&D priorities should not be so niche as to be unlikely to generate knowledge spillovers in the relevant economic sectors. Yet neither should they be too broad lest they encompass excessively expansive fields of science and compromise the very goal of priority-setting.

To chart the possible R&I priorities across the 13 candidate fields, experts, business stakeholders, and other innovators were called on to participate in an online survey. Its goal was to populate the candidate fields with proposals concerning specific R&I programs regarded as promising over the 2014–20 period. A key feature of this round of online consultations was to provide arguments to support individual choices of program. The survey asked invited experts and business stakeholders not merely to nominate or briefly describe promising R&I programs or subfields, but also to back up their proposals with arguments pertaining to their economic and/or societal importance. The arguments concerned are as follows:

- main challenges (societal and economic) which the proposed R&I program or subfields would address;
- conditions which have to be met to ensure the success of the programs; and
- expected results of the programs.

It should be noted again that, of the 1543 individual respondents to the online survey, many were identified through the knowledge maps rather than the nomination and conomination (snowballing) method used for the previous RDI strategy. Among those targeted were scientifically productive or well-networked individuals and organizations.

The Consolidation Phase

The survey yielded a considerable number of proposals for R&I programs within the 13 candidate priority fields, as well as many accompanying arguments. The subsequent goal was, therefore, to consolidate all the information and then whittle down the result to some 6–8 particularly promising R&I subfields for each candidate smart specialization field. The consolidation entailed a clustering of similar proposals, an assessment of the online respondents' support for the various programs, as well as some general cleaning work on the qualitative data collected during the exploratory consultation.

Most of the work was done within 13 expert panels (one per candidate field), each of which had around 12–20 members. As with the previous online consultation, some of the panel members were selected on the basis of their influence and competencies as suggested by knowledge-map metrics (for instance, innovators with recent patents, and top researchers). Others occupied organizationally important roles (e.g., the rector of a leading university) or headed successful businesses in the field. The panels met first in two intensive, two-day sessions of facilitated parallel work (two weeks apart); they then met over the course of several weeks through online communication. Panels were provided with the relevant knowledge maps for their fields, as well as with other analyses and surveys pertaining to the RDI ecosystem and the economy in general. They worked on the basis of a set of predefined smart-specialization-specific criteria to guide them through the consolidation and narrowing down (see later). Panel members also had access to the results of the online survey in a manageable form (i.e., with some clustering and cleaning).

The chief assignment of each panel was to develop, based on the materials earlier and the results of the exploratory exercise in particular, 6–8 "microvisions" for the most promising R&I programs in their candidate field. Each "microvision" was arranged as a compact brief advocating for one program, whose structure followed the preestablished criteria mentioned earlier. These six "smart-specialization-compliant" criteria referred to:

- the R&I program's opportunities and challenges at the time horizon of 2020;
- the specific relevance of these challenges for the proposed R&I program;
- the current RDI capabilities relevant to the program (such as number of researchers, existing research infrastructure, etc.);
- the regional or national economy relevant for the program (business actors, investments in relevant sector, the market/s for relevant products and services, etc.);

- the resources (specifically, researchers, investments, and infrastructure) needed for the program to overcome the challenges; and
- the results expected by 2020 from the R&I program, provided the needed resources are available (specifically, estimates of the numbers of publications in the main scientific flows, patents, and new innovative companies, as well as of the value of new innovative products sold).

The better part of the efforts to generate the set of 6–8 microvisions per field was accomplished during the two intensive, two-day face-to-face sessions, with the remaining fine-tuning—also based on feedback from the project team—left for the following weeks. By the end of this stage, the project team received 90 briefs describing an equal number of R&I programs at the time horizon of 2020 which were considered promising. These programs varied in breadth and range (e.g., compare the very broad program of "Bioenergy: biogas, biomass, biofuels" with the more specific "Assessing the risks of the widespread use of over-the-counter drugs and dietary supplements"), although mostly between rather than within fields. In other words, the level of granularity was better calibrated within fields, which is what we expected. The effort to improve the format and adjust the granularity was limited to the work of panel facilitators.

The Selection Phase

The final list of smart specialization R&I programs was selected by means of a very broad online consultation in which most Romanian organizational and individual RDI actors and stakeholders were invited to participate. In this intensive stage, participants were asked to assess as many of the microvisions in their main field(s) of competence as possible. The emphasis during this phase was on building an *argument-based* consensus regarding the selection, as opposed to merely a broad agreement resulting from the ranking of the proposed R&I programs in terms of their relevance.

To this end, the online consultation followed an adapted roundless,[5] realtime, online Delphi format (Gordon and Pease, 2006; Gnatzy et al., 2011) called Dynamic Argumentative Delphi (Gheorghiu et al., 2014). The platform was developed in-house and was previously tested in a higher education foresight project in 2011 (Andreescu et al., 2012). The questionnaire set comprised the 13 candidate strategic fields, specifically, the 90 R&I programs. It was dispatched to around 44,000 potential respondents—researchers and academics, doctoral students and recent PhDs, members of the scientific diaspora, executives of companies with significant R&D activity, and so on. Each respondent was invited to choose a main and, where desired, secondary field; and fill in the separate survey sheets for each of the 6–8 R&I programs per field. The online consultation period lasted a little over one month.

In light of its goals, the roundless online Delphi was designed to yield both a quantitative evaluation of the R&I programs (to enable the ranking and prioritization); and a set of arguments for and/or against prioritizing these programs. Specifically, each program was assessed quantitatively by the respondents in terms of the six criteria mentioned earlier in the section on the consolidation phase (these corresponded to the six sections of the program survey sheet). Simultaneously, the questionnaire invited the respondents to support each of their evaluations with arguments.

Given the many participants invited, the number of arguments had to be kept in check to prevent the number of arguments from spiraling up. A few default arguments were made available in each survey sheet (they had been drafted by the consolidation-phase panels and occasionally adapted from the argumentative exploratory consultation). Respondents were asked to either select some of the preexisting arguments, add new arguments, or both (without exceeding three selections and/or additions). As new arguments were provided, they became instantly visible to respondents who accessed the survey later and who could, in turn, select the previously introduced arguments and/or add new arguments of their own. The arguments were ranked dynamically: the current frequency of each argument on the program sheet is indicated by a number in brackets. A detailed description of the Dynamic Argumentative Delphi design is available in Gheorghiu et al. (2014).

By the end of the consultation, over 4000 individuals had responded to the questionnaire (some 9% of those who were invited). The figure is relatively large in both an absolute sense and relative to the size of Romania's active research sector (around 27,000 according to Eurostat). The average number of respondents per survey sheet was 161, with the lowest number being 36 (only 8 sheets out of the 90 had less than 50 respondents). As with previous Delphi consultations built around this template, the number of arguments per survey question remained, with a few exceptions, within manageable limits Fig. 14.5.

The procedure for selecting the final smart specialization priorities was carried out on the 90 R&I programs, *not* the 13 fields. Specifically, the quantitative evaluation delivered through the Delphi survey was used to create a simple composite index, with the underlying "economic criterion" weighted at 0.5. The three items considered were are as follows:

- opportunities represented by the subfield (0.25 weight);
- contribution of RDI in the subfield to the challenges (0.25 weight); and
- economic impact (0.5 weight).

The initial list of 90 finalists was ranked in terms of their composite score in the quantitative assessment, and a cut-off threshold was established at the point where the resources deemed necessary for the success of the programs[6] reached the projected R&D budget for the period 2014–2020 (5 billion Euro). The final list consisted of 30 R&I programs—as it happened, exactly one-third of the candidate list. These finalists were then grouped together as a function of their mutual affinities into four broad "smart specializations;" and *an additional*

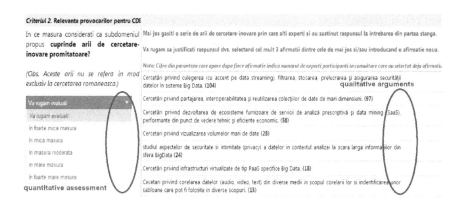

FIGURE 14.5   Quantitative assessment and dynamic ranking of arguments in a roundless online Delphi. Pictured above is the section of the questionnaire corresponding to criterion 2, "relevance of challenges [to which the narrower R&I program is supposed to respond] for RDI." In the left column, participants are asked to assess on a five-point scale (in the drop-down box) the extent to which the subfield consists of promising R&I ideas. In the broad right column, they are asked to support their assessment by selecting from the previously proposed arguments or by proposing new ones. The figures in brackets indicate the frequency of a particular "argument" at that time.

three "national interest" fields responding to pressing societal challenges rather than to the goal of economic competitiveness. Some of the 13 candidate fields were completely omitted as no single associated R&I program made it to the final list. The four smart specialization fields selected were: Bioeconomy, ICT, Energy & environment, and Eco-technologies; the three other (national) priority fields were Health, Space and security, and National patrimony (Annex 14.1).

ANNEX 14.1 List of Titles of Top 30 R&I Programs

Candidate smart specialization field	R&I program title
Agrofood	Innovative technologies and equipment for food and nonfood bioresources
Pharmaceuticals	In vitro/in vivo assessment in designing generic drugs
Health	Early detection, personalized treatment and forecasting in oncology
Biotechnologies	Medical and pharmaceutical biotechnologies
Security	Cybernetic security to increase resilience
Agrofood	Adapting zootechnics, veterinary medicine, fishing and aquaculture to 21st century challenges
Agrofood	Sustainable development of forestry and increasing in competitiveness in Europe
Security	Developing innovative methods and technologies to combat cross-border organized crime, terrorism, and illegal trafficking
Pharmaceuticals	Assessing the quality and risks of widespread use of OTC drugs and dietary supplements
Pharmaceuticals	Personalized therapy and therapeutic monitoring
Pharmaceuticals	Optimizing biopharmaceutical and pharmacokinetic profiles
Space	Dedicated spatial applications: earth observation, GNSS, Satcom
Agrofood	Developing new technologies, practices, and products in horticulture
Agrofood	Safe, accessible, nutritionally optimal products
Transportation	New generation of vehicles and ecological, energy-efficient technologies
Biotechnologies	Bionanotech
Space	Integrated spatial applications
Agrofood	Sustainable production of crops adapted to global climate changes
Biotechnologies	Agrofood biotechnologies
Pharmaceuticals	Molecular design (bio)synthesis, semisynthesis, high-performance screening
Health	Healthy aging and lifestyle
ICT	Analysis, management, and security of large data
Biotechnologies	Environmental biotechnologies
Energy	Increasing consumers' energy efficiency
Socioeconomics	Integrated economic development in rural areas
Biotechnologies	Industrial biotechnologies

(Continued)

ANNEX 14.1 List of Titles of Top 30 R&I Programs (*cont.*)

Candidate smart specialization field	R&I program title
Health	Research on neurodegenerative, neuroinflammatory diseases
ICT	Future internet
Pharmaceuticals	Quantitative systemic pharmacology and toxicology: modeling and forecasting
Environment	Optimal use of conventional and nonconventional water resources in the Danube area

DISCUSSION

Limitations by Design

In our view, the design presented earlier has at least two main limitations if judged against the standard of a full-fledged RIS3 process. The first is the restricted ED setup. The project was primarily designed as a one-off series of consultations (though extending them into the future was contemplated) aimed at selection and, thus, prioritization. The project did not engender any stable, systematic "framework of strategic interactions between the government and the private sector," which is the "essence of entrepreneurial discovery" according to Foray (2015). This is attributable to several factors including:

- the restricted timeframe for the delivery of a tightly structured type of output (the entire strategy and implementation plans);
- the narrow involvement of government beyond RDI agencies, a reflection of current policy routines and/or of a failure to upset or circumvent these routines; and, perhaps, a tactical choice as well (as discussed earlier); and
- the framing of the process as the elaboration of the "next (or new) RDI strategy," which may have blurred the nature of the expectations.

Nevertheless, one may argue that there have been benefits of the process that are relevant to any future effort to put in place an ED mechanism. These would include the communication of smart-specialization terminology; R&D actors getting better acquainted with broader consultations on RDI issues; and their being exposed to and involved in prioritization. Yet, engaging in the same type of process at the beginning of each programming cycle would certainly not do justice to the concept of "entrepreneurial discovery"; more would be needed for that purpose.

Second, it would not be a great exaggeration to say that the core concern behind the design of the Romanian national RIS3 was concentration-enabling prioritization. The succession of consultations, either broadly participatory or in panels, which made possible the progressive shortlisting of smart specialization fields down to the level of R&I programs, was designed specifically so as to make prioritization both feasible and legitimate to the greatest extent possible under the circumstances. Other mandates of the smart specialization doctrine, such as "particularization"—meaning the development of distinctive and original areas of specialization (Foray, 2015, pp. 28–29)—were comparatively less reflected in the process. To what extent the selected specializations reflected a particularization-enabling approach to developing economic strengths remains an open question, and certainly not one which the design sought to explore explicitly.

Indeed, one may argue that, while the prioritization started from a broad set of research specializations associated with the country's most promising economic specializations (JASPERS-ARUP, 2013, pp. 51–52), the link between R&I domains and the current economic structure was weakened over time by the RIS3 design. The knowledge maps themselves represented a form of "STI-mode" knowledge, whereas the sources of knowledge accumulated by doing, using and interacting (DUI-mode) (Jensen et al., 2007) were nowhere nearly as well represented. Arguably, the absence of DUI-mode knowledge sources was because these are harder to tap into and package for such a process. As such, the limitation of the focus on prioritization was practically inherent in the discovery process.

Limitations of Subsequent Use

The draft National Strategy for RDI 2014–2020, which the process described earlier played a central part in formulating, was adopted by the Romanian Government on October 21, 2014. This was around half a year after it had been submitted. Before this date, the draft and the process underlying it underwent a European S3 peer-review procedure.[7] The adopted version is similar to the one originally proposed, except for two key areas: the list of prioritized fields was expanded by political decision, while the governance structure (not described herein) was changed in a few but rather significant ways (more on this below). The Strategy's two key instruments, the National Plan for RDI and the Operational Plan for Innovation (in fact, a priority axis of the new Operational Program Competitiveness) were both delivered to the decision maker at the same time as the NS RDI yet were adopted later. Indeed, the Plan was adopted almost a year after the Strategy.

The first cycle of RIS3-making in Europe is sufficiently advanced for an initial round of evaluation of procedures and outputs. Comparative assessments are mixed but often strike a positive note, even where they point out that "the increasing body of evidence on RIS3 strategies provides ample justification for skepticism" regarding the usefulness of bottom-up approaches and the prospects of implementation (Kroll, 2015b, p. 5). In their recent effort to map smart specialization priorities in Europe, for instance, Sörvik and Kleibrink (2015) (p. 20) conclude optimistically, in response to the concern that smart specializations may not be particularized enough, that "very few regions and countries have developed similar combinations [of priorities]." In their view, this suggests "that there is no significant "copycat" behavior among regions and countries." They also note, however, that "the overall relationship between priorities and the economic and innovation structure seems weak," which they attribute to either mismatching, poor data, the way priorities are oriented towards the future, or "political ambitions and efforts towards structural change connected to EU objectives" (Sörvik and Kleibrink, 2015, p. 20). An additional cause mentioned by Sörvik and Kleibrink, also identified previously in this chapter, is the disproportionate share of supply-side actors in the RIS3-making processes. The R&D sector in Romania, for example, was overrepresented numerically as well as symbolically, at least relative to its share and to the philosophy of smart specialization.

More interesting for the purposes of this article is Karo and Kattel's (2015) recent discussion of the process of RIS3-making, specifically with reference to policy and administrative capacity in the CEE states. In this respect, the experience of Romania's national RIS3 proves rather ambivalent. On the one hand, the process was decentralized and, as such, took place outside the ordinary coordination and consultation routines. The "line ministry" for innovation—the Ministry of Education and Scientific Research—outsourced the project to a consortium and took a hands-off approach throughout the process. In this, it acted atypically if judged against national (and probably CEE) standard operating procedures—the other national strategies aimed at meeting ex-ante conditionalities were usually coordinated by the relevant ministries. The reasons for this can only be guessed (and will be engaged presently in this section). Almost certainly, however, the limited time frame of around one year to meet the ex-ante conditionality played a part, as did the modest capabilities of the Ministry to organize and carry out a systematic consultative process.

On the other hand, the Ministry did change the draft form of the Strategy after public consultations (whose procedure, unlike that of the strategy making, has not been well documented). One glaring change is the expansion of the scope of the four smart specializations. One of the previous candidate fields, "Advanced materials," was included although none of its purportedly promising R&I programs had made it to the final list of selections. Moreover, "Space and Security" were recategorized as smart specializations (they had been originally identified as "national priority" fields) (Table 14.1).

Furthermore, there is no mention in the adopted Strategy of the 30 R&I programs behind the four smart specialization clusterings (they were provided as annexes in the draft version). This immediately raises the question of whether, or to what extent, they will be reflected in the funding streams. Most of the competitive streams of the National Plan for RDI have not been fully implemented yet (the exception being the bottom-up exploratory programs). The nature and substance of the calls will show whether the spirit of the original prioritization

TABLE 14.1 Smart Specialization Fields in the NS RDI 2014–2020

Draft version	Adopted version
Bioeconomy	Bioeconomy
ICT	ICT, space, and security
Energy and environment	Energy, environment, and climate change
Eco-technologies	Eco-nanotechnologies and advanced materials

process (ultimately, the finer granularity) remains relevant or will get lost on the way (perhaps aided by the long delays in implementation).

Additionally, the project's relatively modest suggestions as to changes in governance were also altered, notably concerning the role of the newly founded National Council for Science, Technology, and Innovation Policy (CNPSTI). According to the draft document, this body was to be headed by the Prime Minister and consists of representatives of relevant ministries; its main tasks were to coordinate RDI policy across sectors, carry out strategic planning, and oversee the planning and implementation activities of the Ministry of Education and Research. In contrast, in the adopted version, the Council is a consultative body to the government consisting of ministers and coordinated by the head of the executive. Its key role is to assess the implementation of the National Strategy and publish a yearly report with recommendations. The adopted version of the strategic document also eliminates the Center for RDI Policy, initially envisaged as a permanent arm of the CNPSTI in charge of gathering, integrating, and supplying data on the RDI ecosystem and providing strategic analysis, and expert advice. The Center was replaced by nonpermanent expert working groups, while the National Council's secretariat is provided by the Ministry. This dilution of the Center for RDI Policy's organizational and substantive role suggests skepticism of, or perhaps resistance to, a new specialized agency in charge of smart specialization.

Limitations of "depoliticization"

We mentioned previously that the decision to outsource Romania's RIS3 project may be attributed, in part, to the limited time frame available to meet this ex-ante conditionality; and the questionable capabilities of the public agency in charge of RDI to carry out a systematic process palatable to the European Commission. However, there might have been additional rationales for such a choice. For one thing, the Ministry may have also chosen to dodge, at least during the formulation, some of the anticipated string-pulling behind the prioritization procedure. It may have preferred, more generally, to embark on a process of prioritization *at arm's length*, in which it could conveniently claim no direct involvement; and which, additionally, could be couched in a methodological frame ("foresight") which appeared impartial and democratic (and favored by the Commission). This makes particular sense with a process smacking of "picking winners" and letting losers go. In particular, we should note the current social and political climate in Romania, where accusations ranging from bland rent-seeking to sheer corruption have been especially strong over the past two decades. These accusations have recently resulted in a spate of indictments and convictions in all corners and at all levels of Romanian political life.

The decision to outsource, whatever its likely diverse motivations, was thus without doubt politically and practically convenient for the decision makers. As suggested implicitly throughout this chapter, it probably also resulted in a structurally neater, more systematic priority selection process. One should inquire, however, into the inherent trade-offs implied by this essentially technical solution to setting priorities. We point out three issues.

The first has already been alluded to above: a projected long-term exploratory process with massive business involvement, a multi- or cross-sectoral reach, and an active government presence was not among the bequests of the project elaborating Romania's National Strategy for RDI. While a participant among others in the RIS3-making process, the government was not a facilitator of the discovery process. It certainly did not occupy the driver's seat. As a result, it did not get its feet wet (enough) in the process, and appeared to happily relinquish any pretense of having to make hard choices. One must wonder what this signals about the government's commitment not only to the selected priorities themselves, but to the prioritization process in general, with its attendant risks as well as secondary benefits.

A second point, closely related to the first, is that the project failed to leave behind a governance structure for the RDI ecosystem that would naturally accommodate a continuous ED process, or something akin to the mechanisms needed for an "open economy industrial policy" (Kuznetsov and Sabel, 2014). While designing a governance framework was part of the project's terms of reference, this was at least to a certain extent because it was prescribed as part and parcel of the structure of a properly designed RIS3. However, the effort invested in the governance structure was clearly much more limited than that injected in prioritizing. This was partly because, given the arm's length involvement of the Ministry (and of other relevant line ministries), it was in a sense considered outside the proper remit of the project. The dumbing-down of the proposed governance structure in the adopted version of the Strategy mentioned earlier highlights this drawback.

Finally, as pointed out in the previous subsection, the relevant line ministry occasionally acted as if it could claim the cake of an impersonal and objective priority selection process—and eat it too. It worked creatively with the priorities set through the foresight process, adding a few and reorganizing several others in ways that were arguably at odds with the underlying philosophy of the approach. The decision appeared to be political and was never openly explained, even though it was claimed it had been reached at the end of a public consultation process. Once again, this raises questions as to the real commitment of the government not only to the (original) priorities themselves, but to the discovery process as such.

CONCLUSIONS

We argue that the foresight framework and the associated set of methods have proven amenable to designing a fit-for-purpose (if one-off) "entrepreneurial discovery" procedure for smart specialization. At least in Romania, the challenge of adapting it to a continuous, iterative, *proper* ED process remains a task for the near future. This raises complex issues which the procedure described herein did not address and, arguably, was not designed or expected to. These issues included setting in place a governance structure for the country's innovation ecosystem, which is perhaps the most glaringly missing as well as the most difficult to tackle. As Kroll (2015a; p. 2083) noted in summarizing recent literature on RIS3 implementation: "even with the best of intentions, many policy makers in weak institutional environments would need much more time to move towards an "optimal RIS3 consultation process..."

The implications of the formal delivery of Romania's RIS3 on future concentration of financial and human resources remain, at this date, difficult to predict. The RDI budget for 2015 was dramatically at odds with the commitments made in the strategic document that had just been formally adopted. The figure for 2016 is some 30% higher, although still below commitments. Expectations were high for a while, given that one of the coordinators of the strategy-making process (and a coauthor of this chapter) was minister of education and research for around 7 months between November 2015 and July 2016. However, whatever progress was made during this period was not directly relevant for smart specialization. In any case, the changes suggest that traditional policy routines were not circumvented. Despite the hands-off approach of the ministry during the strategy design phase, which enabled it to capitalize on the analytical intelligence and consultation expertise available elsewhere, the old policy-making style subsequently made an informal comeback through the backdoor after the formulation phase and just in time for implementation. This is not particularly surprising. Lithuania, which made recourse to future-oriented technology analysis in the design of its RIS3, has recently reported concerns of their foresight process being "lost in [the] translation" to implementation (Paliokaitė et al., 2016).

Perhaps more significant for an assessment of the Romanian government's administrative capacity to implement the RIS3 is the future of ED in the country. While the strategy-making process may have passed muster despite its limitations (e.g., the narrow involvement of other ministries), it does not seem to have enhanced the administrative capacity of the relevant public agencies to date, nor set in motion a systematic and iterative discovery mechanism.

ENDNOTES

1. Henceforth, the term RIS3 will be used to denote research and innovation strategies for smart specialization.
2. While Romania is formally split into eight development regions, the respective Regional Development Agencies (RDAs) are weak in terms of their actual prerogatives. Their main role is to coordinate the formulation of Regional Development Plans, supported through structural funds via the Regional Operational Plan (OP). RDAs delivered regional RIS3 before the end of 2015, but it is questionable whether these are "genuine" smart-specialization instruments (Gheorghiu et al. 2016).
3. Three of the authors of this paper served as consultants to the Agency during the making of the strategy. The fourth author was director of UEFISCDI at the time.
4. These partly overlapping domains were: Agro-food, Biotechnologies, Energy, Environment, Health, ICT, Intelligent systems, Materials, Pharmaceuticals, Security, Society and economics, Space, and Transportation.
5. The consultation was technically roundless, although the respondents had the option to keep the questionnaire open and return to it later. Given the argument-based nature of the Delphi and the dynamic ranking of arguments (see caption to Fig. 16.5 and text below for further explanation), respondents were able to gauge the state of the conversation on R&I priorities as it evolved over time and to change their positions accordingly.
6. The original figures proposed by the consolidation-phase panels were "corrected" after the Delphi process, whose respondents were also asked to assess the realism of these estimates.
7. This took place in Dublin on 3–4 July 2014; http://s3platform.jrc.ec.europa.eu/peer-review.

REFERENCES

Aghion, P., David, P.A., Foray, D., 2009. Science, technology and innovation for economic growth: linking policy research and practice in "STIG Systems". Res. Policy 38, 681–693.

Andreescu, L., et al., 2012. Systemic foresight for romanian higher education. In: Curaj, A. et al., (Ed.), European Higher Education at the Crossroads: Between the Bologna Process and National Reforms. Springer, Dordrecht.

EC (European Commission) 2012, Guide to Research and Innovation Strategies for Smart Specialisation (RIS3), May 2012, Available from: http://s3platform.jrc.ec.europa.eu/en/-/guide-on-research-and-innovation-strategies-for-smart-specialisation-ris3-guide-?inheritRedirect=tr ue&redirect=%2Fen%2Fcommission-guides.

Foray, D., 2013. The economic fundamentals of smart specialization. Ekonomiaz 83 (2), 55–78.

Foray, D., 2015. Smart Specialisation: Opportunities and Challenges for Regional Innovation Policy. Routledge, London and New York.

Foray, D., Goenaga, X., 2013. The Goals of Smart Specialisation, S3 Policy Brief Series, no. 1/2013, The European Commission, JRC-IPTS.

Freeman, R.E., et al., 2010. Stakeholder Theory: The State of the Art. Cambridge University Press, Cambridge.

Gavigan, J.P., Scapolo, F., 1999. Matching methods to the mission: a comparison of national foresight exercises. Foresight 1 (6), 495–517.

Gheorghiu, R., Andreescu, L., Curaj, A., 2016. A foresight toolkit for smart specialization and entrepreneurial discovery. Futures 80, 33–44.

Gheorghiu, R., 2015. RIO Country Report: Romania 2014, JRC-IPTS. Available from: https://rio.jrc.ec.europa.eu/sites/default/files/riowatch_country_report/RIO%20Country%20Report%20 2014_Romania_1.pdf.

Gheorghiu, R., Andreescu, L., Curaj, A., 2014. Dynamic argumentative real-time Delphi: lessons from two large-scale foresight exercises, 5th International Conference on Future-Oriented Technology Analysis (FTA), Brussels. Available from: https://www.academia.edu/18708439/Dynamic_argumentative_Delphi_Lessons_learned_from_two_large-scale_foresight_exercises.

Gnatzy, T., Warth, J., von der Gracht, H., Darkow, I.-L., 2011. Validating an innovative real-time Delphi approach—a methodological comparison between real-time and conventional Delphi studies. Technol. Forecast. Soc. Change 78 (9), 1681–1694.

Gordon, T., Pease, A., 2006. RT Delphi: an efficient, roundless almost real-time Delphi method. Technol. Forecast. Soc. Change 73, 321–333.

Grillitsch, M., 2015. Institutions, Smart Specialisation Dynamics and Policy, Papers in Innovation Studies, no. 2015/12, CIRCLE, Lund University.

Hausmann, R., Rodrik, D., 2002. Economic development as self-discovery, NBER Working Paper no. 8952.

Hill, C.W.L., Jones, T.M., 1992. Stakeholder-agency theory. J. Manag. Stud. 29 (2), 131–154.

JASPERS-ARUP, 2013. Analysis and Evidence Base of the R&D&I Market in Romania. Available from: http://www.poscce.edu.ro/uploads/programare-2014-2020/final-report-12-aprilie.pdf.

Jensen, M.B., Johnson, B., Lorenz, E., Lundvall, B.A., 2007. Forms of knowledge and modes of innovation. Res. Policy 36, 680–693.

JRC-IPTS, S3 Platform, website. Available from: http://s3platform.jrc.ec.europa.eu/home.

Karo, E., Kattel, R., 2015. Economic development and evolving state capacities in Central and Eastern Europe: can "smart specialization" make a difference? J. Econ. Policy Ref. 18 (2), 172–187.

Kroll, H., 2015a. Efforts to Implement Smart Specialization in Practice—Leading Unlike Horses to the Water. European Plann. Stud. 23 (10), 2079–2098.

Kroll, H., 2015b. Weaknesses and opportunities of RIS3-type policies. Seven Theses, Karlsruhe: Fraunhofer, ISI September 2015.

Kuznetsov, Y., Sabel,C., 2014. New Open Economy Industrial Policy: Making Choices without Picking Winners, in Making Innovation Policy Work Learning from Experimentation, eds. M.A. Dutz, Y. Kuznetsov, E. Lasagabaster, D. Pilat, OECD/World Bank.

Paliokaitė, A., Martinaitis, Ž., Reimeris, R., 2015. Foresight methods for smart specialisation strategy development in Lithuania. Technol. Forecast. Soc. Change 101, 185–199.

Paliokaitė, A., Martinaitis, Ž., Sarpong, D., 2016. Implementing smart specialisation roadmaps in Lithuania: lost in translation? Technol. Forecast. Soc. Change 110, 143–152.

Paunica, M., Gheorghiu, R., Curaj, A., Holeab, C., 2009. Foresight for restructuring R&D systems. Amfiteatru Econ. 11 (25), 201–210.

Rodríguez-Pose, A., di Cataldo, M., Rainoldi, A., 2014. The role of government institutions for smart specialisation and regional development, S3 Policy Brief Series, no. 4/2014, The European Commission, JRC-IPTS.

Rodrik, D., 2004. Industrial policy for the twenty-first century, UNIDO Working Paper, 2004. Available from: http://www.hks.harvard.edu/fs/drodrik/Research%20papers/UNIDOSep.pdf.

Sörvik, J., Kleibrink, A., 2015. Mapping Innovation Priorities and Specialisation Patterns in Europe, S3 Working Paper Series no. 08/2015, Spain: European Commission, Joint Research Centre.

van de Kerkhof, M., Wieczorek, A., 2005. Learning and stakeholder participation in transition processes towards sustainability: methodological considerations. Technol. Forecast. Soc. Change 72 (6), 733–747.

van der Helm, R., 2007. Ten insolvable dilemmas of participation and why foresight has to deal with them. Foresight 9 (3), 3–17.

WB (World Bank), 2011. Functional review of the Research, Development & Innovation sector, Romania, 2011. Available from: http://documents.worldbank.org/curated/en/810741468294621571/pdf/NonAsciiFileName0.pdf.

WB (World Bank), 2013. Input for Bulgaria's Research and Innovation Strategies for Smart Specialization. Available from: https://rio.jrc.ec.europa.eu/en/file/9491/download/token=JhCjkUCE.

FURTHER READING

Gheorghiu, R., Andreescu, L., Zifciakova, J.,. 2016. RIO Country Report: Romania 2015, JRC-IPTS. Available from: https://rio.jrc.ec.europa.eu/en/file/9491/download?token=JhCjkUCE.

Chapter 15

Advancing Theory and Practice of Smart Specialization: Key Messages

Slavo Radosevic
University College London, London, United Kingdom

Chapter Outline

Academic Highlights

- Smart specialization (SS) is the case of incomplete new industrial innovation policy.
- Different technological levels of countries and regions require different approaches to SS.
- SS is not only a technical exercise, but also a sociopolitical bargaining process.

Advances in the Theory and Practice of Smart Specialization. http://dx.doi.org/10.1016/B978-0-12-804137-6.00015-2

Policy Highlights

- SS approach would need to explicitly recognize the institutional context and capacities necessary for the SS process.
- Integration of global value chains and FDI in an SS approach would need new policy tools.

KEY MESSAGES

The book takes the case of the European Union's SS as an example of "new industrial innovation policy." It explores issues of its design and implementation across developed and less-developed EU regions and countries, as well as in relation to non-EU countries. Furthermore, SS is analyzed in the comparative context of other emerging approaches in industrial innovation policy. The book explores SS in relation to the neo-Schumpeterian approach, new structural economics approach, and the process (evolutionary) view of industrial innovation policy.

Smart Specialization as a Case of Incomplete New Industrial Innovation Policy

First, the evidence presented shows that SS is indeed one of the emerging approaches in the new industrial innovation policy, with which it shares similarities, but also has its strong specificities (Chapter 1). SS selects policy priorities through the so-called "entrepreneurial discovery process," which is based on the idea that no individual stakeholder has a complete view of technological and market opportunities (Chapter 3). However, the process is not only a technical exercise in technology prioritization, but also a political, social, and administrative process.

Whether SS is effectively implemented not only depends on policy capacities but, primarily, on political considerations. For example, Chapter 14 by Gheorghiu et al. explores an attempt of depoliticizing SS, while Chapter 5 shows differences in political attitudes among German regions toward SS. Its implementation requires identifying gaps in a legal, regulatory, and institutional environment, which would need to be addressed to enhance the emerging innovation ecosystems or microsystems of innovation. So, the transformative potential of SS is faced with numerous obstacles (including political, social, and administrative), and is by no means guaranteed by the size of funding.

Conceptually, an SS implies a form of so-called "experimentalist governance." Governance of this kind assumes that policy cannot be run based on the principal–agent logic, which assumes that both agents and principals know what the problem they are solving is. By introducing the entrepreneurial discovery process, SS recognizes that the very process of problem solving (discovering and implementing a regional specialization, which has transformative potential) cannot be resolved within the principal–agent model. Instead, it requires deliberative rather than hierarchical mechanisms of communication and reliance on direct experiences of actors at different levels (Sabel and Zeitlin, 2011). It is based on consultations between firms, regions, countries, and the EC, where objectives and metrics for gauging their achievements are established. Regions and countries are given substantial discretion to advance these goals in ways adapted to their local contexts. However, they are part of a broader monitoring and peer review process, and are expected to undertake corrective actions and modify their goals and metrics. Unlike conventional innovation policy, which is about meeting strategic objectives set a priori by principals, the concept of experimental innovation policy integrates monitoring and evaluation at the policy design stage, as well as throughout implementation (Dutz and Kuznetsov, 2014).

The key experimental features of SS policy, which are outlined in Chapters 2 and 3, by Foray, and Kuznetsov and Sabel, respectively, reside in the process of collective "discovery" of growth opportunities. It is crucial to organize this process with feedback loops and continuous corrections in the light of the discovery of new facts. However, the actual implementation shows that the experimental nature of SS is not only strangled by political and administrative requirements of public administration and funding rules (Chapter 13), but also by undeveloped institutional contexts in less-developed EU regions and countries (Chapters 6 and 12). Those standards and practices seem to be inimical or difficult to adapt to the experimental nature of the new industrial innovation policy process. In that respect, SS still represents a case of *"incomplete" new industrial innovation policy*. SS programs are usually organized as a series of separate individual projects instead of as a portfolio of related and complementary projects. This may lead to a series of successful individual projects, which, however, do not necessarily have critical mass and synergy effects. When taken jointly, they may not result in the emergence of innovation ecosystems or of microsystems of innovation, and will have limited mezzo- or macroeffects.

The experimental nature of SS would require "diagnostic monitoring" instead of conventional interim or end-of-project evaluation. Diagnostic monitoring or problem-solving monitoring is "the systematic evaluation of the portfolio of projects to detect errors as each of the specific projects evolves and to correct the problems (including the weeding out of inefficient projects) in light of implementation experience and other new information" (Chapter 3). While understandably it may be too risky to organize the entire selection and implementation process based on the principles of experimentalist governance, it would be equally expected that some proportion of funds is devoted to funding new areas based on this principle. In a nutshell, SS as it has been applied so far has reduced experimentation only to the initial selection process, while implementation is run as a conventional public funding program.

Challenge of Identifying Country- and Region-Specific Sources of Technological Opportunities

Second, the overall design and procedures of SS formally encourage identification of region- and country-specific sources of new technological opportunities. In fact, it is at the core of SS to encourage regions and countries to reexamine their approach to R&D and innovation. The process of SS is designed in a way that it can be applied in all types of regions; from the most developed to the least innovative. The entrepreneurial discovery process is perceived as a mechanism that can accommodate different technology-upgrading challenges. Indeed, as demonstrated in the case of Scandinavian regions (see Chapter 4) competitive advantage through SS can be promoted in all types of industries based on the industry-specific modes of innovation and knowledge bases. Asheim et al. (Chapter 4) show the importance of both STI mode of innovation, as well as of the experience-based innovation implemented by DUI mode. So, nominally SS shows how a policy that goes beyond "one size fits all" models can be applied to accommodate the needs and potential of heterogeneous European regions.

However, it seems that the identification of region- and country-specific opportunities has been much more of a challenge in less-developed countries and regions. In Southern Europe, past and current funding goes overwhelmingly to ubiquitously improved scientific infrastructure and scientific output in less-favored regions (see Chapter 6 by Tsipouri). This has led to several scientific Pockets of Excellence built over the past years in this area, which are currently challenged to find the best way of commercializing that knowledge.

In both the East and the South of the European Union, significant research infrastructure has been built or is in the process of being built. A nonnegligible number of Research Centers of Excellence, Centers for Collaborative Research, a Network of Technological Centers, and Technology Parks have been created; although in a context of limited demand for their knowledge and services. These potential strengths appear disconnected from the productive system. This is leading or has already resulted in dual R&D and innovation systems: government-financed and basic research oriented academic R&D systems verses less dynamic business sectors with limited demand for academic R&D (see Chapter 12 by Karo et al. and Chapter 6 by Tsipouri).

The linear R&D model of technology upgrading, which is implicit in policies focused on triple-helix actors, captures only a part of the spectrum of technology-upgrading activities. Elsewhere, we show the differing nature of innovation activities in the EU core and periphery (Radosevic, 2016). For example, the share of R&D in innovation expenditures in the European Union "North" (developed European Union) is 73%, while in the EU South and East it is 39% (2010–12). In addition, the shares of the business sector in 2013 were 61, 39, and 35% in the EU North, EU South, and EU East, respectively (ibid., 2016).

The strong R&D focus and neglect of non-R&D innovation can be explained by the fact that academic interests seem to have been better organized, while business participation has usually been weaker and uneven (see Chapter 12 by Karo et al.). SS processes led by ministries or regional agencies for R&D are more likely to result in academic bias and "science push"–based approaches (see Chapter 12). However, this is also due to the neglect of the SS rules and guidelines to take differences in drivers of growth across regions and countries much more into account. Lin points out in Chapter 8 that a different specialization/strategy is needed at varying stages of development. Finally, this is the core assumption of both the neo-Schumpeterian approach as elaborated by Lee in Chapter 9 and of the Schumpeterian approach of Aghion et al. (2011) (see Chapter 2). A new approach should be much more explicit regarding the differences in technology-upgrading challenges across EU28 regions. This should bring into focus-neglected types of innovation, such as practice-based innovation, engineering, workplace innovation, and management practices as the source of firm-level productivity improvements.

Hence, the umbrella role of the entrepreneurial discovery process, as a mechanism promising to embrace a variety of different technology-upgrading paths, should be supplanted. It should be replaced by a much more explicit recognition, inspired by Schumpeterian and neo-Schumpeterian theory, that the countries' and regions' differing distances from the technology frontier strongly affect the scope and type of their innovation and industrial policies. Lin's typology (see Chapter 8) is quite illustrative for less-developed EU regions, as it is based on an industry's distance to the global technological frontier and points to the different facilitating roles of policy in each of the five paths.

Differences in Institutional Thickness and Viability of the Smart Specialization Process

Third, different distances of regions and countries with regard to where they stand on the innovation/imitation spectrum and to the technology frontier mirror their differences regarding the thickness of their institutional networks within which SS processes take place. Readers will notice striking differences in the richness of local institutional policy and support networks when comparing the US Albany, New York region (Chapter 7), Nordic regions (Chapter 4), and German Länder (Chapter 5) with South EU (Chapter 6) and Central and East European countries and regions (Chapter 12). This issue is central to Chapter 10 by Gonchar, Kuznetsov, and Wade, who explore the issue of self-discovery or spontaneous SS in economies characterized by a significant knowledge base and weak institutions (such as Israel, Argentina, and Russia). They also explore whether, under conditions of big interregional differences in innovation and institutional capacities, policy should focus only on leading regions or on those lagging behind too. The evidence in this volume shows that the institutional preconditions differ significantly across the EU28 countries. In cases where there is more scope for institution building for SS, new participatory and coordination practices and experimental policy spaces have not been established (see Chapter 12 by Karo et al.) Even when a broad set of actors from business and academia were formally engaged, they did so mostly symbolically. Such was particularly the case with the business sector, including MNC subsidiaries. So, weakly organized actors in a context of undeveloped interaction mechanisms (private–private and public–private) led to a range of activities where only existing stakeholders with vested interests were engaged.

Moreover, in its initial design, the institutional capacity for SS policies has often been considered as unproblematic, while the major message of new industrial innovation policies is that the institutional context is the key determinant of the effectiveness of these policies, rather than the choice of priorities. Apart from being inclusive and bringing all stakeholders on board, there is little that the current SS approach offers in this respect.

The evidence in the chapters cited earlier shows that the fragmentation of the institutional infrastructure for innovation—the lack of institutionalized links both between R&D and the business sector, and between existing parts of innovation institutions—represents a real constraint to endogenous growth and development in less-developed regions and countries. On the other hand, Gonchar, Kuznetsov, and Wade in Chapter 10 show that even in institutionally weak economies "there are always some regions, firms, sectors, or institutions that are working well." So, the key constraint is not self-discovery of potential growth areas, but how this growth can be sustained by achieving critical mass and cluster coordination. They show that successful first movers do not necessarily generate local clusters. This well resembles the situation in the EU South where the Pockets of Excellence remain isolated enclaves or exclaves (Chapter 6).

Chapter 10's conclusion based on non-EU economies resonates very well with the evidence on SS within the European Union and other chapters in this book. Namely, "wealthy and more developed sub-national regions are well suited for the logic and instruments of (Smart Specialization), and they benefit from a complementarity of policies supported by various funding sources." This raises the question of how realistic it is to rely on SS in places that lack sufficient local resources, competences, and networks, especially when the previous experience of government interventions in promoting economic growth via innovation has been questioned. Gonchar, Kuznetsov, and Wade suggest that such policies would need to include institution-building efforts to ensure adequate public–private and public-to-public coordination. Like the conclusion earlier that SS should reflect different country/region drivers of growth, the policy agenda for advanced and less-developed regions must be designed and implemented differently. Developed regions/countries already have various collective action institutions with a diversity of funding sources. As evidenced in this volume (Chapters 4, 5, and 7), SS in these cases is about further strengthening and building new complementarities.

The discovery of areas of potential growth and technological opportunities for less-developed regions should aim to either discover "new entry points" or enlarge the activities of existing pockets of excellence: individual firms, groups or chains of firms, or research–technology organizations. The mechanisms for their support can be either matching grants or private–public consortia, which are all mechanisms that already exist in the current EU support system. It follows that the challenge is not in the type of funding instrument, but the institutional context in which individual instruments are being deployed. The experimentalist nature of SS calls for two kinds of institutions: micro and mezzo. The microlevel institution is the Schumpeterian development agency, while at mezzolevel there are extensive and varied fora for public–private, private–private, and public–public consultation.

A "Schumpeterian development agency"—introduced in Chapter 3 by Kuznetsov and Sabel—is a generic name for organizations of different institutional affiliations but "with the capability and motivation to experiment, make mistakes, and correct them" and graft experimentalist principles into SS practice and methodology. It can be an autonomous entity that is new or an existing one, which is considered an "island of excellence" in the public or private sector in the country/region. Such an organization has a mandate "to experiment by assembling a portfolio of projects and carefully monitoring the portfolio, yet remaining accountable for the results of the experimentation." Such an agency will use diagnostic monitoring of a portfolio of projects. Examples of such organizations operating for other purposes are the US DARPA agency, the Irish Industrial Development Agency, and, partly, CzechInvest.

The key to the new industrial innovation policy is that it should reach beyond individual organizations as its carriers, as policy needs to resolve information asymmetries among public and private organizations and to enable and sustain entrepreneurial discovery as a collective process. The policy maker is not the principal, and applicants to public programs are not the agents. Policy capabilities, when contained within an individual agent like the "Schumpeterian development agency," are necessary but not sufficient without the capacity to engage in dialogue with the private sector. A competent and autonomous public administration that is not involved in rich information exchange with the private sector will be unable to engage in policy activities in which sector-specific knowledge is essential. On the other hand, only good communications with the private sector, but with weak policy capabilities are also insufficient. In short, SS requires the public sector not only to have a detailed understanding of the specific technology and market context, but also to assess the case for public support on its own merits (see Chapter 2).

In a nutshell, completion of SS as an experimentalist industrial innovation policy would require that it explicitly addresses the institutional context and capacities needed for the SS process. It would require two institutional preconditions for embarking on SS. First, it must have an organization that can operate as a project portfolio manager using diagnostic monitoring as a mechanism to this end. Second, it needs explicit and functional public–private, public–public, and private–private consultative bodies institutionalized under different forms and already active in SS-related areas.

A Neglect of Global Value Chains as Levers of a Smart Specialization Transformative Agenda

Fourth, the new industrial innovation policies are market friendly and designed for the open economy context. SS strategies and their underpinning analyses have difficulties in showing how GVCs that dominate today's global economy can be used as levers of local growth. The analysis of the US leading nanotech cluster in Chapter 7 by Wessner shows the importance of global context and of FDI in shaping the dynamics of local development. The exposition of the original New Structural Economics model by Lin (model 1: catching up industries) in Chapter 8 has at its core the interaction between economies that are losing and those that are gaining comparative advantages in specific industries. The core of the application of short-cycle technologies as a criterion for specialization in Chapter 9 by Lee depends on the assessments of the foreign incumbents: that is, on whether their dominance is about to be disrupted, and whether new technologies tend to emerge more frequently and offer high growth prospects. In addition, the evidence on SS in Scandinavian regions in Chapter 4 by Asheim et al. shows that specialization issues are considered in a global context, which is integral to regions' specialization choices. The experience of SS suggests that the less developed the region, seemingly harder is the integration of an international dimension in its strategic actions (see Chapters 6 and 12 by Tsipouri and Karo et al., respectively).

The EC is aware of these issues and allows for some room for action in this respect. It has a rule that allows regions to spend up to 15% of funds for SS activities outside the region. However, our experience in this respect suggests that less-developed regions are primarily inward focused despite being aware of the need for building levers through interregional and international cooperation (Radosevic and Walendowski, 2016). This gap can be defined as a knowledge and action gap.

Chapter 11 (by Brennan and Rakhmatullin) helps close some of the knowledge gaps by offering a methodological approach to analyzing a country's (region's) position in the GVC. However, the evidence found in the chapters on less-developed regions (see Chapters 6, 12, and 13) shows that the action gap is substantial, that is, regions are mostly inward oriented regarding envisaged activities for promoting technology-based growth. This can be partly attributed to the legacy of past regional policies, which were place-based and thus neglected foreign sources of knowledge as levers of growth.

GVCs/FDI are the least-developed part of the overall SS policy apparatus, but probably also the most important for the EU "periphery." Although considering internationalization "a crucial component of smart specialization strategies" (Foray et al., 2012, p. 94), the Guide for Smart Specialization has perceived it primarily in terms of internationalizing the design process, an international outlook in selection processes, and internationalization as a separate area of activity (cf. internationalization of technology companies). However, globalization is about functional integration, as recognized in Vanguard,[1] a new bottom-up initiative of the more-developed EU regions. The generation of interregional Industry Commons is about demand-led initiatives and facilities, which can be combined with a stronger investment-oriented agenda.

The European Union is the ideal locus for GVC-oriented industrial innovation policy, which is about strengthening the export and technological position of regions/countries by sourcing inputs from regional neighbors. Its regional funds are meant to be spent primarily within the regions unrelated to potential levers, linkages, and learning opportunities that may be generated through interregional links. This does not mean that a variety of tools for interregional collaboration in the European Union is unavailable.[2] However, on the whole, these instruments are mostly focused on the upstream/R&D parts of the innovation spectrum.[3] Regional value chains should become a new direction for investment planning by the European Investment Bank and Structural Funds, especially given the diversity of industrial ecosystems in the EU28. The aim is not to recreate entire supply chains within a country/region, but to utilize extraterritorial linkages that affect a region's/country's positioning in global or regional value chains.

Smart Specialization as a Technical Exercise in Priority Determination and as a Sociopolitical Bargaining Process

Fifth, this volume brings into sharp light the relationship between SS as a technical exercise in priority determination and, conversely, as an exercise facilitated by policy bodies in social, administrative, and political bargaining across many actors. Chapter 8 by Lin introduces the "Growth Identification and Facilitation Framework" as a key analytical framework for deciding on priorities within the New Structural Economics framework. Lee in Chapter 9 elaborates on the "short-cycle technologies" criterion and discusses its merits in relation to Lin's New Structural Economics and the Product Space method by Hausmann and Hidalgo (see Chapter 2). In Chapter 14, Gheorgiu et al. discuss a very thorough and rigorous application of foresight as a mechanism to decide on SS priorities in a neutral manner. Finally, EU SS itself has a very elaborate sequence of steps on how to go about deciding on priorities (see Chapter 2 by Foray). In that respect, they all try to answer the question of *what* or *where* to focus limited resources with the greatest effect. This is a nontrivial problem, especially when both the policy principal and the agent have limited knowledge about potential areas of technology and market opportunities.

However, an experimental innovation industrial policy is even more concerned with the issue of *what* the optimal social and administrative process is, which can generate not only a consensus on priorities, but also encourage actors' willingness to engage in an interactive and cooperative innovation process (see Table 2.1 by Radosevic). It is probably obvious that both sides are equally important and interdependent. Thus, success does not lie in one dimension alone, but in mutual complementarity. Technical exercises are a useful tool but can never be the full answer. Equally, a well-organized process without an external "objective" criterion that could serve as a starting point can be prone to manipulation and presentation of individual interests as general interests.

What can the European Union's Smart Specialization Teach Non-EU Regions and Countries?

Sixth, this volume is based largely on the experience of the European Union, but presented it in a comparative context. In that respect, our evidence shows that differences between EU and non-EU regions regarding the issues of design and implementation of new industrial innovation policies are much smaller than one would think; sometimes, they seem to be nonexistent. This stems from the Schumpeterian logic of the new industrial innovation policy, which recognizes that countries' and regions' varying distances to the technology frontier call for different types of policies. Based on this, the evidence from the European Union contains several valuable lessons for the rest of the world.

Our evidence shows that kickstarting the process of technology-based growth is a complex and difficult task, and that even more serious problems arise in sustaining and enlarging the initial Pockets of Excellence. The case of the US nanocluster nicely illustrates the fragility, the temporary nature, and the questionable sustainability of any success story. The sheer size of the European Union's SS policy effort is not by itself a guarantee of success. Any such attempt is about increasing the probability of achievement, which is by no means guaranteed, and comes as an outcome of a variety of mutually complementary and often unforeseen factors.

The application of the principles of new industrial innovation policy is caught between the features and advantages of experimental policies, on the one hand, and the requirements for prudence and accountability of public funding systems, on the other. The evidence in this volume shows that there are solutions for reconciling these two objectives, but these need deeper changes in the institutional settings, which even many EU regions have to date been unable to meet. How to ensure the monitoring and evaluation of SS strategies, while stimulating a dynamic learning process, is a question that can only be answered in a specific local context.

Finally, any new type of policy carries with it dangers of "isomorphic mimicry": this is where stakeholders can maintain legitimacy through imitating the process of SS (such as entrepreneurial discovery) without making any actual functional changes. The evidence in this volume shows that this is much more widespread than actors engaged would like to believe.

We hope that these lessons represent relevant insights, and will also be food for thought for further study and comparative analyses.

ACKNOWLEDGMENTS

I am grateful to Liviu Andreescu and Imogen Wade for editorial support in revising this chapter.

ENDNOTES

1. See http://www.s3vanguardinitiative.eu/.
2. Examples include: European Territorial Cooperation, ERA-Nets, Joint Technology Initiatives (JTIs), Knowledge and Innovation Communities (KICs), Joint Programming Initiatives (JPIs), European Innovation Partnerships (EIPs), ERA Chairs, Teaming for Excellence and Innovation, and Twinning for Excellence and Innovation.
3. For an exception, see: INNOSUP-01-2016-2017: Cluster Facilitated Projects for New Industrial Value Chains, and INNOSUP-08-2017: A Better Access to Industrial Technologies Developed Overseas.

REFERENCES

Aghion, P., Boulanger, J., Cohen, E., 2011. Rethinking industrial policy. Breugel Policy Brief. Available from: http://bruegel.org/2011/06/rethinking-industrial-policy/.

Dutz, M.A., Kuznetsov, Y. (Eds.), 2014. Making Innovation Policy Work: Learning Form Experimentation. OECD and World Bank, Paris.

Foray, D., Goddard, J., Goenaga Beldarrain, X., Landabaso, M., McCann, P., Morgan, K., Nauwelaers, C., Ortega-Argilés, R., 2012. Guide to research and innovation strategies for smart specialization (RIS 3). European Commission. Available from: http://ec.europa.eu/regional_policy/sources/docgener/presenta/smart_specialisation/smart_ris3_2012.pdf.

Radosevic, S. 2016. The role of public research in economic development. EC, Science, Research and Innovation performance of the EU: A Contribution to the Open Innovation, Open Science, Open to the World Agenda, DG for Research and Innovation, European Commission.

Radosevic, S., Walendowski, J., 2016. A prospective comparative analysis of the national Smart Specialization Strategies in Central Europe. Expert assessment of synergies and areas of potential cooperation related to Smart Specialization Strategies in Central Europe. European Commission, DG Regional and Urban Policy, Directorate F, Operational Efficiency and Central Europe.

Sabel, C.F., Zeitlin, J., 2011. Experimentalist governance. In: Levi-Faur, D. (Ed.), The Oxford Handbook of Governance. Oxford University Press, Oxford.

Index

Printed in the United States
By Bookmasters